Medieval History and Archaeology

General Editors
JOHN BLAIR   HELENA HAMEROW

The Iconography of Early Anglo-Saxon Coinage

THE ICONOGRAPHY OF EARLY ANGLO-SAXON COINAGE

Sixth to Eighth Centuries

ANNA GANNON

OXFORD

UNIVERSITY PRESS

OXFORD

UNIVERSITY PRESS

Great Clarendon Street, Oxford OX2 6DP

Oxford University Press is a department of the University of Oxford.
It furthers the University s objective of excellence in research, scholarship,
and education by publishing worldwide in

Oxford New York

Auckland Bangkok Buenos Aires Cape Town Chennai
Dar es Salaam Delhi Hong Kong Istanbul Karachi Kolkata
Kuala Lumpur Madrid Melbourne Mexico City Mumbai Nairobi
Sao Paulo Shanghai Taipei Tokyo Toronto

Oxford is a registered trade mark of Oxford University Press
in the UK and in certain other countries

Published in the United States
by Oxford University Press Inc., New York

© Anna Gannon 2003

The moral rights of the author have been asserted

Database right Oxford University Press (maker)

First published 2003
First published in paperback 2010

British Library Cataloguing in Publication Data
Data available

Library of Congress Cataloging in Publication Data
Data available

Typeset by Laserwords Private Limited, Chennai, India
Digitally printed and bound
in Great Britain by
CPI Antony Rowe, Chippenham and Eastbourne

ISBN 978–0–19–925465–1 (Hbk.)
ISBN 978–0–19–958384–3 (Pbk.)

Acknowledgements

It is with great pleasure that I wish to acknowledge all the help and support I have received over the years I have been at work on a task that I have greatly enjoyed.

First of all, my deepest gratitude to George and Isabel Henderson, who first suggested the idea of looking at Anglo-Saxon coinage, and to Mark Blackburn of the Fitzwilliam Museum, Cambridge, who has cheerfully and patiently supervised my numismatic work over many years. I have found matching support, kindness, and friendship in Oxford and in London: sincere thanks to Michael Metcalf, Arthur MacGregor, and Nicholas Mayhew for much good advice and access to the Ashmolean and its collection, and equally to Marion Archibald, Leslie Webster, and Gareth Williams at the British Museum for their kindness and generosity in time, advice, and resources.

My gratitude to Lucy Cavendish College, Cambridge, my *alma mater*, and the British Academy for supporting my research, morally and financially. Sincere thanks to the Paul Mellon Centre for Studies in British Art for most generously awarding me a grant to assist with the production of the book.

During my research I have had the privilege of coming into contact with many experts who have given of their time and expertise and helped in innumerable ways. The book is better for their advice, but all the mistakes I claim as my own. For reasons of brevity, I shall simply list their names alphabetically, but each should be followed by a personal tribute of gratitude for the help, inspiration, and in many cases the genuine friendship that I have derived. My sincere thanks go to:

Martin Allen, Mark Atherton, Charlotte Behr, Paul Binski, Donald Bullough, Derek Chick, Mark Clarke, Rosemary Cramp, Philip de Jersey, David Dumville, Bruce Eagle, Richard Emms, Märit Gaimster, Helen Geake, Philip Grierson, Karl Hauck, Jane Hawkes, Michael Herren, Carola Hicks, David Hill, Catherine Hills, John Hines, Jakob Holm, Deborah Howard, David Howlett, Lars Jørgensen, Catherine Karkov, Simon Keynes, Kevin Leahy, John Maddicott, Jean Michel Massing, Rosamond McKitterick, Audrey Meaney, Janet Nelson, John Niles, Éamonn Ó Carragáin, Jennifer O'Reilly, Gale Owen-Crocker, Anne Pedersen, Steven Plunkett, Arent Pol, David Pratt, Anneli Randla, Frank Siegmund, George Speake, Lucia Travaini, Niamh Whitfield, Rotraut Wolf, Michael Wood, Patrick Wormald.

A particular note of gratitude goes to Prof. G. W. de Wit in Rotterdam, who kindly granted me access to his superb collection of over 360 *sceattas* and allowed me to use his photographs to illustrate my work. Having first-hand experience of such an outstanding collection, and being allowed to keep a permanent photographic record of it has been immensely useful. I am also grateful to Tony Abramson, for permission to reproduce coins from his collection.

Many thanks also to the people who kindly helped with the images for the books: Myke Clifford, Ken Jukes, and Sarah Ward.

An enormous debt for their kindness and help is due to my editors, Helena Hamerow and John Blair, and Anne Gelling at the Press.

In the private sphere, I do owe a great deal to the goodwill and interest of very many good friends, and particularly to my family for their loving forbearance. To all my deepest gratitude and affection.

A.G.

Cambridge,
Pentecost 2002

Contents

Abbreviations   x

Introduction   1

PART I. NUMISMATIC BACKGROUND

1. Numismatic Background of Early Anglo-Saxon England   7

    The End of the Roman System   7
    Alternative Uses of Coins   8
    The Beginning of Coinage: Gold Issues   10
    Silver Issues   12
    Offa's Coinage   13
    Manufacturing of Coins   14
    Die-Cutters and Moneyers   15
    Patronage   16
    The Function of the Coinage   17
    Mints   18
    Chronology   18
    Classifications   19

PART II. ICONOGRAPHY

2. The Bust   23

    The Head   25

      Facing Heads   25
      Bareheaded Portraits   30
      Bareheaded Portraits of Offa   31
      Encircled Heads   34
      Confronting Heads   37
      Female Portraits   39
      Heads and Headdresses   42
      Crowns   42
      Diadems   45
      Helmets   51
      Rendering of Drapery   54
      Schematic Drapery   55
      Crossed-Over Drapery   58
      Offa's Drapery   59
      Armour   62

Attributes   63
  Hands   63
  Hands Holding Crosses   65
  Hands Holding Cups   66
  Hands Holding Sprigs   67
  Bust and Crosses   69
  Bust and Vegetation Motifs   71
  Bust and 'Tridents'   72
  Bust and 'Star'   74
  Bust and Sceptre   75
  Bust and Bird   77

3. Human Figures   79
  'Victory' and Angels   79
  The Two Emperors   84
  Single Figure between Crosses   87
  Single Figure with Vegetation Motifs and Crosses   93
  Standing Figures with Cross and Bird   95
  Seated Figures   98
  Two Standing Figures   101
  The Archer   105

4. Animal Iconography   107
  Birds   107
    Birds on Crosses   107
    Birds with Crosses   112
    Birds with Cross and Fledgling   114
    Birds and Snakes   116
    Birds in Vine-Scrolls   117
    Peacocks   120
    The Hen   123
  Lions   125
    Aldfrith's Lions and the Northumbrian Tradition   125
    East Anglian Lions   127
    The Tale of Two Panthers   131
    Facing Lions   134
  Snakes   136
    Motif-Encircling Snakes   136
    Rolled-Up Snakes   138
    Whorls of Snakes   141
    Offa's Snakes   142
  Wolves   144
    The She-Wolf   145

Backward-Looking Animals   148

Fantastic Hybrids   151
   The Female Centaur   151
   Winged Quadrupeds and Other Hybrids   154

5. Reverses with Crosses, Standards/Saltires, and Porcupines   157

   Crosses   157
      Latin Crosses   157
      Greek Crosses   160
      Marigolds   165
      Crossed Instruments   167
      Offa's Crosses   168

   Standards and Saltires   171

   Porcupines   176

6. Conclusion   182

Bibliography   194

Index   219

Abbreviations

BMA	British Museum Acquisition.
BMC	*British Museum Catalogue*: Keary 1887.
CM	Coins and Medals Department, British Museum.
Coin Register	see the *British Numismatic Journal* of the relevant year.
Abramson collection	The private collection of Mr A. Abramson, Leeds.
de Wit collection	the private collection of Prof. G. W. de Wit, Rotterdam.
ex-Subjack	W. L. Subjack collection, sold in London 5 June 1998: see Vecchi 1998.
EMC	Early Medieval Coinage: http://www-cm.fitzmuseum.cam.ac.uk/coins/emc.html
HE	Bede, *The Ecclesiastical History of the English People*, ed. and trans. B. Colgrave and R. A. B. Mynors (Oxford, 1969).
Hunterian	Hunterian and Coats Collection, University of Glasgow: see Robertson 1961.
MEC	*Medieval European Coinage*: see Grierson and Blackburn 1986.
MME	Medieval and Modern Europe Department, British Museum.
MoE	*The Making of England*: see Webster and Backhouse 1991.
T&S	*Thrymsas and Sceattas*: see Metcalf 1993–4.

Introduction

In his introduction to *Thrymsas and Sceattas*, Michael Metcalf stated: 'There are two kinds of book to be written about Anglo-Saxon coins of the seventh and eighth centuries, namely one to set out the arguments which establish where and when the coins were struck, and in what percentage, and another to describe how they circulated and to discuss the purpose for which they were used: one kind of book on numismatics, the other on monetary history.'[1]

This work however will attempt a third way: it will be an art-historical appraisal of Anglo-Saxon coinage, from its inception in the late sixth century to Offa's second reform of the penny *c*.792. Artistically, this is the most exciting period of English coinage, with die-cutters showing flair and innovation and employing hundreds of different designs in their work, yet coins, with the exception of the pioneering work of Baldwin Brown,[2] are rarely included in surveys of Anglo-Saxon art.

Coins have often provided illustrations to history books.[3] However, in contrast to Metcalf's contribution in the book edited by Campbell in 1982, where, albeit from a numismatic perspective, the charm and variety of the types were stressed, and several specimens illustrated,[4] no coin made it onto the pages of Wilson's *Anglo-Saxon Art* of 1984, but only the statement: 'coins provide a fruitful area of stylistic analysis, but, with rare exceptions, show few distinctive or important ornamental traits'.[5] That coins are mentioned, and three specimens illustrated in Laing and Laing 1996,[6] is probably due to the 1991 British Museum exhibition, 'The Making of England', and the catalogue that accompanied it,[7] which stressed the importance of the coinage as a historical document, but more fundamentally presented it as an integral part of the visual culture of the time. The same innovative approach was apparent in the 1997 'Heirs of Rome' exhibition,[8] where emphasis was placed on the iconography of the coinage as a bearer of meaning. These efforts have certainly contributed to a new awareness of the richness of the material.[9]

---

[1] Metcalf 1993–4: i. 1. This work will be henceforth referred to as *T&S*.
[2] Baldwin Brown 1903–37, specifically vol. iii (1915), 57–113.   [3] For example, Wood 1981.
[4] Campbell 1982: 62–3.   [5] Wilson 1984: 15.   [6] Laing and Laing 1996: 84–5.
[7] Webster and Backhouse 1991, here referred to as *MoE*. Marion Archibald, former Curator of Early Medieval Coinage at the British Museum, was responsible for the chapter 'Coins and Currency' (p. 35) and the entries for the coins.
[8] Webster and Brown 1997, with Archibald covering the coinage.
[9] For instance Karkov 1997: 17 and Neuman de Vegvar 1999: 259 use coins as iconographic evidence. A special mention ought to be made of Prof. G. and Dr I. Henderson, who first made me aware of the importance of the subject for art historians.

Although in recent years this early phase of Anglo-Saxon coinage has been the subject of extensive numismatic research,[10] that much can be gained from comparing and contrasting coin iconography from an art-historical stance was demonstrated by Mary Morehart's contributions to the numismatic debate.[11] Her research has shown that there are common interests among art historians, numismatists, historians, and archaeologists and that some of the basic questions that are asked when considering the coinage are indeed the same:[12] hence the desirability of an interdisciplinary approach.

Coins in Anglo-Saxon England were not the continuation of a previous monetary tradition, but a fresh start after nearly two centuries, their inception an act of monetary policy raising questions pertaining to their patronage and function. The artistic merit and variety of the coins, which far exceed contemporary Continental ones, suggest that the designs had a special purpose. The three issues of patronage, function, and design are interlinked.

First and foremost, designs were meant to identify the coin and its issuing authority, so as to foster confidence in its economic value: this had been the minimum required of any coinage since its origin in Antiquity. However, they could also have other functions. The exploitation of the potential of coinage as a propaganda tool goes back to classical times,[13] and it must also have been familiar to the Anglo-Saxons. In the delicate balance between the familiar and the innovative, coins must have played a central role, having the advantages of official sanctioning and wide circulation to support and diffuse new ideas and images. Were the motifs a deliberate manipulation of public opinion and, if so, was this for political or religious ends? Indeed was the coinage, whose introduction is contemporary with St Augustine's mission, instrumental in the promotion of the Christian message? In the range of iconography are we to discover echoes of controversy, of factions, or perhaps of statements to do with cultural or national identity in the choice between Roman and runic alphabets in the inscriptions? Propaganda, however, at any level and whatever the message, must be intelligible to the intended audience, and how the iconography fitted into the visual culture of the time must be borne in mind. Were the prototypes of the images always numismatic,[14] or were they derived from other sources (classical or not), and did they in turn inspire other artistic works? Is there a difference between the iconography of the earlier and that of the later coinages of the period?

---

[10] See the 1984 Oxford congress 'Sceattas in England and on the Continent', proceedings published in Hill and Metcalf 1984; the first volume of *Medieval European Coinage (The Early Middle Ages 5th–10th Centuries)* cataloguing the coins in the Fitzwilliam Museum, Cambridge, edited in 1986 by Grierson and Blackburn (henceforth referred to as *MEC*), particularly chs. 8 and 10; Metcalf's three volumes of *T&S*, cataloguing the coins in the Ashmolean Museum, Oxford; and numerous publications in numismatic journals.

[11] Morehart 1970, 1984, and 1985.

[12] Wicker 1999, specifically on archaeology and art history.

[13] For a discussion of the different views of recent authors on the problems of political propaganda, or lack of it, on Roman coinage, see Bastien 1992: i. 9.

[14] Kent 1961; Whitting 1961.

The conscious use of art for didactic purposes in Anglo-Saxon England is witnessed in the acquisition of paintings by Benedict Biscop for his foundation at Monkwearmouth,[15] but indeed decorated objects had been bearers of meaning since earlier times, as recent research on brooches suggests.[16] How far we can contrast a Christian image with a 'native zoomorphic' one is an issue that will have to be addressed, bearing in mind the fresh role that traditional images may have assumed in a new context. What was the purpose of such a variety of issues, and are they related to each other in some way? Is the iconography always unequivocal or can we detect plays and shifts in the layering of meaning, therefore postulating audiences of varying sophistication and multiple roles for the coinage? Would answers to these questions concerning sources, context, and meaning of the iconography help us to understand who commissioned the coins?[17]

To try and answer these questions, I shall divide the material not into Series and types, according to numismatic practice, but iconographically into four main categories: busts (including attributes and drapery), human figures, animals, and geometrical patterns. Prototypes will be sought, and parallels highlighting the relationship of the designs to contemporary art will enable the material to be viewed within the culture of the time.[18]

Having relied heavily on the research and generous help of numismatists and other scholars, I am aware that many other cultural, numismatic, historical, and archaeological questions could and should be asked of the material gathered, from mints or die-cutters' styles, to the relationship between jewellery and coins, and the apotropaic function of motifs. As an art historian, mine is but one contribution to the subject: my hope is that it will not only serve to enhance understanding and appreciation of early Anglo-Saxon coinage, but will fire the imagination, and encourage further research.

[15] Bede, *The Lives of the Abbots*, ch. 6, Farmer 1988: 190–1. Henderson 1980.
[16] Hines 1997.
[17] *T&S*, i. 16–17; the two polarities (royal versus mercantile coinage) are nowadays not so entrenched.
[18] On account of the great variation in size between coins and *comparanda*, they will not necessarily be reproduced to scale, in order to achieve the greatest possible visual impact when comparisons are being made.

PART I

Numismatic Background

1

Numismatic Background of Early Anglo-Saxon England

The End of the Roman System

In much of the former western Roman Empire the use and minting of coins were continued on the established Roman pattern,[1] albeit with innovations,[2] initially, at least, as a legacy of the old administration. Important changes consisted in a shift from the Roman system of gold, silver, and base metal towards the sole use of gold during the fifth century and in adjusting the weights of the coins to fit in with their particular Germanic system.[3] In Britain, however, the use of coinage seems to have lapsed for nearly two centuries.[4]

The withdrawal of the Roman army from Britain early in the fifth century meant not only that the Romano-British population had to fend for itself, but also the end of the taxation levied to support functionaries and legions and of the need for regular supplies of coins to meet these and other fiscal duties.[5] The breakdown of Romano-British society and its infrastructure was fairly rapid but varied from area to area, as can be seen from the distribution of the finds of the last of the Roman coins to be issued to Britain.[6] The insecurity of the period is reflected in the non-retrieval of buried treasure—precious artefacts, as well as money.[7] Silver coins in particular, often clipped and pared, show the growing shortage of metal.

Taking advantage of the uncertain political situation in Britain, tribes from the Continent—who came to be known as the Anglo-Saxons—established control

---

[1] *MEC* 3.

[2] It has been argued that Roman coinage served fiscal needs, whereas for the Germanic invaders money became an economic means of exchange. See Hendy 1988: 29.

[3] *MEC* 8 ff. and 14.

[4] *MEC* 156.

[5] Kent 1961: 22. Britain had possessed virtually no official mint since the time of Constantine the Great (Kent 1961: 4). As coins had to be imported from other regions of the Roman Empire (Casey 1994: 9, fig. 1), the gold coinage, which served for official payments, offers good evidence for establishing a firm dating for the severance of the province from Rome. The coin evidence coincides with that offered by literary sources (Kent 1961: 21; Campbell 1982: 18–19; and Higham 1992: 69).

[6] Higham 1992: 70.

[7] The magnificence of some of the hoards, for instance the Hoxne treasure (Bland and Johns 1993), allows a glimpse into the wealth of late Roman Britain.

over eastern Britain during the fifth century AD, extending south and west into most of modern England over the next two centuries. The situation in Britain seems to have been very different from that of other provinces of the Roman Empire, where it is appropriate to talk of the continuity of institutions rather than of the collapse of the Imperial organization.[8]

Alternative Uses of Coins

The Anglo-Saxons, though familiar with money from looting and tribute, initially had no need for coins or their orthodox uses. Coins were regarded as bullion or used as jewellery.[9] Evidence from the graves of the fifth to the seventh centuries shows that Roman bronze coins were often pierced and used as decorative spangles on clothes or as pendants,[10] possibly with apotropaic connotations.[11]

Even in the late sixth and early seventh centuries, when coin circulation was just starting with a net import of gold from the Continent,[12] contemporary gold coins from Byzantium, Merovingian France, and Visigothic Spain were still occasionally mounted with gold loops and suspended from festoons of beads or turned into other pieces of jewellery.[13] Two important groups of coins mounted as pendants with suspension loops from the late sixth/early seventh century are the Canterbury St Martin's 'hoard' and the collection of six pieces from Faversham in Kent,[14] a place-name combining the Latin word *faber*, (gold)smith, with the Anglo-Saxon suffix *hām*, suggesting perhaps some continuity in the art of metalwork from Roman to Anglo-Saxon times.[15] Among the most spectacular pieces using coins as pendants is the early seventh-century necklace from Sarre, which includes four gold solidi.[16]

On the majority of the specimens pierced as pendants, the orientation of the obverse with the bust seems to have been a concern.[17] This shows some interest

---

[8] For an account of the problems of the transformation of the Roman Empire: Higham 1992. Webster and Brown 1997 present valuable comparative material.

[9] However, there is some argument for unmounted coins lost at this period having been used in a monetary sense (*MoE* 35). Finds of broken objects and scraps of metal carefully threaded and kept suggest their use as token currency.

[10] King 1988: 224. See also his argument concerning the use of other Roman coin finds from settlements at p. 227.

[11] Meaney 1981: 213 and 220.   [12] Metcalf 1988a: 231.

[13] The fashion is thought to derive from contacts with the Merovingians and, through them, with Byzantium: *MoE* 47; Vierk 1978. Geake 1997: 108 sees a more direct influence from Byzantium. For a list of finds of Merovingian and Visigothic coins in England, other than those from Sutton Hoo: Rigold 1975, and note Metcalf's comment (Metcalf 1988a: 231).

[14] *MoE* 23, nos. 5a–h and p. 53, nos. 34a–f.

[15] Gelling 1978: 80.   [16] *MoE* 48, no. 31b.

[17] On the coin and bead necklace from Brighthampton (White 1988: fig. 43, p. 299) seven out of ten coins are pierced so as to present the wearer, not the onlooker, with the upright view of the bust. This form of 'private viewing' seems to have been widespread, as in the case of the Winkel pendant (Fig. 4.4), and as suggested by Anne Taylor for the orientation of the zoomorphic lobe terminals on cruciform brooches when worn (cf. MacGregor and Bolick 1993: 95–111).

in the iconography, though whether on account of its own artistic merits or for the magic virtues ascribed to the head, and in particular to one in profile, turning away its sight and hence the evil eye, is of course debatable.[18] On coin pendants of the Christian period, the reverse with a cross was probably the preferred side for display,[19] as was the case with the Wilton Cross.[20] It has been argued that such pendants would have been worn as specifically Christian protective amulets, not just as jewels.[21]

The proportion of finds of unperforated coins appears to increase in the Christian period,[22] parallel with the sixth/seventh-century fashion for keeping coins in a purse.[23] The Sutton Hoo purse contained thirty-seven unperforated Merovingian gold coins minted between *c.*575 and *c.*620 (plus three blanks and two billets).[24] Grierson's interpretation of the hoard as a grand Charon's obol has not been universally accepted.[25] The tradition, of classical origin, later adopted by the Franks, is not common in Anglo-Saxon England,[26] and the coins might well represent a statement on the same lines as that made by the other exotic treasures that accompany the burial.[27] The sixteen up-to-date coins in bags from Finglesham and Garton-on-the Wolds deposited after the Conversion (*c.*690–700 and *c.*720–5) might represent a changing attitude to money, but the evidence is ambiguous.[28]

Coins in Anglo-Saxon society must have enjoyed special prestige both before and after the introduction of native coinage. Their status can be compared to that of the medallions and bracteates produced by another coinless people, the Scandinavians, in response to contacts with the Roman world and its gold coinage. These were manufactured from the fourth century onwards, as direct copies of Roman solidi and their multiples, and were worn, in showy mounts, in a fashion derived from the Roman sporting of medallions and ranks of honour.[29] By transforming the image of the deified imperial ruler into that of their god Woden and incorporating symbols and runes from northern mythology, they were a means of showing religious and political allegiances and embraced new

---

[18] Meaney 1981: 220. On the head as the seat of the soul: Harnham, Molleson, and Price 1981: 167. On the reverence paid to the head as bringing good luck: Thacker 1995: 102, for further bibliographical references.

[19] Meaney 1981: 220–1.

[20] *MoE* 27, no. 12. In the Wilton Cross, the back of the jewel guards the upright orientation of the bust, whereas the front has the cross-on-steps reversed. It is possible that the jeweller might not have realized that the cross mounted in this way was upside-down, or one might consider this another instance of 'private viewing' for the wearer, as suggested in n. 17 above.

[21] Meaney 1981: 221. The fact that some of the coins used sometimes had already been worn smooth in antiquity indicates that they were prized for their apotropaic virtues. See White 1988: 99.

[22] Meaney 1981: 216; *MEC* 160; King 1988: 225.

[23] Owen-Crocker 1986: 125.

[24] Kent 1975.

[25] Grierson 1970, 1974.

[26] Geake 1997: 32.

[27] Care Evans 1994: 89.

[28] Geake 1997: 32.

[29] Hauck 1976; Magnus 1997.

ideas as well as advertising their owner's wealth and power in society.[30] It has
been argued that the bracteates originally had a political function and also
served as a sort of special-purpose money within a society of non-commercial
transactions.[31]

Authority established through gifts, forging relationships and bonding individuals together, played an important role in the Germanic world, as testified by
the title of *beagifa*, the ring-giver, often used to describe the king in *Beowulf*.[32]
Apart from being a convenient means of economic exchange, coins in early
Anglo-Saxon society may have been appreciated as an exotic variant on the more
usual prestigious gifts that played such a major role in social interactions.

The Beginning of Coinage: Gold Issues

From the second half of the sixth century the concentration of wealth in Kent, as
witnessed by jewellery and coin finds, indicates how intense and profitable contacts were with the Continent, and with Merovingian Gaul in particular.[33] The
archaeological evidence shows how far trade routes stretched and that the sea
surrounding Britain, far from being a hindrance, facilitated contacts;[34] it is again
through archaeology that the early importance of the ports of Sarre (on the
Wantsum Channel) and Dover is evident.[35] However, the benefits of trade and
the flow of Continental coinage were not restricted to Kent alone.[36]

By the early seventh century, thanks to familiarization with coins, accumula-
tion of precious metals, questions of prestige, and possibly because the demand
for coins outdid the foreign supply, the earliest Anglo-Saxon coins began to be
produced, some copying large Roman solidi, others the smaller Merovingian *tremissis*. Christianity also played an important role: it is symptomatic that the first
coin-like object, which had been produced in England in the late sixth century,
was a looped *tremissis* bearing the name of Bishop Liudhard, who accompanied
the Merovingian princess Bertha to England on her marriage to Æthelberht of
Kent.[37] This extraordinary piece is much celebrated because of its connections
with early Christianity in Kent and the delicacy of its execution. Perhaps the earliest Anglo-Saxon coin intended to have a monetary function, a *tremissis* with the
name of both the mint, Canterbury, and the moneyer, Eusebius, shows strong
Frankish influence and may even have been struck from dies made in Francia.[38]

---

[30] Andrén 1991: 253; Axboe 1991: 200.
[31] Gaimster 1992: 12–13.
[32] See the discussion in Chaney 1970: 148.
[33] Sutherland 1948: 25; Rigold 1975 on coin finds; Chadwick-Hawkes 1981 for Merovingian finds in
Kent.
[34] Adelson 1957; Werner 1961; Verhulst 1970; Carver 1990; Milne 1990; Lebecq 1999.
[35] Chadwick-Hawkes 1981: 51. Sarre and Dover are mentioned as royal toll stations in charters of the
early eighth century. Faversham may also have been a port. See Evison 1979: 61, and maps 2 and 3.
[36] Sutherland 1948: 24.
[37] Grierson 1979; Werner 1991. See Fig. 5.1.
[38] Sutherland 1948: 32; Grierson 1952; *MEC* 161; *MoE* 37, no. 24, where Archibald suggests that
Eusebius might have been a cleric.

Of more robust Anglo-Saxon workmanship are the mid-seventh-century gold solidi copied from Roman originals, some with runic legends.[39]

More sustained coin production began in the second quarter of the seventh century, as exemplified by the contrasting contents of two hoards, possibly divided by about twenty years. Whereas the Sutton Hoo purse (*c.*625) contains only Merovingian coins, the Crondall hoard (*c.*640) shows 70 per cent of the coins as Anglo-Saxon and the remainder Continental.[40] These Anglo-Saxon gold coins, modelled on contemporary Merovingian production, are commonly known as *thrymsas*—but they are probably the *shillings* of Anglo-Saxon laws.[41] The sixty-nine Anglo-Saxon coins from Crondall fall into twelve different types,[42] and the numerous die-links within these, and with contemporary coins found elsewhere, suggest that at this stage, the second quarter of the seventh century, native coin production was quite small. Even taking account of the presence of imported Continental coins, the currency in the mid-seventh century must have been tiny, and the high-value gold coins must only have been used for special transactions.[43] The map of the circulation of Continental gold coins and of the first Anglo-Saxon issues in the first half of the seventh century extends from east Kent and Essex up the Thames and the east coast.[44]

The third quarter of the same century witnessed an increase in coin production, but, parallel to this, a decrease in the gold content, which gradually fell from *c.*40 per cent in the latest coins from Crondall to 15 per cent or even less.[45] This debasement is parallel to events in Merovingian France, where in *c.*675 gold minting was suspended in favour of silver. A comparable weakening of the gold alloy used for Anglo-Saxon jewellery can be observed, even if its dating is less precise than that of the coinage.[46]

Because of the paucity of die-links among the known coins, the 'pale gold' issues are believed to have been produced in slightly larger quantity, and, judging by the location of their finds, seem to have been concentrated mainly in Kent and East Anglia.[47] Among these, two transitional groups, bearing the names of the moneyers Pada and Vanimundus, will influence the successive issues of silver coins.[48]

---

[39] Sutherland 1948: 51; *MEC* 158. On coins with runic inscriptions, see Blackburn 1991.

[40] For the Sutton Hoo coins: Kent 1975; Rigold 1975; for the Crondall hoard: Sutherland 1948. On Anglo-Saxon gold coins: Stewart 1978. Kent 1975 dates Sutton Hoo *c.*625 and associates it with Rædwald, though it could have been deposited any time in the 620s or even marginally earlier. Crondall is dated in *MEC* 127 '650 or a little earlier', while Metcalf prefers *c.*635 × *c.*645 (*T&S* i. 31).

[41] *MEC* 157.

[42] *T&S* i. 30.

[43] *MEC* 161; *T&S* i. 37–8. It has been argued that the hoard had been assembled to pay a *wergild* (Grierson 1970; *MEC* 126).

[44] See maps in *T&S* i. 34–5. However, Metcalf (ibid. 33) points to the absence of Anglo-Saxon gold coins among the single-finds from East Anglia, contrasting it to the presence of foreign ones.

[45] *MEC* 163.

[46] Chadwick-Hawkes, Merrick, and Metcalf 1966: 120. Much as jewellery was often made with metal from old pieces gone out of fashion, it is often in the added elements, such as loops, that one finds standards matching the numismatic.

[47] *T&S* i, map p. 45.

[48] *MEC* 164; *T&S* i. 73–9 and 80–3.

The transition from pale gold shillings (i.e. ones heavily alloyed with silver) to silver pennies (also, if erroneously, known as *sceattas*)[49] was broadly contemporary with the Merovingian reform of the 670s. Although of similar weight and fabric, the new pennies were given distinctive designs and they mark a radical development in English monetary history.

Silver Issues

The earliest silver coinage seems to have been produced and to have circulated mainly in the south-east,[50] with the exception of the coins produced in Northumbria, which bear the name of King Aldfrith (685–704).[51] Very little in the way of foreign coins appears to have come from the Continent during this so-called 'Primary' phase of the early silver pennies, *c.*675–700, to judge from the hoards and grave groups deposited in this period.[52]

The beginning of the eighth century, however, saw a huge influx of coins from Frisia, mirroring the flourishing Anglo-Frisian trade at the time.[53] The Aston Rowant hoard (*c.*710) indicates the effect this had on the English currency, as only a quarter of the 350 coins in the hoard were Anglo-Saxon.[54] This phase, covering the first decade or so of the eighth century, is referred to as 'Intermediate'. It heralds a further expansion in coin circulation in areas such as East Anglia, the East Midlands, the Thames Valley, and the south-west, which in turn stimulates a proliferation of minting activity into Wessex, Essex, East Anglia, and Mercia, leading to the 'Secondary' phase of the silver coinage.[55]

Artistically, this is the golden age of the coins. Apart from the sheer quantity and variety of production, for a period of about thirty years we are confronted with an extraordinary flourishing of inventiveness on the part of the designers and die-cutters, who introduced many new motifs to their repertoire. The numerous specimens show relatively few die-links, suggesting that it was indeed a large coinage, and the profusion and location of the finds (including sites by roads, rivers, and trackways, as possible fairs, ports, or *wics*) indicate a thriving commercial function for the coins.[56]

However, whereas the Primary and Intermediate issues maintained a high

---

[49] On this misnomer, now quite established, see *MEC* 15 and 157.

[50] Metcalf 1984a; *MEC* 167; *T&S* i. 67.

[51] Until the 730s, with the coins of King Eadberht in Northumbria, and the second half of the eighth century with King Beonna in East Anglia and King Offa of Mercia, Anglo-Saxon coins do not bear the name of kings, but follow the Merovingian example of indicating solely the names of moneyers and of mint places. The series of Aldfrith, a king famous for his learning, is an exception, for which the only precedent is to be found in the gold coins with the legend AVDVARLD REGES, ascribed to Eadbald of Kent (616–40). For these, see Fig. 4.25 and Fig. 2.32.

[52] *MEC* 167; *T&S* i. 63–72.

[53] *MEC* 167. For the commercial relations between England and Frisia: Belaiew 1932; Jellema 1955; Lebecq 1983, 1990, and 1997b. See also pp. 176–77 for a fuller discussion.

[54] Kent 1972; *MEC* 167–8.

[55] *MEC* 168; Metcalf 1988a: 236–9.

[56] Metcalf 1974: 1–3; Hinton 1986: 15; *MEC* 169.

silver content (*c*.90–5 per cent), the Secondary phase saw a progressive debasement down to 20 per cent or less.[57] By the middle of the eighth century we are confronted with the virtual collapse of the currency in the south, with output falling, if not altogether ceasing at many mints.[58] Northumbria was not immediately affected, probably on account of its relative isolation, and East Anglia also seems to have been an exception, with King Beonna (749–58 or later), and King Æthelberht I (died 794) managing to raise standards and production in the middle of the century.[59] Their coins were modelled on contemporary Northumbrian issues, which were of finer silver (40–60 per cent), and cited the king's name,[60] while keeping the East Anglian tradition of indicating the moneyers' names.[61]

Offa's Coinage

In the mid-750s Pepin the Short (751–68) had re-established tighter control over the Frankish coinage, bringing it under stricter state monopoly. The coins were thinner and broader, with restored standards of weight and fineness, and incorporating a royal monogram or legend and the mint name.[62] This was also the pattern of the new Anglo-Saxon coinage under Offa of Mercia (757–96),[63] but with two fundamental differences: on the Anglo-Saxon coins the choice of designs remained freer and more artistic than on their Carolingian counterparts, and in addition to the king they named the moneyers, but not the mint.[64] The interest in monetary developments in the Frankish kingdom mirrors commercial links generating the need for some uniformity in the coinage,[65] although Offa's coins were always lighter.

The majority of coins found in this period are in King Offa's name, and they are outstanding in their variety and artistic quality, especially with regard to his portraits and those of his wife Cynethryth.[66] Thirty-seven moneyers are believed to have worked for him at three mint places (London, Canterbury, and somewhere in East Anglia, possibly Ipswich), and one of them, Wilred, was also one of Beonna's moneyers. Offa's reformed coinage on light, broad flans is likely to have begun *c*.760–5 in London, with an awareness of developments in

---

[57] *MEC* 168 and 172. Peter Northover has performed electron probe microanalyses (EPMA) on a large sample of coins (*T&S* iii. 660–79).

[58] *MEC* 187.

[59] Archibald 1985 and Archibald, Fenwick, and Cowell 1995.

[60] *T&S* iii. 576–93.

[61] *MEC* 271 and 278.

[62] Ibid. 204.

[63] Blunt 1961; Chick 1997. A very useful analytical survey of Mercian coinage is presented in Williams 2001a: see particularly pp. 211–19 for a discussion of Offa's times.

[64] *MEC* 278.

[65] As testified by the well-known letter of 796 from Charlemagne to Offa, concerning merchants, *petra nigra* (now generally accepted probably to refer to Tournai marble: Welch 2001: 157), and cloaks (Dümmler 1895: no. 100; Whitelock 1968: no. 197).

[66] See Figs. 2.23*a* and *b*.

Francia and East Anglia.[67] Towards the end of his reign, *c*.792, a new reformed coinage was introduced, and coins were struck on larger, heavier flans, with more standardized designs, stifling the artistic flair of the earlier coinage. The broad flan penny established by Offa remained the principal denomination, with only minor changes, until the fourteenth century.[68]

Manufacturing of Coins

The idea of impressing a design on precious metal to produce a coin—an object giving concrete expression to monetary values—is very ancient, and carried out in order to guarantee its weight and standard and to distinguish issues from those of other locations.[69] Designs can be obtained either by casting metals in prepared moulds or by transferring the design to pieces of metal through the blow of a hammer (the so-called *hammered coinage*), this latter method being preferred in the West, as more difficult to counterfeit.[70] The making of hammered coinage involved three processes: the cutting of the *dies* (the parts carrying the required design), the preparation of the blank metal pieces to be impressed (the *flans,* which must be of a specified metal alloy and of consistent quality and weight), and the actual striking

The eight early medieval coin dies so far retrieved are bars several centimetres long, made in two sections: a shank of wrought iron, which could be replaced if worn, and a die-cap of carbon steel, which carried the design. The manufacturing technique and the handling of the metal show great sophistication.[71] In order to have designs on the two faces of a coin, a blank flan was placed between two engraved dies, so that when the top one was struck with a hammer, both sides would be impressed. The lower one, the *pile* or anvil die, was tapered so as to be fixed firmly into a block of wood, and carried on its die face the design for the *obverse* of the coin. The upper die, the *trussel*, used for the design of the *reverse* of the coin, had a flat head to receive the blows of the hammer. A reversed image of the desired designs and inscriptions was made on the die faces by means of different types of tools: broad- or narrow-headed graving tools and punches. Graving tools would be used to carve away at the metal freehand, while punches with various ready-made patterns could simply be hammered into the die.[72]

---

[67] Chick 1997.

[68] *MEC* 277 and 280.

[69] The earliest coins were struck in western Asia Minor in the seventh century BC and were small pieces of electrum (a natural alloy of silver and gold) stamped with a single design. Nearly a hundred of these were found at the temple of Artemis at Ephesus. Greek tradition, backed by the historian Herodotus, records the Lydians as the first people to have struck and used coinage of silver and gold. Grierson 1975: 9–10; Carradice 1995: 21.

[70] Grierson 1975: 94 ff.

[71] Archibald, Lang, and Milne 1995: 175.

[72] For a description of the various stages involved in the striking of hammered coinage, see Grierson 1975: 100.

Because the shock caused by the hammer blows ruined the trussel faster than the pile below, requiring frequent substitution, the more intricate design was reserved for the lower die, that is for the obverse of the coin. Often a number of trussels would be issued with each pile,[73] and a series of matchings can sometimes be followed through so-called *die-chains*, which enable coin sequences and relations to be worked out.

Die-Cutters and Moneyers

Preparing the dies was the prerogative of the *die-cutters*, but no name or information regarding them has come down to us from early Anglo-Saxon times. Because of the responsibility and artistic skills required, it is often argued that die-cutters may have been jewellers by training, although some of the techniques required would have been those of an ironsmith, capable of forging and hardening high-grade iron.[74] In fact it must have been a special skill practised by a very small number of people. It is interesting to consider the special position that not only smiths, but particularly goldsmiths held in Anglo-Saxon society. In the earliest code of laws to have come down to us, King Æthelberht of Kent in the early seventh century protected them by a particularly hefty *wergild*.[75] Goldsmiths were highly trained and specialized craftsmen, not just forgers of exquisite jewellery, but veritable 'image makers' to their employers, furnishing them with prestigious artefacts. One can imagine, after the introduction of minting, die-cutters falling in the same category.

The *moneyers* whose names appear on the reverse of most coins after the mid-eighth century were far more numerous than the die-cutters and their roles appear to have been quite distinct. Through the careful study of details of coin designs, one can often identify the hand of individual die-cutters working for several moneyers.[76] In the eighth and ninth centuries it was usual for the dies of all the moneyers of a particular mint to be cut by a single die-cutter, while in the later Anglo-Saxon coinage one die-cutter might furnish several mints in a region or even all mints in the country.[77] Conceivably a die-cutter could also have been a moneyer, but in that case he would have been holding two separate offices concurrently, rather than one flowing from the other.

The function of the moneyers was to act as guarantor of the issue and its quality. Their role no doubt varied from period to period and place to place, but where documentary evidence of their status is available, it suggests that they

---

[73] A ratio of 2 : 1 or 3 : 1 was not uncommon; Archibald, Lang, and Milne 1995: 193.

[74] Jessup 1950: 38, is sceptical, and suggests that if the two roles coincided, the work must have been kept separate, seeing no artistic links between the two productions. How the designs on the coins fitted into the metalwork tradition will be discussed later. In Merovingian France, Abbo and Eligius were both jewellers and moneyers. *MEC* 99.

[75] Attenborough 1922: 4, item 7.

[76] Chick 1997.

[77] Blackburn and Lyon 1986. In the later eleventh century, when die-cutting had in principle been centralized in London, the office of royal die-cutter was hereditary: Stewart 1992: 78.

were usually men of moderately high standing and wealth.[78] It is likely, in practice, that the moneyers organized the production of the coins largely through employees, arranging the necessary finance and security, and accounting to the king or other person from whom they held their office. From Offa's reform onwards, we can see how many moneyers were involved, but in the earlier coinages moneyers are not often named, and when they are, a single moneyer may be responsible for an entire issue (e.g. Pada or Æpa). The role of the moneyer, then, may have changed significantly with Offa's reform.

Patronage

If die-cutters were responsible for the artistic work in cutting the dies, and moneyers stood as guarantors of the quality of the coins produced, who commissioned the coinage, and what degree of control was maintained over issues such as the fineness of the metal used and the choice of design for the dies? Trying to determine at which stage of production the motifs were chosen and by whom is of particular relevance to the art historian.

On the question of whether royal authority or private enterprise lay behind the beginning of Anglo-Saxon coinage, opinions are divided. Bearing in mind that developments in Anglo-Saxon coinage often shadowed monetary events in Merovingian France, where Pepin's reform of *c.*755 reorganized the output firmly under royal control, and that coins inscribed in south-east England carried the names of moneyers rather than kings, authorities such as Grierson and Blackburn see the coinage as stemming from private enterprise, self-regulating in as far as the coinage needed widely accepted standards, before it slowly came under royal control.[79]

Metcalf, on the other hand, believes in strong royal involvement from the start on account of the tight control exercised by kings over their realms. He sees the moneyer as a craftsman licensed by the king by means of a contract binding him to his authority. He is inclined to interpret many of the designs as explicitly representing the sovereign,[80] thus being more relevant than any explicit inscription in affirming royal authority to a largely illiterate population.[81] As stated in laws surviving from the tenth century, the privilege of minting coins could be granted

---

[78] *MEC* 98 ff. In the later Anglo-Saxon period, a number of moneyers have been identified among witnesses to royal charters: Stewartby 1998: 151. In eleventh-century Winchester, their landholdings rank them, with goldsmiths, second only to royal officers. Blackburn has argued that in the late eighth and ninth centuries, they were prominent people drawn from the mercantile community, rather than the royal court, for the same individuals continued in office even when political control of the region changed: Blackburn 1995: 555.

[79] *MEC* 158 ff. Mark Blackburn (personal communication) would now see some degree of royal regulation of the currency, if not control of production, from an early date.

[80] Much of what he considers to be royal iconography is, however, open to debate; see, for instance, Morehart 1985.

[81] *T&S* i. 12 ff.

by the king to his bishops:[82] Metcalf sees them as preserving much older provisions and has suggested that some images in the anonymous silver phase reflect minting by ecclesiastical authorities under strict royal control.[83] Marion Archibald has put forward the idea that some of the coinage may have been issued from monastic foundations, and has suggested that some coins may represent saints.[84]

Much as Metcalf uses iconography as a key to the attribution of coinage to kings and ecclesiastics, he is conscious of the many mistakes made due to incorrect chronology or new finds changing the distribution map of a particular coin.[85] Indeed the awareness of the dangers of bending the interpretation of an image to suit one's particular theory ought to be ever present when offering a precise attribution.[86]

The Function of the Coinage

Whether by royal command or private initiative, there were hard financial considerations behind the introduction of coinage in England, and its control would have brought considerable financial benefits. It is tempting to speculate that, as at the time of Edwin's acceptance of Christianity,[87] decisions would have been taken after a full consultation, the strongest lobbying being on the part of those who had the most interest in the control of the coinage. The question of the function of the coins, whether they were originally intended just as another prestigious commodity in social interactions or already understood as a means of commerce, as currency proper, is relevant for the full understanding of the forces behind its inception and expansion.

Again, scholars are divided on the issue.[88] Some favour a minimalist approach, stressing the importance of gift exchange and interpreting coins as primitive valuables in political and social reciprocity, hence underplaying the importance of coinage in commercial transactions.[89] Others, on account of the volume of coinage in circulation, which they estimate from the number of die-links, and because of their wide distribution as finds, arrive at diametrically opposite

---

[82] See King Athelstan's Grateley decrees (c.925–40; Attenborough 1922: 115): 'In Canterbury there shall be seven minters, four of them the king's, two the archbishop's, and one the abbot's. In Rochester three, two of them the king's and one the bishop's . . .'. Coins were also issued with the names of the archbishops of Canterbury and York and the bishop of London, some also naming the king from whom their authority derived.

[83] *T&S* i. 10–25.

[84] See her entries in Webster and Brown 1997: 224–5 (nos. 57–62), and p. 236 (no. 102), and also her reading of the MONITASCORVM legends as *moneta sanctorum* (unpublished lecture, see *T&S* 435).

[85] *T&S* i. 18 ff.

[86] Boon 1992: 82 has published an instructive article on the interpretation by the seventeenth-century scholar Chifflet of an early Anglo-Saxon shilling (the 'Two Emperors' type) and of a Celtic coin showing three heads in profile as portraying the Arian versus the Catholic view of the Trinity.

[87] *HE* II, 13.

[88] See Hodges 1989: ch. 6, for a discussion of theories relating to the passage of coinage from primitive valuable, to primitive money, to currency.

[89] Grierson 1961; Hendy 1988; Vince 2001: 184.

conclusions as to the economic function of early coinage.[90] Clearly there was a development in the perception and use of money, and much as 'an understanding derived only from the design of the coins may turn out to be superficial',[91] changes in the function of the coinage might be mirrored in the choice of designs.[92]

Mints

Few Anglo-Saxon coins before the tenth century indicate the mint places at which they were struck,[93] but it is the established numismatic practice of mapping the concentration and distribution of finds which helps with the attribution of certain issues to particular regions or mints.[94] However, whereas some attributions and dating are universally accepted and secure,[95] others shift as new finds change the balance of data.

Canterbury is named as the mint on the earliest gold coinage,[96] as is London, only shortly after.[97] They are likely to have been the most important mints in southern England, as they were until the late ninth century and later. York and a mint in East Anglia appear to have started striking in the gold phase,[98] but their output only became really substantial in the eighth century. Southampton/Hamwic was a productive mint in the Secondary phase,[99] but the later West Saxon issues, which may have come from Winchester, were of more political than economic importance. Rochester is first identified as a mint *c.*810 and flourished for only fifty years.[100] The find distributions suggest that in the Secondary series there may have been a number of other mints operating, e.g. in East Anglia,[101] Essex, and eastern Mercia,[102] but they are difficult to locate with confidence. What precisely 'mints' were remains unclear, and might simply signify a place where moneyers' activities were regulated or coordinated.[103]

Chronology

The lack of royal inscriptions and the complexity of many parallel series in the early Anglo-Saxon coinage makes it much harder to date precisely than the

---

[90] Metcalf 1965 on the volume of Anglo-Saxon currency; Grierson 1967 for a contrasting view.

[91] *T&S* i. 24.

[92] This might be argued for the switch to geometric reverses on Offa's coins.

[93] As Series L, *T&S* iii. 373, 406–15.

[94] Metcalf 1984*a* and 2001: his methodology of regression analysis is very promising, but relies on very precise recording of single finds.

[95] In the later eighth and ninth centuries issues in the names of local rulers are clearly more helpful.

[96] *MEC* 160–1.

[97] *MEC* 161–2 and 186; Vince 1990: 112.

[98] For York, see *MEC* 163 and Blackburn 1994; for East Anglia, see Plunkett 2001: 77–8.

[99] Metcalf 1988*c*; Morton 1999.

[100] *MEC* 273.   [101] Newman 1999: 41–4.   [102] Williams 2001*a*: 212.

[103] Pagan 1986: 49.

issues of later centuries. Whereas earlier attempts at chronology based on stylistic associations and inferred progressions failed,[104] it was the careful cross-comparison of the contents of the fifteen English and eight Continental hoards containing Anglo-Saxon silver pennies that allowed Blackburn to establish a more reliable and objective chronology among the later gold and early silver coinages.[105] Even so, extrapolation has been necessary to date many types that have not been found in any hoards.

Support for this chronology can be derived from the decline in the weight of coins and the metals that constitute the alloys, assisting the construction of relative chronologies for a range of different issues.[106] These can, however, only be regarded as tentative, pending the discovery of corroborative evidence, for we cannot be sure that debasement and weight reduction progressed in parallel at different mints.

Archaeology also contributes occasionally.[107] For instance, not only did the excavation at Southampton prove successful for understanding the location and function of the Anglo-Saxon *wic* and its mint,[108] but the find of a coin of Aldfrith stratified in an early eighth-century context helped to attribute the issue firmly to King Aldfrith of Northumbria (685–704), and not to Aldfrith of Lindsey (786–96).[109]

Classifications

In contrast to the lamentable lack of interest shown by art historians, numismatists have dedicated much research to various aspects of Anglo-Saxon coinage, mostly concentrated on the classifications of the various issues and the establishing of dates and origin.[110] Whereas the early gold coins only amount to about 125, centred around the Crondall hoard exhaustively studied by Sutherland and later by Stewart,[111] there are several thousand silver pennies of the later seventh and eighth centuries. Rigold made a fundamental contribution to their understanding by distinguishing Primary, Intermediate, and Secondary phases in the issues, and then subdividing the coins in series, distinguished by letters of the alphabet, some functioning as aides-mémoires, such as *H* for *Hamwic*.[112] His arrangement has been widely adopted, but the classification of the coinage is extremely complicated, as it is also divided in types, originally from the numbering of the coins in the *British Museum Catalogue* (*BMC* Types 1–54),[113]

---

[104] *MEC* 155.   [105] *MEC* 184–9.

[106] See Chadwick-Hawkes, Merrick, and Metcalf 1996.

[107] See Casey and Reece 1988, and in particular the article by Dolley advocating links between archaeologists and numismatists.

[108] Andrews 1988.

[109] Metcalf 1988*c*, report on coin no.125, context SOU31/1703.6184.

[110] *MEC* offers excellent sections on the literature dedicated to the coins at pp. 155 and 267–8.

[111] Sutherland 1948; Stewart 1978.   [112] Rigold 1960 and 1977.   [113] Keary 1887.

subsequently added to by Hill (Types 55–76)[114] and Stewart (Types 77–109).[115] In some literature, references are made according to the arrangement and numbering devised by North.[116] In my references to the coins I shall conform to the traditional division into series and type, as followed by Metcalf in his standard work on this coinage, *Thrymsas and Sceattas in the Ashmolean Museum Oxford*, here abbreviated as *T&S*.

[114] Hill 1953.   [115] Stewart 1984.
[116] North 1980. For an annotated concordance among types and series, see *T&S* iii, 681–5.

PART II

Iconography

2

The Bust

One of the most enduring legacies of Roman coinage is that of busts on coins. No matter how debased the image might appear to be, the appeal of classical proto-types is evident. Though Rome cannot claim to have introduced portraiture to coinage,[1] it used it extensively to put forward political propaganda.[2] On Roman coins portraiture passed from renderings of great realism to mystically idealized anonymous representations influenced by Hellenistic fashion, that is from stan-dard profiles of Western type to three-quarter or frontal portraits of Oriental inspiration.[3] With the advent of Christianity and the absorption of Greek abstract ideas of kingship and authority, models became more stylized with greater emphasis put on the symbols of authority rather than the physiognomy of the king.[4]

As Donald Bullough points out, it is now very difficult to appreciate the full impact that these images, whether 'representations or presentations',[5] would have had on the people, because we see the coins in isolation, divorced from all the reinforcing ritualizing propaganda of the Imperial machinery.[6] The perceived effectiveness of the imagery is evident from the close adherence to the convention of portraiture on the independent coinage of the Barbarian states.[7]

Portraits, whilst retaining their charismatic importance on coins, and many of the features of Roman prototypes, such as the positioning of the bust, headgear, and attributes, were flexible enough to accommodate different tastes and traditions, as well as artistic experiments and subtly changing propaganda messages. It is the variety of Anglo-Saxon responses that will be examined in the following sections, because these peculiarities are particularly valuable, as they

---

[1] Lysimachus of Thrace (323–281 BC) used the head of the deified Alexander the Great on his coinage. Later, portraits of living rulers became common. Grierson 1975: 15.

[2] Bastien 1992: i. 9 gives an overview of the different positions of recent scholars on the question of political message, or lack of it, on Roman coinage.

[3] Reece 1983: 168 ff.

[4] Grierson 1982: 30. The shift towards impersonal busts is partly due to a decline in skills, but also to the idea that the concept of majesty should override individual features and weaknesses. MEC 11.

[5] Reece 1983: 173.

[6] Bullough 1975: 227. Garipzanov 1999 discusses the Carolingian period.

[7] As the majority of Germanic coinages are modelled on *tremisses* (one-third of a solidus), it is the profile bust that was normally imitated. MEC 11.

allow us glimpses into 'native' customs and taste, and alternative sources of inspiration.

Among these, for instance, are bearded portraits. Anglo-Saxon coins on the whole show clean-shaven faces, but those with beards are independent from Roman coins portraying curly-bearded emperors.[8] The types of beards reproduced might mirror local fashions, or make a particular statement.[9] One might wonder if the striking arrangement of the runes spelling the end of the name of the moneyer Tilbeorht on the East Anglian coins of Series R,[10] recalling a throat beard under the chin, as seen on the Undley bracteate and the Sutton Hoo whetstone,[11] may be a conscious archaism. Frontal portraits show beards either long and flowing, or W-shaped,[12] and often incorporate a moustache. Sometimes moustaches alone are featured, recalling well-attested Celto-Germanic portraiture styles,[13] and they are also occasionally greatly exaggerated.[14]

The spiky hairstyles, typical of many Anglo-Saxon issues, find counterparts among Merovingian coinage.[15] On both sides of the Channel Celtic coins could have provided a source of inspiration, in spite of their chronological remoteness, because then as now, accidental finds would have been comparatively common, and would have provided the impulse for new designs.[16] Moreover, similar images in other prestigious media would have made the imitation desirable.[17] Interaction between the Anglo-Saxon and Celtic communities is a factor that cannot be substantiated, but should not be undervalued,[18] especially with regard to metalwork.

Besides the multiplicity of sources, factors such as the ability and sensitivity of the die-cutter, the ambitions of the patron, and questions of allegiance must account for the variety of responses we find on the Anglo-Saxon coins.

[8] Bastien 1992: i. 24.

[9] Bearded/moustachioed figures also appear on eighth-century sculpture at Repton, Ruthwell, Bewcastle, and Rothbury.

[10] See Fig. 2.31b. These are quite remote from classical coins with frontal bearded figures, such as those of Heraclius (cf. Kent and Painter 1977: 181, nos. 724 and 738).

[11] For a discussion of the heads on the Sutton Hoo whetstone, see Bruce-Mitford 1978: ii. 323–4. Five out of the eight heads on the whetstone have 'abnormal beard forms', but these are rendered with the same technique used for other beards/hair. Comparison with the iconography of the Undley bracteate (see Fig. 4.54), where the female head of Roma was converted into a male, either because it was misunderstood, or in order to fit a particular message, supports an all-male interpretation for the heads on the whetstone.

[12] See Figs. 2.7 and 2.8.

[13] See discussion at 'Facing Heads'.

[14] For instance see Fig. 2.7a and Fig. 3.14.

[15] One might compare the similarities between the 'Portrait-and-Cross' type (Crondall 36, *T&S* i, pl. 3, no. 71) and the Merovingian coin from Saint-Bertrand-de-Comminges, moneyer Nonnitus (*MEC* pl. 21, no. 434).

[16] Compare for example the Anglo-Saxon coins of the VERNVS and SAROALDO types (*T&S* i, pl. 8, nos. 146–7 and 151–4) with the Celtic coins of Commius, 30–45 BC and Tasciovanus, 15–10 BC (Van Arsdell 1989: 130, no. 355–1; p. 382, no. 1816-1). According to classical writers, Celts treated their hair with lime to make it stand up intimidatingly (Green 1992: 154), but it is also true that exaggerated hair rendering is a common trait amongst 'barbarian' coinages. See Fig. 2.20.

[17] See the head from the handle-mount of the Aylesford bucket (Megaw and Megaw 1989: 187, fig. 316).

[18] Faull 1977, on British survival in Anglo-Saxon Northumbria, argues for the similarities between the two communities and their integration by the time of Christianization.

Fig. 2.1. *a.* lvndiniv, gold shilling, *c.*640 (*T&S* 55 = Crondall 57. The Ashmolean Museum, Oxford); *b.* detail from the portrait of St Luke, The Gospels of St Augustine, MS 286 fo. 129ᵛ, 6th century Corpus Christi College Cambridge (The Master and Fellows of Corpus Christi College, Cambridge).

THE HEAD

Facing Heads

The lvndiniv coin from Crondall is dated around the early 630s on account of its fineness (*c.*64 per cent).[19] Baldwin Brown and Kent believed it to represent an ecclesiastic, perhaps Mellitus,[20] bishop of London in the province of the East Saxons 604–16.[21] The attribution is now seen to be anachronistic, but a link to the Roman mission is possible. Mellitus had been among the second wave of missionaries sent to England by Pope Gregory with 'all such things as were generally necessary for the worship and ministry of the Church, such as sacred vessels, altar cloths and church ornaments, vestments for priests and clerks, relics of the holy apostles and martyrs, and very many manuscripts',[22] among them, quite probably, the Gospels of St Augustine.[23] The lack of modelling on the coin suggests that the prototype was not derived from a medallic precedent: the similarity between the portrait on the coin and the pensive expression of the Evangelist suggests that this or a similar Latin manuscript may have been the model (Fig. 2.1). The shape of the neckline is also comparable.[24]

A detail, visible on some specimens only,[25] might provide a further link to the Gospels of St Augustine. The band framing the head, which Sutherland calls 'experimental "guilloche-hatching" ',[26] could have been inspired by the motif behind the head of St Luke. This pattern was used extensively as a framing device from classical times, in either its single or double form, for metalwork, mosaics,

---

[19] Stewart 1978: 148.
[20] Baldwin Brown 1903–37: iii. 74; Sutherland 1948: 41 ff.
[21] At the time of King Sæberht, nephew of Æthelberht of Kent. *HE* II, 3.
[22] *HE* I, 29.
[23] *MoE* 17. Marsden 1999: 287–9.
[24] The curved line that borders the profile of the neck has been interpreted by Baldwin Brown as a *pallium*, and therefore the head on the coin is considered by him to be that of an archbishop, either Augustine or Laurentius (Baldwin Brown 1903–37: iii. 74). This detail, however, might have apotropaic connotations and compares to the lunette shape on which some figures on the coins stand (see Fig. 3.10).
[25] The Crondall examples (Sutherland 1948: 53–9) are all struck from the same obverse die, but some details are off the flan. Ex-Subjack, 1 differs.
[26] Sutherland 1948: 45.

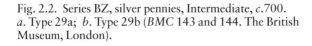

Fig. 2.2. Series BZ, silver pennies, Intermediate, *c.*700.   Fig. 2.3. Detail from the
a. Type 29a; *b.* Type 29b (*BMC* 143 and 144. The British   haunch of the bird mount on
Museum, London).   the Sutton Hoo shield, first
                                                                      quarter 7th century (© The
                                                                      British Museum, London).

and sculpture.[27] From the seventh century onwards it is more frequent as a single 'rope' framing panels,[28] in consciously classicizing fashion, as can be seen on the Hexham plaque, which is often compared to the Merovingian St Mumma reliquary;[29] however, the three-dimensional modelling of the casket is very different from the flat style of the plaque, whose prototype may also have been derived from a manuscript illumination. If one could speculate about churches displaying matching artefacts in different media, so as to impress audiences with a 'total experience', perhaps coinage too may have been part of the experiment.

A scarce issue of the late seventh/early eighth century, Intermediate Series BZ, Type 29, shows facing heads in both linear and modelled styles (Fig. 2.2).[30] Metcalf postulates that Type 29b, 'in a flat and inferior linear style', must have been copied from 29a by a less skilled die-cutter;[31] however, the similarity between Type 29b and the Hexham plaque, which stems from the sophisticated milieu of St Wilfrid, indicates otherwise, and suggests a different explanation. The two styles, in fact, are contemporaneous and well established.[32] Both are

[27] See the framing of the panels on the Esquiline treasure caskets, late Roman, fourth century AD (Kent and Painter 1977: 44–5).

[28] Raspi-Serra 1974: 34, with references to Merovingian parallels; Pugliese Carratelli 1984: 253–4, figs. 145–9; p. 268, fig. 159.

[29] For the Hexham plaque, see *MoE* 138, no. 104, and for St Mumma reliquary (Abbey of Fleury, Saint-Benoit-sur-Loire), of the mid-seventh century, see Hubert, Porcher, and Volbach 1969: 281, fig. 311.

[30] The two Types are linked by their reverses (bird-on-cross); see *T&S* i. 133–7. On some specimens of Type 29b it is possible to see little hands in the *orans* position at the side of the figure, probably misinterpreted as part of a legend by later copies. Both Types have three crosses above the heads, but a gender differentiation may be debatable.

[31] *T&S* i. 136.

[32] For the deep modelling of 29a we can find metalwork parallels on terminal lobes of great square-headed brooches (Hines 1997: 38, fig. 17, Duston, Mucking II 643 and Berinsfield 102; Leeds 1949, pl. 9, Linton Heath 9) and late fifth to sixth-century button brooches (MacGregor and Bolick 1993: 54, e.g. no. 3.1). The modelling flattens as the face becomes more abstract (e.g. no. 3.11). For the linear style, see the seventh-century pendant from Ash, Kent, with four faces in repoussé (*MoE* 25, no. 8) and the carvings on St Cuthbert's coffin (G. Henderson 1987: 116, figs. 166–8).

Fig. 2.4. The 'York Group', pale gold shillings, *c.*670 (*a.* CM 1850, 5-6-1; *b.* CM 1979, 10-10-1. The British Museum, London).

Fig. 2.5. Detail from the symbol of St Matthew, Book of Durrow, MS A.4.5 (57), fo. 21ᵛ, mid 7th century, Trinity College Library, Dublin (The Board of Trinity College Dublin).

found among the treasure from Sutton Hoo (the modelled faces on the whetstone and the helmet's plaques and the linear ones on the haunch and tail of the bird on the shield) and both styles will have influenced the coinage (Fig. 2.3).

A small group of gold *tremisses*, known as the 'York Group' on account of its Northumbrian provenance, geographically too remote to have been represented in the Crondall hoard, but arguably datable by it,[33] presents us with an arresting image (Fig. 2.4). Prototypes for the obverse have been sought either in a Byzantine frontal bust or a Constantinian 'camp gate',[34] and the design interpreted as a figure or a building.[35] The discovery in 1991 of a specimen from Burton-by-Lincoln has made the reading of the image as a 'standing figure between two crosses' more compelling, though his identity, and the function of the crosses, has not been resolved.[36] Blackburn interprets the radiating lines around the face as hair and beards; however, these compare to the garnets surrounding the face on the appliqué of Sutton Hoo (Fig. 2.3), which puts the image in the tradition of fine royal metalwork and links Northumbria and East Anglia.

The two crosses suggest an apotropaic function, like the double wreath-ties of the facing busts of the so-called 'Triquetras Eclectic Group',[37] or crosses flanking

---

[33] Their fineness (50–60 per cent gold) would place them among the baser and later Crondall coins, *c.*640s (Blackburn 1994: 207 ff.). Pirie 1992: 14, however, questions the fairness of such a parameter.

[34] Pirie 1992 discusses the literature.

[35] *T&S* i. 51 favours the first option, whilst North (1980: i, no. 27/1) and Pirie (1992: 14 ff.) the second. Pirie suggests that the image might represent one of the Northumbrian ecclesiastical stone buildings commissioned by Benedict Biscop and Wilfrid and executed by foreign craftsmen, who would have needed payment with coins, to which they were accustomed.

[36] Blackburn 1994: pl. 21, no. 6.

[37] *T&S* iii. 422–5. These coins, related to Secondary Series K, will be discussed in detail at 'Diadems'; see Fig. 2.39.

Fig. 2.6. Series H, Type 49, silver pennies, mid/late Secondary. *a*. variety 1a (*BMC* 192. The British Museum London); *b*. variety 2a (*T&S* 285. The Ashmolean Museum, Oxford).

Fig. 2.7. *a*. Series Z, Type 66, silver penny, early/mid Secondary (3589, de Wit collection); *b*. Series Q, Type QIG, silver penny, mid/late Secondary (3094, de Wit collection).

standing figures.[38] A numismatic precedent exists in coins of Justinian, where the emperor is shown facing, with double wreath-ties and two crosses.[39] The impression of the Anglo-Saxon image is that of unassailable strength, to which the 'armour' contributes: its treatment is reminiscent of the symbol of St Matthew in the Book of Durrow (Fig. 2.5), which Henderson has compared to other images, in metalwork and stone, all equally rigid and impenetrable.[40] In the same vein, the reverse of the York specimen illustrated on p. 27, now at the British Museum, shows four faces, similar to those on the obverse, arranged around a square carefully subdivided, as if for *cloisonné*; the prongs at the corners of the square might be interpreted as raised arms in the *orans* position. The iconography on the coins professes Christianity and alludes to a strong belief in its physical protective power.

A moustached face comparable to those of Series BZ, Type 29a, and sharing the grave expression of the York group, appears on coins of Secondary Series H, Type 49.[41] From among the many variations of the obverse, which show a well-modelled round or kite-shaped head, surrounded by a cowl made up of pellets—recalling that of the Sutton Hoo whetstone—and a variable number of roundels/bosses, two varieties are illustrated here (Fig. 2.6).[42]

On coins of Early/Mid-Secondary Series Z, Type 66,[43] and of Secondary Series Q, Type QIG,[44] the hair has a characteristic bell-shape and curls outwards (Fig. 2.7). Prototypes and *comparanda* can be found in Anglo-Saxon and Continental

[38] See 'Single Figures between Crosses'. Compare also Series BZ, Type 29b, in Fig. 2.3, with prominent crosses as pseudo-inscription arranged as a protective canopy over the head.

[39] See the copper coin of Justinian, *c*. AD 550 in Reece 1983: 237, fig. 203*c*.

[40] G. Henderson 1987: 48–9, figs. 54–7.

[41] *T&S* iii. 321 ff. It is a large issue, centred at Hamwic, spanning a long period of time.

[42] It is thought that the permutations in the number of roundels are indications of different issues: *T&S* iii. 326. Similar roundels also appear on some reverses (see Fig. 4.19); the overall impression is of Celtic influence: see for instance the silver disk from Manerbio (Italy), first century BC (Megaw and Megaw 1989: 167, fig. 268).

[43] *T&S* i. 137. The high silver content points to an early date, *c*.710; finds are mainly from Norfolk.

[44] *T&S* iii. 491–2, and i. 133–4, where Metcalf suggests Series Z and Q might be from the same mint.

Fig. 2.8. *a–b*. Type 30, silver
pennies, late Intermediate/early
Secondary, Type 30b (*T&S* 430
and 431. The Ashmolean
Museum, Oxford).

metalwork.[45] Type QIG was for many years known from only one coin, found at
Carlisle (illustrated on p. 28), and bracketed with Series Z facing heads. There
are now six specimens,[46] with Northumbria/Norfolk provenances (where
known). A fundamental difference between Series Z and QIG, as between Types
29b and 29a of Series BZ (Fig. 2.2), is the absence of moustache. It is possible to
postulate female portraits commemorating influential ladies, perhaps saints or
abbesses, just as female-oriented iconography has been proposed for other artistic works for female patrons and audiences.[47]

   In addition to a moustache, coins of Series Z have a W-shaped/forked beard,
which also characterizes the contemporary coins of Series BZ, but differs from
the beards of coins of *c.*720, late Intermediate/Secondary Series X, of Danish
origin, known as the 'Wodan/monster type'.[48] Types 30a and b,[49] a delicately
engraved group only found in England, with derivative obverses, and regarded
as Anglo-Saxon, opt for W-shaped/forked beards (Fig. 2.8). As Metcalf points
out, both English and Danish coins make use of a familiar image derived from a
common stock, which he perceives as Germanic and Scandinavian.[50] A gold seal-
ring matrix from Postwick (Norfolk)[51] offers an interesting comparison, as the
facing head, on account of the W-shaped markings that appear under the chin
and the wild hair, relates to those illustrated above. Its prototype is to be found
in images of Medusa, which were widely used as good-luck charms in the Roman

---

   [45] Dunston brooch (footlobe) (Hines 1997: 37, fig. 17*a*; see also Berinsfield 102, fig. 17*c*); brooch from
Gammertingen, Baden-Württemberg (Klein-Pfeuffer 1993: pl. 92, no. 74; pp. 214 and 344). *Pace* Callmer
1984: 20–1, the Series Z coin he illustrates at Fig. 14 *does not* have annulets at the ears.
   [46] There are five in de Wit's collection (including the Carlisle find) and one ex-Subjack, 62.
   [47] See Farr 1997*a* for a thought-provoking discussion on the waning position of women in a Roman-
ized Anglo-Saxon church.
   [48] Whereas earlier scholars attributed the series to England, a Frisian source was later suggested on
account of the Hallum and Terwispel hoards. Because of the numerous and well-datable finds from Ribe
and nearby Dankirke, Metcalf suggests a Danish origin, with Ribe as the mint-town: *T&S* ii. 277;
Bendixen 1981*b*. Distribution of the English finds and of Anglo-Saxon imitations: East Anglia and South,
including Hamwic.
   [49] *T&S* iii. 527–31.
   [50] *T&S* i. 134.
   [51] The Postwick matrix, believed to be of Merovingian type and inscribed with the name
Baldehildis (possibly Bathilda, *c.*635–80, queen of Clovis II), was found by a metal detectorist in 1998,
and acquired in 2000 by the Norwich Castle Museum.

world: many are known from Roman Britain, fashioned as cameos or in jet. The original features of Medusa, traditionally with wings over the forehead and surrounded by serpents, became gradually blurred and misunderstood, until the snakes were turned into an ornamental zigzag border, eventually simplified in a W-pattern, easily taken for a beard.[52]

The wild hair of Danish Series X and related coins has given rise to the label 'Wodan', which, whilst useful as a mnemonic device, links their iconography solely to the Germanic pantheon.[53] Both Bendixen's appreciation of the prevalence of such masks in Merovingian and Scandinavian art and Metcalf's embracing of the more neutral description of 'facing head',[54] modelled on Salin's 'le masque humain',[55] help to convey a wider gamut of ideas and images shared not only by Germanic tribes, but also by Celts and Romans.[56]

The rich iconography of male facing heads on all these coins is close to moustached counterparts in the native Anglo-Saxon and Scandinavian tradition, and their Roman and Celtic precedents.[57]

Bareheaded Portraits

Thrymsas labelled 'London derived',[58] known from the Crondall hoard (*c*.645) and a few other finds,[59] have profile bareheaded portraits cut at the neck and framed by a band of hatching similar to the LVNDINIV types.[60] The hair is indicated by three thick strands swept back, in a style familiar in contemporary Anglo-Saxon metalwork, as seen in the Dorchester barrel-lock;[61] the face, however, is clean-shaven (Fig. 2.9).

[52] A devolution can be seen in Romano-British Medusa jewellery comparing the images of Medusa in Henig 1978: pl. 50, no. 725, Allason-Jones 1996: 25, no. 3, and Henig 1978: pl. 52, no. 731. Henig 1978: pl. 51, nos. 727–8, show crosses on Medusa's head comparable to that on the Postwick matrix. Toynbee 1964: 372 suggests that similar female heads lacking wings and snakes represent maenads.

[53] Hill 1952: 2, however, suggested a derivation from Byzantine coins showing the head of Christ. On some Merovingian buckles the iconography of the head is turned to Christian by the addition of inscriptions. See Salin 1949–59: iv. 271.

[54] Bendixen 1981*b*: 64; *T&S* ii. 275.

[55] Salin 1949–59: iv. 272. He considers the head to represent an original pagan protective god, and then, in Christian times, the Holy Face (p. 277). Salin's own opinion for the *sceattas* is stated at p. 221: 'un masque divin, peut-être solaire'.

[56] Compare for instance the footplate frame and terminal lobe of the great square-headed brooch from Barrington A (Hines 1997: 178, fig. 92*b*), the masks on the rim of the silver quoit brooch from Howletts (Smith 1923: 54, fig. 58), the buckle from Corbie (Salin 1949–59: iii. 227), and the Romano-British head from the pediment of Sulis Minerva Temple, Bath.

[57] One could compare the iconography of the coins with the detail of the hand-grip of a wagon from Dejbjerg Mose (Denmark), the silver coin of the? / Taurisci (Megaw and Megaw 1989: 167, nos. 268 and 266), and a Cunobelin bronze coin (Van Arsdell 1989: 403, no. 1963-1). See also the bracteate from Gerete (Webster and Brown 1997: pl. 57), the buckle from Aker, seventh century (Magnusson and Forman 1976: 17), the masks of the Oseberg funerary cart, ninth century (Wilson 1980: figs. 12 and 13), and the moustache on the Vendel and Sutton Hoo helmets. Great square-headed brooches, which furnished many comparisons, originated in Scandinavia (Hines 1997: 1). See also Bruce-Mitford 1974: 11; Biddle and Kjølbye-Biddle 1985: 262.

[58] Sutherland 1948: 86. Metcalf, however, doubts this, on account of alloy and distribution (*T&S* i. 59–60).

[59] Sutherland 1948, Crondall 60–8, and *T&S* i. 60.

[60] See discussion above, p. 25.

[61] May 1977: 64, 73–5; MacGregor and Bolick 1993: 268, no. 59.1.

Fig. 2.9. *a* and *c*. 'London Derived', gold shillings, *c*.640 (*a*. *T&S* 24; *c*. *T&S* 32 = Crondall 63. The Ashmolean Museum, Oxford); *b*. copper-alloy barrel-lock from Dorchester, 7th century (1993.50. The Ashmolean Museum, Oxford).

Some influence from Celtic iconography may well be postulated, especially when comparing the strong similarities between a left-facing specimen from the Crondall hoard and certain Iceni coins.[62]

Bareheaded Portraits of Offa

The majority of portraits of Offa (757–96), show him bareheaded, even when the head is framed by a halo.[63] The elegant quality of the execution and the introduction of name and royal title suggest a conscious imitation of classical models, old and new, often drawn via the Anglo-Saxon artistic tradition, which, as Keary pointed out, was 'fully capable . . . of furnishing Offa with designs for his coins'.[64]

Arguably his most striking and elegant portrait is that showing him with hair dressed in voluminous curls (Fig. 2.10).[65] Although numismatic precedents for the hairstyle can be found amongst the coinage of Hadrian and of his successors,[66] and even amongst Anglo-Saxon gold issues of the LICINIVS type,[67] if we look to Insular manuscripts and sculpture for *comparanda*, it is striking how the curly hairstyle is consistently employed in representations of King David (Fig. 2.11).[68] Unlike the flat pattern-making of other wavy heads, such as in the

---

[62] Compare Crondall 63 (*T&S* i, pl. 2, no. 32) with the coin of the Iceni, *c*.20–15 BC in Van Arsdell 1989: 196, no. 665–1.

[63] See Fig. 2.54.

[64] Keary 1875: 215.

[65] Blunt 1961: pl. 5, nos. 37–41 (moneyer Eadhun) and 46 (moneyer Alhmund); pl. 6, no. 74 (moneyer Pehtwald).

[66] Hadrian, however, has wavy, rather than curly hair, and also a beard, as do his (curlier) successors, Antoninus Pius and Marcus Aurelius (Bastien 1992: i. 24–5; iii, pls. 49–57 and 62–5).

[67] See Fig. 2.26*b*.

[68] Representations of David with curled hair are to be found in the Durham Cassiodorus (fos. 81ᵛ and 172ᵛ; Wilson 1984: 42, no. 31 and p. 62, no. 53) and in the Vespasian Psalter (historiated initials, fos. 31 and 53, *MoE* 198, no. 153). For a full discussion and coverage of the David iconography: Henderson 1986, and 'Images of Power: The case of King David' in Webster and Brown 1997: 226–30. It must be noted though that a curly hairstyle is also a feature of the angel at Breedon-on-the-Hill (Fig. 2.25).

Fig. 2.10. Penny of Offa of Mercia
(757–96), moneyer Eadhun (*MEC* 1126.
The Fitzwilliam Museum, Cambridge).

Fig. 2.11. Detail of the St Andrews
Sarcophagus (St Andrews Cathedral
Museum, Fife, Scotland), late 8th century
(photograph courtesy of Dr I. and Prof.
G. Henderson).

Lindisfarne Gospels,[69] these images of King David appear to emphasize the voluminous tridimensionality of the curls, inviting a parallel with other representations of him, as for instance on the 'David Plates'.[70]

   Donald Bullough, whilst accepting the supposition that early medieval representations of King David were considered 'types' of contemporary kingship, and
indeed citing the David Plates as such visual allegory, rejects similar intentions or
interpretations for eighth-century Western images of David.[71] However, that
parallels between Old Testament and contemporary ideals of kingship were
drawn is apparent from writings of Bede and Alcuin.[72] Such virtues as shown by
the figure of David were attractive and useful qualities for kings,[73] and could be
said to be part of the *Zeitgeist*.[74] If Charlemagne saw himself as a new David, and
was so referred to by his friends and counsellors,[75] it would be no surprise—
although we have no remaining evidence—if Offa chose to show himself as an
embodiment of the ideal of David. As for the correct 'reading' of such an image
by the audience, in spite of caveats,[76] the manipulation of the David iconography

   [69] See curly portraits of Matthew's symbol and spectator, Mark and Luke, Lindisfarne Gospels, fos.
25ᵛ, 94ᵛ, and 137ᵛ (Backhouse 1981: 40, 46, and 50).
   [70] The David Plates, from the 'Second Cyprus treasure', AD 613–29/30 (Kent and Painter 1977: 109,
no. 184). See ibid. 102 on the affinity between the iconography of the plates and other cycles, supporting
the theory postulating common prototypes and illustrated Psalters, now lost, in the fourth and fifth centuries. Arguably, some of these may have been known in Anglo-Saxon England.
   [71] Bullough 1975: 238 ff.
   [72] See Dümmler 1895, letters of Alcuin to Charlemagne, e.g. nos. 41, 177, 178, 249. Wallace-Hadrill
1975: 185, and 1971: 72–88, discusses the conceptions and ideals of kingship in Bede and Alcuin. For
Bullough, however, Bede shows 'little enthusiasm' for parallels between 'the "literary-historical" David
and the English kings whose historian he was' (Bullough 1975: 238).
   [73] Nelson 1995: 423 ff. Henderson 1994: 79–81 and 92–3 stresses the importance of understanding the
iconography as an expression of secular kingship.
   [74] The iconography of the St Andrews Sarcophagus may be seen in this context: Henderson 1998: 155.
   [75] Dümmler 1895, e.g. letters nos. 72, 112, 118, 121.
   [76] Bullough 1975: 238; Henderson 1986: 100.

Fig. 2.12. Pennies of Offa of Mercia (757–96). *a.* moneyer unknown; *b.* moneyer Ibba; *c.* moneyer Dud (*BMC* 30; CM 1955, 7-8-351; CM 1896, 4-4-18. The British Museum, London).

in Insular renderings assures familiarity both with the contents and with the channels of transmission,[77] making likely that understanding of the ideal royal hero that Offa would have been keen to convey.

Such an exaggerated hairstyle would not pass unnoticed, nor would the refined dignity of his many portraits. Certain eye-catching coins of the moneyer Alhmund represent Offa with a hairstyle with fringe and tightly escheloned curls.[78] Around his neck some dies show a necklace with a pendant. Other bare-headed representations of Offa show him with a variety of coiffures and often mystically heaven-gazing (Fig. 2.12). It is possible that Offa's coinage may have employed such hieratic portraits,[79] and the iconography of King David,[80] in order to stress 'otherworldliness' and the sacrality of kingship.

All these different portrait coins clearly show the wealth and breadth of the sources of inspiration available to Offa's die-cutters, as well as his interest in experimenting with new models. The iconography of the coins is derived not only from Roman prototypes, but also from exotic models, as in the case of the gold coin (BMA 14),[81] imitating a *dinar* of Calif Al Mansur.[82] Although much of the contemporary Mercian art is lost, what remains makes us wonder about the wide-ranging, educated, and cosmopolitan tastes of Offa's court.[83]

[77] Henderson 1986: 101 and 107 ff.; Webster and Brown 1997: 226.

[78] I favour the distinction between Alhmund and Ealmund advocated by Metcalf 1963: 41. Alhmund's known coins are: *BMC* 8 and Hunterian 305, from the same die, and Blunt 43, Chur, ex-Ilanz hoard (all with cross reverses, see below); specimens from Shalford (*Coin Register* 1984: no. 21), nr Derby (*Coin Register* 1986: no. 88), and the one illustrated in the *Numismatic Circular* (vol. 97, Nov. 1989, no. 5892) reproduce the hairstyle, plus a large and elongated eye with double-headed torque reverses.

[79] Such experiments call to mind those of Constantine I (Reece 1983: 175, figs. 143*g–j*).

[80] The 'David hairstyle' occurs on coins of the moneyers Eadhun, Alhmund, and Pehtwald, all associated with the London mint (Stewart 1986: 41), and also combining the upward gaze.

[81] Blunt 1961: pl. 4, no. 5.

[82] The Abbasid coin is dated 773/4 and the skilful Anglo-Saxon copy adds Offa's name, upside-down in relation to the elusive Kufic inscription (Blunt 1961: 50, pl. 4, no. 5). For Offa's gold coinage, see Blunt and Dolley 1968. Possible Islamic influences on Anglo-Saxon coinage are discussed at 'Standing Figures with Cross and Bird'.

[83] For instance, the friezes at Breedon-on-the-Hill are believed to reflect Coptic and Near Eastern models (Jewell 1986: 108–9 and Plunkett 1998: 215 ff.). See also 'The Mercian Supremacy' section in *MoE* 193–253 and the various contributions in Brown and Farr 2001.

Fig. 2.13. *a*. Series B, Type Bx, silver penny, Primary (*BMC* 26. The British Museum, London); *b*. penny of Offa of Mercia (757–96), moneyer Alhmund (*MEC* 1123. The Fitzwilliam Museum, Cambridge).

Fig. 2.14. Detail of shaft from Otley (Church of All Saints, Otley, Yorkshire), 8th century (photograph courtesy of Dr J. Hawkes).

Encircled Heads[84]

Leafy wreaths, symbols of the triumphant emperor, were sometimes used on classical coinage to encircle portraits or inscriptions on the reverse, exploiting the decorative potential of the ties fastening the branches and of the top central jewel.[85] Besides such wreaths, which could be considered outward signs of triumph, Imperial coinage, especially in the East, used haloes as a manifestation of the superior mystical aura emanating from the emperor, or indeed to suggest sacred isolation.[86]

On Merovingian coinage, both gold and silver, circles of pellets are regularly found on the reverse, separating the central motif (usually a cross) from the inscription.[87] This practice is imitated in England, but their use around the bust, either completely surrounding it or forming a canopy around the head, appears to have been an Anglo-Saxon innovation, perhaps influenced by classical wreaths and haloes, but there is unlikely to have been any political connotation. More than just decorative enhancement, however, they might have served an apotropaic function comparable to that of cowls on coins and other artefacts.[88]

A motif used over an extensive period in Anglo-Saxon coinage, circles resting on the shoulders of a bust, and separating it from an inscription, are met with from the gold coins of 'benutigo', possibly earlier than 630, to the Intermediate

[84] The 'guilloche-hatching' forming a halo-like background to bareheaded busts has already been considered (see above, 'Facing Heads'). Circles of pellets bordering the perimeter of the flans will not be discussed: they are a common feature and may be compared to the organization of motifs into fields by means of frames, often multiple, typical of Anglo-Saxon art.

[85] See for instance the highly decorative reverse of the silver multiple of Constantius (Bastien 1992: iii, pl. 188, no. 2).

[86] Bastien 1992: i. 167. Elsner 1998: 84. In a Christian context, haloes are found from the second century, and reserved for representations of Christ and the saints from the fourth century.

[87] Examples: *MEC* pls. 20–9.

[88] See discussion regarding Figs. 2.6 and 2.7.

Fig. 2.15. Series K, Type 32a, silver penny, Secondary (*BMC* 151. The British Museum, London).

Fig. 2.16. Series O, silver pennies, Type 38 Secondary. *a.* (*BMC* 108. The British Museum, London); *b.* (*T&S* 374. The Ashmolean Museum, Oxford).

Type Bx (680–700), to the coins of Offa at the end of the eighth century, and beyond (Fig. 2.13).[89] On illiterate coins as well as Offa's legend, annulets or crosses begin and end the sequences of letters/symbols, implying quasi-magical associations for the inscription. Fused with the circle in a band, the whole can be interpreted as a 'canopy' above the head, a favourite way of portraying figures and organizing space in manuscripts, sculpture, etc.,[90] but also a much older way of suggesting a protected space (Fig. 2.14).[91] The crest on the York helmet,[92] with zoomorphic bands bearing Christian inscriptions, offers a three-dimensional counterpart.

The idea of a self-contained, niche-like space is apparent on coins of Secondary Series K, Type 32a where the heads, flanked by knotted wreath-ties and a hand-held cross as apotropaic attributes, become visually detached from the geometrically rendered bust (Fig. 2.15).

At the beginning of the sequence of Secondary Series O, Type 38 features a head framed by a pseudo-legend and by a pelleted circle resting on an ornamental curve, taken to represent the bust (Fig. 2.16a).[93] This element, however, might represent a torque, worn as insignia on the chest in the manner of the Roman army, and as seen on some bracteates, hence the design could be interpreted as talismanic.[94] This design changes slowly to the point where inscription and

[89] 'benutigo' (Sutherland 1948: pl. 1, no. 17: for its fineness and dating: Stewart 1978: 149); Series Bx (*T&S* i, pl. 5, nos. 97–9). Offa's coins adopt the device extensively (see the plates in Blunt 1961: *passim*). See also ninth-century coins from Wessex and Mercia (*MEC* pls. 57–8).

[90] See canon tables collected under arcades, and the organization of motifs and roundels under arcades in the panels of embroidery of the chasuble of SS Harlindis and Relindis (*MoE* 184, no. 143). See also the sculptural panels at Breedon and Castor, the 'Hedda' stone at Peterborough, and the shaft at Gloucester (illustrated in *MoE* 240–1).

[91] See the Niederdollendorf Stele (Engemann and Rüger 1991: 141, fig. 86b).

[92] *MoE* 60, no. 47; Tweddle 1992.

[93] *T&S* iii. 470.

[94] Graham-Campbell 2001: 33; see the bracteate from Maglemose, Præstø (Mackeprang 1952: pl. 4, no. 4).

Fig. 2.17. *a*. pendant from
Bacton, Norfolk, 7th century
(© The British Museum,
London); *b*. pendant from
Wieuwerd, Friesland (imitat-
ing solidus of Justinian), 7th
century (Rijksmuseum van
Oudheden, Leiden).

Fig. 2.18. *a*. Series B, Type
BIB, silver penny, Primary; *b*.
Series J Type 85, silver penny,
early Secondary (*T&S* 101 and
293. The Ashmolean Museum,
Oxford).

torque become assimilated and resemble the ornamental border of bracteates, or
of some seventh-century jewelled coin-pendants, like the one from Bacton (Fig.
2.17). Speake interprets the Bacton pendant's *cloisonné* border as a double-
headed serpent torque: others, including the Frisian craftsman of the Wieuwerd
jewel who, according to Speake, copied the Bacton pendant, only saw it as plait-
work.[95] The motif of the interlinked jaws might have been interpreted in isolation as an interlaced snake. As such, it makes an interesting comparison with a
series of coins of Offa by the moneyer Pendred, where the encircling label is split
in two by the insertion of a coiled snake above the portrait: its apotropaic character is evident.[96]

    The ancient motif of the *uroborus*, the snake biting its own tail,[97] appears on
both obverses and reverses of coins of Primary Series B and its copy, Secondary Series J, Type 85: it is then replaced by a plain surround of pellets in other
types of Series J (Fig. 2.18). Arguably, its apotropaic function is left to the magic
of the protective circle, a device, however, common throughout the Series. Parallels can be seen with the iconography of Secondary Series H, where the facing
heads are either partially or entirely surrounded by pellets.[98] The motif of

[95] Speake 1970. See also discussion below, in 'Birds and Snakes'. The Bacton pendant's interlaced
border is fundamental for the understanding of the plaited snake on the Obrigheim brooch (Fig. 4.11).
[96] See below, Fig. 4.51. For coins of Offa by the moneyer Pendred: Blunt 1961: pl. 6, nos. 76–8.
[97] Speake 1980: 91.
[98] See Fig. 2.6.

Fig. 2.19. Series J, Type 37, silver penny, Secondary (*T&S* 299. The Ashmolean Museum, Oxford).

Fig. 2.20. Celtic coin, found at St Nicholas at Wade, Thanet, Kent (Amgueddfa ac Orielau Cenedlaethol Cymru/National Museum & Galleries of Wales).

encircled heads on the coinage seems therefore to hark back not so much to classical numismatic prototypes, but to indigenous traditions and beliefs.

Confronting Heads

In the Secondary Series J, Types 37 and 72 employ confronting twinned heads in the distinctive style with quill-like hair and pearled diadem that Series J derives from Primary Series B (Fig. 2.19).[99]

Late Antiquity presents us with two numismatic traditions of double portraiture.[100] In the West, busts are shown as differentiated portraits in profile, whilst in the East representations are usually frontal, icon-like, portraying rank difference by means of size, but stressing family resemblance.[101] According to Miles, the Byzantine iconography of two rulers on either side of a cross[102] was borrowed by the Visigoths for coinage struck during the joint rule of Egica and Wittiza, *c*.698–702.[103] This in its turn is believed to have inspired a similar Merovingian gold coin from *Vellavorum civitas*,[104] and silver denarii from Savonnière, said to represent the local patron saints, Gervasius and Protasius.[105]

Whether these Merovingian coins can be considered precedents of the Anglo-Saxon issues is open to question.[106] A recently found Celtic coin from Kent has also been proposed as prototype (Fig. 2.20), persuasive not only

---

[99] For Series B, see illustration above, Fig. 2.13. [100] Bastien 1992: ii. 661–8.

[101] Compare for instance the reverse of the gold multiple of Constantine I showing Caesars Crispus and Constantine II, AD 317, with that of Licinius I and II, AD 320, and the gold solidus of Heraclius and his father AD 608/9 (Kent and Painter 1977: 164–5, nos. 373 and 375, and p. 181, no. 738).

[102] As on the gold solidi showing Heraclius and his father AD 608/9, mentioned in the previous note.

[103] Miles 1952: 53. The Visigothic busts, however, are all in profile, with the one exception of an issue from Cordoba. See *MEC* pl. 14, nos. 278–83.

[104] Belfort 1892–5: no. 4697 and Prou 1892: no. 2115 *bis*.

[105] The Merovingian silver denier from Savonnières (Belfort 1892–5: no. 4582 and Prou 1892: no. 342) is illustrated in Bendixen 1974: 97A. The Merovingian iconography might have been independently inspired by Byzantine issues (Bendixen 1974: 92). For the Savonnières coins as representations of Gervasius and Protasius: Lafaurie 1963: 72; Nau 1982: 477 n. 12.

[106] Sellwood and Metcalf 1986: 181–2. See discussion below.

iconographically, but also conceptually, as the sacred symbol of the inverted bucranium between the heads could be interpreted as theoretically equivalent to the cross on the Anglo-Saxon coins.[107]

Aside from numismatic precedents, in the Roman world, the iconography of people facing each other was also commonly used to signify a relationship,[108] as we find on marriage rings, devotional medals, or gold-glass.[109] It could easily acquire new meaning by cross-reference to related images: if the Merovingian coins were dedicated to the patron saints at Savonnière, it is possible that on our coins the image might commemorate SS Peter and Paul, whose 'most holy fetters' made into 'a cross with a golden key' were sent to Oswiu's wife at York by Pope Vitalian.[110]

In a Christian context the image also suggests the iconography of the 'tree of life' flanked by two creatures,[111] a motif conflating and transforming many traditions, evolving from geometrical, ornamental arrangements on Oriental silks to the symbolical dimension of the inhabited double scrolls in Anglo-Saxon England. A distinction however ought to be made between inspiration and imitation,[112] derivation and meaning. Whatever the source for the design of Types 37/72, what was its contemporary, relevant meaning to the patron, and did it differ from that of its 'audience'?

Metcalf, who ascribes the Series to York, sees it mirroring a political cooperation between church and state, with the two heads representing a king and his bishop.[113] The image may have been politically relevant in early eighth-century Northumbria, mirroring an ultimately Visigothic precedent, where the undifferentiated, symbolical portraits of the equally royal co-rulers would have been an apposite statement of unity. However, the image could be chosen for use in a devotional context, as the unique gold-leaf cross from the grave of a warrior at Ulm-Ermingen (Baden-Württemberg; Fig. 2.21), closely copying the iconography of an Anglo-Saxon coin, testifies.[114] It may also be noticed that the same iconography is shared by the brooch from nearby Berghausen.[115] The same Type

---

[107] This symbol will be discussed in detail at 'Bust and "Tridents"'.

[108] The iconography is discussed in Cabrol and Leclercq 1907–53: *Mariage, Pierre, Saint*, and *Paul, Saint, passim.*

[109] In particular, see the Roman bezel of a gold ring and the devotional medal with SS Peter and Paul, both fourth century, illustrated in Cabrol and Leclercq 1907–53: *Mariage*, p. 1942, no. 7693; *Pierre, Saint*, p. 939, no. 10221, and Dalton 1901: no. 636.

[110] *HE* III, 29; Henderson 1999: 66.

[111] Koch 1982: 53. See 'Two Standing Figures'.

[112] Scheers 1992: 42.

[113] *T&S* iii. 343–4.

[114] Nau 1982 discusses the gold-leaf cross from Ulm-Ermingen and its relation to Series J, Type 37 *contra* Seewald 1981. Vierk 1975 examines the crosses as religious votive offerings and apotropaic symbols of affiliation. Nau 1982: 478 dates the cross to the first quarter of the eighth-century, but it is possibly earlier (mid-late seventh century). Like other Continental metalwork closely related to Anglo-Saxon coins (discussed at pp. 112, 114, and 116) this creates a problem with the dating of the coins, which deserves further research.

[115] The brooch from Berghausen (grave 40, Koch 1982: pl. 31B) is discussed and illustrated in Klein-Pfeuffer 1993: 183 and 317–19, fig. 19.

Fig. 2.21. Gold-leaf cross from Ulm-Ermingen, Baden-Württtenberg (Ulmer Museum, Ulm, Inv. Prä. A 41.1).

Fig. 2.22. Anglo-Saxon gold solidus naming the Roman Empress Helena, early 7th century (CM 1864, 11-28-195. The British Museum, London).

is also behind a gold bracteate from Odense, and indeed a find from Dankirke confirms that these Anglo-Saxon coins were known and copied in Denmark.[116] Apart from testifying to patterns of interaction—monetary, cultural, and personal—the jewels also strongly suggest the possibility that at a personal level the image on the coins was understood principally as apotropaic.

Female Portraits

The majority of female images surviving from early Anglo-Saxon times are religious, and as such likely to refer to conventional models for dress and headgear.[117] It is also questionable how far secular representations, such as on the Franks Casket, where women appear with hooded cloaks, or on a Pictish stone sculpture, where a bareheaded queen is shown riding side-saddle, her cloak fastened by a large penanular brooch, can be considered true portraits of contemporary women.[118]

It is tempting to interpret the facing figures with no beard or moustache on the coins of Intermediate Series BZ, Type 29b and Secondary Series Q, Types QIF and QIG as female,[119] but, as discussed earlier, such identification ought to be

---

[116] For the gold bracteate from Odense (now in Copenhagen): see Bendixen 1974: 92 and 96, fig. B, and for the 'Anglo-Saxon' coin Series J, Type 37 (perhaps a Frisian imitation, *T&S* iii. 357) found at Dankirke: see Bendixen 1981*b*: 99, no. 42. On bracteates used as *oboli*: Vierk 1975: 141.

[117] See for instance the representation of the Virgin on St Cuthbert's coffin, the Book of Kells (fo. 7ᵛ), the Genoels-Elderen book-cover (G. Henderson 1987: figs. 222, 221, and 209), the Ruthwell Cross, and the panel from Breedon-on-the-Hill (Lang 1988: figs. 11 and 16).

[118] For the Franks Casket, see Fig. 2.62*a*, and for the principal rider on the late eighth-century sculpture at the Hilton of Cadboll, see Alcock 1993: 231, fig. 28.3. It is debatable whether some of the faces carved on the Sutton Hoo sceptre are female. See Bruce-Mitford 1978, ii. 323–4 and above, n. 11.

[119] See Fig. 2.7, and *T&S* iii. 491–2.

supported by stronger evidence of female patronage or cult of female saints at a securely established mint-place.[120] It may be salutary to remember that contemporary gender-related questions, whilst worth asking,[121] are difficult to answer as we lack firm evidence on many counts. However, two remarkable landmarks are unique to Anglo-Saxon England monetary history.

Amongst the first experiments in Anglo-Saxon coin making, and medallic in character, is the splendid early seventh-century gold solidus bearing on its obverse a bust with the inscription 'Helena' (Fig. 2.22).[122] We can postulate that a particular devotion to the Empress Helena, who was, according to widely circulating legends, the finder of the True Cross, may have been behind the choice of iconography, but we cannot speculate regarding the possibility of its having been commissioned specifically by or for a female patron/queen. As for the rendering of the drapery, described by Sutherland as a 'jewelled and embroidered "collar"',[123] it shows a love of sumptuousness comparable to similar elaborate treatments on other 'male' coins, but gives us no idea of 'female costume'.

More extraordinary, indeed unique at the time, is the coinage struck between *c.*787 and *c.*792 in the name of Offa's queen, Cynethryth.[124] Prof. Stafford makes a strong case for the special position of the queen in Offa's political strategies as his legitimate consort, and bearer of his rightful heir,[125] and Williams suggests her coinage, all by the moneyer Eoba, may reflect a grant of Offa to Cynethryth.[126] In either case, the coinage in her sole name, and portraying her as *Regina M[erciorum]*, is a unique phenomenon: the inspiration is likely to have come from Roman precedents, in line with the many Roman models Offa chose for his own portraiture.[127] The often-quoted near-contemporary Byzantine issues of the Empress Irene are indeed anachronistic and do not compare stylistically.[128] It is reasonable to assume that Offa's intentions were political,[129] and the number of dies recorded indicates that the volume of Cynethryth's coinage was significant; its distribution, different from Offa's, suggests that it may have fulfilled more than one role.[130]

Produced under the aegis of one moneyer, Eoba, the coins fall in two categories (Fig. 2.23). Some issues are portraits of the queen with elaborate hair-

---

[120] See Fig. 3.27.

[121] See particularly Fell 1984, and Farr 1997*a*.

[122] The piece conflates motifs from three Roman fourth-century bronze coins, and had presentation value rather than a monetary function (Sutherland 1948: no. 21; Kent 1961: 10; Rigold 1975: no. 116*a*; and *MoE* 37, no. 22).

[123] Sutherland 1948: 78. In its stiffness it differs greatly from the Roman prototype's soft drapery.

[124] For a discussion of Cynethryth, praised for her piety by Alcuin yet an evil queen in later legends: Fell 1984: 90 ff.

[125] Stafford 2001: 37–41.

[126] Williams 2001*a*: 216.

[127] As for instance the beautiful solidus/mancus by the moneyer Pendred (*MoE* 106, no. 76*b*).

[128] *MEC* 279–80; Zipperer 1999: 124.

[129] Blunt 1961: 47.

[130] Derek Chick, personal communication.

Fig. 2.23. Pennies of Cynethryth, wife of Offa of Mercia (757–96), moneyer Eoba (*a*. CM, before 1838. The British Museum, London; *b*. MEC 1132. The Fitzwilliam Museum, Cambridge).

styles, mostly incorporating diadems, often with softly gathered drapery, while others use the same obverse dies employed for Offa himself. Coming from such an efficient administration as Offa's, these 'mules' (obverses with Offa's male portrait, reverses with Cynethryth's name) are no accident, but possibly reflect the significant production requirements.[131]

A less competent engraver is believed to have been responsible for the portrait of Figure 2.23*b*, often regarded as 'ugly'.[132] However, the large and elongated eye, the thick neck, and pelleted drapery can be compared with the contemporary solidus of the moneyer Ciolheard (Fig. 2.24),[133] and suggest a new set of aesthetic values. The portraits in fact seem to combine numismatic precedents with echoes from other media. The florid, well-modelled features are reminiscent of Eastern Mediterranean influences, possibly to be seen in the context of an ongoing dialogue with the Carolingian Court. The angel at Breedon (Fig. 2.25) can also be seen in this context:[134] here, too, facial type, neck, and eyes compare well with those on our coins, which must therefore be considered as sophisticated experiments in a new direction.

If some of the 'male portraits' carrying the name of Cynethryth might be baffling, it is worth noticing how carefully both the names of Offa and Cynethryth were inscribed and turned into attractively balanced patterns on the coins.[135] This indicates, if not an increase in literacy, at least an awareness of the potential of inscriptions as bearers of authority akin to representations of the monarch,[136] so that it would have been the name of Cynethryth rather than her countenance that might have mattered to the beholder.

---

[131] I am grateful to Derek Chick for discussing the issues raised here with me.

[132] For the coin of Cynethryth, and questions regarding its authenticity: *MEC* pl. 52, no. 1132.

[133] On Ciolheard's solidus (*MoE* 106, no. 77*b*), see Pagan 1965: 10.

[134] A late eighth-century dating for this carving (Plunkett 1998: 219; Jewell 2001: 256–8), rather than tenth-century (Parsons 1976) might be supported by the comparison with the iconography of these coins.

[135] A precedent could be seen in the coins of Beonna, king of East Anglia from 749; Archibald 1985.

[136] Thomas 1998 discusses how further readings can be found in the disposition of inscriptions, so we might suppose an attentive public.

Fig. 2.24. Gold *mancus* of the moneyer
Ciolheard, end of 8th century (CM 1984,
12-21-1. The British Museum, London).

Fig. 2.25. Detail from the Angel
panel from Breedon-on-the-Hill,
Leicestershire, 8th century (The Conway
Library, Courtauld Institute of Art).

Heads and Headdresses

On Roman Imperial coins (and imitations) busts often wear crowns, radiate
crowns, diadems, and helmets. Though fundamental differences existed between
these attributes in the classical world,[137] by the time the Anglo-Saxons introduced them on their coins these distinctions would have been blurred, and it is
the symbolic as well as the decorative potential that is exploited, often conflating
discrete details.

Crowns

Whilst crowns, symbols of victory, were originally made up of leaves attached to
a band done up at the back of the head by means of ties, radiate crowns derive
from Greek representations of the god Helios with rays emanating from his
head. The two types were merged, conflating the idea of power suggested by the
ties to the divine character symbolized by the rays.[138] Leaves, ties, and rays
offered interesting pattern-making possibilities to Anglo-Saxon die-cutters.

We see laurel-crowns on certain coins from the Crondall hoard (*c*.645) of the
LEMC and LICINIVS types (Fig. 2.26).[139] On the LEMC coins, crown and portrait
are in linear style,[140] whereas on the LICINVIVS group they are modelled, even

---

[137] Bastien 1992: i. discusses the various types in detail.

[138] Ibid. 103–16.

[139] As Kent 1961: 10, noted, LICINIVS is actually derived from a number of prototypes: this is wholly in
line with the eclectic artistic trends of the time and suggests that die-cutters had access to a repository of
models.

[140] Sutherland 1948: 75, described LEMC Crondall 26 as having 'hair rendered by "porcupine quills"'
but LEMC Crondall 27–33 as having 'hair resembling a laurel-wreath'. Undoubtedly Crondall 26 is of a
different design, while the comparison with the LICINIVS coins helps us understand the laurel-crowns on
the others.

Fig. 2.26. *a* and *b*. LEMC LICINIVS, gold shillings, *c*.640 (*T&S* 45 and 36 = Crondall 29 and 47. The Ashmolean Museum, Oxford).

Fig. 2.27. Anglo-Saxon gold shilling, *Concordia Militum* type, *c*.650–60 (CM 1903, 10-5-1. The British Museum, London).

though, in spite of the delicate rendering of the portrait, the ties at the back are calcified in a pattern of three.[141]

Radiate crowns allow great opportunities for pattern making and ornamented designs. The first Anglo-Saxon issue to present this feature is a base gold shilling, *c*.650–60, copied from the Roman *Concordia Militum* type.[142] On the Anglo-Saxon coin the crown has become rather over-sized, and whereas on Roman originals the spikes stand proud and distinct from the hair, now they merge with it, forming a pattern of triangles in fields of dots (Fig. 2.27). This design proved very influential, as can be seen from Rigold's diagram, which shows how this coin (SIIi) inspired the crowns of Primary Series A coins (Fig. 2.28).[143] These in turn influenced Series C, and Secondary Series R, so that a creative pattern of continuity can be followed.[144]

It is interesting to note how seemingly trivial details are perpetuated. A feature derived from the classical world, for instance, is the single jewel sometimes adorning the front of crowns. This is reproduced on Anglo-Saxon coins by an annulet or a dot, quite distinct from the other annulets seen at the back of the head, which might be either fragments of legends, mintmarks, or introduced to balance the composition.[145] Whatever the case, the element was felt to be

---

[141] The looped knot of the ties of the prototype (e.g. Bastien 1992: iii, pl. 182, no. 8) might have been misunderstood as a third ribbon, although sometimes Roman coins show three, or even four ties (Bastien 1992: i. 154).

[142] The two coins can be seen juxtaposed in *MoE* 105–6 no. 73*a* and 73*b*.

[143] Although these series follow one another over a period of *c*.50 years and were struck in Kent and East Anglia, they are linked through the reverses (see Fig. 5.19). Series A, minted in Kent, end of the seventh century; *T&S* i. 85 ff.

[144] Blackburn and Bonser 1985: 61 ff., believe Series C (with runic legend 'æpa') is a direct successor of Series A, and minted in Kent. Metcalf, however (*T&S* i. 106 ff.), reserves judgement, as the distribution of finds is unhelpful in assigning Series C to Kent or East Anglia. Series R (with runic inscriptions, among them 'epa') has definitively an East Anglian distribution (*T&S* iii. 502 ff.). It was the principal coinage of East Anglia, minted over a long period, using a conservative design, directly continuing a primary coinage design (bust/standard) to the end of the *sceatta* coinage (*T&S* iii. 502). The pattern A-C-R leads from Kent to East Anglia, with a stylistic link between A and C, but a different hand for R (*T&S* i. 116).

[145] See Rigold's scheme, above.

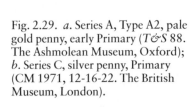

Fig. 2.29. *a*. Series A, Type A2, pale
gold penny, early Primary (*T&S* 88.
The Ashmolean Museum, Oxford);
b. Series C, silver penny, Primary
(CM 1971, 12-16-22. The British
Museum, London).

important to the meaning of the design, and therefore included. The sense of
horror vacui that these coins convey to us must be understood against the wish
to pack all the necessary information into such a small area.

Series A (Fig. 2.29*a*), presumably in order to accommodate the broken 'A'
element behind the head,[146] has a better fitting crown, on a pelleted band. Rigold
suggests that the drapery is derived from a Pada type (PIIA, in his diagram), but
it also recalls that of the LICINIVS coins (Fig. 2.26), and comes to resemble a
shield over which floats the disembodied head.[147] Series C, which substitutes a
runic legend 'æpa' for the Latin one, also has a similarly neat crown, but adds
a neck in the form of a stylized triangle below the chin (Fig. 2.29*b*).[148]

Series R moves towards abstraction and pattern making. The crown opens up
like a frieze, while the modelling of the face is flattened. Figure 2.30*a* shows a
coin where the 'A' behind the head has become a zigzag, and a rare retrograde

---

[146] According to Rigold 1960: 10, this is derived from the 'Two Emperors' type (SII.v in his diagram).
[147] Drapery will be treated in detail below.
[148] For the triangular element, see 'Schematic Drapery' and Fig. 2.46.

Fig. 2.30. *a*. Series R, Type R7, silver penny, Secondary (*T&S* 409. The Ashmolean Museum, Oxford); *b*. Series R, Deriv R3, silver penny, Secondary (3031, de Wit collection).

Fig. 2.31. Series R, silver pennies, Secondary. *a*. Type R 10, moneyer Wigræd; *b*. Type R11, moneyer Tilbeorht (*MEC* 715 and CM 511-1993. The Fitzwilliam Museum, Cambridge).

specimen (Fig. 2.30*b*) where matching zigzags are used for crown, drapery, and behind the bust.[149] On both the neck is made up of a triangular element.

Towards the end of the sequence of Series R, coins of the moneyers Wigræd and Tilbeorht of East Anglia bring a distinctive elegant geometry to the obverse: the crown is smaller and its band blends in with the profile, while the runes making up their names interplay with the design (Fig. 2.31).

Diadems

In the classical world diadems, originally derived from the fillet Greeks bestowed on victorious athletes, evolved into symbols of conquest and absolute power. In the process they became richly encrusted with gems and pearls, even developing *pendilia*, pearl cordonets trailing each side, a fashion enthusiastically adopted in the Byzantine world.[150] Orthodox patterns are not strictly followed in Anglo-Saxon renderings, and, as customary, we often find a conflation of ideas. Whereas, theoretically, only one gem adorned crowns, whilst a single or a double row of pellets rendered the bejewelled band of the diadem, radiate crowns too were sometimes elevated on such pelleted bands,[151] and flamboyant hair could rise above the diadem to resemble a radiate crest. To the Anglo-Saxons, distinc-

---

[149] The coin of Fig. 2.30*b* (Deriv R3: *Numismatic Circular*, 96 (1988), no. 126) is a retrograde version of the one discussed in *T&S* iii. 510, from the Garton-on-the-Wolds grave-find. The reverse in a triple dotted border (see Fig. 5.5*e*) appears identical. Another version, with bust looking right and with a reverse with a smaller cross and lacking the pellets between the arms (cf. Hunterian 15), is also in the de Wit collection.

[150] Bastien 1992: 143–66.

[151] See Fig. 2.29. It is doubtful whether one could interpret the pellets as a rendering of curly hair. In Series R occasionally the crowns extend beyond the pellets, making such an interpretation plausible, but on other coins in the same Series the pellets form a border to the crown in its entirety (contrast *T&S* iii, pl. 23, nos. 391–5, and pls. 24–5, nos. 396–428). It might be better to regard pellets as decoration.

Fig. 2.32. AVDVARLÐ, gold shilling, *c*.640 (Tangmere find, CM.2259-1977. The Fitzwilliam Museum, Cambridge).

Fig. 2.33. WITMEN MONITA, gold shilling, *c*.640 (CM 1935, 11-17-915. The British Museum, London).

Fig. 2.34. WUNEETTON, gold shilling, *c*.640 (*BMC* 6. The British Museum, London).

tions among classical symbols of power were purely academic:[152] condensing them was already acceptable in Roman times, and increased the allusive as well as the decorative potential, particularly with ties and *pendilia*.

A pearled diadem with crossed-over ties is featured on one of the finest and earliest coins in the Crondall hoard,[153] minted in London. The issue, now known in five specimens,[154] although undistinguished in style, is outstanding on account of the legend inscribed around the bust:[155] AVDVARLÐ REGES (Fig. 2.32). The coinage is generally attributed to Eadbald (616–40),[156] who succeeded his father Æthelberht as king of Kent in 616 and, after a period of apostasy, was baptized and 'promoted and furthered the interest of the Church to the best of his ability'.[157] The king appears to stress his conversion to Christianity by means of crosses on the coin's obverse and reverse, and his adoption of *romanitas* (diadem) and literacy (Latin inscription).

[152] Arguably any subtle distinction between the various headdresses of classical times was by then blurred, and only the general symbolism perceived.

[153] Mean fineness: 69.75 (Williams 1998: 139).

[154] Williams 1998. The five specimens are: Crondall 90 (Sutherland 1948: pl. 4, no. 23; Ashmolean Museum, Oxford); Pas-de-Calais (New York); unknown provenance (Hunterian collection, Glasgow); Tangmere, Sussex (Fitzwilliam Museum, Cambridge); Shorne, Kent (British Museum). Whilst all obverses are from the same die, all reverses are from different ones.

[155] The legend on Crondall 90 is the most complete, but whether the sixth letter is a B or inverted R is debatable (see below). The final barred D has been interpreted as a contracted genitive ending (Archibald 1997: 152 and Sean Miller, in Blackburn 1998*b*: 3; Williams 1998: 137).

[156] Attribution first proposed by Amécourt 1872: 78, supported by Sutherland 1948: 52; Stewart 1978: 145; *MEC* 161; Blackburn 1998*b*: 3; Williams 1998: 137.

[157] *HE* II, 5–6. However, in *HE* II, 8, a letter by Pope Boniface to Justus praises his part in the conversion of a king whose name is rendered in Latin as Aduluald. This is explained (Kirby 1991: 39, and McClure and Collins 1994: 378 n. 83) as a scribal error for Audubald, archaic form of Eadbald, whose conversion had, however, been attributed by Bede to Laurentius (*HE* II, 6). Hunter Blair 1971: 8, postulated a Kent divided not only into two bishoprics, but also governed by two kings, Eadbald in Canterbury and an otherwise unrecorded king, whose name he transliterated as Æthelwald, in Rochester. The coin might perhaps confirm the spelling of the name as Auduarld, a form that cannot be taken as an archaic version of the name 'Eadbald', but that appears in the St Petersburg manuscript of the *Historia Ecclesiastica* as Adulualdi and had been corrected and glossed at an early date to Eadbaldi (Hunter Blair 1971: 7–8; Yorke 1990: 32).

The type most heavily represented in the Crondall hoard is the WITMEN MONITA, with twenty-one specimens (Fig. 2.33).[158] The bust wears a pearled diadem, with two ties, and the modelling and the severity of the composition suggest a not-too-distant classical model. Variations in fineness allow the dies to be tentatively arranged into some chronological sequence,[159] enabling us to consider as prototype of the series two coins with the same, but recut, obverse die.[160] WUNEETTON coins are not represented in the Crondall hoard, but the type appears to be the likely continuation of the WITMEN coinage. Whilst closely following their prototype, they show important changes in the rendering of the hair, indicated by stiff strokes, and in having diadems with three ties.[161] In some specimens the presence of a diadem is only to be guessed at on account of the ties, until these too merge in the pattern with the quills of the hair (Fig. 2.34). Hair must have carried great symbolism in Anglo-Saxon England:[162] indeed, the designs which allow scope for the hair to be developed into flamboyant patterns seem the most readily imitated.

On Pada's coinage, a pale gold transitional issue (*c*.655–80),[163] portraits with diadems are rendered in two different styles (Fig. 2.35):[164] one features a rounded face, wavy hair, and a prominent cluster of curls on the neck below the ties, whilst a more severe portrait with spiky hair has a double diadem with a central rosette.[165] As Rigold's scheme shows,[166] some details derived from Pada's coins contributed to Primary Series A, but other elements, such as the double diadem from which spiky hair develops, were also influential on Series B. Indeed, a double diadem with prominent central decoration is the headgear chosen for these other Series of Primary coins. The halo originally surrounding the bust, as we have seen, eventually develops into a circular frame around the head. The distribution of Series B shows coinage spreading from Kent to East Anglia and the East Midlands,[167] and a line of descent is evident for the coins of Secondary Series J,[168] where we find comparable representations, with a detached head in a ring

---

[158] *T&S* i. 30 and 57–9.

[159] Ibid. 40. The specimen illustrated here is *not* from the Crondall hoard; it is now in the British Museum collection.

[160] The coins from the same recut die are Crondall 69–71, illustrated in Sutherland 1948: pl. 3, nos. 21–3. The difference concerns the drapery, and will influence all the derivatives.

[161] The WUNEETTON type (Stewart 1978: 148; *MEC* 163). The drapery continues the modified style of Crondall 69–71.

[162] See above.

[163] Pada was formally identified with King Peada (d. 656) (Sutherland 1948: 54), but anachronistically, and the name is now thought to represent a moneyer (*MEC* 163).

[164] A third style of portraiture, the helmeted type, will be discussed at Fig. 2.42*b*. For the subdivision of the coinage, see *T&S* i. 73–9.

[165] This type of portrait might have been inspired by prestigious Visigothic prototypes, such as the coin illustrated in *MoE* 36, no. 21. The numerous finds of Visigothic coins in England testifies to the fact that they were well respected in trading on account of their fineness.

[166] See Fig. 2.28.

[167] See map in *T&S* i. 103. Series BII is also found in Northumbria.

[168] Five types with different reverses are assigned to Series J, which Metcalf attributes to York (*T&S* iii. 341 ff.).

Fig. 2.35. Series Pa, transitional pale gold
shillings of Pada, *c*.670–80 (*a. MEC* 668; *b.*
MEC 669. The Fitzwilliam Museum,
Cambridge).

Fig. 2.36. Series G, silver penny,
early Secondary (CM 1922, 11-5-45.
The British Museum, London).

featuring a double diadem and spiky hair, either singly or duplicated confronting
a cross.[169]

Possibly related to these are the coins of Series G,[170] an early Secondary coinage with finds widely scattered in England, arguably attributed to
Quentovic, an important port from Roman times, and the most direct route
between England and the Continent.[171] Some particularly fine busts are obviously classically inspired: the gaze is heavenward, as in the mystical portraits
of Constantine,[172] the modelling sensitive, and the diadem carefully rendered,
albeit low on the forehead, as tends to be the case on Anglo-Saxon coins
(Fig. 2.36).

In the Intermediate series, coins labelled VER because of the inscription legible
on some specimens, have busts with either diadems (and spiky hair) or crowns
(Fig. 2.37). The diademed busts exist in two versions, one with the bust laterally
reversed, and incorporating as a chin the E of the original legend VER. Scholars
differ over whether the design represents a gradual evolution or a degeneration,
from or towards 'porcupines', and over the place in the sequence of the specimen
with crowned busts.[173] If we accept that the crowned specimen heads the

---

[169] See Fig. 2.13*a* and 2.19.

[170] Series G (*T&S* ii. 266–74) comprises the earlier, refined Type 3a (reverse with 'standard') and the
subsidiary G2 (muled with reverses of Series J, Types 36 and 85). Metcalf believes it to be Continental,
from Quentovic (*T&S* ii. 266), but the many English finds and the fine workmanship suggest an Anglo-
Saxon origin 'from a site participating in foreign trade' (*MEC* 170).

[171] Quentovic: Leman 1990; Weiller 1999: 222–3; Lebecq 1999: 57–9 points out that already among
the Sutton Hoo and Crondall hoard coins there were two from Quentovic; it was from here that
Archbishop Theodore sailed to England in 668 (*HE* IV, 1) and Wilfrid was supposed to land in 678 on his
'direct route to Rome' (*Vita Wilfridi*, ch. 25). Metcalf sees it as a port predominantly used by pilgrims
(*T&S* ii. 269).

[172] See for instance the coin of Constantine, *c*. AD 328 in Reece 1983: 175, fig. 143*i*.

[173] Metcalf (*T&S* i. 142), explains the sequence of the design putting at the beginning of the series a
'porcupine/plumed bird' which will develop into a head 'probably in response to the commercial standing
achieved by Series A, B and C'. However, if we follow de Wit/Blackburn and Bonser's reversed order
(Blackburn and Bonser 1984*a* and de Wit 1984) which culminates in a 'porcupine' lookalike, and consider the adoption of this design on some English derivatives (Series T), we can postulate a conscious
movement towards a design used over a large commercial area. It is possible that the V of the legend, often
with a central pellet (see *BMC* 26 and *T&S* i, pl. 8, no. 149), may have been misunderstood for a jewel,
precipitating the interpretation of the E as a pattern.

Fig. 2.37. *a*. VER group, silver penny, Intermediate (*T&S* 147. The Ashmolean Museum, Oxford); *b*. Series F, silver penny, Intermediate (CM 1971, 12-16-77. The British Museum, London); *c*. Two Emperors' type, gold shilling, *c*.660–70 (*T&S* 79. The Ashmolean Museum, Oxford).

sequence, then in the subsequent abstract, illiterate composition of the image, the substitution of the crown with a diadem and spiky hair serves to underline the importance of hair as a symbol of power, and to explain the success of 'porcupines'. It certainly was an influential 'look' copied by other types, such as the SAROALDO,[174] whereas the curly heads of Intermediate Series F, also with an elongated diadem, do not seem to have met with much success (Fig. 2.37*b*).[175] Wreath-ties are definitively essential elements of the iconography, even when merged with spiky hairstyles, as we saw above, or rendered incongruously, as in the gold 'Two Emperors' type, where they are suspended in space (Fig. 2.37*c*).

Playfulness and flamboyance are evident in the renderings of the wreath-ties of Secondary Series K, where they are knotted in a variety of ways (Fig. 2.38).[176] The decorative potential of wreath-ties with knots and floating ribbons had already been exploited on Roman coins,[177] and it could be that such examples, which would have appealed to the Anglo-Saxon taste for interlace, served as prototypes. A most striking comparison for such elaborate knots is with Scandinavian metalwork: the so-called *Guldgubbar*,[178] votive foils dating from the sixth to the ninth century, found all over Scandinavia, or the sixth-century silver gilt pendants representing Valkyries, the long hair dressed in a special knot symbolizing high status.[179]

Some coins related to Series K, grouped as 'Triquetras' on account of the reverse cross design, show a frontal bust with a knotted wreath-tie each side (Fig. 2.39). Metcalf compares them to girls' plaits and calls them incongruous.[180]

[174] See *T&S* i. 147–51.
[175] Series F, a close copy of a Merovingian coin type from Auxerre, is now firmly believed to be English, with several different variants (most of which are represented in the Aston Rowant hoard, *c*.710) and widespread north-easterly distribution, pointing possibly to a Middle Anglian origin. *T&S* i. 125–32.
[176] For Metcalf's chart of wreath-ties see ibid. 387.
[177] See for instance the gold multiple of Constantius (Bastien 1992: iii, pl. 147, no. 5).
[178] On *Guldgubbar*, or 'embracing couples', see Magnus 1997: 205–7, fig. 94*a–c*.
[179] For the Swedish Valkyrie pendants: Magnusson and Forman 1976: 89–90.
[180] *T&S* iii. 422.

Fig. 2.38. Series K, Type 42, silver penny, mid/late Secondary (*T&S* 311. The Ashmolean Museum, Oxford).

Fig. 2.39. 'Triquetras' type, related to Series K, mid/late Secondary (*T&S* 344. The Ashmolean Museum, Oxford).

Although the desire to balance the composition symmetrically may have contributed to such duplication,[181] the iconography finds a counterpart in the *orans* figure at the centre of the cross-bracteate from Spötting, with hair similarly dressed in two knots at the side of the head.[182] On account of its custodial function,[183] the object is suggestive of a further, apotropaic dimension derived from placing a figure between two powerful symbols.[184]

Long hair knotted by both ears,[185] however, is a comparatively rare detail found in Insular art and on the Continent, apparently used specifically in images of Christ in Majesty: in Anglo-Saxon England it appears on the coffin of St Cuthbert, and on sculpture at Hoddom and Rothbury, and differentiates Christ from other figures.[186] Whether this is a further layer of meaning alluded to on our

[181] The double *pendilia* of classical models might have offered inspiration, as for instance on the solidus of Eudoxia (Bastien 1992: iii, pl. 224, no. 1), the representation of the Empress Theodora in Ravenna, or the ivory plaque with an unidentified royal lady, now in the Bargello Museum, Florence (Pugliese Carratelli 1982: 23, fig. 6, and 1984: 534, fig. 457).

[182] For the cross-bracteate from Spötting see *Die Alamannen* 1997: 256, fig. 270. Another similar image from Tissø in Denmark shows a full-size female figure, with raised arms supporting two very large hair-knots at the side of the head (Jørgensen 2002).

[183] Vierck 1975: 134 ff.

[184] As discussed for 'Single Figure between Crosses'.

[185] For obverses of Series K, Keary (1887: i. 12) refers to 'hair and dress of Saxon character', and Baldwin Brown (1903–37: iii. 85) points to the 'picturesque knots' as an original Anglo-Saxon trait related to their 'feeling for knot-work' as a significant artistic tendency. His later statement (p. 110) that *interlace* on tomb-furniture does not appear until the seventh century, thus furnishing a chronological parameter for coins with 'interlaced long hair', is mistakenly taken by Hill 1952: 266, as referring to busts with 'Saxon hair'. Alcuin's letter to Æthelred of Northumbria (Whitelock 1955: no. 193, p. 776) does refer to hairstyles in which 'you have wished to resemble the pagans'. For Owen-Crocker 1986: 113 ff., it is unlikely that Alcuin should be referring to the Vikings, but to Northumbria's own pagan past (see Rives 1999: 285 on knotted hair in Roman historiography and iconography. I am grateful to Dr Maddicott for this reference), and backward sense of fashion, remote from Frankish influence. See, however, the sophistication in the iconography of knotted hair in Hawkes 1996: 81.

[186] Hawkes 1996: 81.

Fig. 2.40. Series L, Type 13, late Secondary
(4179, de Wit collection).

coins is debatable: we can only note that the knots are turned into emphatic *Chi-*
cross signs.[187]

Coins of Secondary Series L opt for two or three straight wreath-ties. As on
particularly fine portraits of Series K,[188] the hairstyle supporting the diadem is
sometimes rendered by Xs, which are also used to reproduce the texture of the
tunic worn by the figures on the reverse. One wonders if the hatching is another
way of portraying the texture of hair, or representing caps in precious fabrics
(Fig. 2.40).

Wreath-ties on diademed portraits of Offa eschew decorative motifs: here too
they are represented straight, well clear of the head; sometimes they are curiously
arched downwards, as if weighed down by their pelleted ends.[189]

Helmets

Helmets appear on Roman Imperial coins from the second half of the third
century, as symbols of authority.[190] Originally they were of Greek type, betraying
the strong Hellenistic influence, but from Constantine I, on account of a shift
towards a more Oriental fashion, it was the richly ornate and bejewelled Persian
helmet that was preferred.[191] Arguably, this might be the first form of helmet to
be copied on Anglo-Saxon coins, on the coinage inscribed with EAN,[192] known
from four specimens in the Crondall hoard (*c*.640), all from one die, recut (Fig.
2.41).[193] In the Germanic world, with an elite based on warrior values, the

[187] If the image on the Anglo-Saxon coin does refer to Sight as one of the senses, as I suggest in the
Conclusion (see p. 187), in view of the many biblical warnings to guard eyes to avoid sin (e.g. Matthew
5: 29), such 'defence' would be totally appropriate.

[188] Cf. Fig. 2.38.

[189] Compare for instance the diadems of Dud and that of Eoba ((Blunt 1961: nos. 27–8 and 52).

[190] According to Alföldi 1934: 99, helmets, originally martial accoutrements of emperors' parades,
came to be used as everyday crowns when troubled times meant that emperors were permanently dressed
in uniform.

[191] Bastien 1992: i. 201–23.

[192] Compare a *nummus* of Constantine I (e.g. Bastien 1992: iii, pl. 171, no. 10) and the EAN Types,
Crondall 94 and Crondall 91 (Sutherland 1948: pl. 4, nos. 27 and 24).

[193] Sutherland (1948: 96) arranges the coins postulating alterations transforming a head with upright
hair 'resembling a radiate crown' and a pearled diadem with one long tie (fig. 1*c*) to something akin to a
bejewelled helmet with cheek-piece (fig. 1*b*). Metcalf, however, on account of the fineness of the coins,
would prefer to place the sequence, and recutting, in reverse order (*T&S* i. 41, cf. his arrangement on pl.
3, nos. 63–6. The fineness in his revised order goes from 63 to 35 per cent). Examining the originals, it

Fig. 2.41. EAN, gold shilling, *c.*640 (*T&S* 64 = Crondall 93. The Ashmolean Museum, Oxford).

Fig. 2.42. *a.* CRISPVS/'delaiona' type, gold shilling, *c.*660–70 (CM 1934, 10-13-1. The British Museum, London); *b.* Series Pa, transitional pale gold shilling of Pada, *c.*670–80 (4307, de Wit collection).

helmets worn by the Romans were very much admired and imitated, not so much as practical objects affording protection in battle, but as symbols of status to be paraded.[194] The surviving Anglo-Saxon and Scandinavian helmets, classified by Steuer as *Kammhelme*,[195] were not the only types produced, witness the representations on the foils of the helmets themselves, or that worn by the figure on the Finglesham buckle.[196]

Just as diadems and hairstyles offered great scope for exuberant displays in the iconography of rank, helmets gave rich opportunity for compact and intricate overall patterns, imitating filigree and pellets, traditional metalwork techniques, as can be seen considering the CRISPVS/'delaiona' coin (Fig. 2.42*a*). The design was clearly very influential, as we find it inspires other types. Among the post-Crondall, pale gold issues, the 'Two Emperors' coins evolve from a bust sporting a double 'pearled' diadem towards a martial-looking head wearing a helmet-like skullcap, albeit with no crest. The wreath-ties are completely detached, but evidently still meaningful.[197] Equally, pale gold/transitional issues of Pada's with a

appears that vertical strokes were added on the skullcap above the bejewelled band, perhaps to represent hair. Also, proposing the Constantinian coin as a prototype, at the head of the series would be the portrait with the cap-like helmet, with ties added as additional symbols of rank, or, as Sutherland puts it (ibid. 54) expressions of the personal caprice of the individual represented. Sutherland (ibid. 53–4), because of the strong individuality behind the EAN portraits, was inclined to believe them royal, but, although the inscription is clear, a particular attribution remains impossible.

[194] Steuer 1987: 191. Alkemade 1997: 184 discusses fighting equipment as prestige-goods. The decorations on helmets (Sutton Hoo: zoomorphic crest, nose and eyebrow protectors, foils with warriors; Benty Grange: crest with boar and cross on nasal; Coppergate: bands with inscriptions with prayers intersecting to form cross, zoomorphic finials, and interlace) do serve a symbolically protective function, combining invocations of Christian protection with the pagan ideology of asking for victory (Steuer 1987: 202 ff.).

[195] Steuer 1987: 200.

[196] Tweddle 1992: 1122 ff. and fig. 556. Finglesham buckle: *MoE* 22, fig. 2. See also the discussion in Pedersen 1994–6: 28–36 on Danish artefacts showing similar headgear.

[197] See above, Fig. 2.37*c*.

bust with crested helmet,[198] show unquestionable affinity with the 'delaiona' type (Fig. 2.42*b*).

Metcalf postulates a Roman prototype for helmeted Pada (PIA–B) issues,[199] and whilst the Roman character of the portrait is unquestionable, they are modelled closely on the texture (pellets/annulets and short oblique traits) of the 'delaiona' coins. The crested helmets seen on the other transitional Series VA,[200] bearing the name of the moneyer VANIMVNDVS, also reflect the contemporary taste for surface patterning of the 'delaiona' and Pada coins (Fig. 2.43). On account of their higher gold content, the coins of Pada with helmeted obverses can be considered to head the series,[201] and to have been replaced by diademed ones. Metcalf considers that the helmeted bust was chosen because of some perceived social or political appropriateness;[202] however, though helmets are thought to have had the function of early Germanic crowns,[203] it is debatable whether any are represented among the later Secondary Series coinage.

A feature sometimes interpreted as a helmet is the pelleted crest that surmounts the diademed bust on some specimens of Series T, thought to be the output of a single mint and engraver; Metcalf classifies these coins as having busts either crested/helmeted, or bareheaded.[204] However, when specimens are compared,[205] the crest seems to be derived from degenerated lettering.[206] As for coins of Series Q, one might wonder if the line of pellets taken to represent the crest of the helmet has not in fact a numismatic precedent in the *appendice perlée*,[207] so common on Merovingian coinage (Fig. 2.44).

Among the Secondary Series coinage, certainly, no representation resembles any of the recovered Anglo-Saxon helmets (Benty Grange, Sutton Hoo, Coppergate, and Wollaston), or those on the Franks Casket, which clearly indicate nosepieces, neck protections, and finials (Fig. 2.45).[208] We might question

[198] For Pada types with diadems, see Fig. 2.35.

[199] *T&S* i. 75.

[200] Ibid. 44.

[201] Ibid. 74. Within these helmeted coins, the gold content (PIA: 30 per cent and PIB: 26 per cent) might also suggest a movement parallel to that in the 'Two Emperors' series, away from the Roman prototypes towards native taste.

[202] *T&S* i. 75.

[203] Chaney 1970: 137; Steuer 1987: 196–7.

[204] *T&S* iii. 545–51 and 546.

[205] Compare *T&S* iii, pl. 26, nos. 443–4.

[206] A similar crest surmounts a bust of a coin with a DE LVNDONIA inscription (de Wit collection), with a small cross in front of the face comparable to those of Series T, and carrying on the reverse a porcupine design (as on Series T) and the inscription SCORVM. The DE LVNDONIA legend links this coin to a specimen badly worn, but with a clear pelleted crest, reading ELVNOOIIV+, with a 'Celtic Cross' reverse (*BMC* Type 14, *BMC* 93, laterally reversed bust, ex-Thames hoard, illustrated in *T&S* iii. 427). This reverse in turn connects to a coin from Tilbury (were there were also found three, or possibly four, Series T coins, *T&S* iii. 548) with on the obverse a crested bust (*T&S* iii, pl. 20, no. 345).

[207] Belfort 1892–5, when describing *appendices perlées* of Merovingian coins, oscillates between descriptions of helmets, hats, or haloes: numerous examples of these can be found in his first volume. See for instance the Merovingian gold *tremissis*, mint of Orléans, moneyer Bertulfus, Prou 632; Belfort 489 illustrated in *Die Franken* 1996: ii. 1136, no. 36.

[208] For a discussion of the helmets on the Franks Casket, see Webster 1982: 26–7.

Fig. 2.43. Series VA, transitional pale gold shilling of 'Vanimundus', *c.*660–70 (The Ashmolean Museum, Oxford).

Fig. 2.44. Series Q, Type QIH (*T&S* 385. The Ashmolean Museum, Oxford).

Fig. 2.45. Detail with helmet from the back panel of the Franks Casket, 8th century (MME 1867, 1-20, 1. © The British Museum, London).

whether helmets were symbols of regal authority at all for the Anglo-Saxons. The Repton relief, believed to represent King Æthelbald,[209] shows him bareheaded, though equipped for battle, and no coin of Offa's represents him wearing a helmet, despite a very varied iconography. It could be inferred that by the eighth century helmets had ceased to be symbols of supreme leadership, and were possibly only used by the royal entourage and elite warriors.[210] This might reflect a desire on the part of the king to stress civic virtues. Moreover, unlike on Roman coins, no weapon is ever included among the attributes that accompany Anglo-Saxon busts. It seems to be the image of the king as peacemaker and patron of commerce that is being promoted on the coinage.[211]

Rendering of Drapery

The great variety of drapery found on Anglo-Saxon coinage draws inspiration from Roman, Byzantine and Merovingian prototypes and tends towards geometry, symmetry, and pattern making, as comparisons between some of the early issues and their Roman prototypes clearly show.[212] It is important to note that

[209] Biddle and Kjølbye-Biddle 1985 and Webster and Brown 1997: 225, no. 63, fig. 99.
[210] Steuer 1987: 197. For Webster and Backhouse 1991: 61, the majority of fighting men would have been protected by simple blocked leather headgear. According to Ian Meadows (Northamptonshire Archaeology), the Coppergate helmet would fit *inside* the helmet recently found at Wollaston, which, though much less ornate, allowed room for substantial padding, suggesting a fighting rather than a parade helmet.
[211] Sawyer 1977: 158 argues that whilst traders needed the protection of kings, these gained from commerce both wealth and prestige and could extend their control through the activities of the merchants.
[212] Compare for instance the Roman coin, minted at Trier, from Chapmanslade and the Anglo-Saxon gold solidus of Empress Helena (Bland and Orna-Ornstein 1997: pl. 31, no. 309/1; *MoE* 37, no. 22); the coins of Crispus and 'LICINIVS' (Kent 1961: pl. 1, no. 8; Sutherland 1948: pl. 2, no. 12); the radiate from Antioch found at Wareham and the Anglo-Saxon shilling *Concordia Militum* type (Bland and Orna-

the Roman coinage circulating in Britain and used as prototypes consisted of coins minted in different provinces of the Empire, with significant variations in design and technique between mints, and with a certain degree of simplification and linearity already evident.

The tendency towards pattern making is apparent not only in the transposition from Roman prototypes to the first imitative coins, but also later, as Anglo-Saxon models inspired further native production.[213] In the extensive use of intricate decorations we might perceive the taste for precious braiding, particularly around the neckline,[214] and behind the geometrical shape of the body and the use of punches for texture, a strong native metalwork tradition in the interpretation of classical prototypes. On the coinage, as well as in portrayals in contemporary manuscripts or sculpture, classical drapery does not seem to be fully understood, but is simplified and arranged with an eye to symmetry and detailed decorative texture.[215] In spite of the widespread use of brooches in the Roman and Germanic world, and in Roman and Byzantine coinage, no early Anglo-Saxon coin features them until some of Offa's issues,[216] mirroring the waning of the fashion for brooches from the mid-seventh to the late eighth century.[217]

Behind particularly prestigious issues we might postulate the coming to light of fine classical specimens, stimulating experiments in a new direction,[218] but it must be stressed that not all prototypes or sources of inspiration were numismatic.

Schematic Drapery

It has been already been noted that the obverse of the gold shilling copied from the *Concordia Militum* Roman type is among the prototypes of the Primary Series A,[219] where the shape of the body becomes geometrically rationalized in a segment of circle, with a pelleted texture matching the crown.[220] The same rendering, as we saw, is continued in Secondary Series C and the baser Series R (Fig.

Ornstein 1997: pl. 22, no. 156/1; Sutherland 1948: no. 23, pl. 2, no. 2); the coin of the reign of Domitian from Skellow and the Anglo-Saxon 'delaiona' (Bland and Orna-Ornstein 1997: pl. 8, no. 262; Kent 1961: pl. 1, no. 13).

[213] As in the recutting of the drapery on the WITMEN coins (Sutherland 1948: pl. 3, nos. 20 and 25).

[214] Beside the WITMEN coins (Fig. 2.33), see the 'Helena' solidus (Fig. 2.22).

[215] Compare for instance the drapery on the figure of St John in the Lindisfarne Gospels, fo. 210ᵛ (Backhouse 1981: 54, fig. 33), or on the figures on the lid of St Cuthbert's coffin (Wilson 1984: 51, fig. 42) with the coin of Series J, Type 36 (*T&S* iii, pl. 18, no. 301).

[216] See Fig. 2.53. The coinages of Offa and, later, Alfred follow classical numismatic precedents more closely.

[217] Owen-Crocker 1986: 117–18.

[218] As in the case of Series K, whose iconography, both for reverses and obverses, is particularly sophisticated.

[219] See Fig. 2.28.

[220] It is likely that the rendering of the bust as a semicircle may have been influenced by the visual ambiguity between shoulder and shield, as seen on the LICINIVS coins (Fig. 2.26*b*).

Fig. 2.46. Series R, Type R3,
silver penny, Secondary (*T&S*
398. The Ashmolean Museum,
Oxford).

Fig. 2.47. *a–b*. Series R, silver pennies,
Secondary, Type R 10: moneyer Wigræd (CM
1914, 4-11-3. The British Museum, London;
MEC 714. The Fitzwilliam Museum,
Cambridge).

2.46) with a tendency towards transforming the various elements of the composition into a pattern.[221]

Series R has a stylized triangle made up of double rows of pellets or lines below
the chin: whether it was understood as a neck over round shoulders, or as
drapery, with the shape below as a shield, is debatable; however, the motif of an
accentuated triangle is certainly found on early metalwork and particularly on
bracteates.[222] Hines considers it derived from the gathering of folds fastened by
a brooch,[223] and our coins may be consciously modelled on earlier images. A
further archaism of the coins is the rendering of nose and eyebrow with one
angular band, a profile recalling Style I, so that the effect, plus the substitution of
runes for the Latin legend, is far removed from Roman prototypes, and harks
back to Germanic metalwork traditions. Towards the end of Secondary Series R,
the coins in the name of the moneyer Wigræd are noteworthy. In some issues the
rune 'æ' is elongated flamboyantly to reproduce drapery, whilst in others the
geometry of the X (rune 'g') is wittily exploited by doubling it in the rendering of
the drapery, which also mirrors the triangles of the crown (Fig. 2.47).

In the Secondary Series busts are often presented frontally, though heads are in
profile. In spite of a superficial similarity in the adoption of semicircles for the
shoulder-line, some coins of Secondary Series K perhaps incorporate different
classical traditions. Besides fourth-century Roman prototypes, Byzantine-style
frontal busts may also have been influential, as they would have afforded better

[221] See Fig. 2.30.

[222] See the bracteates from Kingston Bagpuize (Hines 1993: pl. IV, A: back), and Hjørring
(Mackeprang 1952: pl. 3, no. 16), *c*. fifth century, and also the belt-furniture from Mucking, Essex, early
fifth century (Campbell 1982: 23, fig. 19). A very base silver coin from Tilbury imitating Series L, Type 18,
also shows a similar triangular rendering (*T&S* iii, pl. 20, no. 334).

[223] Hines 1993: 219, on brooches on the bust of the Roman coins and medallions that served as
prototypes for A bracteates, especially of the 'West Scandinavian Group' (Mackeprang 1952).

Fig. 2.48. Series K, silver
pennies, mid/late Secondary.
a. Type 32a; *b.* Type 33 (*T&S*
307. The Ashmolean Museum,
Oxford; *BMC* 160. The British
Museum, London).

opportunity for symmetry, and their sumptuous drapery could inspire interesting pattern making. Although generally an Anglo-Saxon artistic trait, the rigid
geometry of decorations and pellets of the busts recalls Byzantine representations of heavily bejewelled empresses.[224] Decorative stiff collars of pellets alternating with wire are employed either following the contour of the shoulders or
of the neckline (Fig. 2.48).

Visigothic prototypes, which are also schematic copies of frontal Byzantine
models,[225] are apparent in the trapezoid bust of some of Pada's issues.[226] This
shape is mirrored in the stately 'saddleback' drapery of the rare style 'A–B' of
Series K, which combines the richness of pearled texture and the fall of drapery.
In spite of parallels for 'saddleback' frontal busts and profile heads in Merovingian gold coinage, such renderings are quite rare among Anglo-Saxon issues.[227]
This type is known from only four coins,[228] but is echoed in the design of some
copper-alloy coin-brooches.[229] Close parallels for such rendering are to be found

[224] See for instance the mosaic of the Empress Theodora, San Vitale, Ravenna (Webster and Brown
1997: pl. 36), the ivory of Ariadne (?) (Bargello, Florence), and the solidus of Eudoxia (Bastien 1992: iii,
pls. 264, 263, and 224, no. 1).

[225] Visigothic *tremisses*, well known in England and much appreciated on account of their high gold
content, were often mounted in jewellery. Rigold 1975: 661.

[226] See Fig. 2.35*b*.

[227] See the Merovingian coin: Moutiers-en-Tarentaise (found near Diss, Norfolk; *MEC* pl. 20, no. 411)
and the Anglo-Saxon 'Celtic Cross with Rosettes' type (from Wangford, Bury St Edmunds, *T&S* iii. 430,
now de Wit collection).

[228] Apart from the two mentioned in Metcalf and Walker 1967, nos. 15*a–b* (*BMC* 158 and Hunterian
102), there is one in Mr Abramson's private collection in Leeds, and a specimen in the Woodham Walter
hoard (Webster and Brown 1997: 230, no. 75).

[229] The two coin-brooches are from two villages near Thetford: Icklingham and Thompson. The find
from Icklingham is in the Ashmolean Museum (Reg. No. 1909. 465; Hinton 1974: no. 15), and is much
worn. The brooch from Thompson (in a private collection, Gannon forthcoming) allows a better understanding of the Oxford specimen, and shows a *left-facing* bust with two straight wreath-ties ending in
pellets. Two crosses, possibly apotropaic, flank the tiered drapery, and there is a short pseudo-inscription.
As the brooches are quite worn, it is difficult to establish if the border was made up of pellets or if
these were simply suggested. Hinton proposes a date of mid to late eighth century, but the brooch
from Thompson (a recent metal detector find) is from a site said to have yielded mainly ninth-century
material. Interestingly, Diss, Wangford (see above), Icklingham, and Thompson all centre around
Thetford.

Fig. 2.49. *a*. Series K, Type 33, silver penny, mid/late Secondary (*BMC* 158, Abramson collection); *b*. pendant from the Wieuwerd hoard, incorporating solidus of Phocas, Friesland, 7th century; bracteate from the Wieuwerd hoard, Friesland, 7th century (© Rijksmuseum van Oudheden, Leiden).

in German imitations of Byzantine solidi and their reproductions as bracteates, as seen in the Wieuwerd hoard, where the closeness to draped Byzantine proto-types is evident (Fig. 2.49).[230]

Crossed-Over Drapery

Many Anglo-Saxon coins drew inspiration from the crossed-over Roman *trabea* of Consular coinage, heavily encrusted with pearls when worn by the emperor, and from the Byzantine scarf-like *loros*, also elaborately embroidered with jewels.[231] However, the Anglo-Saxons would have also been familiar with another type of crossed-over dress of late classical origin, and early Persian ancestry,[232] with richly ornamented bands, as represented on the Sutton Hoo helmet (Fig. 2.50).[233] The transitional coinage of VANIMVNDVS shows a similar garment crossed right over left, sumptuously decorated with pellets, annulets, and wire bands,[234] which can be compared with the equally rich garment worn on gold coins of the 'delaiona' type, albeit shown in profile.[235]

The martial, metallic stiffness of the earlier coinage contrasts with the softer drapery of Secondary Series K, Type 42. This resembles precious cloth, suggest-ing more peaceful connotations, love of refinement—and trade in luxury goods (Fig. 2.51). The coins of Series K, Type 42 are close to classical models, even

---

[230] The pot-hoard, made up of 39 pieces of gold jewellery and coin ornaments, was found in 1866 in Friesland and is dated *c*.620 (*MEC* 124). See Lafaurie, Jansen, and Zadoks-Josephus Jitta 1961.

[231] For a discussion of the *trabea* and the *loros*: Bastien 1992: i. 284 ff.; Grierson 1982: 11, and compare the illustrations of Constantius II (in the *Calendar of 354*: see Salzman 1990) and of the solidus of Majorian, AD 457–61 (Bastien 1992: iii, pls. 195 and 227, no. 2), with the solidus of Justinian II, AD 705–6 (Kent 1961: 1, no. 15).

[232] Almgren 1983: 15, discusses Germanic élite warriors wearing such clothes.

[233] As the 'dancing warriors' are arranged symmetrically, the coats overlap correspondingly. For a Scandinavian example: Webster and Brown 1997: 199, fig. 90.

[234] *T&S* i. 80–4, and see Fig. 2.43.

[235] See Fig. 2.42.

Fig. 2.50. The dancing warriors scene from the Sutton Hoo helmet (drawing after Care Evans 1994: 48. © The British Museum, London).

Fig. 2.51. *a*. Series VA, transitional pale gold shilling of 'Vanimundus', *c*.660–70 (The Ashmolean Museum, Oxford); *b*. Series K, Type 42, silver penny, Secondary (CM 1935, 11-17-202. The British Museum, London).

showing the neckline of an undergarment,[236] which on the earlier VANIMVNDVS coins (VaB) was substituted by a conspicuous annulet. Series K, Types 33 E–F and Series L, Types 15 and 16, however, reproduce the shawl-like effect with V-shaped folds radiating from a central point and fanning out at the shoulders.[237] Here, only the texture of the prototype remains, but the rendering is certainly very effective.

Offa's Drapery

The drapery on Offa's coinage falls into two categories. While some coins follow the Anglo-Saxon convention of presenting the body as a frontal geometrical shape, albeit with innovative combinations of decoration and experiments, others seem freshly inspired by Roman prototypes, and reject ideas of symmetry in favour of classical drapery or even the nude.

Among traditional Anglo-Saxon renderings, examples range from the schematic, triangular body of the moneyer Udd, to others that, whilst remaining strictly linear and abstract, effectively allude to mass in a third dimension by means of concentric lines. The triangular body and the inner circle framing the head (Fig. 2.52*a*) produce what Chick has termed a 'keyhole' effect, which he sees as characteristic of a distinctively East Anglian portrait coinage.[238] We may

[236] Notice, however, the two lines on the neck of Bacchus seen on the gem illustrated at Fig. 2.64, a representation which I believe to have been the prototype for Type 42a.

[237] Compare Series K, Type 33 E–F (Metcalf and Walker 1967: pl. 7, no. 30), and Series L, Types 15 and 16 (*T&S* iii, pl. 19, nos. 327 and 329).

[238] Chick 1989: 192.

Fig. 2.52. Pennies of Offa of
Mercia (757–96). *a.* moneyer
Udd; *b.* moneyer Ibba (CM
1896, 4-4-17b and *BMC* 19.
The British Museum, London).

note the similarity to coins of Series R, where the body is also triangular, and
assume a continuation of a regional style for the obverses.[239]

Renderings suggesting muscular shoulders and chest (Fig. 2.52*b*) are found
on coins of Ibba, Eadhun, and Alhmund,[240] Offa's moneyers associated with
the London mint.[241] The treatment can be compared to the 'rounded shoulder'
version of the standing figures seen on the reverse of Secondary Series L, Types
15b and 16, also associated with London.[242] The style of drapery finds no equivalent in surviving contemporary Mercian art: it is, however, reminiscent of the
distinctive schematic renderings found in the earlier miniatures of the Echternach Gospels and derivatives, where drop-shaped elements are arranged in tiers
to represent the body in different planes.[243] It is interesting to notice similarities
between this style of Offa's drapery and that of the coin-like roundels with busts
forming the frame of the Late Saxon Fuller brooch.[244]

Portrait coins more directly inspired by classical models tend to present the
king in sumptuous fashion.[245] Ornamented braids are carefully detailed, suggesting a keen contemporary interest in such fashion.[246] On some coins by Dud

[239] See Fig. 2.30. Chick (1989) points out how such peculiarly East Anglian obverses are teamed with
conventional reverses comparable to the Canterbury/London production.
[240] Blunt 1961: pl. 5, nos. 37, 39, 46, 61, 62, 64, 65, and 67. The one portrait coin in the name of
Œthilred (Blunt 1961: pl. 6, no. 71), East Anglian moneyer of the second half of the eighth century
(Stewart 1986: 31), has similar but pointed shapes scored in a herringbone pattern.
[241] Chick 1997: 52. Stewart 1986: 41 postulates one gifted engraver working at the London mint for
these and other moneyers.
[242] See coins of Series L, Types 15b/16 in Metcalf 1976: pl. 12, nos. 2–3.
[243] Contrast this with the more monumental and realistic rendering of the drapery of St John in the
Barberini Gospels, fo. 124ᵛ (*MoE* 206, no. 160), but compare the rigidity of the body of the Echternach
evangelist (G. Henderson 1987: 74, fig. 102) with the still geometric but softer rendering of the drapery
on Offa's coins.
[244] See 6.2.
[245] For the drapery, one can compare the multiple solidus of Constantius II (Bastien 1992: iii, pl. 190,
no. 11) with the coin of Offa by the moneyer Pehtwald (Blunt 1961: pl. 6, no. 74); the gold solidus of
Honorius (Reece 1983: 236, no. 202*d*) with the coin of Offa by the moneyer Dud (Blunt 1961: pl. 4, no.
27); the solidus of Majorian (Bastien 1992: pl. 227, no. 4) with the coin of Offa by the moneyer Tirwald
(*Coin Register* 1996: no. 170).
[246] Apart from the type of dress and the style chosen to portray it, many coins present elaborate borders
to the garments (see for instance Blunt 1961: pl. 5, nos. 38, 47, 48, 52, 63, 66).

Fig. 2.53. Penny of Offa of
Mercia (757–96), moneyer Dud
(*MEC* 1124A. The Fitzwilliam
Museum, Cambridge).

Fig. 2.54. Pennies of Offa of Mercia (757–96):
a. moneyer Dud (*BMC* 12. The British Museum.
London); *b*. moneyer Ethilvald (*MEC* 1128. The
Fitzwilliam Museum, Cambridge).

(Fig. 2.53) the gathered folds suggest the presence of a brooch, but do not show it.[247] It is debatable whether such ornament can be discerned on Cynethryth's coins: one possible instance has a pellet misplaced on top of the shoulder, serving no practical function.[248]

The idea of representing the bust naked might have derived from classical inspiration, but its treatment on Offa's coinage, realized by various moneyers, is original.[249] A chain with a pendant, sometimes described as heart-shaped,[250] appears prominently between Offa's wide bare shoulders on certain coins of the moneyer Alhmund (Fig. 2.13*b*).[251] The portrait of Figure 2.54*b* is very Roman; however, the effect recalls coins of Secondary Series O, Type 38, where the pelleted circle framing the head rests on a torque.[252]

[247] Gale Owen-Crocker (personal communication) points out that, with the exception of the iconography of the Franks Casket, where brooches are portrayed several times, there is a gap in our evidence for the use of brooches from the Migration period to the tenth century (when they appear in manuscript art). Coins of Alfred in the London style, inspired by similar Roman prototypes, carefully copy the brooch by means of an annulet, but misunderstand its function in the ordering of the folds (*pace* Blackburn 1998*a*: 117). These are actually more naturalistically reproduced on Offa's issues, as can be seen by contrasting Blackburn and Dumville 1998: pl. 8, nos. 20–31, with suggested prototype L of pl. 11 and Offa's coins illustrated in Blunt 1961: pl. 4, no. 27, and pl. 7, nos. 116–19. The drapery should not result in V-shaped folds, but should radiate from the brooch.

[248] See Fig. 2.33*a*.

[249] On such coins by the moneyer Ethilvald and the moneyer Babba (Lockett 1920: pl. 10, no. 1; pl. 6, no. 2) to the right, after the king's name, there is a triple branching spray, interpreted as a palm branch signifying victory and peace by Lockett 1920: 78, and as a jewel by Blunt 1961: 42.

[250] The pendant is so described by Lockett 1920: 77.

[251] According to Derek Chick (personal communication), the very first in the series of these extraordinary coins of Alhmund does *not* represent a jewel.

[252] See Fig. 2.16. On the coin by Babba mentioned above, the head is surrounded by a circular pelleted frame resting on a heart-shaped bust. It is possible that the die-cutter was attempting a witty synthesis between a jewel, perhaps a prestigious acquisition, and the representation of the body.

Fig. 2.55. Detail with armour from the lid of the Franks Casket, 8th century (MME 1867, 1-20, 1. © The British Museum, London).

Fig. 2.56. Series W, silver penny, Intermediate or early Secondary (*T&S* 155. The Ashmolean Museum, Oxford).

Armour

On Roman coins pellets were used to simulate the textures both of the *lorica squamata*, a type of armour, and of the *lorica hamata*,[253] mailcoat. Archaeological and artistic evidence for the use of mailcoat in Anglo-Saxon England comes from Sutton Hoo and Benty Grange,[254] and from the figures in mailcoat on the lid and back panel of the Franks Casket (Fig. 2.55), some with long flexible sleeves, as worn by the warrior on the Repton Cross.[255]

It is particularly among the gold and early Anglo-Saxon coins that we encounter representations of busts that might be understood as clad not in drapery, but in military attire, with texture rendered by pellets. The representations on the gold coins of the 'Constantine' and 'Two Emperors' types recall the figures of the Franks Casket who wear 'pelleted' mailcoats.[256] The pellets give a three-dimensional feel to the rendering of these coins, unlike the linear style of those of the 'York' group, which can be likened to flat *cloisonné* metalwork.[257] Intermediate Series W presents many variations in the representation on the obverse of figures between crosses: some are half-length busts, possibly with a beard, clad with pellets (Fig. 2.56).[258] These can be compared to an eighth-

---

[253] Bastien 1992: i. 259: the *lorica squamata* is believed to be of Assyrian origin, and the *lorica hamata* to be Celtic.

[254] Sutton Hoo: Bruce-Mitford 1978: ii. 234–7; Benty Grange: Meaney 1964: 72.

[255] For the Repton Cross figure: Biddle and Kjølbye-Biddle 1985: 242, fig. 3; Webster and Brown 1997: 225, no. 63, fig. 99.

[256] For these coins, see Figs. 2.59 and 2.37c.

[257] See Fig. 2.4, and compare also the *cloisonné* of the shoulder clasp from Sutton Hoo (Wilson 1984: 17, fig. 7).

[258] Corpus: Blackburn and Bonser 1984b: 235, and see *T&S* i. 152–7. Apart from the type discussed here, some figures are half-length, but with no pellets, others are full-length, either with a body made up of pellets or wearing a garment with a vertical row of pellets down the front.

century gilt-bronze plaque from Alrachsheim, Switzerland,[259] with a bearded king between two crosses, crowned with feathers and wearing a garment covered in roundels surrounded by dots, like that worn by King Agilulf on the gilt-bronze helmet plaque from Val di Nievole.[260] The similarity of the iconography would seem to point to a Continental link,[261] at least in inspiration.

The comparisons suggest the possibility that the pellets might be used to indicate not mail, but prestigious textiles. Mindful of Care Evans's caveat when discussing the coat covered with pellets of the fallen warrior on the Sutton Hoo helmet,[262] we might postulate that the texture of special material, perhaps of a weight particularly suitable as protective clothing in battle, might be rendered with granulation or annulets. Whether mail or material, the effect would have stressed the exclusive quality of the garment and the special status of the wearer.

ATTRIBUTES

As on classical coins, a range of additional features appear on the obverse of Anglo-Saxon coins, complementing the image and its meaning. On certain coins the attributes are hand held, suggesting a more personal interaction to them, whilst on others they are simply featured near the bust.

Hands

Before examining hand-held attributes, hands, in themselves symbolic, need considering. Among the first Anglo-Saxon coins, a gold shilling of *c*.650–60, a close copy of the *Concordia Militum* type,[263] has on its reverse clasped hands, a device for peace on Roman coins, but also symbolic of marriage and harmony on rings and jewels (Fig. 2.57).[264]

The ancient gesture of the raised hand, a sign of menace, but also apotropaic and of benediction, of *adlocutio* or *adventus,* was important in the notion of imperial power and exploited on Roman coinage in all its nuances. Its positive

---

[259] Salin 1949–59: i, pl. 4.

[260] Webster and Brown 1997: 118, fig. 49.

[261] The design of the reverse (see Fig. 5.6*b*) is also found among Merovingian coins: *MEC* 170, suggests that these are copied from the Anglo-Saxon ones, whilst *T&S* i. 153, compares the obverse with later Anglo-Saxon types.

[262] Care Evans (Bruce-Mitford 1978: 237–9), warns about positively identifying mail in graphic representation and discusses granulation as texture.

[263] See Fig. 2.27.

[264] A Roman prototype for the reverse of the coin is illustrated in *MoE* 105–6, no. 73a: coin of Marius, AD 286. The device was also common for marriage rings, referring to the *Dextrarum iunctio* rite (see the one from Grovely Wood, Wiltshire, in Johns 1996: 63, fig. 3.24, and fig. 3.25, and the ring illustrated in Buckton 1994: 47, no. 26).

Fig. 2.57. Anglo-Saxon shilling,   Fig. 2.58. Series K, Type 33 variant (*T&S* 306;
c.650–60 (*BMA* 2, CM 1903, 10-5-1.   drawing courtesy of Prof. Metcalf, by permis-
The British Museum, London).   sion of the RNS).

religious overtones, related to the cult of *Sol invictus,* were translated to Christianity, and adopted on the coinage of Constantine and his successors.[265] Originally an oratory valedictory gesture, it was adopted in a religious context as a sign dismissing and blessing the congregation, and, whilst originally one blessed with the open hand, from the third century certain customs began to be fixed regarding the disposition of the fingers.[266]

The right hand raised in the gesture motif is also found on the traditional decoration of great square-headed brooches with parallels pointing to Scandinavia.[267] Indeed expressively used open-palmed hands often appear on Scandinavian bracteates, not only in imitation of Roman coins, but in conjunction with inscriptions in narrative context.[268]

A unique variant of the Secondary Series K, Type 33 shows a bust with a hand raised in the gesture which we now associate with the Roman, trinitarian blessing before a cross (Fig. 2.58).[269] Metcalf has argued that such a hand, innovating on the more common design of Series K (bust and cross), is unambiguously priestly in its gesture, and therefore postulates that the coin might have been an issue of Archbishop Berhtwald of Canterbury (693–731).[270] Berhtwald succeeded Theodore of Tarsus (668–90) at Canterbury,[271] and one might wonder if by then the common gesture of blessing would not have been performed in the

[265] Bastien 1992: ii. 559 ff. See for instance the *aureus* of Constantine, ibid. iii, pl. 170, no. 3.
[266] Cabrol and Leclercq 1907–53: *Bénir*, p. 746.
[267] See the details of the raised hand on the great square-headed brooches from Dartford and Kempston, and on the pressed foil from Snartemo, Norway, illustrated in Hines 1997: 28, fig. 12*a–d.* See also the Merovingian belt fittings from Morrens (Salin 1949–59: iv. 366, fig. 156).
[268] See the Scandinavian bracteates from Store Salte, Rogoland (Mackeprang 1952: pl. 4, no. 6) and Skåne (Andrén 1991: 249, fig. 4*d*).
[269] For the actual coin, see *T&S* iii, pl. 18, no. 306. The obverse with the hand is in rather poor condition. Smith and Cheetham 1875–80: *Benediction*, p. 199. The fact that the hand is the left one may be due to confusion between dies (producing mirror-like images) and prototype.
[270] Metcalf 1988*b*: 126.
[271] Brooks 1984: 76–8.

Greek style, with thumb and finger ring touching, as we see in a carving at Breedon-on-the-Hill, in manuscripts or on the Tassilo Chalice.[272] It is possible that on the coin the hand gesture may be rhetorical, pointing to the cross as a statement of affiliation,[273] but a deeper meaning may not be excluded.[274]

Hands Holding Crosses

It is generally held by numismatists that the Anglo-Saxon *tremisses* showing a profile, half-length figure with a large outstretched hand are derived from coins of Constantine (Fig. 2.59).[275] The large size of the hand might be due to the influence of late antique figural style, as Jane Hawkes argues for the same peculiarity on Anglo-Saxon sculpture.[276] The Anglo-Saxon coins show a cross behind the open hand, and it has been suggested that this iconography might represent oath taking, with the hand resting on the cross.[277] This hypothesis cannot be verified, but it is a fair assumption that the purposeful reworking of the image of the ruler in profile,[278] with his hand raised high, holding and displaying the cross,[279] is a statement of religious allegiance and of exaltation of the cross. The end of the shaft on which the cross is mounted is clearly visible and in its proportions the cross is reminiscent of contemporary Byzantine examples used to bless the faithful.[280]

Hands holding crosses are also found in the iconography of later Series.[281] Certain coins of Series W and Series Q show a half-bust and bent arm (Fig. 2.60), as on the 'Constantine' *tremisses*, whereas some coins of Series G, and especially among the Secondary Series K, show a cupped hand. Among coins with

---

[272] For the angel at Breedon-on-the-Hill, see Fig. 2.25; for the Tassilo Chalice (*MoE* 168, no. 131); and see the examples of the finger position on fo. 9ᵛ and fo. 150 of the Stockholm Codex Aureus (ibid. 199, no. 154).

[273] See the representation of King David on the fragment of textile from the Convent of SS Harlindis and Relindis, Aldeneik, Belgium, illustrated in Stiegemann and Wemhoff 1999: ii. 463, VII.22.

[274] See discussion in Conclusion.

[275] Sutherland 1948: 39 and 80, and *T&S* i. 47. See for instance the *follis* of Constantine in Bastien 1992: iii, 174, no. 3.

[276] Hawkes 1996: 85.

[277] *T&S* i. 49, suggests the possibility that the coinage might be connected with the founding of *Medeshamstede* by King Wulfhere (658–74).

[278] Numismatic precedents from Constantinople present the emperor frontally, as, for instance, on the gold solidus of Heraclius, AD 610–13 (Kent and Painter 1977: 180, no. 723).

[279] It may be argued that the hand is not actually holding the cross. The representation on other coins (for instance Series W, Fig. 2.56, and Series U, Fig. 3.10) testifies to the difficulties involved in the rendering of grips on such a small scale. It is also possible that the open hand was a gesture conveying further significance, as discussed above.

[280] See the miniature of St Gregory the Great in the 'Incipit' to Book II of Bede's *Historia Ecclesiastica* (St Petersburg, Lat. Q.v.I; Scharer 1999: 193, fig. 9.2), the figure on the silver book-cover from Antioch (Kent and Painter 1977: 87, no. 149), and the silver bowl with the bust of a military saint (Buckton 1994: 121, no. 135) both seventh century. See also the flamboyant iconography on the slab from Narbonne, eighth century (Hubert, Porcher, and Volbach 1969: 100, fig. 118). Numerous examples of comparable crosses survive (for instance Buckton 1994: 105–6, no. 114, and see the display in the Ashmolean Museum).

[281] Arslan 1992: 822 underlines the fact that the cross is a cross-on-globe.

Fig. 2.59. 'Constantine' type, pale gold shilling, *c*.660–70 (CM 1896, 4-4-10. The British Museum, London).

Fig. 2.60. Series Q, Type QI, silver penny, Secondary (3918, de Wit collection).

Fig. 2.61. Series K, Type 20/18, silver penny, Secondary (*T&S* 317. The Ashmolean Museum, Oxford).

full-length figures, gripping hands are only indicated by pellets, with the exception of coins of Series U, Type 23b, where the fingers are differentiated.[282]

Hands Holding Cups

Coins of Secondary Series K, Type 20 show a bust with a hand holding a cup instead of a cross, although coins of Type 20/18 also place a cross above it, sometimes made up of pellets (Fig. 2.61).[283]

The fact that the cup takes the place of the cross might suggest that it is actually a religious figure holding a chalice;[284] however, the attribute can be clearly identified with a palm cup. Archaeologically, glass palm-cups are known from burials and are datable between the seventh and eighth century, and they differ in shape and size from those intended for liturgical use which usually have a knob and stem.[285]

The Franks Casket differentiates between two types of cups: a palm-cup and one with a stem (Fig. 2.62):[286] the scenes on the front panel portray a contrast between mythological and Christian, profane and sacred settings. The two different types of cups, one with drugged beer, one with offerings to Christ, probably mirror this intentionally.

---

[282] *T&S* iii. 554–5.
[283] Some coins of this type have four dots over the cup, in an arrangement still suggestive of a cross.
[284] *T&S* iii. 391.
[285] For Anglo-Saxon palm-cups, see Harden 1956*b*: 138, fig. 25X; see Ryan 1990 for a discussion of early medieval eucharistic chalices (including the Tassilo Chalice, ibid. 303, pl. 10). In Hexham Abbey the shape of a chalice is carved on a grave slab.
[286] Palm-cups are shown on the front panel (Weland the Smith and Beadohild), and on the back (seated figure); chalices appear on the front (with one of the Wise Men) and on the right-end panel (under the runes 'bita'). Webster 1999 and Lang 1999 for the latest interpretations of the iconography programme.

Fig. 2.62. Details with Weland and Magus from the front of the Franks Casket, 8th century (MME 1867, 1-20, 1. © The British Museum, London).

It is likely that the cup on our coins is to be interpreted as secular, alluding to hospitality and generosity, kingly qualities in pagan times, and desirable also in a Christian context.[287] However, the Anglo-Saxon riddles understood as meaning 'cup' alert us to a complex interpretation of the object, where dichotomies between sacred and profane contexts, feasting and the Eucharist, sin and Salvation, wine and Blood, are all material for metaphysical meditations.[288] The image on our coins might suggest similar comparisons and invite a careful use of the cup: while it may make merry and win friends, it might also cause inebriation and fall from grace.[289]

Hands Holding Sprigs

Coins of Series K, Type 42 present another variation on the iconography of the hand holding an attribute: sprigs, arranged by Metcalf in four groups (Fig. 2.63). Vegetation motifs are extraneous to traditional Germanic art; they are of Mediterranean origin and, as in other areas of the Germanic world,[290] they testify to the appreciation and display of imported luxuries. Such motifs become current in Anglo-Saxon manuscripts, metalwork, and sculpture from the eighth

[287] See feasting as bonding in *Beowulf*, inscriptions with the theme of hospitality as 'political medium' on bracteates (Andrén 1991: 249) and *HE* III, 6 describing King Oswald as a Christian host and alms-giver.

[288] Williamson 1977: nos. 9, 61, and particularly riddle 28*a*, as discussed by Whitehurst Williams 1992: 25–30.

[289] See also further discussion and suggested interpretation in Conclusion.

[290] This is the interpretation for the *appliqué* with plant motif from the Lombard shield of Stabio, seventh century (Pugliese Carratelli 1984: 244, fig. 118; Menis 1990: 191).

Fig. 2.63. Series K, Type 42, silver
penny, Secondary (*T&S* 311. The
Ashmolean Museum, Oxford).

Fig. 2.64. The Bacchus Gem, Roman, 2nd
century AD (© Cambridge Antiquarian
Society).

century, not only in the form of vine-scrolls, but also as learned quotations from the antique.[291]

The model for the coins is derived from Roman gems representing Bacchus holding his *thyrsus*, as on the gem found at Cambridge (Fig. 2.64).[292] As the reverse of these coins is also copied from a 'Bacchic' gem, showing a panther with a *thyrsus*,[293] we might postulate that two such gems associated with the cult of Bacchus might have been found together, and served as sources of inspiration.[294]

It is possible to see in the iconography of our coins a multiplicity of allusions: *crux foliata*,[295] perhaps even a vine-scroll on account of the berries, bringing salvation to the soul, or a medicinal plant bringing healing to the body.[296] Its

[291] See the binding of the St Cuthbert Gospel, *c*.698, with plant motif possibly of Coptic inspiration (*MoE* 121, no. 86), and compare the plant details on fo. 129ᵛ of the Gospels of St Augustine with that of fo. 9ᵛ of the Stockholm Codex Aureus (*MoE* 17, no. 1; p. 199, no. 154). The vegetation filling the background of the miniature of the Evangelist St John (Barberini Gospels, fo. 124ᵛ; *MoE* 205, no. 160) is also worth noticing.

[292] The Cambridge Bacchus Gem has been published several times (Henig 1978: pl. 27, no. 99; Hutchinson 1986: 437, no. Ge-3; Alexander and Pullinger 2000: 90–1, fig. I.3). Comparisons can be drawn between the rendering of details such as the two lines on the neck of Bacchus (interpreted on the coins as the border of a tunic), the drapery and the two long cork-screw locks, turned into interlaced wreath-ties.

[293] See Fig. 4.37*b*. On Bacchus' panther: Hutchinson 1986: 145.

[294] On Bacchus in Roman Britain: Hutchinson 1986; on the reuse of Roman gems by the Anglo-Saxons: Henig 1978: 160–1; Cherry 1999: 143, on a Jupiter Serapis intaglio which the monks of Durham provided with an inscription linking it with King Oswald.

[295] See below, Fig. 2.67.

[296] Revelation 22: 2: 'and the leaves of the tree were for the healing of the nations'. Anglo-Saxon medicine and magic were based on the virtues of plants: Riddle 1965; Cameron 1993. In the Book of Kells branches held by angels are interpreted as hyssop, a plant prescribed in the Old Testament and Christian liturgy for purification rituals: Farr 1997*b*: 145.

Fig. 2.65. Detail of the Magi from the front of the Franks Casket, 8th century (MME 1867, 1-20, 1. © The British Museum, London).

Fig. 2.66. MONITASCORUM type, silver penny, Secondary (3794, de Wit collection).

sensory vividness is indicated by the fact that the sprig is hand held, and close to the nose.[297] The two ideas of deliverance, spiritual and physical, are intentionally juxtaposed, and invite contemplation, as we saw for the iconography of the cup.[298]

Frankincense and myrrh,[299] burnt in the worship of God and emperors, and also praised for their medicinal virtues, appear, with gold coins, as gifts from the Wise Men on the Franks Casket (Fig. 2.65).[300] They are worthy gifts from wise kings, and as such an attribute that would associate their bearer with wisdom.[301]

Bust and Crosses

The Anglo-Saxon inclination to exploit all available space with details conveying meaning is apparent also in the coinage, where the space around the bust is filled with inscriptions—more or less garbled but often 'rationalized'—symbols, and crosses.

Crosses and sprigs, attributes that on some series, as we saw, are hand held, are also found in other series simply placed in front of the bust (Fig. 2.66). Some of these crosses seem to be mounted on shafts, comparable in proportion to those featured on the reverse of the same coins,[302] where they appear to be about the size of the figure holding them: presumably, then, they are not

[297] See Conclusion.

[298] See the idea of the riddle discussed at p. 67.

[299] Incense, 'the prayers of saints' (Rev. 5: 8), was also burnt in Anglo-Saxon England as a departure ceremony (Bede, *Lives of the Abbots*, ch. 17; Farmer 1988); myrrh, associated with the memory of the Saviour, was also used as an analgesic (Cabrol and Leclerq 1907–53: *Encens* and *Myrre*). Riddle 1965: 188; Atchley 1909.

[300] On the Magi: Flint 1991: 364 ff.

[301] Further allusions are also possible, such as to Aaron's rod and the tree of life: Howlett 1974: 45, on associations with Wisdom.

[302] See for instance *T&S* iii, pl. 19, nos. 324 and 326.

Fig. 2.67. *a*. Series L, Type 15,
silver penny, Secondary (*T&S*
323. The Ashmolean Museum,
Oxford); *b*. lead ampulla from
Palestine, 6th century (no. 9,
Museo del Duomo, Monza,
Italy).

cross-sceptres,[303] but large processional ones.[304] Sometimes the cross appears to
be mounted on a base, perhaps for use on an altar.[305] A cross potent, mounted on
a similar base,[306] is shown on the obverse of a 'Victory' type coin, with a winged
Victory/Angel holding a wreath over it as a crown.[307]

Series L, Type 15, where the cross springs between two stems ending in pellets,
presents an even more poignant image: this is the *crux foliata*, where the cross
truly becomes 'the tree of life', synthesis of death and resurrection,[308] as we see
on *ampullae* from Monza (Fig. 2.67). The motif is of Oriental origin,[309] and was
favoured for altar screens, sarcophagi, and church sculpture from the sixth
century onwards in Rome, Ravenna, Milan, Pavia, Constantinople, etc.[310] It is
also commonly found in Merovingian Francia as a decoration for sarcophagi,
besides being used on coinage.[311]

---

[303] *T&S* iii. 392, describes them as cross-sceptres: the existence of such an object as a royal symbol in
Anglo-Saxon England, however, is doubtful.

[304] The so-called Rupertus Cross (*MoE* 170, no. 133) is an impressive survival of this type contemporary with our coins, and it exemplifies the 'theatrical quality of early Anglo-Saxon church furniture'
(ibid. 171). The tenon at the foot would have fitted into a base.

[305] *T&S* iii, pl. 20, no. 345, See *MEC*, pl. 23, nos. 471–2 for similar bases on the reverse of
Merovingian coins.

[306] A large cross potent, a kingly gift for the altar, is shown in the *Liber Vitae* of the New Minster,
Winchester (British Library, Stowe 944, fo. 6ʳ), eleventh century (Wilson 1984: 184, fig. 231). Of the
famous Cross of Eligius (*c*.600) only a fragment survives (Bibliothèque Nationale, Paris), but a fifteenth-
century Flemish painting by the Master of Saint-Gilles (National Gallery, London) shows it in its setting
(Hubert, Porcher, and Volbach 1969: 242, figs. 266–7).

[307] Compare *T&S* iii, pl. 21, no. 351 obv. (and below, Fig. 3.3*a*). See also ibid. pl. 19, no. 331, for a
cross on a pyramidal base of three pellets.

[308] Casartelli Novelli 1992: 552.

[309] On Oriental influences in the West in the early Middle Ages: Bréhier 1903.

[310] The volumes of the *Corpus della scultura altomedievale Italiana* offer many examples that would
probably have been seen by Anglo-Saxon pilgrims. Among the many variations, see the seventh/eighth-
century altar with a cross sprouting branches on which a bird perches (Raspi-Serra 1974: fig. 313).

[311] See the illustration of stone sarcophagi, seventh/eighth century in the Musée Carnavalet, Paris, Périn
1980: 30, no. 18; Périn 1996: 12; Merovingian gold coin, Rodez, Saint-Bernard-de-Comminges (*MEC* pl.

Fig. 2.68. *a–b.* Series L, Types 15b and 16, silver pennies, late Secondary (*BMC* 96 and 98. The British Museum, London).

The choice of such a motif on the Anglo-Saxon coin shows awareness of the symbolism attached to the cross,[312] mirrored in the sophisticated interlocking imagery of tree and cross in *The Dream of the Rood*,[313] and displayed in the use of the vine-scroll, which turns crosses so decorated into *cruces foliatae*. The iconography of the coin might be understood as corresponding to that of Series K, Types 32a and 42, and of reverses with figures holding crosses and/or trees of Series L, K, and related.[314]

Bust and Vegetation Motifs

Coins of Series L, Types 15b–16 alternate obverses with a bust facing either a cross or a sinuous sprig: these have as reverses a figure holding either a branch (or bird) and a cross, or two crosses (Fig. 2.68).[315] Such interchange in the iconography suggests a deliberate correlation between the cross and the branch, as in the portrait of St Luke in the Lichfield Gospels, where, as Prof. Henderson points out, by holding a flowering rod, the Evangelist alludes to Aaron and the Old Testament, whilst the cross represents the church and the New Testament.[316] The message is one of concordance and continuity between the two traditions, and important in the interpretation of the coin reverses. Another similar juxtaposition is probably presented in the Codex Aureus, where the capitals of the architecture framing the portrait of St Matthew bear representations carrying a scroll and a book, probably the Old and the New Testament. A plant is shown by

22, no. 447). It is also used in Carolingian manuscript illuminations, e.g. Harley MS 2788, fo. 9, early ninth century, Rosenbaum 1955: 14, where the motif is derived from sarcophagi in Ravenna.

[312] Youngs 1999: 293.

[313] On *The Dream of the Rood* see Szarmach and Oggins 1986 (part 3: 'Interdisciplinary Approaches'). Such images may have been drawn from experience, as the 'hastily made' cross Oswald put up at Heavenfield, clearly from a freshly felled tree (*HE* III, 2).

[314] These are discussed at p. 88 and p. 93.

[315] See also Figs. 3.19, 3.20. The iconography also appears on two of the embroidered roundels on the *chemise* of Sainte Bathilde (Vierk 1978: 529–30, fig. 5.3).

[316] The portrait of St Luke, Lichfield Gospels, 218, is discussed and illustrated in G. Henderson 1987: 122–4, fig. 180.

Fig. 2.69. Series L, Type 16, silver
penny, late Secondary (*BMC* 156. The
British Museum, London).

Fig. 2.70. WITMEN MONITA, gold shilling,
c.640 (*T&S* 5 = Crondall 73. The
Ashmolean Museum, Oxford).

the figure carrying the scroll, whereas a *Chi*-cross is inscribed on the book:[317]
perhaps this alludes to the fulfilment of the Covenant.

Not only do the obverses of Series L and related coins respond to those of
Series K, Types 32/42 and their rich allegorical meanings,[318] but we can see the
motif reproduced in a variation allusive to the Eucharist (Fig. 2.69). Arguably
such complex exegetical allusions may have been apparent to only a few of the
beholders of our coins,[319] whilst to less sophisticated audiences the motif would
have recalled the vine-scroll in its basic interpretation.[320] Contrary to Baldwin
Brown's theory that sees relics of paganism clinging to coinage, with Christian
crosses boldly discarded in favour of *pagan* flowering stems,[321] the vegetation
motif should be interpreted as profoundly Christian.

Bust and 'Tridents'

The gold coins of the WITMEN group in the Crondall hoard (*c*.640, Fig. 2.70) add
in front of the bust an attribute in the shape of a 'trident' on a bifurcated base.
Sutherland equated it with the 'trident' featured—with decussate cross and
crozier on similar stands—on the reverse of an ABBONI MANET coin, also from
the Crondall hoard.[322]

As can be seen in some specimens, where the whole of the 'trident' is visible on

---

[317] The Stockholm Codex Aureus, fo. 9ᵛ (*MoE* 200, no. 154).

[318] See discussion at pp. 67 and 69. See also G. Henderson 1987: 122–4, and 'Tree of Jesse' imagery
(Isa. 11: 1).

[319] Howlett 1974: 50 stresses the familiarity of the exegesis of the relevant biblical texts.

[320] Youngs 1999: 293 considers the motif of a cross superimposed onto a plant on a modest eighth-
century Northumbrian plaque 'established iconography'.

[321] Baldwin Brown 1903–37: iii. 101–2 (specifically about the reverse of a Series L-related coin from
Youlbury).

[322] Sutherland 1948: 33. For the ABBONI MANET and further discussion of the attribute on the reverse
of the coin, see 'Crossed Instruments'.

the flan of the coins, there is a further bifurcation of the central prong, mirror-image of the base of the object.[323] This feature does not appear on the related WUNEETTON type,[324] perhaps because they copied WITMEN coins with 'trident' tops off the flan, or had different prototypes.

Series J, Type 37, in the Secondary phase, shows a cross mounted on an upside-down 'trident' between confronted heads.[325] This was once taken as support for theories of cooperation between state (trident) and church (cross),[326] especially as the earliest specimens, with the upright divided either by a pellet or actually severed below the noses, seem to distinguish two parts.[327] Parallels in Continental metalwork, however,[328] with figures or animals flanking a cross with elaborate base, are demonstrably derived from tree-of-life iconography:[329] therefore the 'trident' base of Series J is simply a rationalized representation of the roots of the cross as the tree of life.

Undoubtedly, as iconographically the 'trident' alternates with a cross in front of busts, we are confronted with an object with some sacro-ceremonial function. It may be a cross/*candelabrum*,[330] with occasionally a further extension on its top, or the frame for a standard, recalling the Sutton Hoo iron stand.[331] The reverse of some 'Constantines' from Coddenham perhaps shows one 'dressed' with drapes, crosses, etc. (Fig. 2.71).[332] The 'trident' might fit Bede's description of the Roman-inspired *tufa* carried before Edwin of Northumbria.[333] Some conflation, if not confusion, must have taken place between various Roman insignia of this type,[334] but certainly such standards were understood and used as symbols of authority.[335] We might postulate a juxtaposition of cross/ 'trident', religious/secular insignia, and issues of theatricality and symbolism in the displaying of a *crux gemmata* and a dressed standard bearing earthly treasure.

[323] See Sutherland 1948: pl. 3, nos. 25, 26, 28, 29, 30, 32, and pl. 4, nos. 1, 2, 3, 11, 13, 14.

[324] See Fig. 2.34. The WUNEETTON type is not represented in the Crondall hoard, possibly because geographically remote (Stewart 1978: 151), though the legend WUNEETTON, apparently a corruption of WITMEN MONITA, might suggest it is a post-Crondall successor of that coinage (*MEC* 163).

[325] See Fig. 2.19.

[326] *T&S* iii. 344, but see discussion below.

[327] Ibid. 351 considers the coins from Garton-on-the-Wolds and one from York as stylistic starting-points.

[328] See Klein-Pfeuffer 1993: pl. 5, no. 19; pl. 27, no. 128; pl. 4, no. 18.

[329] Koch 1976: 22–3; Koch 1982: 56; Klein-Pfeuffer 1993: 163.

[330] See 'Crossed Instruments'.

[331] Bruce-Mitford 1978: 403–31; Care Evans 1994: 86, no. 74.

[332] The reverse of these *tremisses* has been described as a lyre-shaped object (Sutherland 1948: 80 and Rigold 1960: 12) or a standard (Bruce-Mitford 1974: 12). For 'Constantines' see Figs. 2.59 and 2.72.

[333] *HE* II, 16. Edwin had been a guest at Redwald's East Anglian court, whence he might have derived the use of standards (Bruce-Mitford 1974: 11 ff.; Henderson 1972: 215). See also discussion of the term *tufa* = foliage (Bruce-Mitford 1978: 430–1), and the suggestion that the grid and basket of the Sutton Hoo stand could have been used to display foliage, feathers, etc.

[334] Bruce-Mitford 1974: 13 ff.; Neuman de Vegvar 1986: 5.

[335] Chaney 1970: 139; Raw 1992: 172.

Fig. 2.71. 'Constantine' type (reverse), pale gold shilling, *c.*660–70 (CM 1896, 4-4-10. The British Museum, London).

Fig. 2.72. 'Constantine' type from Billockby, pale gold shilling, *c.*660–70 (The Fitzwilliam Museum, Cambridge).

Bust and 'Star'

In a variant of the hand-and-cross obverse of the 'Constantine' type,[336] the coins from Billockby (Fig. 2.72) and Coddenham 285 present a star-shaped object with annulets in front of the face. Unfortunately we lack specific *comparanda* for what is a very carefully reproduced object on both specimens.[337]

Classical coinage motifs might be behind the attribute. Roman coins often show stars: these were symbols of eternity associated with legends concerning the death and deification of Caesar, but were also used in the iconography of living emperors, until they eventually became so degraded in the Late Empire as to be used as mintmarks.[338] Stars were adopted for Constantine's triumphal imagery and conflated with the *Chi-Rho* monogram:[339] on a medallion, perhaps of Mauricius Tiberius, mounted on a bracelet found in Constantinople, the traditional star to the left of the emperor incorporates a *Chi-Rho* (with closed and reversed loop) and has eight limbs.[340] When Roman coins were imitated, such marks were noted and carefully reproduced, as testified by the gold bracteate from Undley, based on the obverse and reverse of a fourth-century 'Urbs Roma' coin minted at Trier,[341] which includes *two* stars with eight points ending in pellets.

Another possible source of inspiration for the motif may have been the stars, usually ending in pellets, which are ubiquitous on Byzantine medical-magical

---

[336] See Fig. 2.59.

[337] One wonders if the object might be folding scales (MacGregor and Bolick 1993: 257, nos. 53.1–2), which have perforated arms. These pivot on a central section to which a pointer and stirrup handle are attached. Scales would be a fitting attribute, guaranteeing the weight of the coins.

[338] Bastien 1992: 684. See for instance the *aureus* of Trajan (issued by Hadrian) and the *nummus* of Constantine II (Bastien 1992: iii, pl. 48, no. 1; pl. 190, no. 4).

[339] Cf. Bastien 1992: iii, pl. 172, no. 5.

[340] The gold medallion (Mauricius Tiberius?) from a bracelet of the Small Gold Treasure of Constantinople, second half of sixth century (Ross 1962–5: ii. 4 and pl. 6).

[341] See Fig. 4.54: a second star is just visible under the left spiral. Webster and Brown 1997: 237 and 117, fig. 48.

amulets.[342] These, as well as pilgrims' badges and tokens from Palestine, would have been regarded with great veneration on account of their association with holy places.[343]

Unusually for Anglo-Saxon art, the composition of the 'star' and annulets on our coins is asymmetrical: moreover, the Billockby coin introduces an independent limb with a third annulet. Such deliberately scalene compositions recall the monograms used as control marks in Byzantine silver stamps. In the Sutton Hoo treasure, the Anastasius dish and four other silver vessels present control stamps and it is conceivable that these marks might have been understood as signs of prestige—and possibly imitated.[344] However, whether the 'star' represents a pseudo-monogram, imitating silver stamps, a star-shaped symbol of authority in the Constantinian tradition, or something else entirely, is unfortunately so far unclear.

Bust and Sceptre

The VANIMVNDVS MONE issues,[345] spanning the transition from gold to silver, show a helmeted bust with an attribute with a rounded finial, presumably a sceptre (Fig. 2.73). No particular Christian significance can be assigned to the emphatic cross formed by the wreath-ties intersecting the sceptre on the Anglo-Saxon coin, as this is a conspicuous feature also on the ring of Childeric,[346] who was not Christian, and on Roman models. The iconography shows close parallels with Roman coins with profile busts in military accoutrement, while Consular issues, where a cross replaces the sceptre,[347] inspire the rich robes.[348] The iconography also recalls the influential Constantinian issue of 315–16, with the emperor carrying a spear on his right shoulder, the prototype for many representations of Christ Triumphant carrying his cross.[349]

The royal burial at Sutton Hoo, besides the whetstone, included the remains of what has been interpreted as a wand, which, in its speculative reconstruction,[350] is closely related to Roman models,[351] and recalls the light sceptre on the

---

[342] As on the silver pendant, Eastern Mediterranean, sixth/seventh century (Mundell Mango 1986: 265, no. 93, fig. 93.1; cf. stars on ring at p. 265, no. 92, fig. 92.1). For amuletic marks: Buschhausen 1995: 55.

[343] See for instance the star on the *ampulla* now in Monza illustrated at Fig. 5.12*b*.

[344] For the hexagonal control stamp on the Anastasius dish, Sutton Hoo, see Cruikshank Dodd 1961: 58, no. 4.

[345] Name of a Merovingian moneyer, copied on this Anglo-Saxon transitional group (*MEC* 164).

[346] MacGregor 1999: 133, and p. 162, fig. 10.

[347] This was implemented in 422 by Theodosius II (Kent and Painter 1977: 186).

[348] See the *follis* of Constantine, and the solidus of Valentinian III (Bastien 1992: iii, pl. 144, no. 7; pl. 223, no. 6). The drapery is discussed above.

[349] For example: the left-hand panel of the Genoels-Elderen book-cover (*MoE* 181, no. 141). Grabar 1971: 237 ff., discusses the Christian takeover of the imperial iconography, with examples. For the solidus of Constantine, see Bastien 1992: iii, pl. 184, no. 4.

[350] Bruce-Mitford 1978: 401, fig. 286.

[351] See discussion on contemporary sceptres and the antique tradition, ibid. 350–8.

Fig. 2.73. Series VA, transitional pale
gold shilling of 'Vanimundus', *c*.660–70
(CM 1983, 10-24-3. The British
Museum, London).

Fig. 2.74. Series K, Type 42 (*T&S* 313. The
Ashmolean Museum, Oxford).

VANIMVNDVS MONE coins. Hand-held 'sceptres', be they whetstones or wands,
are believed to have become part of the Germanic tradition of power and sacral
insignia,[352] albeit formally influenced by Roman and Celtic example.[353]

If Bullough was bemused at the 'indifference' to the lance as symbol of
authority in representations of Germanic kings (Childeric's ring being the only
exception) whilst it was such a common attribute on contemporary imperial
coinage,[354] we might equally wonder at the lack of sceptres on our coins. Indeed,
the VANIMVNDVS MONE is the sole issue to portray one, and the CARIP coin with
a seated figure holding a cross and a long-staff on its reverse is also unique:[355]
both are isolated copies from classical prototypes. The answer might lie with the
original significance of such attributes for the Anglo-Saxons and the possible
coincidence of religious and political roles in early Anglo-Saxon kingship.[356] The
evidence of the coins suggests that, in spite of Roman precedents and of poten-
tially being disguised as crosses by the wreath-ties, sceptres were soon replaced
with hand-held crosses,[357] perhaps because they were felt to be too charged with
connotations of the old religion to be used for images intended to underline
allegiance to Christianity.[358]

[352] A caveat (Bruce-Mitford 1978: 352) suggests that some may have had more humble functions.
[353] Chaney 1970: 145. In the publication of the finds, formal similarities between the whetstone and
classical sceptres were emphasized, especially regarding the spherical knob ends (Bruce-Mitford 1978:
352, with Celtic comparative examples discussed at pp. 364 ff.). On the appeal to *romanitas*: Deanesly
1943.
[354] Bullough 1975: 229. Chaney 1970: 145 on the long-staff as a variant of Woden's spear. Spears,
however, are far from being an exclusively royal attribute, as testified by grave-finds and iconographical
evidence. See for instance King Agilulf's plaque (Webster and Brown 1997: 118, fig. 49), the Finglesham
buckle (*MoE* 22, fig. 2), and the Sutton Hoo helmet plaques (Fig. 2.50).
[355] See Fig. 3.22*a*. The iconography is a variant on the seated figure with bird and cross, also classically
inspired.
[356] Chaney 1970: 11.
[357] See above.
[358] Bruce-Mitford 1978: 377, suggests a similar reason for the burial of the whetstone at Sutton Hoo.

Bust and Bird

Coins of Secondary Series K, Type 42, although linked by the same animal reverse,[359] have busts with different attributes: a cross, a sprig, and a bird; Series K, Type 20, with a standing figure holding a cross and a bird as reverse, features a similar bust with a cup.[360] On the obverses of these types the hands holding the cross, the sprig, and the cup are prominent; however, on the one with a bird this is simply perched on the shoulder. There are two variations to the bird, its head either turned towards or away from the bust (Fig. 2.74).[361]

Arslan particularly highlights the iconography of bird and bust as innovative among the 'barbarian' coinages, introducing motifs peculiar to their culture, and he quotes in particular the Western imitation of a *tremissis* of Justinian I, where the head of a Germanic-style bird of prey confronts the bust.[362] On many sixth/seventh-century pagan Scandinavian bracteates derived from Roman imperial medallions, a bird, generally identified with Woden's raven, replaces the classical winged Victory,[363] a change that may be taken as indicating a shift towards more positive connotations for ravens, transformed from symbol of death to symbol of victory.[364]

As with all of Series K, the iconography of these coins presents a wealth of references. If ravens were of sacral importance for kings claiming descent from Woden,[365] the handling of birds of prey, such as hawks and falcons in the royal hunt, and their portrayals on coins and other artefacts,[366] allows some continuity in the symbolism. The Christian counterpart of ravens as hunters/food-providers for saints, as in the legends of Paul and Antony in the desert, or of St Cuthbert, would have suggested striking parallels, as would the iconography of the Evangelist St John.[367]

The tale of Gregory the Great, recounting how he was inspired with divine wisdom and dictated his writing by a white dove, was first recorded in England in the *Liber Beati Gregorii*.[368] However, our coins seem to testify to the earlier knowledge of the story at Canterbury, a place of well-attested devotion and links

---

[359] See *T&S* iii. 395.

[360] See the relevant sections above.

[361] Other coins are illustrated in Metcalf and Walker 1967: pl. 7, nos. 23–6.

[362] Gold Western imitation of a *tremissis* in the name of Justinian I, unknown provenance, sixth century (Arslan 1992: 796, pl. 1, no. 2).

[363] See for instance the gold bracteate from Funen, sixth century (Axboe 1991: fig. 6, p. 190).

[364] Lukman 1958: 133.

[365] Chaney 1970: 132–3.

[366] See discussion at 'Standing Figures with Cross and Bird'.

[367] Ó Carragáin 1988; Bede, *Life of St Cuthbert*, ch. 20 (Farmer 1988: 69). On the eagle as symbol of St John the Evangelist: Braunfels 1968–76: 111.

[368] On the legend of Gregory (from the *Liber Beati Gregorii*): Scharer 1999: 195, and see the miniature of St Gregory from the ninth-century Metz Sacramentary fragment illustrated ibid. at fig. 9.3. See also the splendid miniature of Gregory the Great in the *Registrum Epistolarum*, Trier Stadtbibliothek 171/1626, c.983 (Gameson 1997: 25, no. 3).

to Gregory, and probably connected with Series K.[369] An attribute reminiscent of past symbolism and contemporary royal associations, the bird might have represented a potent contrast between Woden's raven, foretelling death,[370] and the white dove, inspiring with divine wisdom.[371]

---

[369] Scharer 1999. As mint-place of Series K, *T&S* iii. 384 suggests 'East Kent, and perhaps a place on the banks of the Wantsum Channel rather than Canterbury'; however, it is possible that this speculative mint-place was connected to Canterbury.

[370] Chaney 1970: 134, on an incident related in the *Life of St Gregory*, where a crow 'sang with evil omen'.

[371] See discussion on Series K at Conclusion.

3

Human Figures

Many reverses of the Intermediate and Secondary phases have human figures either singly or in pairs, sitting or standing, and with a variety of attributes.

'Victory' and Angels

Among the many figures representing Virtues in Roman art and coinage, that of Victory must be counted among the most influential of Roman-inspired reverse coin designs.[1] Quite apart from formal variations,[2] the subtlety with which it could be used as propaganda for military or political achievements facilitated its passage to a more idealized sphere. The move, already effected in stoic circles, where Victory had come to signify abstract philosophical and moral triumphs, culminated with Christianity to symbolize virtuous triumph and ultimate victory over death.[3] Iconographically, in addition to the traditional wreath and palm carried by Victory, still appropriate symbols of triumph for the new ideology, other specifically Christian attributes were added, such as long crosses.[4] The shift from pagan to Christian mirrors a readjustment not only in the meaning, but in the perception of Victory, which, together with other Virtues of pagan times, became an Angel, a personification of the celestial power of God.[5] In the Lombard regal gold coinage (c.690–774), during the reign of Cunincpert (688–700), the traditional Victory transformed into the Archangel St Michael (Fig. 3.1).[6]

Anglo-Saxon moneyers would have had many different models of Victory to draw on, not only from Roman examples, numismatic and others, but from

[1] *MEC* 11.
[2] Vermeule 1957: 358 identifies seventeen types among them, adapted from standard decorative motifs in other media commemorating triumphs and mirroring different political aims and ideals.
[3] Tomasini 1964: 16, and Cabrol and Leclercq 1907–53: *Anges*.
[4] *MEC* 11. Tomasini 1964 sees subtle propaganda at play in the choice of distinct positions and attributes for the Victories used as reverses for Eastern and Western Empire coinages.
[5] Mattingly 1937: 117.
[6] Arslan 1984: 428 explains the political statement meant by the change. The iconography seems to have been chosen because of associations between St Michael and the Lombard kingdom, but the special devotion of Cunincpert for the archangel would also have been a determining factor in the change (*MEC* 64).

Fig. 3.1. *Tremissis* of Liutprand (712–44), king of the Lombards (*MEC* 322. The Fitzwilliam Museum, Cambridge).

Fig. 3.2. Gold coin, probably Anglo-Saxon, late 6th century (CM 1896, 4-4-11. The British Museum, London).

Byzantine, Burgundian, Alemannic, Merovingian, Visigothic, and Lombard coins,[7] appealing to *Romanitas* and with political or religious overtones. It is surprising that more extensive use of it was not made.[8] Indeed, the find of a gold coin on the seashore at Weymouth, with a striding Victory on its reverse, led Stewart to propose that this and another gold coin with a facing Victory, unprovenanced, could represent an early and unrecognized phase of Anglo-Saxon coinage, contemporary to the time when the Victory was used as a reverse on Continental coins, before being replaced by crosses (*c*.578–82).[9] His suggestion has encountered scepticism, mainly because an English origin is debatable for both.[10] However, the iconography merits consideration, as they both derive from influential, albeit discrete, classical models. Whereas the Victory from Weymouth (A94) is in profile, advancing right, with raised legs, flowing drapery and wing suggestive of Visigothic precedents,[11] that illustrated here is frontal, with outstretched arms holding wreaths and with a wing (indicated, as on the previous specimen, by a serrated bar on the left) balanced by floating drapery to the right (Fig. 3.2). The head is radiated, and the overall impression is one of symmetry. A possible model might be seen in the Victory crowning two emperors, as on coins of Licinius I and Licinius II, also reinter-

---

[7] Rigold 1975: 653 ff., on early finds of foreign coinage in Anglo-Saxon England.

[8] The little hand-held Victory on the reverse of the SKANOMODV solidus will not be considered here, as its Anglo-Saxon origin is debatable (Blackburn 1991: 141).

[9] Stewart 1978: 150; the advancing Victory coin (A94) is illustrated at p. 163. For the facing Victory, see also the coin from the Glendining sale catalogue, 20 Sept. 1978, lot 1, from a different die. Unfortunately the other Victory coin (included in Sutherland 1948, no. 84, ex-Montagu sale) is equally unprovenanced.

[10] The two coins could be compared to the Merovingian *tremisses* illustrated in *MEC* pl. 22, nos. 459–60.

[11] See the Visigothic *tremissis*, imitating 'Justinian', from Ash, Kent (Rigold 1975: 664, fig. 429, no. 37).

Fig. 3.3. *a.* 'Victory' type silver penny, Secondary (*T&S* 351. The Ashmolean Museum, Oxford); *b.* detail from the early 8th-century panel at Hovingham, North Yorkshire, showing the Annunciation angel (© Corpus of Anglo-Saxon Stone Sculpture).

preted in a Christian context and well represented in gold-glass roundels.[12] This would be another example of the Anglo-Saxon tendency to select and adapt part of a design to fit on small coin flans.[13]

In the Secondary Series, silver pennies of Type 22 (the so-called 'Victory' *sceattas*) portray a winged figure looking right and proffering a wreath.[14] The figure has replaced the billowing drapery of classical coinage with a much closer-fitting garment, resembling that worn by the static angels at the end of the Hovingham panel or by other figures on our coins, as if constricted by the narrowness of the space they inhabit (Fig. 3.3).[15]

Metcalf comments that on the coins the wings are always divided in two segments, one twice the size of the other, in correspondence to the angle at which the forearm is held.[16] This can be explained by considering how on classical examples of Victory carrying palms, the stem cuts through the wing roughly keeping that proportion. Vermeule notes that on Roman coins, irrespective of whether the Victory is walking left or right, the same attributes are always carried in the same hands: a palm in the left and a wreath in the right hand.[17] This is not the case on our coins, and indeed the adaptation of the iconography of classical models presents difficulties. If, conceptually, the iconography of Victory could

---

[12] Compare the *nummus* of Licinius I and Licinius II (Bastien 1992: iii, pl. 162, no. 8) with the gold-glass roundel with Christ crowning Peter and Paul (Engemann 1968–9: pl. 8*a*).

[13] See the 'Two Emperors' and reverses with standard/altar.

[14] *T&S* iii. 440–3.

[15] Hawkes 1993: 254

[16] Metcalf (*T&S* iii. 440) suggests the possibility that it might be a banner.

[17] Vermeule 1957: 360. It follows that the image was not merely reversed as in a mirror, but thought in three dimensions and possibly copied from statues, etc.

easily serve to portray angels,[18] the difficulty of keeping close to a vaguely remembered classical model is evident when we consider the awkward pose of the Annunciation angels at Hovingham (see above), or of the Genoels-Elderen ivory diptych.[19] The angel holds up his right hand in the gesture of speech and in the left he has a branch or staff, but in order to show it in front of the wing, as classical Victories do, he is made to cross his arms clumsily. The problem is avoided in the panel from Fletton, where, however, the angel becomes curiously left-handed (Fig. 3.4).[20] On coins, the difficulty of reproducing arms in different positions, and on figures in diverse stances, is compounded by having to engrave on a die that would moreover reverse the image, as in a mirror.

The figure on Type 22 holds a wreath in the left hand, but in a less expansive manner than Roman Victories, and cradles a staff in the right arm, so that it crosses over the large wing, clearly important for the reading of the image as an angel. The composition, apart from the presence of the wing, is similar, though reversed, to the Durham Cassiodorus illumination of King David as warrior.[21] To the side of the Angel of Type 22 there are some garbled letters, shadows of some legend,[22] tending towards a pattern. The coin illustrated above, probably towards the end of the production because of its lower fineness,[23] decisively turns this into a cross potent on a box-shaped base, perhaps an altar.

Some of the reverses of Type 22 feature frontal winged figures flanked by crosses and standing on a triple-strand torque-shape.[24] They lack arms, but their rectangular bodies, legs, and wing patterns show similarities with the figure on the obverse (Fig. 3.5). An innovative image, its prototype might be sought in the Victory/Angel of the 'Two Emperors' gold coinage: it seems that the die-cutter sought to give a body to the figure, barely visible apart from face and wings, hovering behind the emperors.[25] Of the known specimens of Type 22 showing this reverse, all from different dies, the coin illustrated as Fig. 3.5 has the highest silver content,[26] and might head the series. The rectangular body of the figure on the reverse is divided in two parts, the lower bearing a faint X-pattern, as if the top bar and the crossed struts of the emperors' throne had been interpreted as part of the figure's body.[27] The two crosses nestling under the wings might be understood as apotropaic. The shared features of the obverse and reverse figures

---

[18] Reinterpreting the traditional attributes of wreath and palm in a Christian context of triumph.

[19] For the Genoles-Elderen book cover, see *MoE* 180, no 141.

[20] The confusion between left and right hands/feet seen in the Book of Kells (Rynne 1994: 313) might also be explained in the light of the difficulty in adopting and adapting classical models to represent different activities and poses.

[21] Alexander 1978: no. 17, p. 46. The model is believed to originate from a sixth-century Italian prototype, perhaps from Vivarium.

[22] *T&S* iii. 441.

[23] Ibid. 442.

[24] For the other reverse and the torque-shape see 'Single Figure between Crosses'.

[25] For the 'Two Emperors' see Fig. 3.8.

[26] There are three listed in *T&S* iii. 442 (two with metal analysis), and one in the de Wit collection.

[27] Personally observed on a specimen of the Ashmolean Museum (illustrated here) and on the one in the de Wit collection (3503).

Fig. 3.4. Detail from frieze at Fletton, late 8th century (photograph courtesy of Dr J. Hawkes).

Fig. 3.5. Reverse of 'Victory' type silver penny, Secondary (*T&S* 350. The Ashmolean Museum, Oxford).

Fig. 3.6. 'Triquetras' eclectic group silver penny, Secondary (*T&S* 343. The Ashmolean Museum, Oxford).

suggest that they belong to the same genus, if not the same species: perhaps they are both angels of distinct orders. The main diagnostic difference is the lack of arms on the reverse figures: this could suggest the depiction of multi-winged seraphim, as opposite to anthropomorphic angels or archangels.[28]

A Secondary phase type, assigned to the 'Triquetras' group on account of its reverse pattern, shows a facing figure with large outspread wings and outstretched arms held in the *orans* position, unencumbered by attributes (Fig. 3.6).[29] The figure of the *orans*, signifying *pietas*, was used on Roman coinage of the second and third centuries AD and was adopted early on as an appropriate image in a Christian context, as testified by its appearance in catacombs, murals, gold-glass, and on sarcophagi.[30] There are precedents of *orans* representations, with or without wings, in the early Merovingian coinage,[31] and indeed Amécourt considered the type among the most interesting manifestations of the emancipation of Christian art in Gaul.[32]

In Anglo-Saxon England the *orans* figure would have been known not only from local Roman heritage,[33] but (with or without wings) from numerous imported Christian artefacts, such as pilgrims' flasks, gold-glass, manuscripts, and from examples seen abroad. Lombard sculpture provides the closest parallel to the iconography of our coin: the figure of St Michael from Monte S.

[28] See for instance the representations of seraphim on the Crucifixion page of the Durham Gospels, fo. 38ᵛ (*MoE* 114, no. 81, and see G. Henderson 1987: 83) and on the Clonmacnoise Plaque no. 2 (Bourke 1993: 176, fig. 21.1*a*). For Anglo-Saxon angels/archangels, see St Cuthbert's coffin side (Battiscombe 1956: pl. 9).

[29] Four specimens with this iconography are known: those mentioned in *T&S* iii. 424 and two in the Woodham Walter hoard (Webster and Brown 1997: 230, no. 75).

[30] Cabrol and Leclercq 1907–53: *Orant, Orante, passim.*

[31] Ibid., figs. 9099–102.

[32] Amécourt 1877: 175 ff.

[33] As in the wall painting at Lullingstone, Kent, mid-fourth century (Potter 1997: 63, fig. 47).

Angelo, in the Lombard Duchy of Benevento,[34] a much-revered site known to have been visited by Anglo-Saxon pilgrims.[35] It is conceivable that with the spread of the cult of St Michael to the West, this iconography may have travelled to England and may have been chosen for a coin. A devotion to St Michael the Archangel in England is known from church dedications,[36] as in the oratory near Hexham mentioned by Bede,[37] and on account of his reputation as a healer one could postulate that the angel on these coins might specifically represent St Michael, as on Lombard issues.[38] The iconography, however, as with the Secondary silver pennies, and unlike the early gold coinage, does not follow numismatic precedents, but typically is more eclectic in its source of inspiration.

The Two Emperors

The 'Two Emperors', used by several joint emperors of the late fourth century,[39] is one of the most commonly found types of Roman solidi in Britain.[40] It represents two emperors sharing power, sitting on one throne, together holding the orb, and was adopted during a delicately balanced political situation. Behind them, forming a canopy over their heads with her wings, is a Victory, counterbalancing on a celestial level the earthly impression of strength given by the crossed struts of the throne.[41] Apart from being reproduced on a pseudo-coin pendant (Fig. 3.7),[42] and having furnished a pattern for one of the Victory/Angels discussed above, the iconography of these coins twice served as model for Anglo-Saxon issues, in the gold coinage of the mid-seventh century and in Alfred's reign in the ninth century.

The 'Two Emperors' is one of the most common types among Anglo-Saxon shillings. Apparently post-dating the Crondall hoard, its production is put at *c*.660–75, as the colour of the metal varies noticeably between the coins. On account of the smaller flans of our coins compared to the Roman prototype, the iconography had to be focused on the detail of the three heads only. These are

[34] For the carving of St Michael, Monte S. Angelo, eighth century, see Rotili 1966: pl. 64, fig. 103. Although the Lombard sculpture shows the Archangel slaying the dragon, there are undeniable points of contact with our coin, in the symmetrical stance and the shape of the head, which is typical of eighth-century Lombard taste (see for instance the figures on Ratchis's altar (Pugliese Carratelli 1984: 266, nos. 154–5)), and which is used by Rotili 1966: 101–2, for dating.

[35] Bailey 1996: 26. The Anglo-Saxon name Eadrihd and three runic names (Anglo-Saxon/Frankish) appear among eighth-century graffiti scratched by pilgrims on the walls of the sanctuary (Arcamone 1980: 287; Mastrelli 1980: 332), testifying to the Anglo-Saxon presence at the site. Visits of other Anglo-Saxon groups are also recorded in chronicles (Carletti and Otranto 1980: 24).

[36] Farmer 1978: 278 mentions Malmesbury (Wilts.), Clive (Glos.), Stanmer (East Sussex), and the Hexham oratory.

[37] *HE* V, 19.   [38] Henderson 1999: 152 ff., especially 154 n. 59.

[39] The type was produced between the reigns of Valentinian I, AD 364–75, and Theodosius I, AD 379–95, and was issued, with variations, by nine associated emperors (Whitting 1961: 30).

[40] Blackburn 1998*a*: 113.

[41] Webster and Brown 1997: 236, nos. 99 and 102 show the Anglo-Saxon coin and one of its Roman prototypes (solidus of Valentinian II).

[42] The reverse of the pseudo-coin pendant copies a solidus of Honorius on the obverse (MacGregor and Bolick 1993: 156, no. 23.6).

Fig. 3.7. Pseudo-coin
pendant (reverse with 'Two
Emperors'), unprovenanced
(1942.220. The Ashmolean
Museum, Oxford).

Fig. 3.8. 'Two Emperors'
type pale gold shilling,
c.660–70 (*T&S* 79. The
Ashmolean Museum,
Oxford).

Fig. 3.9. Silver penny of
Alfred of Wessex
(871–99), struck at
London, moneyer Cenred
(CM 1896, 4-4-63. The
British Museum, London).

modelled, while the rest of the composition is linear and the haloes, rather than
encircling the heads, stop with horizontal traits at the side, and minute pellets,
also used to suggest the feathers on the wing, indicate the hair. The drapery is
economically rendered, but respects the difference in the fall of folds. The struts
of the throne are prominent, as is the orb, symmetrically held by skeletal hands.
The general impression is of balanced elegance (Fig. 3.8). Other coins dated
slightly later on account of the much poorer alloy take as their prototype the
Anglo-Saxon copy, and so misunderstand one important detail, as there are now
two orbs side by side.[43]

Although beyond the period examined here, the pennies struck by Alfred
(871–99) and Coelwulf II of Mercia (874–9) offer an interesting comparison in
the perception of the iconography, as the broader flans of that coinage allowed a
return to the Roman prototype in its entirety (Fig. 3.9).[44] Some scholars believe
that the 'Two Emperors' iconography was deliberately chosen as politically
appropriate, though this has been doubted by others.[45] Blackburn suggests that
a renewed interest in Roman prototypes, stimulated perhaps by the fortuitous
find of a hoard, might be behind the choice of this design and its careful reproduction from an original Roman coin, postulating an aesthetic/scholarly interest,[46] rather than exploitation of the image for propaganda purposes. However
close to the Roman prototype,[47] the Anglo-Saxon copies differ in one important

[43] *Pace* Whitting 1961: 30, and *T&S* i. 46, on some dies the second orb degenerates from the loop in
the drapery on the figure on the right, which on certain issues takes the shape of a large annulet (brooch?)
placed centrally on the chest (see *MoE* 64, no. 52*a*).

[44] See *MoE* 284, no. 262*a–b*, and Blackburn and Dumville 1998: pl. 7, nos. 5–6.

[45] Blackburn 1998*a*: 113.

[46] Alfred uses an innovative range of Roman models, several of them from late solidi (Blackburn
1998*a*: 113).

[47] Notice the distinctive rendering of the togas and the reproduction of the palm-branch between the
figures. A prototype from Londinium (Kent and Painter 1997: 172, no. 506) is closer than the issue proposed by Kent 1961: 30 and pl. 1, no. 11.

detail: in contrast to the hieratic, frontal pose on solidi, there is greater interaction between the kings, indicated by the twisting of their bodies, so that they
now sit facing each other.[48] It is difficult not to believe an intentional message
in the reworking of the image or that the introduction of such suggestive
iconography would have gone unnoticed.

We see that the image was understood to be laden with meaning and capable
of manipulation when we consider an illumination of the 'Magnificat' in
the Corbie Psalter, which bridges the time span between the shillings and the
Alfredian coinages.[49] The illumination takes as its model the iconography of the
'Two Emperors', as a meditation on the theme of humility contrasted with
earthly glories. Instead of two rigidly seated emperors sustained by the grace of
God, we have the compliant figures of Mary and Elizabeth submitting to the will
of God. Although the iconography of a *sacra conversazione* presided over by a
third figure goes back to that of Christ blessing marriages or crowning Peter and
Paul,[50] common in late Roman jewellery and gold-glass, it is interesting to note
that the prototype of the initial is actually numismatic.

It is possible that the image on the Anglo-Saxon shillings could have been used
both in secular and religious contexts. Archibald suggests that they may have
been issued by a religious foundation with two patron saints,[51] such as the
monastery of SS Peter and Paul in Canterbury—and one might even wonder
whether they might allude to instances of co-rulership or overlordship in Anglo-
Saxon England.[52] On the other hand, both the secular and the religious possibilities of interpretation might come together to mirror a facet of the political
background still common to Anglo-Saxon England in the 660s: the baptism of a
king under the sponsorship of another.[53] Such ceremonies would have been a
very public way of advertising and reinforcing existing ties between kings, and
as Higham argues, far from being concerned solely with furthering religious
conversion, baptismal sponsorship signified subtle political relationships.[54] In
balancing the two, the iconography of the 'Two Emperors' would have offered a

[48] The borders of the Roman togas are substituted for the symmetrical juxtaposition of the kings' legs,
creating an impression of modelling under drapery rather than flat pattern. Also, it may be argued that the
struts of the throne are understood as arms entwined, thus adding a further dimension of companionship.

[49] Initial M of the 'Magnificat', fo. 136^v, Corbie Psalter, c.800 (Hubert, Porcher, and Volbach 1969:
200, fig. 209).

[50] The roots of this iconography are actually pre-Christian: Cabrol and Leclercq 1907–53: *Mariage*.

[51] Webster and Brown 1997: 236, entries 99–102. Archibald stresses that the monastery, under its later
name, St Augustine's, enjoyed minting rights. However, if appeal is made to late antique iconography for
such an identification, one ought to be aware that the two apostles are represented alone, with a *Chi-Rho*
or with the figure of Christ between them, but to my knowledge never with an angel. The iconography of
Secondary Series J, Type 37 ('Confronting Heads') is actually closer to such models.

[52] Yorke 1997: 157–62.

[53] Angenendt 1986: 758, lists the sponsorship of: Æthelberht to Rædwald (East Anglia) and Sæberht
(Essex), Edwin to Eorpwald (East Anglia), Oswald to Cynegyls (Wessex, 635), Oswiu to Peada (Mercia)
and Sigiberht (Essex), Wulfhere to Æthelwald (Sussex, 661), Anna to Cenwalh (West Saxon, c.646),
Æthelwald (East Anglia, 655–64) to Swidhelm (Essex).

[54] Higham 1997: 102 ff.; Charles-Edwards 1998: esp. 59–62.

perfect tool for advertising the new pseudo-spiritual kinship of godfather-godson, or indeed any cooperation between kings. Although the lack of inscriptions frustrates any secure attribution, the perpetuation of the 'Two Emperors' type in Anglo-Saxon coinage suggests meaningful choice rather than fortuitous chance.

Single Figure between Crosses

The motif of the figure holding two tall crosses first features on coins of the Intermediate/early Secondary Series W, and then, with the figure sometimes balancing on a lunette, on the reverse of the silver pennies of the Secondary Series U, followed by Series Q, L, Y, K/N related, and CARIP eclectic groups, in the Celtic Cross and Victory/Angel types.[55] As can be expected considering the widespread distribution of the types and the many mints and die-cutters involved, there are many variations in details of stance, costume, and hairstyle (Fig. 3.10). For instance, the hands holding the crosses are generally represented by pellets, but on some coins of Series U, Type 23b thumbs and fingers are differentiated, whereas a coin of Series L has a hand tightly clutching one of the crosses, and the other holding a globe.[56] These skeletal 'grips' are comparable to those on Series K and the Franks Casket.

As for the derivation of the design, Whitting suggested that the iconography mis-copied degenerated Byzantine coinage,[57] but even assuming familiarity with Roman coins featuring upright figures between standards,[58] the images on our coins are not particularly close to classical prototypes. The closest parallel can be found among experimental Merovingian gold coinage where Christian designs (chalices, monstrances, crosses, sometimes varied with monograms, alphas and omegas, pendants, etc.) were added to the Roman repertoire.[59] The figure of the *orans*, already signalled as important in transforming the classical Victory into a Christian angel, can be seen 'modified' with crosses and other attributes on a gold *tremissis* found at Domburg (Fig. 3.11).

The iconography of this coin, possibly Christianizing a well-known motif, expresses the talismanic protection obtained through entrenchment between sacred symbols:[60] the man is defended not only by the crosses at his side, but by

---

[55] See the relevant chapters in *T&S* (vol. i for Series W, vol. iii for all the other series), and the various examples illustrated here.

[56] See *T&S* iii. 555 and 560–1, and pl. 21, no. 360.

[57] Whitting 1961: 31, and the bronze *follis* of Constans II, 641–68 which he illustrates on pl. 3, no. 16.

[58] Constantinian solidi with reverses of the *Principi Ivventvtis* type (figure with three standards) from the mint of Siscia are commonly found in Britain (Dr Orna-Ornstein, personal communication).

[59] *MEC* 118–20.

[60] A parallel is found in the protection charm known as the 'St Patrick's Lorica', quoted in Salin 1949–59: iv. 344–5, and Godel 1963: 301. Still sung in the Roman Catholic Church, it expresses the idea of being protected by Christ in front, behind, below, above, on all sides.

Fig. 3.10. *a*. Series U, Type 23b; *b*. K/N-related Type 23a, silver pennies, early Secondary and mid/late Secondary (*T&S* 447 and 352. The Ashmolean Museum, Oxford).

Fig. 3.11. Merovingian gold coin, uncertain mint (*MEC* 532. The Fitzwilliam Museum, Cambridge).

one above his head, and two E-shaped signs.[61] The duplication of the symbols is not simply a balancing of the composition, but a response to religious as well as superstitious needs. The facing busts flanked by crosses on *tremisses* of the York group and their sense of impenetrability have already been discussed above.[62]

The motif of crosses beside the figure of the *orans*, originally almost space fillers at the side of the head, spread from Coptic Egypt, especially via the iconography of St Menas (Fig. 3.12), and was very influential on the figurative art of the Christian West.[63] Whilst many sarcophagi with representations of the soul in heaven, standing between flanking crosses or palms emblematic of Paradise, testify to the popularity of the iconography in the context of burial,[64] representations on seventh-century Merovingian buckles feature the talismanic *orans* in a secular context,[65] as on the Alrachsheim plaques.[66] It is interesting to compare these Christian images to the pagan cult figure of the Finglesham buckle:[67] they all can be said to share the iconography of safety between sacred symbols.[68]

---

[61] Amécourt (quoted by Belfort 1892–5: iii. 306) suggested that what on some coins is generally interpreted as a Latin cross with pendilia might represent a monogram formed with the cross and a sideways E (for *ecclesia*), which is a possible suggestion for the two Es on our coin. However, these Es also feature on a copper alloy ring, probably late antique (Henig 1975: 68, fig. 296), where these might be understood as schematic renderings of the beasts flanking the *orans* (cf. the abbreviated versions of the motif on the buckle from Cras-Chalet, illustrated in Deonna 1949: pl. 1*b*, no. 21, and that from Boussières, in Salin 1949–59: iv, pl. 6).

[62] Fig. 2.4.

[63] Badawy 1978: 361, discusses Coptic influences and ways of transmission.

[64] Cf. Cabrol and Leclercq 1907–53: *Orant, Orante*, figs. 9081–4, and the stele of the matron, ibid., fig. 9096; Salin 1949–59: ii. 136, fig. 71 (sarcophagus from Lens).

[65] See Deonna 1949 and Salin 1949–59: iv. 310–40 and in particular, the buckle from Villechevreux, Haute-Saonne (p. 313) with crosses at the side of the *orans*. In a Scandinavian context, see the bracteate from Welschingen-B (Hauck and Axboe 1985: ii, pl. 166, fig. 389*a*).

[66] Salin 1949–59: i, pl. 4.

[67] *MoE* 22, fig. 2.

[68] The spear is a symbol of Woden, similar in shape to the rune T, often found discretely engraved on spearheads, swords, etc. in Kentish graveyards of the seventh century, and which might stand for Tiw (Wilson 1992: 117).

Fig. 3.12. St Menas's flask,
Coptic Egypt and gold-glass
roundel with figure of *orans*
(1889.940 and Loan 65. The
Ashmolean Museum,
Oxford).

In the identification of the figures, one must beware of conflating discrete personages, legends, and images.[69] For instance, the iconography, if not the story,[70] of the aerial flight of Alexander the Great drawn by griffins tempted by bait would have been known in Anglo-Saxon England, as it occurs commonly among Coptic textiles.[71] Representations are based on official Roman art, as found on coins showing the apotheosis of the emperor in his chariot, but assimilate ascensions of many gods and heroes,[72] so that there are many variations on the iconography (Fig. 3.13).[73] It is tempting to see a trace of the iconography of Alexander's legend in the figure of some exceptional coins of Series U, Type 23c (Fig. 3.14),[74] where two animals are represented beside the head of a man with an exaggerated moustache, holding crosses. An explanation for the strange moustache might be in the misunderstanding of the arms supporting bait. Less debatably, the image might be simply a rearrangement of the iconography of the ampullas of St Menas

[69] It is in fact difficult to separate images of St Menas between the camels from those of St Thecla and of Daniel in the lions' den, or even representations of non-Christian heroes, such as Gilgamesh, master of the beasts. See Kühn 1941–2.

[70] The story of the flight is in the *Epistola Alexandri ad Aristotelem*, found in the Nowell Codex (Cotton Vitellius A XV), with the only copy of *Beowulf*. Porsia 1976: 69–82, argues for the knowledge and use of this and other classical texts at the Wessex school at the time of Aldhelm. See also Herren 1998: 102.

[71] Settis-Frugoni 1973: figs. 27, 31–3. For Rice 1956 the Alexander's flight iconography was behind the Alfred Jewel and he cites a seventh-century Oriental textile from Münsterbilsen as prototype (p. 217, fig. 1). Similarities between this figure (holding floriated staffs), the Book of Kells, fo. 12[r], and the Archangel on St Cuthbert's coffin are discussed in Stevenson 1993: 16–17. See also the recent discussion on the jewel in Kempshall 2001.

[72] Rice 1956: 216.

[73] Thompson 1971: 56. Compare the multiple solidus of Constantius II (Bastien 1992: iii, pl. 194, no. 2) with the seventh-century Coptic textile illustrated here (Fig. 3.13*a*). Coins and textiles renderings are usually very similar, apart from the necessities of symmetry for the textile, so that there are two whips or sceptres (see also the eleventh-century Byzantine gold ring in Settis-Frugoni 1973: 196, fig. 63). Later these are shown with baits for the griffins. For the iconography of Alexander's flight: Settis-Frugoni 1973; Schmidt 1995.

[74] Two coins are known: one from Shalbourne, now in the Ashmolean Museum, and one in the de Wit collection, ex-Subjack 86, with obverses from a similar die. Series O, Type 21 from East Kent (*T&S* iii. 472–4), known from four specimens from the same die, features a similar moustachioed figure with pellets for breasts.

Fig. 3.13. Details from 7th-century Coptic textiles showing Alexander's flight (*a*. Brussels, Musée du Cinquantenaire; *b*. Monpezat-de-Quercy, church of St Martin. After Settis-Frugoni 1973, figs. 27*a* and 31. Istituto Storico Italiano per il Medioevo).

and the camels, or a representation of Daniel in the lions' den, or even recall the beginning of the Canticle of Habakkuk, 'you will be revealed in the midst of two animals'.[75] In any case the exotic, ultimately Eastern origin of the iconography is unquestionable. The overlapping iconography between such 'masters of the beasts' in secular and religious context and the conflation of themes contribute to the difficulty in separating what Ingeld has to do with Christ.[76]

The lunette shape on which figures balance, as featured on several coins, and on Fig. 3.10*b*, might recall the Christian metaphor of the church as a boat offering safe passage to salvation, following the interpretation given to some Merovingian coins, where a cross is believed to be a replacement for the mast.[77] In Scandinavian mythology the boat is a means of reaching the Other World, albeit pagan.[78] On some Anglo-Saxon coins the double-banded shape does indeed suggest a vessel,[79] and the image might portray a saint travelling by boat to proclaim the gospel.[80]

On the other hand, the iconography of our coins could allude to otherworldliness and refer to a sacred, but removed, space, as in the Bronze Age carvings from Scania,[81] where such shapes appear in a funerary context, or the stylized acanthus calyxes opening to reveal a soul on Coptic tombstones, a form of abbreviated vine-scrolls.[82] Parallels for the horizontal bar connecting the crosses

[75] See, however, the discussion on the Loveden, Risley, and Finglesham Men in Fennell 1969.

[76] Letter of Alcuin to Bishop Speratus, *c*.797 (Bullough 1993; Dümmler 1895: 183, no. 124).

[77] See the Merovingian *tremissis* in Fig. 3.25*a* (and also Belfort 1892–5: 374, nos. 1345–6). Cf. Cabrol and Leclercq 1907–53: *Navire*. In earlier iconography the boat represented life and the striving to reach harbour (Paradise).

[78] Ellmers 1986: 348–9 discusses the iconography specifically for Gotland: see for instance the slab from Rikvide, Gotland, seventh century (p. 358, fig. 10).

[79] See Fig. 3.10*b*.

[80] Apart from the journey of St Peter, there are many accounts of saints travelling by boat and of miracles connected with sailing (for instance, Farmer 1988: *Life of Cuthbert*, ch. 3, pp. 46–7 and ch. 21, pp. 70–1; *Life of Wilfrid*, ch. 13, pp. 118–20). See also Morton 1999: 49–55 on travels by sea.

[81] Slab 8 from the Kivik grave, Scania (Ellis Davidson 1967: 48–9, fig. 7).

[82] See the tombstone of Apa Dorotheos (Beckwith 1963: no. 127).

Fig. 3.14. Series U, Type 23c, silver
penny, early Secondary (Shalbourne find,
The Ashmolean Museum, Oxford).

Fig. 3.15. Detail with civilians from the
back panel of the Franks Casket, 8th
century (MME 1867, 1-20, 1. © The
British Museum, London).

and framing the figures on some coins can be found on Merovingian stone sarcophagi,[83] where they probably mean safety in Paradise: by analogy, it is possible that the figures on our coins could represent souls in Paradise. While the
pellet endings are characteristic of torques,[84] earthly treasure of a certain weight
and value, the shape on which the figures stand recalls the plate of a balance
where souls, treasures *par excellence*, are weighed,[85] so that the iconography
might also be a 'sermon in miniature'.

Metcalf had proposed royal status for the figures, as he thought the heads were
covered by *cynehelm*, helmet-crowns.[86] Interpreting these features as *appendices
perlées*,[87] or diadems, is problematic; although on some specimens wreath-ties
are clearly portrayed.[88] Comparisons with the Franks Casket reveal closer
parallels not with the helmets (always with prominent cheek-pieces), but with
the hairstyles of the civilians (Fig. 3.15): such 'detached' hairstyles are probably
due to the size of the figures.[89]

As for the clothes that the figures on our coins wear, whilst some have simple,
three-quarter length tunics, others have kilts,[90] sometimes carefully modelled,

---

[83] Notice the decorations at the side of the sarcophagi from Saint-Geneviève, Paris (Bourla's water-
colour, 1850), second half sixth century (Périn 1980: 19, fig. 9). See the coin illustrated at Fig. 3.10a, but
also the coins of Eadberht and Archbishop Ecgeberht illustrated in *T&S* pl. 28, nos. 464–6, particularly
coin no. 464, where a crozier replaces one of the crosses, and see below, Fig. 3.16.

[84] The finials on some specimens, although minute, are distinctly zoomorphic (cf. *T&S* iii. 567).

[85] Proverbs 16: 2.

[86] Metcalf 1972 attributed the coinage to Æthelbald of Mercia, a claim untenable because of Blackburn's revised chronology (Blackburn 1984). According to Metcalf, wreath-ties are visible on early dies of
Series U, Type 23d, and simplified later (*T&S* iii. 555; see fig. 11a). Chaney 1970: 137 ff., for the *cynehelm*
as royal attribute.

[87] For these, and the iconography of helmets, see the relevant section above.

[88] For instance some coins of Series U, Types 23b and 23d (*T&S* iii, pl. 27, nos. 445 and 449).

[89] On contemporary sculpture it is often difficult to distinguish hair from haloes. A comparable rendering can be found on a fragment of the cross-shaft at Urswick, Lancs., dated ninth century on account
of its eschewing classical dress; though the identity of the people represented is obscure, they are described
as 'seemingly without haloes' (Bailey and Cramp 1988: ii. 148–50, fig. 565). See also the figure on the
capital from San Pedro de la Nave, Zamora, second half of the seventh century (Hubert, Porcher, and
Volbach 1969: 87, fig. 101).

[90] Compare the illustrations in Figs. 3.19b–c and 3.20a, and also the figure on the arch-stone from
Nantes (Hubert, Porcher, and Volbach 1969: 53, fig. 65).

Fig. 3.16. Series Y, silver penny issued by
King Eadberht of Northumbria (738–57)
and Archbishop Ecgberht (*T&S* 465;
drawing courtesy of Prof. Metcalf, by
permission of the RNS).

Fig. 3.17. Series O, silver penny, mid/late
Secondary (*T&S* 380. The Ashmolean
Museum, Oxford).

revealing the thighs beneath. Some have hatched tunics, perhaps representing precious fabrics, rather than mail.[91] The Franks Casket's Magi (and one of the figures on the lid) offer good parallels to a peculiar attire seen on some of the coins of the Secondary Series Y, issued jointly in York by King Eadberht (738–57) and his brother, Archbishop Ecgberht (734–66), where the figures seem to wear horizontally gartered leg coverings (Fig. 3.16).[92]

The interpretation of the pellets seemingly hanging at the hem of some of the kilts is problematic. Whilst they match the pellets that appear on crosses, at elbows, as terminals, and on the coins' outer circles, their positioning seems to represent more than metalwork technique. They lack contemporary archaeological counterparts,[93] although later literary evidence indicates that small bells were occasionally hung on the lower hem of priestly copes.[94] It is also possible they may have been derived from the erroneous rendering of a design that was being copied.[95] The fact that pellets appear at the corners of trapezoid kilts, however, might be a way of rendering the fullness of the material in three dimensions, as the volutes used in Insular style for the folds of vestments.[96]

[91] See Fig. 2.40.

[92] See Figs. 2.65 and 2.55. Prof. Gale Owen-Crocker (personal comment) agrees that these might be representations of loose trousers tied at intervals round the legs with thin thongs, possibly a regional fashion.

[93] K. Leahy (Scunthorpe Museum) signals some later medieval finial balls, possibly comparable, found at Newbald, a prebend of York (personal communication). On the cross-shaft from Nurnburnholme (St James), ninth/tenth century (Bailey and Cramp 1988: fig. 710) the figure grasps a stole which is said to end with 'two large globular terminals' (Bailey and Cramp 1988: 190), but see below.

[94] Dodwell 1982: 32 and 301 n. 87.

[95] See for instance the Coptic textile (the first known example showing the iconography of the flight of Alexander) from Monpezat-de-Quercy, seventh century (Settis-Frugoni 1973: 149, fig. 31, illustrated above, Fig. 3.13*b*), where the wheels of the cart may have been misunderstood as part of his attire.

[96] See the rendering of the garments of the symbol of St Matthew in the Echternach Gospels, fo. 18ᵛ (G. Henderson 1987: 74, fig. 102), and those of the figure on the cross of Muiredach (Owen-Crocker 1986: 125, fig. 120) which can be compared to those at Nunburnholme (Bailey and Cramp 1988: fig. 710) discussed above, and also the 'curls' at the hem of the kilts of the figures on the lid of the Franks Casket (Webster 1999: 234, fig. 19.3).

Besides tunics being girdled and usually worn with a cloak, as testified by contemporary literary and artistic evidence,[97] the coins show the continuation of a
simpler, older style of tunic,[98] three-quarter length, either plain or decorated with
vertical lines, presumably reproducing pleats, as portrayed on the Hexham
plaque (Fig. 3.17).[99]

What can be said about the identity of these figures? Undoubtedly, that they
support and proclaim the redemptive/apotropaic power of the cross, but as for
their particular status, and indeed whether they represent living or dead characters, or a particular saint, or even Christ, the question remains open. Even for the
coins of Ecgberht it is probably more appropriate to argue that the figure represents not a portrait of the archbishop, but a 'badge' appropriate to his position.

Single Figure with Vegetation Motifs and Crosses

A unique coin found at Tilbury shows a figure facing left between what appear
to be twigs, some apparently growing from his left arm. The design has been
described as a cross between Struwwelpeter and the Green Man,[100] but an
explanatory prototype may be found among Roman gems, which the Anglo-
Saxons knew, appreciated, and reused.[101] A similar representation of Heracles
carrying a lion skin on his left arm and attacking Hydra with a club, perhaps
rendered in a provincial linear style, with simplified details, may have been
admired for its classical resonance, but reproduced with no understanding of its
true iconography (Fig. 3.18).

Whilst echoes of the composition, when identified, are still recognizable in the
Anglo-Saxon rendering, both Hydra and the lion's skin have been interpreted as
twigs, complete with buds. The figure, in a simple tunic and streaming pigtail,
has lost the dramatic vigour of the prototype and seems to be tentatively finding
his way through vegetation. It being the only known coin with this design, it is
impossible to know whether such transformation was due to an original mis-
reading of the image,[102] or if the elements gradually degenerated into vegetation,
with the iconography adapted to represent different native or classical myths,
or even earthly Paradise. It is possible that knowledge of the luxuriant foliage
used on late antique sarcophagi to frame figures or episodes may also have been
responsible for the transformation of the image.[103] In any case the prototype, a
precious antique object, gives an insight into both the kind of material used as
sources of designs and to the fascination with classical images.[104]

---

[97] Owen-Crocker 1986: 121–3.   [98] Dodwell 1982: 173.   [99] *MoE* 138, no. 104.
[100] *T&S* iii. 452.   [101] Henig 1978: 160–1.
[102] As a cultural parallel, it is interesting to note the point that Herren 1998 makes when quoting the
several mistakes made in the Anglo-Saxon glossing of Roman or Greek mythological names, as these
show the great interest in the material in late seventh/early eighth-century Anglo-Saxon England.
[103] An indirect influence of such art in the use of foliage in the Romulus and Remus panel of the Franks
Casket is discussed by Webster 1982: 21.
[104] See Figs. 2.64, and 4.37*b*.

Fig. 3.18. *a*. Type 23e, silver
penny, Secondary (*T&S* 361.
The Ashmolean Museum,
Oxford); *b*. Roman gem, Heracles slaying Hydra, 1st century
BC, Museo del Castello.
Collezioni Civiche Archeo-
logiche U. Formentini—Castello
di S. Giorgio, La Spezia, Italy
(inv. 1342, inv. Fot. L 2962).

The interpretation of the iconography of vegetation motifs has already been
discussed for the obverse of coins with busts, where the interchange between
crosses and sprigs has been seen as deliberate and justified in relation to textual
exegesis. The meaningfulness of such a juxtaposition finds support among the
coins of Secondary Series L, K, and related issues, where, as a variant to the
iconography of figures between crosses, figures are shown between a cross and a
plant or between two plants (Fig. 3.19).

The coins are not related in style but in conception. They invite a comparison
between the cross and the uprooted tree, once a living plant, in the same manner
as we read in the *Dream of the Rood*.[105] Transmutation is also a recurring theme
in the metaphors of Anglo-Saxon riddles, a number of which invite meditation
on the idea of living trees becoming wood, out of which objects such as spears,
cups, or boats can be fashioned.[106] The complexity of the analogies of some of
the riddles suggests a sophisticated audience sensitive to subtle connections and
actively searching for patterns of meaning. Similarities between the aesthetic
pleasure to be found in the interweaving of seemingly disparate ideas in Anglo-
Saxon literary art and interlaced patterns in graphic art have been suggested by
Whitehurst Williams.[107] Interlace has been seen as an underlying organizing
principle in the complexity of *Beowulf*,[108] an idea refined by John Niles's perception of the structure as composed of symmetrically arranged roundels.[109] This
image suggests a way of organizing concepts or events as self-standing medallions or miniatures within a complex framework, again reminiscent of the visual
arts.[110] It is particularly helpful as it suggests a mentality and an intellectual
framework in which coins may have been seen as the perfect embodiment of
riddles, or indeed of sermons in miniature.

[105] Swanton 1996, especially lines 28–30.
[106] Williamson 1977: 229 and 345; Niles 1998.
[107] Whitehurst Williams 1992: 24.
[108] Leyerle 1967: 14. Consider also Aldhelm's notoriously tortuous style (Lapidge and Herren 1979;
Lapidge and Rosier 1985).
[109] Niles 1977.
[110] See arrangements in arcades, frames, and roundels discussed at 'Encircled Heads'.

Fig. 3.19. *a* and *b*. Series L, Type 16; *c*. CARIP group, silver pennies, late Secondary (*T&S* 329, 330, 339. The Ashmolean Museum, Oxford).

Though the image of the tree is loaded with ancient pagan connotations,[111] the sinuous plants with berries on several of the coins suggest a biblical reference by recalling the 'true vine' as provider of food and refuge.[112] On some coins the crosses are held with two hands, underlining the religious commitment, with the figure protected between the 'true vine' and the cross. Although the plant motifs vary on the coins, they often terminate in a pointed turgid bud, of classicizing, eastern Mediterranean taste that finds parallels in a variety of media.[113]

Standing Figures with Cross and Bird

Coins of Series K, Types 20 and 20/18, and of Series L, Types 18 and 19, show a standing figure on a lunette-shaped base, holding a long cross in the right hand and a bird in the left. On some variants, an additional T-shaped perch appears below the bird (Fig. 3.20).

As prototypes of this iconography, Whitting suggested early Arab-Byzantine issues,[114] most recently explored by Oddy.[115] On this coinage, of the last quarter of the seventh century, the robed Byzantine emperor was replaced by the standing caliph, often shown wearing 'native' clothes, and the *orb cruciger* by a falcon on a stand. Contacts with Syria and Palestine, direct or indirect, through commerce, gifts, or pilgrimages, are well attested,[116] so knowledge and imitation of such coins are not improbable. Undeniably there is a formal similarity between the Anglo-Saxon and the Arab coins: the splayed shape of the kilt and the

---

[111] As does the world-tree Yggdrasil in Norse mythology and Woden's sacred ash.

[112] John 15: 1. The theme of the inhabited vine is discussed in detail below, at 'Birds in Vine-Scrolls'. See also Wamers 1993: 38.

[113] See for instance the binding of the St Cuthbert Gospel of St John, and the plants on the Barberini Gospel, fo. 124b (*MoE* 121, no. 86; p. 205, no. 160).

[114] Whitting 1961: 31.

[115] Oddy 1991: 59–66.

[116] Levison 1946: 42–4, on the interest in the geography of the Holy Land and pilgrimages of Arculf and Wilbald.

Fig. 3.20. *a* and *b*. Series L, Type 18 and Series K, Type 20/18, silver pennies, Secondary (*T&S* 331 and 318. The Ashmolean Museum, Oxford); *c*. Series L, Type 19, silver penny, Secondary (*BMC* 105. The British Museum, London).

modelling of the chest, characteristic of the London coins, find counterparts among some Umayyad issues, as do the expansive gesture and drapery.[117]

These models might have appealed not only on account of their exotic connections, but particularly because of their iconography: a stately figure with a bird. On one level, we might read it as simply representing falconry, whose prestige in Anglo-Saxon England is testified by a reference in *Beowulf* describing it as a suitably heroic and fashionable pastime,[118] and by Archbishop Boniface's correspondence with Æthelbald of Mercia and Æthelberht of Kent.[119] The controversy over the identification of the standing figure holding a bird next to a T-shaped perch on the Bewcastle Cross alerts us to the complexity of the iconography.[120] The figure has been interpreted as representing either an aristocratic benefactor with his falcon, or St John with his eagle; modern scholarship is inclined to see it as the layman mentioned in the inscription.[121] As the attribute is shared, and indeed legends often connect saints with birds,[122] a certain ambiguity is unavoidable,[123] and purposefully recalls cross-references between the two contexts, the sacred and the secular.

A comparable ambivalence between Christian and secular symbolism features in the legend of the saint-king Oswald and his attribute, the raven,[124] which may

[117] Compare for instance the two Arab coins illustrated in Oddy 1991: pl. 19, no. 8, and pl. 20, no. 22, with the Anglo-Saxon coin illustrated above (Fig. 3.20*b*, *BMC* 105) and the one in *T&S* iii, pl. 19, no. 332. The modelling and drapery on the Arab coins seems to have also influenced some of Offa's issues from London (see 'Offa's Drapery', above).

[118] *Beowulf*, lines 2262–5: 'ne god hafoc | geond sæl swingeð' (Alexander 1995: 148).

[119] Boniface's correspondence: Dümmler 1892: 337, no. 69 (Æthelbald) and p. 391, no. 105 (Æthelberht). For accounts of falconry in Anglo-Saxon England: Oggins 1984 and Hicks 1986: 162–3.

[120] The T-shape of the perch itself is not 'neutral': it has been compared to a tau cross (Bailey 1996: 67).

[121] Ó Carragáin 1986, 1987; Bailey and Cramp 1988: ii. 69–70; Kitzinger 1993: 11–12; Bailey 1996: 66–9; Karkov 1997. Bailey and Cramp 1988 and Karkov 1997 also note and discuss similarities with our coins.

[122] For instance, Cuthbert and Guthlac (Bede, *Life of Cuthbert*, Farmer 1988: ch. 12, p. 58, and chs. 19–20, pp. 68–70; Felix, *Life of St Guthlac*, Colgrave 1956: ch. 39, pp. 120–5).

[123] Compare the ambiguity of the mounted figure on the Repton Stone (Biddle and Kjølbye-Biddle 1985: 254–7, 271–3, 287–90). The same iconography is used in the portrayal of St George killing the dragon (Pugliese Carratelli 1984: 337, fig. 239).

[124] Clemoes 1983; Thacker 1995.

be recalled to understand the iconography both at Bewcastle and on our coins. Some elements of Oswald's story not found in Bede, who was more concerned with Oswald's orthodox miracles and devotion to the Cross, were handed down in Reginald of Durham's *Life of St Oswald*.[125] According to Reginald, after the defeat at Maserfelth, as Oswald's brother Oswiu was searching for his *membra disiecta*, a raven flew off into an ash-tree with the king's severed right arm. The story further relates miracles connected with the place and the tree sanctified by the body of Oswald.[126] The *Life* unwittingly includes sacral pagan elements, among them the ash and the raven, both connected to Woden, and these are found in the legends and iconography of the cult of St Oswald spread on the Continent by Anglo-Saxon missionaries, and appear as his attributes even in the later Middle Ages.[127] The spread of the cult of St Oswald in England made him the dominant English royal saint, even outside Northumbria,[128] with Mercian royal patronage attested from *c*.700, and running through the whole of the eighth century.[129]

The iconography of the coins of Series K and L—showing crosses, trees, birds, and cups—presents, if not a direct reference to St Oswald, a perpetuation of elements connected with sacral kingship and its symbols,[130] as mirrored in his legend.[131] The figures with birds on our coins, and the one at Bewcastle, may well represent secular figures, but the attribute, allusive to the iconography of saints and to the Evangelist St John,[132] goes well beyond that of a fashionable pastime.[133] The coins, conflating past and present themes and symbols, and portraying stately and perhaps otherworldly figures, ultimately allude anagogically not to earthly, but to eternal kingship. Such a complex reading would have been familiar to people accustomed to exegetical interpretations: how far the meditation was carried and the message understood would have depended on the sophistication of the audience;[134] however, it was certainly reinforced by its presence in 'public' media, as on the coins and the cross at Bewcastle.

---

[125] Tudor 1995, on the manuscripts and traditions. [126] Ibid., 190.

[127] Rollason 1989: 127–9; Baker 1949 and 1951; Clemoes 1983; Jansen 1995. At Regensburg, the thirteenth- and fourteenth-century statues of St Oswald (Stancliffe and Cambridge 1995: pls. 16 and 20) show a raven and a ciborium, possibly derived from Bede's account (*HE* III, 6) of the silver dish given as alms (Clemoes 1983: 12). The permutation of the dish into a cup in the legend could be a return to what may have been considered a more appropriate attribute (see 'Hands Holding Cups').

[128] Thacker 1995: 112. Bewcastle is not far from Hexham, whence Wilfrid promoted the cult of King Oswald (Rollason 1989: 113; Thacker 1995: 107 ff.) and from where his cult indeed spread (*HE* III, 2 and 9–13). Artistic similarities between the Bewcastle Cross and sculpture fragments from Hexham (Bailey and Cramp 1988: ii. 70) suggest links between the two communities.

[129] Thacker 1995: 113; G. Henderson 1987: 129. [130] Rollason 1989: 127.

[131] Compare the various attributes on obverses and reverses of coins of Series K, Type 20, Series L, Type 18, and Series L, Type 16 (*T&S* pl. 18, no. 314 and pl. 19, nos. 331 and 329): crosses, cups, and birds seem to interchange with a purpose.

[132] See 'Bust and Bird'.

[133] I would particularly strongly argue against the label 'fashionable nobleman-falconer' for the Bewcastle figure, because the birds (as echoed in Oswald's legend) carry far richer connotations than those of a fashion accessory being paraded, but I would agree with Karkov 1997: 20.

[134] Alexander 1997: 107. Bailey 1996 (61–76) refers to the concept of *ruminatio* (Leclercq 1957: 70–3), as a key to the proper reading of monuments. This is in line with the other 'riddles' discussed above.

Fig. 3.21. Detail of the lower front
panel of the Bewcastle Cross, Bewcastle, Cumbria, 8th century, (photograph
courtesy of Dr J. Hawkes).

Fig. 3.22. *a*. CARIP group; *b*. Series L, Type 13,
silver pennies, late Secondary (3895 and 4179,
de Wit collection).

Seated Figures

A rare iconography showing seated figures occurs in Anglo-Saxon coinage in
two variations. On an unpublished CARIP coin a figure sits on a chair with a
scrolled back, looking at the cross held in his left hand, and clutching a staff in
his right. A London-related type, known from only three specimens,[135] with the
inscription VNOONN+ on the obverse, has a figure sitting on a similar chair,
holding a cross with his left hand and turning towards the bird perched on his
right (Fig. 3.22).

There are numismatic precedents for enthroned figures with staffs and birds in
Greek coinage, subsequently imitated by Celts and Romans, where a Victory
takes the place of the bird, and eventually also by Scandinavian bracteates.[136]
The motif appears on other artefacts with many variations in the figure represented, stance, type of chair, and attributes.[137]

Seats were charged symbols of authority in the Roman world, as witnessed
by the *sellae curules*, represented unoccupied on coins, supporting insignia
of power, and by the richly ornamented sixth-century examples on ivory dip-

---

[135] The specimens are: *BMC* 92; de Wit collection, and ex-Subjack 48.

[136] See for instance the tetradrachma of Alexander and the silver multiple of Hadrian illustrated in
Bastien 1992 (iii, pl. 250, no. 7 and pl. 54, no. 6); the Celtic coin from the Lower Danube (third century
BC) in Megaw and Megaw 1989: 179, no. 298; and the bracteate from Várpalota-B (Hauck and Axboe
1985: i, pl. 274, fig. 206*a*). See also the Merovingian coin reading REDONIS+ (Prou 1892: pl. 9, no. 5, and
p. 168, no. 492).

[137] For instance, the representation on the domed silver casket of the Esquiline treasure, late fourth
century AD (Kent and Painter 1977: 45, no. 89).

tychs.[138] In the Germanic world, the seated figure bore symbolic importance,[139] with additional overtones derived from the classical world, as in the plaque of Agilulf,[140] or in the complex at Yeavering.[141] It has been argued that possession of the throne was a necessary condition of royal authority and an attribute of the Germanic king in his hall, and Anglo-Saxon texts give an unequivocal picture of the *giftstol* as one of the royal insignia.[142] Philologists have sought to unravel this term—literally the chair from which gifts are given—in the context of lines 168–9 of *Beowulf*. For DuBois,[143] interpreting the role of the king in pagan Anglo-Saxon society not only as chieftain, but as intermediary between Woden and his people, *stol*, a synecdoche used to convey a wide gamut of ideas ranging from hall to kingdom, takes on a particular meaning with the signifier *gifu*. Semantically, *gifu* means 'gift', recalling *Beowulf*'s descriptions of the king as bountiful ring-giver.[144] On a spiritual level the word can also signify 'gift of divine grace', so that the *giftstol* would have connotations both of throne and of altar,[145] with a sacral function for the king understood and acceptable both in a Pagan and a Christian context.[146]

No secular Anglo-Saxon throne has survived,[147] but one might be represented on the back of the Franks Casket (Fig. 3.23); in a religious context, however, two complete bishop seats in stone survive at Hexham and Beverley.[148] Whilst these must have shared some of the symbolism associated with the king's throne,[149] and resemble Continental examples,[150] they are not comparable to the thrones

---

[138] See for instance Sydenham 1952: pl. 23, no. 808, for Roman republican coins with empty *sellæ* (the distinction between *sella* and throne is discussed in Mathews 1993: 104–9). The iconography of consular diptychs (see that of Rufus Gennadius Orestes, seated on his *curule* chair) in Webster and Brown 1997: 125, fig. 53, would also have played an influential role in promoting the motif of seated figures associated with power (Wood 1997: 124).

[139] Bullough 1975: 236 ff.

[140] Webster and Brown 1997: 118, fig. 49. The plaque conflates imagery of the Roman and Barbarian worlds.

[141] Hope-Taylor 1977. It is postulated that the structure resembling a segment of Roman theatre would have been for an assembly to be addressed by a king seated on a dais in front of it. However, this would have been unlike the imperial custom of the *consistorium*, i.e. 'standing committee', whose members stood while only the emperor sat (Mathews 1993: 109), and is more reminiscent of the kind of oligarchic council presided over by Edwin (*HE* II, 13).

[142] Chaney 1962: 516–17.

[143] DuBois 1954: 547.

[144] See discussion on the king as *beaggifa* in Chaney 1970: 148.

[145] DuBois 1954: 547.

[146] Chaney 1962: 516.

[147] Chaney 1970: 135 infers its role through literature—and we are left to wonder about the status of the pensive 'chairperson' on the sixth-century pottery lid from Spong Hill, North Elmham, Norfolk, presumably from a cremation urn (Campbell 1982: 35, fig. 32; Hills 1990).

[148] For the Hexham seat, see *MoE* 148, fig. 10, and for the one from Beverley, Bailey and Cramp 1988: ills. 885–7. For these, the term *friðstol*, 'peace stool', was also used (Rollason *et al.* 1999: 198, 221).

[149] Chaney 1962: 518–19, on laws concerning the right of sanctuary: nine nights' asylum could be granted to those seeking protection by the king's throne, while the church could allow seven. Nine was the king's number, sacred from the pagan Germanic past, whilst the number seven was sacred in the Mediterranean tradition and meaningful in an ecclesiastical context.

[150] Cabrol and Leclercq 1907–53: *Chaire Épiscopale*. The more spectacular examples incorporating precious material (like Bishop Maximian's throne at Ravenna), however, suggest a different patronage.

Fig. 3.23. Detail of the seated
figure on the back panel of the
Franks Casket, 8th century
(MME 1867, 1-20, 1. © The
British Museum, London).

Fig. 3.24. Series N, Type 41b, silver pennies, mid-
Secondary (*BMC* 175. The British Museum, London;
T&S 369. The Ashmolean Museum, Oxford).

shown on the coins. These, though different from the 'Throne of Dagobert',[151] a self-conscious copy of a *sella curulis* of classical Antiquity, have the same look of 'movable furniture', which would allow them to follow the king in military campaigns or peaceful progresses.[152]

The contrast between the two styles is clear on the illuminations of the Evangelists in the Lichfield Gospels. St Luke's throne is solid, with finials in the shape of canine heads, comparable to the stone fragments from Monkwearmouth and Lastingham;[153] St Mark's is a light and airy construction, with gracefully curved zoomorphic elements, maybe rendering a structure in wood and metal. The closest parallel to the thrones on our coins is that on the Franks Casket (Fig. 3.23), where the uprights terminate in simple volutes, rather like on the throne of St Matthew in the Echternach Gospels.[154] The style of the throne may be native, independent of classical sources.[155]

Some may argue that our coins show the first positive representation of an Anglo-Saxon king on his throne,[156] exercising power by God's grace, as indicated by the cross, and mighty in temporal matters, even hawking, as symbolized by his control of the bird, and the image might be compared to that of the seated King David, also holding a cross, on a fragment of the embroidery of SS Harlindis and Relindis.[157] It could, however, equally be argued that the figure

---

[151] Webster and Brown 1997: 41, no. 19.

[152] If the constant rebuilding noticeable at Yeavering was due not to enemy raids, but to the will of each generation to rebuild more splendidly (Dixon, *MoE* 67–70), a mobile throne to be handed down could signify continuity through transformation.

[153] For the portraits of St Luke and St Mark in the Lichfield Gospels, pp. 218 and 142, see G. Henderson 1987: 122 and 126, figs. 180 and 185; for the stone fragments, see *MoE* 151, nos. 111–12.

[154] For the symbol of St Matthew, the Echternach Gospels, fo. 18ᵛ, see G. Henderson 1987: 74, fig. 102.

[155] It is not surprising that royal, as opposed to ecclesiastical, thrones should appear on evangelists' miniatures, as even Dagobert's throne finds counterpart in the miniature of the Evangelist St John in the Emmeran Gospels. The reciprocal allusion might serve to stress the God-given position of the king and the holy status of the throne.

[156] The first official image of a king is the tenth-century miniature on the frontispiece of the Cambridge CCC MS 183, of Athelstan presenting a book to St Cuthbert (Wallace-Hadrill 1971: 96).

[157] See Stiegemann and Wemhoff 1999: 462–3, no. VII.22.

suggests an Evangelist enthroned, in particular St John with his attribute, and might represent spiritual power.[158] As with the standing figures with birds discussed above, the charged ambiguity between temporal and celestial symbols and attributes may be intentional and thought provoking.

Two Standing Figures

In dialectic contrast to the iconography of the single figure standing between two crosses, some series feature two figures flanked by two crosses and with a third between them.[159] The crosses are sometimes held, sometimes suspended, and differ in size and rendering. The figures shown also vary in stance, attire, and style; occasionally they stand on a straight baseline (Fig. 3.24). Do these coins represent a duplication of the 'single figure between crosses' motif, arranged in a frieze? Though conceptually related, with the crosses having a similar apotropaic function, and sometimes also alternating with that iconography,[160] it is differentiation between the figures that prevails, presumably indicating separate identities.

Classical numismatic prototypes for a two-figure iconography abound. Kent illustrates a Roman coin of the *Gloria Exercitus* type with a single standard and juxtaposes a Merovingian copy:[161] indeed Roman coinage presents several variations on the basic motif, especially among the provincial imitations found in Roman Britain.[162] These already show schematic simplifications which are possibly behind the misunderstood details on the Anglo-Saxon coins, such as the 'long arms' which are a peculiarity of some specimens.[163]

Merovingian *tremisses* with the two figures motif, looped as pendants, were found in the so-called Canterbury St Martin's 'hoard' and in a grave at Faversham; the motif also inspired an Anglo-Saxon pseudo-coin pendant formed by two back-to-back gold relief plates (Fig. 3.25). Some Merovingian coins re-elaborated the composition: an interesting type from Le Mans has two figures flanking the *menhir*, surmounted by a cross, that was by the cathedral,[164] while others apparently turn the figures into angels.[165]

---

[158] On the *seated* figure of St John on the Ruthwell cross, see Hawkes and Ó Carragáin with Trench-Jellicoe 2001.

[159] Series N, Types 41a, 41b, and 41b/a; Series Q, Types QIA and QIB; Types 30 and 51 and 'Celtic Cross with Rosettes', Type 58.

[160] As among the 'Celtic Cross with Rosettes', Types 58 and 106 (*T&S* iii. 428 and 430, sections V and VII).

[161] Kent 1961: 10 and pl. 1, nos. 1 and 3.

[162] See for instance the imitation from Chapmanslade, Wiltshire (Bland and Orna-Ornstein 1997: pl. 33, no. 690/1).

[163] On some particularly fine specimens in the de Wit collection it is clear that the 'long arms' are actually renderings of long cloaks, terminating at the hem with a pellet.

[164] Salin 1949–59: iv. 376–7, fig. 166c. Salin also comments on the Christianization of *menhirs*.

[165] See the Merovingian silver coin and the Merovingian pendant from Viernheim, Hessen, illustrated in Klein-Pfeuffer 1993: 184, fig. 57.7 and p. 492, no. 382 (see also p. 184, fig. 57 for other examples of pendants). Klein-Pfeuffer (ibid. 186) interprets the lines of pellets which extend the arms of the figures to the ground as rendering wings, features unknown in the Germanic world. This is in parallel with the development of 'long arms'/cloaks on the Anglo-Saxon coins.

Fig. 3.25. *a.* looped gold Merovingian *tre-missis*, struck at Campbon, Nantes (found at King's Field, Faversham, Kent) late 6th–early 7th century (MME 1884, 12-21, 11. The British Museum, London); *b.* pseudo-coin pendant from Compton Verney, Warwickshire (1948.135. The Ash-molean Museum, Oxford).

Fig. 3.26. Breedon-on-the-Hill, paired figures, late 8th century (photograph courtesy of Dr J. Hawkes). Series N, Type 41a (*MEC* 704. The Fitzwilliam Museum, Cambridge).

To numismatic derivations, obviously important, must be added the influential iconography stemming from the original Oriental tree-of-life motif,[166] which is often met with in Germanic metalwork.[167] Such 'heraldic' compositions, however, differ substantially from classical compositions that represent interaction between two figures. Though symmetry also played a part in these, the figures are differentiated, and symbolize active collaboration, as between Victory and *Libertas* or a contract such as marriage.[168] Moreover, images of interacting people represent concentrated narratives, and they are often found on medallions and bracteates believed to illustrate mythological episodes.[169] The versatility of such iconography and its ease of movement from profane to sacred,

[166] Koch 1982: 56. Klein-Pfeuffer 1993: 163, on the acceptance of the Oriental motif of the tree of life because equated to the Germanic world-tree Yggdrasil; Riemer 1997: 449, caption to fig. 513, for the interchange of animals/men and trees/crosses.

[167] See for example the seventh-century repoussé brooches with birds from Hüttlingen and with figures from Kirchheim, Baden-Würtenberg (Klein-Pfeuffer 1993: 368, no. 125; p. 379, no. 149), and the seventh-century belt-fitting from ?Morrens (Salin 1949–59: iv. 366, fig. 156).

[168] See the gold solidus of Magnentius, 350–3, rev. VICTORIA AUG LIBROMANOR (Kent and Painter 1977: 169, no. 435) and the gold-glass roundel with a representation of marriage, fourth century (Cabrol and Leclercq 1907–53: *Mariage*, p. 1923, fig. 7662).

[169] See the reverse of the fourth-century gold medallion from Aak (Lowrie 1947: 78, fig. 33) and the obverse of the contemporary gold medallion from Viken (Webster and Brown 1997: 197, fig. 87), and Hauck 1976 for interpretations.

is clearly exemplified by Coptic textiles, where images of grape harvesting served as ideal templates for representations of Peter and Paul.[170]

Anglo-Saxon coins with two figures also take their inspirations from classical sources expressing concerted action: an interesting juxtaposition is with the historiated initial to Psalm 26 in the Vespasian Psalter, believed to represent the covenant between David and Jonathan, one of the earliest examples of 'narrative' illuminations.[171] The men hold two spears (one centrally between them) and shake hands. Other parallels can be drawn with sculpture. In contrast to the typical arrangement of single figures under individual arcades, the paired personages at Breedon-on-the-Hill share the same space. Their identity is uncertain, the lack of haloes perhaps indicating worthies rather than saints. Their proximity and mirroring postures suggest solidarity of intent, like the facing characters on the coins (Fig. 3.26). A fine coin in the de Wit collection features two people with seemingly 'pointed heads': an illuminating parallel can be found among the Mercian sculpture, this time with the slab from Peterborough, where the two figures, possibly foreign learned bishops, wear Frigian caps.[172] Another interesting comparison is with the sculpture at Hornby, which portrays two figures under a vine, and the miracle of the five loaves and two fishes:[173] the many layers of abstract meaning that can be teased out of this representation alert us to the fact that it may be futile to look just for one explanation (or identification) of the figures.

Much as the general iconography of two figures with crosses is comparable, there are many variations among the coins. Similar in the linearity of their style and in the swathing cloaks with symmetrically arranged folds, two coins of Type 30b and Series N, Type 41b recall the schematic drapery seen on much Anglo-Saxon work, from manuscripts to the St Cuthbert's coffin, from the Franks Casket to the sculpture at Wirksworth in Derbyshire. Though the style might appear 'primitive',[174] the complexity of the iconography at Wirksworth, most recently discussed by Hawkes,[175] suggests great sophistication and learning. The figures on our coins (unfortunately unprovenanced) might derive their style (and possibly content) from the same source as the Wirksworth sculpture. The fact that they are cowled and muffled perhaps signifies that they are female, and it would be interesting if they could be linked to a monastery ruled by an abbess (Fig. 3.27).[176]

[170] Compare for instance the fourth/fifth-century Coptic textiles in Wulff and Volbach 1926: pl. 69, nos. 6729 and 6847, pp. 43–4.

[171] Henderson 1986: 99. *MoE* 198.

[172] For the Peterborough slab, see Cramp 1977: 207 and Jewell 2001: 258. On the connotations of Phrygian caps and the spiritual, see Elsner 1997: 190.

[173] Bailey 1996: 59–61, and pl. 2.

[174] Wilson 1984: 85, describes the slab's figural style as 'extremely primitive' and Metcalf (*T&S* iii. 528) pronounces 'coarse' that of Type 30b.

[175] Hawkes 1995.

[176] In terms of economic importance Wirksworth (a double monastery under an abbess, and a dependency of the royal foundation at Repton) supplied lead to Canterbury in the ninth century (Campbell 1982: 226–7).

Fig. 3.27. Type 30b (*BMC* 146. The British Museum,   Fig. 3.28. Type 30a (*BMC*
London); detail from the slab at Wirksworth, Derbyshire,   145. The British Museum,
8th century (photograph courtesy of Dr J. Hawkes).   London).

In contrast to the heavily dressed representations above, coins of Type 30 have naked figures, carefully detailed. Type 30a includes coins with two moustachioed nude males, one diademed and in profile.[177] They hold a cross between them, and grip long sceptres. Their nudity, like that on the Finglesham buckle and the plaque from Grézin,[178] recalls the heroic Germanic past, and combined with royal and Christian attributes may typologically juxtapose old and new heroes, perhaps the Old and the New Adam. On Type 30a one of the figures appears to have breasts, while the other has large moustaches. The male/female pair finds counterpart in Merovingian metalwork, interpreted by Salin as symbolizing fertility,[179] but perhaps now meant to represent Adam and Eve (Fig. 3.28).

Another variation on the two figures is met with among the apparently imitative coins found in the north-eastern area of circulation of Series N: here the facing figures have bird-like heads.[180] Such iconography is not unique to the coins, but occurs also on certain cross-slabs, whose wide distribution suggests a visual legacy among ecclesiastical foundations, presumably of common, ancient origin.[181] If the motif on our coins and on the slabs is the Christian Adoration of the Cross,[182] the bird-men from Papil, apparently supporting between their

[177] *T&S* iii, pl. 26, no. 431. See also coins of Type 51, ibid., nos. 432–3, and of Series N, pl. 22, nos. 368–72, which also seem to represent naked males.

[178] Finglesham buckle (*MoE* 22, fig. 2). The identification of the fifth/sixth-century terracotta plaque from Grézin (Saint-Germain-en-Laye, *Guide*, p. 208, fig. 160) with Christ, as in Psalm 90 crushing the adder, seems generally accepted, as is the apotropaic character of the phallus (ibid. 208; Engemann and Rüger 1991: 147–8). Christ is already understood as the New Adam by St Paul (Rom. 5: 14; 1 Cor. 15: 22).

[179] Compare Type 30a, *BMC* 145 (illustrated in *T&S* iii. 528) with the seventh-century buckle from Picardy illustrated and discussed by Salin (1949–59: iv. 257, fig. 67 and p. 258). Salin states that these images are sometimes accompanied by the apotropaic 'monstre regardant en arrière', which appears also as a reverse to the coins of Series N.

[180] *T&S* iii. 464–5.

[181] Harbison 1986, and in particular the grave-slab from Lancaster (ibid. 83, pl. 4.12*d*, discussed at p. 65).

[182] Compare the iconography with that of the cross of Arboe, as understood by Deonna 1949: 127, pl. 1*b*, 25.

Fig. 3.29. The 'Archer' type, silver penny, Secondary, obverse and reverse (3134, de Wit collection).

Fig. 3.30. The archer of the Ruthwell Cross, Ruthwell, Dumfriesshire, 8th century (© Corpus of Anglo-Saxon Stone Sculpture).

beaks a human head, hark back to heathen times, and likewise the character on the Franks Casket, the warrior in a wolf-mask from Gutenstein, or the figures from the Kivik grave-slab, also with bird-masks.[183] They suggest a ceremonial sacrality for such costumes that must have continued to be understood well beyond pagan times. Once again we witness a variety of responses to a well-established iconography across various Series, which suggests access to a wealth of artistic models to suit the patrons' particular intentions, and perhaps even to promote local cults.

The Archer

The motif of the archer, found on a few coins of the Secondary series, has been the object of a detailed study by Morehart,[184] who put it in the context of contemporary eighth-century Anglo-Saxon art adapted from the inhabited vine-scroll of Christian tradition. If Morehart's arguments and illustrations concerning the familiarity of the motif of the archer shooting at a bird, and its Mediterranean derivation, are persuasive, her interpretations of the figure simply as 'one more of the denizens of the inhabited vine-scroll'[185] requires further comment (Fig. 3.29).

The vine-scroll is indeed the setting in which archers and birds are commonly presented, and for Morehart, this was the iconography which, though extending over both faces of the coin, the audience would have understood.[186] In making this connection, however, the interpretation would have been not, as she advocates, purely secular, concerning the hunt,[187] but religiously charged. It is indeed

---

[183] For the grave-slab from Papil, Shetland: Ritchie 1989: 8; for the right-hand panel of the Franks Casket: *MoE* 102, no. 70; for the now-lost scabbard from Gutenstein: *Die Alemannen* 1997: 437, fig. 502; for Slab 8, Kivik grave, Scania; Ellis Davidson 1967: 49, fig. 7 and p. 48, where the Kivik iconography is interpreted as representing a ceremony performed by people in bird-like costumes.

[184] Morehart 1984.   [185] *T&S* iii. 439.

[186] Morehart 1984: 188, but see Gannon, forthcoming.

[187] Following Shapiro 1963, who considered the vine-scroll and its inhabitants purely decorative and fashionable.

Fig. 3.31. The 'Archer' type (*T&S* 349.
The Ashmolean Museum, Oxford); detail
of the archer from the lid of the Franks
Casket, 8th century (MME 1867, 1-20, 1.
© The British Museum, London).

in a scriptural context that an explanation has been sought for another archer,
that on the Ruthwell Cross (Fig. 3.30).

This figure has been variously interpreted. Negative readings, either as a
symbol of the Devil,[188] or of Ishmael,[189] have been rejected as inappropriate by
Raw.[190] She points out how in the patristic tradition—where arrows are polyva-
lent images, not only signifying attacks by the Devil, but divine punishment and
also the Scriptures themselves, either delivering God's message, or providing the
ammunition for heretics to poison souls—Hrabanus presents the archer as a
symbol of the preacher, whose mission it is to convey the Word of God.[191] For Ó
Carragáin the apparent paradox of the archer's violence is resolved by considering Bede's commentary on Habakkuk,[192] where the image of the drawn bow is
interpreted as giving a warning sign that, when taken seriously, will ensure the
safety of the person aimed at. Indeed, the archer at Ruthwell is represented not
with a quiver of arrows but with a satchel with a squarish object inside, possibly
the Scriptures from which he takes his ammunition.[193]

It is in this light that our coins should be interpreted. The archer represents the
preacher: his arrow, not pointed, but with a rounded finial, intended to stun
rather than kill (unlike those that Egil the Archer uses in earnest on the Franks
Casket, Fig. 3.31), aims God's words and warnings of his punishment at the soul
(the bird on the reverse) in order to instil fear, leading to repentance.[194] Linked by
the familiar and well-understood iconography of the vine-scroll, obverse and
reverse combine to deliver an important moral lesson.

---

[188] Saxl 1943, referring to Psalm 91: 5 'Thou shall not be afraid . . . of the arrow that flieth by day'. Also
Atherton 1993, and Henderson 1999: 210.
[189] Kantorowicz 1960, interpretation accepted by Beckwith 1966, concerning the archer on the mid-
eleventh-century ivory cross at the Victoria and Albert Museum (Backhouse, Turner, and Webster 1984:
12–3, no. 125). Ishmael was seen as a type of persecutor.
[190] Raw 1967: 393, on the same reliquary cross. Webster (Backhouse, Turner, and Webster 1984: 123)
accepts Raw's positive interpretation as suitable for a pectoral cross and underlines further Christological
themes.
[191] Raw 1967: 393, for relevant quotations in the *Patrologia Latina*; Ó Carragáin 1987–8: 62 n. 86.
[192] Ó Carragáin 1987–8: 41–2. Third Canticle of Habakkuk, verse 9: 'Thou wilt surely take up thy
bow'.
[193] Ó Carragáin 1987–8: 42, and personal communication, after his close inspection of the sculpture.
[194] Ó Carragáin 1987–8: 42.

4

Animal Iconography

Pagan Germanic art had favoured the representation of animals and invested it with apotropaic qualities.[1] The new Christian animal iconography (Evangelists' symbols, doves, peacock, the fauna in the vine-scrolls, etc.) was accepted and integrated into a tradition which saw it not as purely decorative, but as a potent symbolic image.[2] It is not surprising that, just as in contemporary sculpture, manuscripts, metalwork, and embroidery, many of the reverses of the Secondary series show animals, real or fantastic. These representations must be analysed in the context of the culture of the time, and therefore as potential for metaphors.

BIRDS

Whilst the gold coinage, following Merovingian numismatic prototypes, had crosses as reverses,[3] the Primary coins of Series B introduced birds to this iconography. Birds will indeed dominate amongst the reverses of the whole of the early Anglo-Saxon coinage, and their importance can be understood in a Christian context.[4]

Birds on Crosses

Several groups of coins sharing the iconography of a bust or head with diadem and spiky hair on the obverse, and of a bird surmounting a cross on the reverse, are gathered under the classification of Series B.[5] Some issues have unintelligible legends on both sides, cordoned by a torque of pellets, sometimes snake-headed, and though they differ in details, their iconography is consistent

---

[1] Salin 1949–59: iv. 140 ff.
[2] Kitzinger 1980: 160; Hicks 1993: 5.
[3] See Chapter 5.
[4] Schmidt and Schmidt 1982, particularly doves: 110–19, eagles: 34–40, peacocks: 94–6.
[5] Rigold 1960 published a Corpus of Series B; *T&S* i. 94–105 and 158–65 updates it. The main Types are: BX, BI (Subtypes: BIA–G), BII, BIII (Subtypes: BIIIA and BIIIC) and BIV (Continental imitation). BIIIB (= *BMC* Type 85) is now reclassified as part of Secondary Series J with *BMC* Type 37 (with confronting heads), etc. (*T&S* iii. 341–67). The early Series BZ (Type 29a–b) also has bird-on-cross reverses (*T&S* i. 133–9).

Fig. 4.1. Series B, silver pennies, Primary. *a*. Type BX (*BMC* 123. The British Museum, London); *b*: Type BIB (*T&S* 101. The Ashmolean Museum, Oxford); *c*. Coptic bronze lamp, 4th–6th centuries (Inv. 938 MBVA, Musei Vaticani, Città del Vaticano).

(Fig. 4.1).[6] Rigold regarded the coin iconography of the bird on a cross as original Anglo-Saxon, rejecting any Merovingian numismatic precedent.[7]

Conceptually close models may have developed in imitation of Roman and Christian standards or sceptres.[8] Coptic bronze lamps present us with several examples where the reflector above the handle is in the shape of a cross topped with a bird (Fig. 4.1*c*),[9] and there is also an interesting bronze lamp in the shape of a ram with a cross and bird on its head.[10] Following Early Christian precedents,[11] the bird on the coins can be identified as a dove,[12] in a Christian context a symbol of the Holy Spirit,[13] appropriately set on a cross. In Insular metalwork

[6] *T&S* i 94. The birds on some coins also detail feet. For the iconography of motif-encircling snakes, see p. 136–8.

[7] Rigold 1960: 11. Indeed, the often-mentioned *tremissis* from Laon (Prou 1892: no. 1051) differs from the Anglo-Saxon coins: although Klein-Pfeuffer 1993: 159 still considers it important as a prototype (see her illustration 46 at p. 158), the bird is actually identified as a crested phoenix or peacock by Lafaurie 1974: 138.

[8] See for instance the Roman grave-slab from Straßburg (*Die Alamannen* 1997: 114, no. 105) and the Christian standard on fo. 133r of the Corbie Psalter (Hubert, Porcher, and Volbach 1969: 198, fig. 207). For eagles topping imperial staffs and their Christian rendering compare Hubert, Porcher, and Volbach 1969: 135, fig. 149; p. 137, fig. 151, and p. 178, fig. 188. For Dagobert's eagle-topped sceptre: Gaborit-Chopin 1989: 266, fig. 6.

[9] See Bénazeth 1992: 123, no. E 20502, where other examples are also mentioned, and those in the Vatican collection, in Conticello de' Spagnoli and de Carolis 1986.

[10] Cabrol and Leclercq 1907–53: *Agneau*, col. 895, no. 209. The lamp, originally published by De Lasteyrie in 1853, has no provenance, but can be safely ascribed to the sixth/seventh century, as it resembles similar zoomorphic lamps (see for instance *Die Franken* 1996: ii. 810, fig. 656 and Bénazeth 1992: 126, no. E 11865 and De Lasteyrie 1855: 229).

[11] For a Byzantine example of a dove on a cross with scalloped (stepped) edges: Mundell Mango 1986: 234, no. 64. See also the pattern on the dress of one of Theodora's companions in the mosaics of San Vitale, Ravenna (Pugliese Carratelli 1982: 399, fig. 353).

[12] However, on some issues the bird has the long neck and stance of a swan. Wittkower 1977: 39 refers to the *Physiologus* bird Caladrius, described as swan-like and sharing the positive attributes of the eagle, with which it was often confused. Possibly the swan's whiteness and elegance made it a suitable alternative to the dove on the coins. See also p. 114. The bird might also represent a phoenix, often shown on a palm-tree (Schmidt and Schmidt 1982: 96–100).

[13] Schmidt and Schmidt 1982: 110 ff. and Meehan, quoting Adomnán's *Life of Columba* (Anderson and Anderson 1991: 5), where it is stated that 'often in sacred books a dove is understood to signify mystically the Holy Spirit'.

Fig. 4.2. *a*. Series J, Type 85, silver penny, Secondary (*T&S* 293. The Ashmolean Museum, Oxford); *b*. detail of the birds from the front panel of the Franks Casket (MME 1867, 1-20, 1. © The British Museum, London); *c*. copper-alloy belt-chape, Northumbria, second half 8th century (MME 1989, 3-3, 3. The British Museum, London).

there are two three-dimensional dove-shaped mounts that may perhaps have similarly topped crosses.[14]

The main body of Series B (BX, BIA/B/C, and BII) is seen as the organized output of an official production, albeit with imitations,[15] and BIIIB as a separate later issue (now designated Series J). BIIIA and BIIIC,[16] once considered unskilful copies,[17] deserve further comment. As Metcalf notes,[18] the main difference between these two types is in the birds, which on Series BIIIA are comparable to the plump ones of Fig. 4.1, but on BIIIC are schematic, and similar to those of Series J, Type 37 (see Fig. 4.3). Metcalf considers BIIIC a synthesis between Series J, Type 37, and Type 85 (= BIIIB, Fig. 4.2), as it combines the simple bird of the former with the slim Latin cross flanked by large annulets with pellets of the latter; therefore it post-dates both types, adding as an innovation two groups of three pellets below the cross.[19] On account of the fineness of the metal, however, there is no reason why BIIIC and Types 37 and 85 could not all be contemporary.[20]

The bird of Type 85, although conceptually related, is innovative compared with the modelled birds of Series B (see Fig. 4.1), as it is executed in a linear style of simple elegance (Fig. 4.2). The nearest parallels, allowing for differences in

---

[14] Dove-shaped bronze mounts from Kilpatrick, Co. Westmeath (overall height: 4.05 cm), and Whitby (similar dimensions), seventh/eighth century (Swan 1995: 77–8, figs. 3e–4). Peers and Radford (1943: 55, no. 32) see the Whitby mount as part of an ornamental bowl or shrine. Compare also Ross 1962–5: i, pl. 41, no. 69.

[15] Namely: BID-G (*T&S* i. 94).

[16] Illustrated in *T&S* i, pl. 8, no. 157, and iii, pl. 18, no. 305.

[17] Rigold 1960: 21–2.

[18] *T&S* i. 158–9.

[19] Ibid. 159; iii. 364.

[20] See metal analysis in *T&S* iii. 671, for nos. 293, 296–9, 304.

Fig. 4.3. *a*. Series J, Type 37, silver penny, Secondary (*T&S* 296. The Ashmolean Museum, Oxford); *b*. silver penny, possibly of Offa of Mercia (757–96), *c*.757–60, (Cabinet des Médailles, Bibliothèque Nationale, Paris).

material, can be drawn with the Franks Casket, which is chronologically and, arguably, geographically, close to the coins of Series J,[21] where the birds are similarly simplified with comparable wing-scrolls, tail feathers, and S-necks, and also with the spiral wing joint of a Northumbrian belt-chape.[22] Similarities can also be noted comparing the rendering of birds in the Lindisfarne Gospels.[23]

Variations are many: on some coins, whilst keeping the general simplicity of the pattern, the designs break the continuous swooping line, detaching the wing and adding details to the head, or concentrate all the features into a few traits, as in Types 37 (Fig. 4.3*a*) and BIIIc.[24] Such innovations suggest that within the concept of a coin with a bird on a cross, differences were not only acceptable, perhaps testifying to die-cutters vying with each other to produce more and more elegant designs, but also desirable for differentiating between issues.

The whorl of birds of Type 37 (Fig. 4.3*a*) has been discussed by Morehart, who indicated precedents in Germanic metalwork and confuted theories that saw it created afresh on the coins from the multiplication of the single bird-on-cross design.[25] If the design of the whorl of birds can be seen to fit in the Germanic artistic tradition and cosmology,[26] its message might be translated in a Christian context and used to express an exegetical visualization of quadripartite cosmic

[21] *T&S* iii. 341 ff.

[22] *MoE* 137, no. 101.

[23] Although wing-scrolls are common in the rendering of birds in Insular manuscripts, they more commonly roll in the opposite direction to those on the Franks Casket and coins. Contrast the birds in the corner of fo. 29 of the Lindisfarne Gospels to those that appear in the borders of the same page (Backhouse 1981: 45, fig. 26), and see Meehan 1994: 57–65 for examples of birds in the Book of Kells.

[24] See above for discussion on re-sequencing of Type BIIIc. Other examples of 'broken' Type 85 (= BIIIb, 8) are illustrated in *T&S* iii. 348, and see also pl. 17, no. 293.

[25] Morehart 1970: figs. 1–2. Examples closer to our coins than those illustrated by Morehart are to be found among the openwork discs grouped as Type VII D in Renner's classification (Renner 1970: 169–70, pls. 24–5, nos. 506–14), all dated sixth/seventh centuries, to which can be added the fine specimen from Kleinlangenheim (Pescheck 1975: 216, fig. 7.3). Although on these discs the Germanic eagles are substituted by tamer-looking birds, a Christian interpretation of this change in iconography is generally rejected (Renner 1970: 87).

[26] See the discussion on whorls of three/four animals combining the magic of the solar symbol of the wheel to that of the animals, and its subsequent Christianization, in Salin 1949–59: iv. 231–40.

harmony schemes, with an orthogonal cross as the source from which Redemption flows to the four points of the compass.[27] A unique coin, believed to be of Offa of Mercia, conceptually related, has on one side four birds nestling at the side of the cross (Fig. 4.3*b*).[28]

Morehart acknowledged that no ornament with birds similar to those of Type 37 had been found in England, and pointed to contacts through the Rhine trade route in the late seventh and early eighth centuries to explain similarities with the Continental metalwork.[29] The interaction, however, is complex, trade being but one facet of it, and the ties of cultural affinity were strengthened through the missions to convert the Frisians and the Germani, with whom the Anglo-Saxons felt particularly strong blood-ties.[30] Coins of both Types 37 and 85, as finds show, circulated widely in England and were exported to the Continent, to the Rhine and beyond.[31] As a confirmation of these contacts, we have already noticed the gold cross from Ulm-Ermingen, which is modelled on the iconography of the obverse of Series J, Type 37.[32] A definite and very close relationship also exists between coins of Type 85 and a gold pendant found at Winkel (Fig. 4.4). The pendant is dated to the seventh century by Klein-Pfeuffer, who believes it to be inspired by Merovingian coins.[33] The jewel, however, exhibits all the traits which Metcalf considers essential for 'the best style' on coins of Type 85: four pellets in front of the bird, a group of three to the left and right of the cross, plus two annulets with a central pellet.[34] It appears to have been produced as a bracteate using a particularly fine coin of Type 85 as a cliché, so it cannot have been produced earlier than the coin it is modelled on.[35]

As for the place of origin, the Winkel pendant may be Anglo-Saxon or Continental, as comparable filigree, showy borders of annulets and suspension loop are found both on Continental and on Anglo-Saxon pieces.[36] Be that as it

[27] Esmeijer 1978: 47–53, esp. 50; McEntire 1986: 349. The composition is conceptually comparable to many Gospel book illuminations where the Evangelists or their symbols are represented together under the arms of the cross (O'Reilly 1998). The four birds might represent the spreading of the Gospels to the Four Corners of the world. See also the book-mount discussed at n. 174 below.

[28] The penny, which was found in France, is attributed to King Offa by Archibald and Dhénin (*MoE* 248, no. 213, and see *T&S* iii. 608) and is believed to precede his reformed coinage.

[29] Morehart 1970: 4. For hoards and site-finds of Anglo-Saxon coins along the Rhine, see Op den Velde, De Boone, and Pol 1984: map 1, p. 119.

[30] *HE* V, 9; Boniface's letter of 738 (Talbot 1954: 96). For the Anglo-Saxon missions to Frisia and Germany in the eighth century: Levison 1946: 45–93; Mayr-Harting 1972: 262–73; McKitterick 1991 and 1994.

[31] *T&S* iii. 345 and 352. See also Stiegemann and Wemhoff 1999: i. 261, no. IV.138.

[32] See Fig. 2.21

[33] Klein-Pfeuffer 1993: 493–4, pl. 84, no. 385; pp. 158–9, fig. 46.3; p. 640. The Landesmuseum Mainz bought the Winkel pendant in 1901 from the finders, but the grave-context is unknown.

[34] These pellets in the annulets, which Metcalf defines as 'a good art-historical criterion because . . . such a trivial detail' (*T&S* iii. 345), might actually have served to identify issues.

[35] Although I have not examined the brooch personally, I am indebted to John Hines, Michael Metcalf, Patrick Périn, Frank Siegmund, George Speake, and Leslie Webster for discussing technicalities, dating, and iconography with me.

[36] See, for instance, *MoE* 52, no. 33*b*, the rendering around the embroidered pendants on the *Chemise* of St Bathilde (Vierk 1978; *Les Francs* 1997: fig. 31) and Stiegemann and Wemhoff 1999: i. 229, no. IV.53. Mazo Karras 1985: 164, comments on the finer, more regular filigree of Anglo-Saxon jewels compared to Continental examples.

Fig. 4.4. Bracteate gold pendant from Winkel, Hessen (after M. Klein-Pfeuffer, *Merowingerzeitliche Fibeln und Anhänger aus Preßblech* (1993), Taf. 84, 385).

Fig. 4.5. Series B, silver penny, late Primary (CM 1971, 12-16-9. The British Museum, London).

Fig. 4.6. Q-related silver penny, Secondary (4314, de Wit collection).

may, it is not surprising to find it along the Rhine and in the Hessen region, where Boniface and other missionaries operated.[37] The pendant copied a design that was thought handsome and prestigious, with a Christian image that must have been ascribed with apotropaic qualities.[38] The Winkel pendant and the other pieces discussed might be seen to testify not just to commercial links but to personal contacts with missionaries, which would explain the special reverence in which coins of Series J seem to have been held.[39]

Birds with Crosses

The reverses of the coins of Series B, Type BII, in addition to the cross on which the birds are perched, feature a smaller cross in front of the birds, perhaps a way of differentiating productions, but also allusive to a different type of iconography (Fig. 4.5).

The Coptic world presents us with numerous examples of birds carrying crosses in their beaks. Doves appear iconographically interchangeable with eagles,[40] and the birds are presented in various stances and with additional attributes: *alpha* and *omega*, sprigs or grapes. They are to be found in innumerable sources, sculptural and pictorial as well as on textiles across the Mediterranean world and beyond.[41] In early Christian iconography, especially on

[37] Reuter 1980: 78.

[38] The Winkel pendant (Fig. 4.4) was mounted so that it is right-way-up for the wearer, like the Wilton Cross (*MoE* 27, no. 12), for 'private viewing'.

[39] Further examples of the iconography that Series J shares with Continental jewellery are discussed below.

[40] Eagles, however, will come to be preferred among Germanic brooches (Koch 1982: 55), but they are often difficult to distinguish indubitably from doves (Klein-Pfeuffer 1993: 146–7).

[41] See examples in Völkl 1963: 270, fig. 68, and p. 272, fig. 70. Doves are iconographically interchangeable with eagles: compare the Coptic stele of eagle with *bulla* and *crux ansata* in Badawy 1978: 220, no. 3.215 and the Coptic textile illustrated in Du Bourguet 1964: 159, D107, where the bird is described as a dove. Eagles dominate among Continental brooches (Koch 1982: 55).

Fig. 4.7. *a*. Series E 'plumed bird' variety, silver penny, Intermediate (CM 1971, 12-16-60. The British Museum, London); *b*. Series Q Type QIII, silver penny, mid/late Secondary (3885, de Wit collection); *c*. Series Q, Type QIIA, silver penny, mid/late Secondary (Abramson collection).

sarcophagi, doves are commonly represented in profile next to a cross (or sacred monogram) in pairs, sometimes resting on it, but more often as supporters.[42] This is the arrangement seen on the St Radegund reading-desk;[43] however, such a composition in its entirety would of course have been difficult to fit on a coin: it was handsomely attempted on a Q-related coin, which shows two backward-looking birds flanking a cross fourché, a design that remains unique (Fig. 4.6). Whether the iconography of some Merovingian gold coins from Bordeaux with a striding bird carrying a cross in its beak might be understood as a simplified detail from a more complex composition with two birds flanking a cross, and as a direct prototype of Anglo-Saxon coins, is a debatable point.[44]

Birds carrying crosses in their beaks feature on two disc-brooches found at Hamwic: one, with hatched lines above the bird, recalls the 'plumed bird' variety of Series E, a coinage well represented in Hamwic excavations,[45] and crosses are also associated with the peacocks of Series H, from Hamwic.[46] Slim long-legged birds appear with many variations on coins grouped as Series Q. Whilst most are associated with crosses,[47] on some coins these are replaced by triquetras, presumably with a similar religious/apotropaic function, or are created by wittingly crossing the raised wing with a bar (Fig. 4.7).

As for the identity of the bird, the long legs and beaks indicate waders, appropriately, considering the coastal attribution of the Series.[48] Janet Backhouse, discussing the birds in the Lindisfarne Gospels, suggested that they were given

---

[42] See for instance, Hubert, Porcher and Vollbach, 1969: 136–7, figs. 150–1.

[43] *Die Franken* 1996: 601, fig. 449.

[44] See Prou 1892: no. 2170.

[45] *T&S* ii. 206–9; Morton 1999. For the Hamwic lead-alloy disc-brooch (31/1653), see Hinton 1996: 4–5, fig. 1 and p. 103. See also discussion at 'Porcupines' and Fig. 5.26a.

[46] For these birds of Series H, see 'Peacocks'.

[47] Not all birds of Series Q are shown with crosses: crosses are, however, featured on the obverse of these coins (see *T&S* iii, pl. 23, nos. 383–4).

[48] Metcalf 1984*b*: 200; *T&S* iii. 486.

Fig. 4.8. Series J, Type 36, silver penny, Secondary (*T&S* 301. The Ashmolean Museum, Oxford).

Fig. 4.9. *a* and *b*. bracteate brooches from Darmsheim, Baden-Württenberg and Deidesheim, Rheinland-Pfalz (after M. Klein-Pfeuffer, *Merowingerzeitliche Fibeln und Anhänger aus Preßblech* (1993), Taf. 9, 43 and Taf. 10, 46).

'characteristics with which [the artist] felt at home'.[49] This observation is no doubt relevant also with regard to the iconography of the coins, where we are justified in discerning discrete species of birds. In response to the request of the patron, the realization of a given concept seems to have been open and variable, depending on the available prototypes and the experience of the die-cutters, welcoming witty innovations, perhaps in answer to the need of differentiating mintmarks.

Birds with Cross and Fledgling

Series J, Type 36 presents a complex iconography. The bird carries a cross in its beak, like the coins examined earlier, and in addition has a smaller bird on its back (Fig. 4.8).

A close parallel to this image can be found in Continental metalwork: a brooch from Darmsheim features a backwards-turning bird with two smaller ones in the field, certainly a meaningful innovation on the more common motif of a bird carrying a cross in its beak found among Alemannish/Frankish brooches (Fig. 4.9).[50] The bird on these brooches, with the curved beak characteristic of predators, is an eagle, whose representation passed seamlessly from pagan Germanic iconography to symbolize Christ victorious,[51] via Imperial Roman and Barbaric numismatic tradition.[52] For Hauck, the iconography of the Darmsheim brooch shows the Christianization of a very Germanic image, and represents a passage from the Old Testament,[53] where the eagle is said to

---

[49] Backhouse 1989: 167–9: the birds, whilst undoubtedly inspired by Mediterranean models, were 'credible in a Northumbrian setting'.

[50] Klein-Pfeuffer 1993: 327, no. 43, and p. 330, no. 46; see also pp. 151–4 for other examples.

[51] Schiller 1971: 120 ff., on the eagle as symbol of the Resurrection and Ascension.

[52] Klein-Pfeuffer 1993: 146–8; Hauck 1984 on Christian and pagan representations on bracteates. See the light series of Ostrogothic follis (*MEC* 31–3 and pls. 6–7, nos. 101–9).

[53] Deuteronomy 32: 11: 'Like an eagle teaching its young to fly, catching them safely on its spreading wings, the Lord kept Israel from falling'.

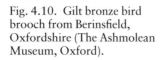

Fig. 4.10. Gilt bronze bird brooch from Berinsfield, Oxfordshire (The Ashmolean Museum, Oxford).

Fig. 4.11. *a*. Series J, Type 72, silver penny, Secondary (*T&S* 303. The Ashmolean Museum, Oxford); *b*. bracteate brooch from Obrigheim, Rheinland-Pfalz (after M. Klein-Pfeuffer, *Merowingerzeitliche Fibeln und Anhänger aus Preßblech* (1993),Taf. 53, 249).

encourage its fledglings to fly by carrying them on its back, prefiguring Christ saving souls through his Resurrection and Ascension.[54]

The iconography must have been widespread, as a fragment of a seventh-century Coptic textile showing a bird, more dove-like, similarly carrying another on its back testifies.[55] In the West the motif must have been known and adapted from discrete traditions: on the Continent it was integrated in the iconography of backwards-looking predatory birds, whilst the Anglo-Saxon coins might have looked to other prototypes. The birds on coins of Series J, Type 36 can be said to share the iconography both of the eagle/Christ saving the faithful and of the dove, supporter of the cross, thus conveying a complex message. The syncretism is an indication of the wealth of models available to die-cutters: we must envisage as prototypes portable artefacts considered precious, whatever their particular artistic merit or intrinsic value, simply because originating from the late antique culture of the Christian Mediterranean.[56]

It is interesting to find that such iconography also occurs in later times amongst bird brooches. A find from Berinsfield, in the shape of an eagle with fledgling on its back,[57] parallels Type 36, and is unique in England, as more commonly such three-dimensional brooches represent birds with crosses on their backs (Fig. 4.10).[58]

[54] Hauck 1984: esp. 15.

[55] Du Bourguet 1964: 145, D68, X 4679.

[56] Hubert, Porcher and Volbach, 1969: 209 ff.; Koch 1982: 55.

[57] MacGregor 1998: 9. Bird brooches are not common in Anglo-Saxon England (MacGregor and Bolik 1993: 154). The Berinsfield brooch can be dated to the late Viking time (mid-eleventh century; Leslie Webster, personal communication). For bird brooches see Pedersen 2001.

[58] Brooches with birds with crosses have been found in Norfolk, Essex, and Lincolnshire, fitting in with the distribution of finds of coins of Series Q (*T&S* iii. 485), some of which also present such crosses (Fig. 4.7c). See also the brooch from Wünnenberg-Fürstenberg mentioned in n. 108 below. I am indebted to Arthur MacGregor for discussing the Berinsfield find and furnishing examples of related brooches.

Fig. 4.12. *a.* the snake on the Obrigheim brooch (after K. Hauck, 'Missiongeschichte in Veränderte Sicht', 1984, Abb. 12*c*); *b.* the snake on the gilt-bronze disc from Standlake, Oxfordshire; *c.* the snake formed by the cloisonné border on the coin-pendant from Bacton, Norfolk (© Oxford University Press, 1980. Reprinted from George Speake, *Anglo-Saxon Animal Art and its Germanic Background* (1980) by permission of Oxford University Press, figs. 10*i* and 11*a*).

Birds and Snakes

Coins of Series J, Type 72 show a backwards-looking bird confronting a snake.[59] The iconography of backwards-looking birds is very commonly found in the Germanic tradition,[60] but the Obrigheim brooch in particular shows some 'interlace' around the bird, which brings the motif closer to that of our coins (Fig. 4.11).

Whilst Hauck interpreted this as a coiled snake trampled by an eagle,[61] signifying the triumph of Christ over death,[62] Klein-Pfeuffer has not shared his reading, but has preferred to explain the interlaced design as purely due to *horror vacui*.[63] Comparisons with Germanic metalwork clearly confirm Hauck's zoomorphic reading (Fig. 4.12). Hauck's interpretation of the brooch as representing the combat between eagle and snake finds strong support in the iconography of the coins of Type 72, which, in common with others of Series J, share a religiously charged iconography mirrored on Continental metalwork finds.[64] On the coins we witness the ongoing battle between Good and Evil, with the bird and the snake engaged in active fight, whereas the submissive position and back-twisted head of the snake encircling the bird on the brooch signifies the defeat of Evil.[65]

It is possible that a vestige of the iconography of the bird triumphing over the snake might also be seen on a unique coin of Series Q, where the bird, protected

---

[59] Wittkower 1977: 16–44, on the diffusion of the symbol, especially pp. 38–9.

[60] Klein-Pfeuffer 1993: 147–50.

[61] For the rendering of coiled snakes, compare Hauck 1984: 26, figs. 11*a*/*b* and the gilt-bronze disc from Standlake (Speake 1980: fig. 10*i*).

[62] Hauck 1984: 17. The iconography of eagle and snake also belong to St John: his Gospel (the eagle) triumphing over Evil (the snake) (Wittkower 1977: 39).

[63] Klein-Pfeuffer 1993: 153 and 268 n. 1088.

[64] See above for Type 36 and Types 37 and 85, and the obverse of Types 37 and 72.

[65] See 'Encircled Heads' for the apotropaic connotations of snake frames.

Fig. 4.13. Series U. *a*. Type 23c; *b*. Type 23b, silver pennies, Secondary (*T&S* 452 and 446. The Ashmolean Museum, Oxford).

by a cross, tramples over a snake.[66] Perhaps other coins of Series Q might also be perpetuating the iconography of the battle between Good and Evil, albeit degenerated, with the snake represented by pellets,[67] or indeed might be showing the outcome of such fight, with the snake hacked to pieces.[68]

Birds in Vine-Scrolls

The vine-scroll, plain or inhabited, as a single frieze or part of a tree of life, is one of the most enduring motifs derived from the Mediterranean world.[69] Before becoming emblematic of Jesus' words in John 15: 1–8, 'I am the true vine', visualized as a framework where creatures, especially birds, representing human souls, could safely abide, the decorative potential of the motif had already been widely used in classical art, as testified by countless artefacts.[70] In Anglo-Saxon England vine-scrolls are ubiquitously found in countless variations in sculpture, metalwork, manuscripts, embroidery, and carving, as a visualization of salvation and Paradise.[71] It is no surprise that the motif should be used extensively and in many variations on the coins. Series U, with 80 per cent silver content among the earliest of the coins of the Secondary Phase, around the 710s, introduces the iconography of the bird-in-vine (Fig. 4.13).

The rendering of the birds is schematic: wing, legs, tail, and neck spin out from a central double spiral, the main difference within the Series being the treatment of the wing, detailed with hatching on Type 23b, but always ending in a scroll.

---

[66] Ex-Subjack 67, now de Wit collection.

[67] For snakes' bodies made up of pellets, see Fig. 4.1*b*. For the relevant Series Q coin see Fig. 4.7*b*.

[68] This is the fate of the snake in the so-called 'Nine Herbs Charm' (fos. 160ʳ–163ᵛ, MS Harley 585, British Library, believed to be eleventh century), where Woden, with nine magic sticks, 'sloh ða þa næddran þæt heo on viiii tofleah' (fos. 161ʳ⁻ᵛ). The spell was first published by Cockayne 1864–6.

[69] Wilson 1984: 64 prefers the neutral term 'plant-scroll', as used in the *Corpus of Anglo-Saxon Sculpture*. However, the substitution of native vegetation (brambles instead of vines, berries instead of grapes) is a translation in the vernacular indicating a mature understanding of the symbolic value of the motif. See also Backhouse, Turner, and Webster 1984: 126–7, no. 131.

[70] For a selection from Roman Britain, see Potter 1997: 'Mosaic of the wrestling cupids' from Colchester (p. 6, fig. 1), Corbridge lanx (p. 81, fig. 76), sword sheath (p. 48, fig. 30), Samian ware bowl (p. 72, fig. 61).

[71] Wamers 1993: 38. See discussion of its origin and usage in Bailey 1996: 52–4.

Fig. 4.14. Anglo-Saxon
bronze sheeting for a
bucket, 8th century, Birka,
Sweden (after Egil Bakka,
'Some English Decorated
Metal Objects Found in
Norwegian Viking
Graves', *Humanistisk
Serie*, 1963, No. 1,
Universitetsforlaget Oslo).

The design can be compared to the decoration of a bronze bucket lost to a Viking raid, which shows similarly presented birds in vine-scrolls or nestled in the branches of a tree of life (Fig. 4.14).[72]

The ornament on the bucket closely resembles the Croft on Tees cross-shaft fragment,[73] where animals abide in the scrolls developing symmetrically from a tree of life (Fig. 4.15). The left-hand-side bird in particular preserves the splayed-out pose of the birds of Series U, the raised wing and the interlocking with the vine. The same stance is seen at Breedon.

On several coins the design of the birds is calligraphic, with the upright scrolled ending of the wing, and general disposition of limbs suggestive of a *Chi-Rho*.[74] Such a reading has been proposed for the emphatic X-shapes created by the interlace and wings of the animals on the Gandersheim Casket,[75] but countless other examples suggest a similarly intentional allusion.[76] As Susan Youngs puts it, these images are 'not evocative, but invocative',[77] proclaiming Faith in the hope of protection. On the coins, the birds abiding within the vine-scroll strengthen the significance of the image by recalling the *Chi-Rho* shape.

The abbreviated renderings of the birds of Series H, Type 39 are even closer to the fluid shape of a *Chi* initial on a *Christi autem* Gospel page. Just as 'limbs' are

---

[72] Bucket from Birka, Sweden: Wilson and Klindt-Jensen 1966: 44; Youngs 2001: 211–16.

[73] Henderson 1983: 252, aptly compares the carving at Croft on Tees to metalwork.

[74] Lewis 1980 discusses the symbolic associations of the *crux decussata* and the preoccupation with the *nomen sacrum*.

[75] Stiegemann and Wemhof 1999: ii. 458 ff.

[76] See the Gandersheim Casket (*MoE* 177, no. 138; Webster 2000); the Witham pin-set (*MoE* 227, no. 184, and here, Figs. 4.29*b* and 5.17); the Fetter Lane sword-hilt (*MoE* 221, no. 173); the nasal of the York helmet (*MoE* 60, no. 47, which shows several Xs, see below, Fig. 4.61*b*), all late eighth century. Innumerable examples appear in the Book of Kells (e.g. fos. 114, 124, 187ᵛ, 218), and allow a Christian reading of the interlocked beaks on the jamb of the west door of St Peter's, Monkwearmouth, and related images (G. Henderson 1987: figs. 38, 39, 213, 216, 218, and 231). The crossed paws of the beast on the Ruthwell Cross provide confirmation of their recognition of the Saviour (Ó Carragáin 1999: 193, fig. 16.1).

[77] Youngs 1999: 293.

Fig. 4.15. Detail of cross-shaft fragment from Croft on Tees, North Yorkshire, late 8th century (© Corpus of Anglo-Saxon Stone Sculpture).

Fig. 4.16. Series H, Type 39, silver penny, mid/late Secondary (*T&S* 283. The Ashmolean Museum, Oxford).

added to manuscript letters, which transform them into zoomorphic shapes, the anatomical correctness on the coins is maintained to allow the primary reading of the bird-in-vine motif (Fig. 4.16).[78] The design on the reverse of the coin allows double focusing, either on the plain cross or on the rosettes,[79] again inviting the recognition of a cross shape among vegetation. Birds of Series H, Type 39 are comparable to those of Series U in position and details such as stumpy tails and bent wings; the vine-scroll, however, is simply a meandering line of pellets.[80]

Different models to represent the same iconography were adopted in various regions: on some specimens the birds are more naturalistic, and often face backwards.[81] One such backward-looking birds-in-vine is paired with the archer/preacher motif: obverse and reverse are related—Salvation, as the well-meaning blows of the archer/preacher remind us, is found abiding and feeding in the True Vine.[82] Among the many birds-in-vine prototypes available, ours is poised between the delicate relief from York and the dynamic sculpture from Breedon (Fig. 4.17).[83]

A classical prototype, like the 'She-Wolf' on its obverse,[84] must have inspired the reverse of Series V, which shows the bird frontally: a rarer iconography. Eagles appear thus on Roman insignia, coinage, and gems,[85] and must have served as prototypes for the symbol of St Mark in the Book of Durrow,[86] or the

[78] For example, see the *Christi autem* initial, Book of Durrow, fo. 23, and the initial E, *Collectio Canonum*, Cologne, Dombibliothek Cod. 213, fo. 4ᵛ, both eighth century (G. Henderson 1987: 65, fig. 80; 90, fig. 128).

[79] *T&S* iii. 324. See also Fig. 5.5h.

[80] G. Henderson 1987: 108 on interlace formed by dotted lines in metalwork and manuscripts.

[81] See also the specimen from Tilbury, now de Wit collection, illustrated and discussed in *T&S* iii. 430.

[82] See 'Archer'.

[83] Compare also the birds in the vine on the side of the Ormside Bowl (*MoE* 172–3, no. 134).

[84] See Fig. 4.53.

[85] Eagles on Roman gems (for instance Henig 1978: pl. 21, no. 696) or brooches had specific connection with Jupiter (Johns 1996: 176).

[86] Book of Durrow, fo. 84ᵛ (see G. Henderson 1987: 52, fig. 61).

Fig. 4.17. *a*. unpublished type, silver penny, Secondary (4030, de Wit collection); *b*. detail from the York Minster cross-shaft fragment, 9th century (© Corpus of Anglo-Saxon Stone Sculpture); *c*. detail of frieze at Breedon-on-the-Hill, Leicestershire, late 8th century (© The Conway Library, Courtauld Institute of Art).

majestic eagle embedded—sideways—at the side of the door of the church at Brixworth,[87] but our bird is busy feeding, like at Easby and Jedburgh, rather than aggressively displaying (Fig. 4.18).

Although frontal, classically inspired birds appear in the repertoire of inhabited vine-scrolls,[88] Metcalf doubts that the vegetation offering food and refuge to the bird is a vine-scroll.[89] Indeed, its symmetrically formal arrangement is perhaps more reminiscent of the laurel wreaths that often surround Imperial eagles: the classical wreath/vine-scroll combination recalls simultaneously Rome, source of Christianity, and themes of spiritual nourishment, a conflation also suggested for the 'She-Wolf' motif.[90] The frequency of occurrence and variations, in coinage and contemporary and later artefacts, testifies to the fascination with the bird-in-vine motif and the wealth of models available. To the sophisticated eucharistic/Christological interpretation must be added the more basic but universal apotropaic appeal of the motif.[91]

Peacocks

It may be argued that the pelleted 'vine' that the birds of Series H, Type 39 busily peck at is of secondary importance to the bird motif and its splayed-out pose, which were earlier compared to manuscript lettering. In view of such subordination it is no surprise that other coins in the Series (Type 49) not only abandon the vine device, but transform the bird. Pellets are still a feature on some

[87] Bailey 1996: 56–7, fig. 30.
[88] Apart from Easby and Jedburgh, see also the birds in the vine-scroll on the Bewcastle Cross, and that on the top of the Ruthwell Cross. The similarity between the bird of Series V and that at Easby confirms that similar prototypes existed in Anglo-Saxon England independently of Carolingian art (but see Bailey 1996: 54–5).
[89] *T&S* iii. 572.
[90] See below; Gannon, forthcoming.
[91] *T&S* iii. 572.

Fig. 4.18. *a*. Series V, silver penny, Secondary (*T&S* 453. The Ashmolean Museum, Oxford); *b*. detail from the cross shaft from Easby, Yorkshire, early 9th century; (© Corpus of Anglo-Saxon Stone Sculpture); *c*. detail from the screen fragment from Jedburgh, Borders, early 9th century (© Corpus of Anglo-Saxon Stone Sculpture).

Fig. 4.19. Series H, type 49, silver pennies, mid/late Secondary. *a*. variety 2a (*T&S* 285. The Ashmolean Museum, Oxford); *b*. variety 5a (CM 1935, 11-17-282. The British Museum, London).

specimens,[92] contouring wing and tail as on Insular manuscripts and metal-work,[93] but on many coins the tail pellets are within a rounded shape suggestive of the 'eyes' on the trailing tail of a peacock. The disposition of the limbs of the bird and additional symbols create a sense of dynamic spiralling movement beautifully adapted to the shape of the flan: there seems little doubt that Type 49 birds are meant to represent peacocks (Fig. 4.19).[94]

Peacocks, often met with in Christian art,[95] are Christological symbols of immortality and of the Resurrection, because their flesh was reputed to be incorruptible.[96] However, whilst certainly known in Romano-British art,[97] and of

[92] Namely Type 49, var. 1a and 2b.
[93] Backhouse 1981: 71.
[94] Hill 1952: 12, happy with the *BMC* label 'fantastic birds', believes them to be cranes or herons. Metcalf (*T&S* iii. 326) suggests a crested peacock; however, he considers the raised wing of Type 39 to have been interpreted by the die-cutter as a tail raised in display (surely, one would expect a 'wheel'?) and the 'bag-shaped element' as the wing of the bird. This seems an unnecessary complication: the 'bag-shaped element' is indeed the round tail with eye-feathers, typical of peacocks. The raised wing appears a common affectation: cf. Fig. 4.13, and see the embroidered roundels on the *Chemise* of St Bathilde (Vierk 1978: 352, figs. 3 and 12).
[95] Schiller 1971: 177.
[96] St Augustine (*The City of God*, XXI, 4) and Isidore of Seville (Lindsay 1911: ii, lib. XII.48).
[97] See the fourth-century mosaic from Rudston villa, North Yorkshire (Potter 1997: 62, fig. 46).

Fig. 4.20. Detail of fo. 32ᵛ, the Book of
Kells, MS A.1.6 (58), mid-8th century,
Trinity College Library, Dublin (The Board
of Trinity College Dublin).

course from Christian artefacts from the Mediterranean world,[98] peacocks were
not familiar to the Anglo-Saxons and were often assimilated to other birds used
in comparable Christian contexts.[99] With the exception of those found in profusion in the Book of Kells (Fig. 4.20),[100] clearly identifiable peacocks are difficult
to find.[101] Our coins can therefore claim to be amongst the earliest (surviving)
representation of peacocks in Anglo-Saxon art. We can assume the image to have
been derived from a prototype less generally common and well known than, for
instance, the bird-in-vine motif, and therefore probably intended to create a
remarkable impact.

A sculptured panel in Pavia, traditionally said to be from Abbess Theodata's
sarcophagus, and believed to have been executed at the time of King Liutprand
(712–44),[102] shows striking similarities with our coins (Fig. 4.21). In its rendering of the classical image of peacocks flanking a chalice, the Pavia sculpture
shares the sense of dynamic motion of our coins through details such as the
upright wing and splayed legs.[103] Particularly noteworthy are the rosettes and
concentric circles, which also feature on the coins,[104] suggesting that the coins
may have indeed been inspired by a model close to that at Pavia,[105] with the
die-cutter selecting motifs as required. Occasionally a cross (which at Pavia tops
the chalice) is placed in front of the bird.

[98] Dodwell 1982: 151 brings to our attention the report of a silk chasuble with a design of peacocks
worn by St Aldhelm in the late seventh century.
[99] For instance doves, especially paired, flanking a cross/tree of life or drinking from a chalice, symbolizing spiritual rebirth.
[100] Meehan 1996: 57 ff.
[101] The ninth-century peacock pair on the Masham column is now unfortunately quite worn (Hawkes
1999: 209, fig. 17.5). The Æthelwulf ring, first half ninth century, usually described as featuring peacocks
(Smith 1923: 114–15, fig. 143; MoE 268, no. 243), shows griffin-hybrids, with ears, fleshy toes, wings,
and tails exactly paralleled on a tile from Sorrento Cathedral (Pugliese Carratelli 1982: 226, no. 145 and
p. 256), and these are presumably derived from similar outlandish models.
[102] Pugliese Carratelli 1984: 270, no. 167, and p. 280.
[103] The peacocks at Pavia deserve contrasting with the more naturalistic and static ones at Brescia and
Cividale (Pugliese Carratelli 1984: nos. 178 and 190).
[104] See Metcalf 1988c for the classification of the coins in varieties according to the details displayed.
[105] It is possible to speculate that the panel itself might have been admired and copied. Pavia was the
capital of the Lombard kingdom and a convenient stopping place for Anglo-Saxon pilgrims on their way
to Rome and beyond, and for merchants wanting to purchase Byzantine silks, often adorned with peacocks (Dodwell 1982: 151–2).

Fig. 4.21. Panel from Pavia, Lombard, early 8th century (Musei Civici di Pavia, Italy).

These symbols were perhaps used to differentiate issues,[106] but the cross will certainly have evoked additional devotion, and possibly also the rosette.[107] The disc-brooch from Hamwic already mentioned also has a cross in front of the bird, whilst a brooch from Wünnenberg-Fürstenberg features a bird with a rosette on its back.[108]

Series H, Types 39 and 49 belong to Hamwic,[109] a prosperous commercial centre and an important port of entry for luxury commodities.[110] If Type 49 was developed as a distinguished 'local badge', it is interesting to note that the iconographical choice is of a prestigious foreign model with strong religious overtones.

The Hen

A delicately engraved coin in the de Wit collection features a hen as motif. The iconography is unique but not unexpected, as hens are frequently met with in vine-scrolls,[111] presumably on account of their meekness and patience, but also as symbols of a day-to-day existence, totally trusting in Divine Providence (Fig. 4.22).[112]

A further allegorical significance was gained because of their motherly protective instinct, referred to by Jesus: 'even as a hen gathereth her chickens under her

---

[106] *T&S* iii. 326. Roundels varying in number frame the obverses of Type 49 (see Fig. 2.6), whilst for Type 39 a rosette-pattern alternates visually with the cross (see *T&S* iii, pl. 17, pp. 283 and 284).

[107] On the connotations of rosettes, see 'Greek Grosses', Figs. 5.7 and 5.8.

[108] See above. The Wünnenberg-Fürstenberg brooch *c*.800 (Stiegemann and Wemhoff 1999: 222, no. IV.44) can be compared with one from Osnabrück (ibid. 359, no. IV.47) featuring a bird with a cross on its back and a few other examples found in England, including the one from Berinsfield (Fig. 4.10). Although later in date, the iconography is maintained.

[109] *T&S* iii. 321.

[110] Hinton 1982: 102–3; Morton 1999.

[111] See also the architectural frieze at Santa Maria de Quintanilla de las Viñas (Burgos), end seventh/early eighth century (Brenk 1977: pl. 341).

[112] Luke 12: 24.

Fig. 4.22. *a*. the 'Hen', unpublished type, silver penny, Secondary (4030, de Wit collection); *b*. details from the friezes at Breedon-on-the-Hill, Leicestershire, late 8th century (© The Conway Library, Courtauld Institute of Art).

Fig. 4.23. *a*. miniature from the *Cinegetico* of pseudo-Oppiano (cod. Gr. Z. 479 (=881), fo. 43ᵛ), Byzantine, 6th century (Biblioteca Marciana Venice); *b*. group of hen with chicks, silver gilt on wood, 7th century (Museo del Duomo, Monza, Italy).

wings':[113] hens came to symbolize Mother Church, gathering and protecting the faithful. The extraordinary group from Monza, traditionally said to have been a gift of Pope Gregory the Great to Queen Theodolind of the Lombards, probably represents the church she founded, and the seven parishes it covered.[114] Jesus adds to the image of safety and refuge under tender wings the implied rebuke to 'dumb clucks' shunning safety,[115] which explains the double vignette of the Byzantine manuscript (Fig. 4.23).

We cannot be sure which reading was intended on the Anglo-Saxon coin, but certainly the church simile would have been known, as would other positive associations of cocks as harbingers of dawn as Christ-the-light.[116] However, why the iconography was not continued remains speculative, but might be due to chickens being linked to pagan customs and burials,[117] or to other common

---

[113] Matt. 23: 37; Luke 13: 34. See the mosaic at Beit Alpha, sixth century (Grabar 1966: 115, fig. 122).
[114] Conti 1983: 46–9, on dating, technique, and further interpretations.
[115] *Dictionary of Biblical Imagery*, 1998: 'Birds', p. 94.
[116] Schmidt and Schmidt 1982: 45.
[117] Conti 1983: 46.

Fig. 4.24. Detail of fo. 67[r],
the Book of Kells, MS A.1.6
(58), mid 8th century,
Trinity College Library,
Dublin (The Board of Trinity
College Dublin).

observations: in the Book of Kells, for instance, they are about to mindlessly peck the seed in the Parable of the Sower (Fig. 4.24).[118]

LIONS

The contrasting roles lions played in Antiquity and in the Bible,[119] as killers or protectors, as symbols of the Devil or St Mark or even Christ, the 'Lion of Judah',[120] were resolved in the *Phisiologus*, where the positive aspects were emphasized through allegories relating to Christ.[121]

As for artistic representations, the models available ranged from relatively naturalistic Roman examples (statues, mosaics, jewellery, silverware, or manuscripts)[122] to stylized oriental patterns, such as textiles,[123] which provided variety but also led to a vagueness as to the true anatomy of the animal. For instance, in some Gospel books, such as Durrow, the mane is not truly understood, but is treated as an all-over body pattern,[124] whilst the Lindisfarne model is more realistic.[125] Moreover, lions, leopards, and panthers often seem to be interchangeable.[126] On account of the choice of prototypes available, it is not surprising to find that there are numerous variations amongst the lions featured on the coinage.[127]

Aldfrith's Lions and the Northumbrian Tradition

Aldfrith, king of Northumbria (685–704), praised by Bede and his contemporaries for his learning and keen love of books,[128] produced the first silver coinage

---

[118] Parable of the Sower: Matt. 13: 17–22; Mark 4: 3–25; Luke 8: 4–18.
[119] Schmidt and Schmidt 1982: 78–86.
[120] Gen. 49: 9.
[121] Curley 1979: 3; Neuman de Vegvar 1997: 172–82.
[122] See the lions from Shorden Brae Mausoleum (Corbridge Museum; Higham 1993: 33), the gems illustrated in Henig 1978: pl. 20, and examples in Potter 1997: 62 and 90, nos. 46 and 90.
[123] See below.
[124] G. Henderson 1987: 42, 44, 52, 79, 91, nos. 42, 44, 64, 112, 130.
[125] On the diversity of styles available in late Antiquity, see Henderson 1999: 99 ff.
[126] Hutchinson 1986: 145.   [127] Gannon 2002
[128] *HE* IV, 26; V, 15; Farmer 1988: 75.

Fig. 4.25. Penny of King Aldfrith of
Northumbria (685–704), late Primary
(CM.2172-1997. The Fitzwilliam Museum,
Cambridge).

Fig. 4.26. The lion of St Mark, fo. 75ᵛ,
Echternach Gospels, MS lat. 9389, late
7th/early 8th century (Bibliothèque
Nationale, Paris).

in Northumbria. The coins are remarkable because, uniquely at the time, they are inscribed on the obverse with the king's name, implying the importance of literacy for Aldfrith and the expected recipients (Fig. 4.25).[129]

The animal on the reverse has been variously described as a 'crude beast' or a pantomime horse, and its tail has been mistaken for a tree.[130] The various odd details that mystify at first sight, however, belong to a far nobler creature, and go back to the kind of prestigious models likely to have appealed to the taste of a patron such as Aldfrith: the coins, in fact, portray a classical *lion courant*. The sinuous body finds precedents in late Roman work, such as the tigress handle from the Hoxne treasure,[131] a type that may have inspired animals such as the lion of the Echternach Gospels (Fig. 4.26).[132] Though the lion's movement is compressed by the restriction of the coin, the design still manages to convey a sense of leaping movement, which must be understood entirely in the classical tradition:[133] manuscripts and textiles could have been equally influential in the transmission of details, such as the triple-tufted tail or the long open snout.[134]

---

[129] On Aldfrith's coinage: *T&S* i. 117–19.

[130] Interpretations of the designs are discussed in *T&S* i. 118. The detail of the pellet in the mouth, visible on some specimens only, will be discussed in the next section.

[131] Bland and Johns 1993: 24–5; Webster and Brown 1997: pl. 31.

[132] Henderson 1999: 50 draws a parallel between the lion on Aldfrith's coin and the one in the Book of Durrow (see Fig. 4.36). However, the similarity does not extend to the stance of the animals, as the Durrow lion is in fact motionless (Dynes 1981: 37–8). Dransart 2001: 235 notes this type of lion with exaggeratedly narrow groins as a pictorial form used for the symbol of St Mark on Insular illuminated manuscripts of the late seventh and early eighth centuries, and also in the Pictish sculptures of David rending the lion's jaws at St Andrews and Kinneddar.

[133] The lions on the spoon from the Thetford treasure, late fourth century (Johns 1983: 120, fig. 34, no. 66), and on Coptic textiles (e.g. Du Bourguet 1964: F78, AC 293; Kybalová 1967: 92, no. 44) are good examples of *lions courants*, whilst the detail of the 'tail cocked over its back' is featured in several of the examples mentioned here.

[134] For further examples of triple-tufted tails, see Kybalová 1967: nos. 30 and 36 and Muthesius 1997: fig. 108*a*.

Fig. 4.27. Silver penny of King Eadberht of Northumbria (738–57), Series Y, Class B (*T&S* 455. The Ashmolean Museum, Oxford).

Another lion, although stiffer than Aldfrith's, and so self-consciously formal that it could be described as 'heraldic' and thought of as a royal badge,[135] is continued on the coinage of later Northumbrian kings. These coins, classified as Series Y, have been studied and subdivided by Booth.[136] Inscriptions still play an important role on the obverses, whilst a vast array of mintmarks differentiating issues (such as crosses, triquetras, and annulets, in various combinations) indicates a well-organized output (Fig. 4.27).

The animal of Series Y is sometimes described as horse-like—indeed on some dies there seem to be long ears or even horns:[137] these, however, are exaggerated stylized upright manes.[138] Other mannerist features, such as the long-toed limbs, the prancing stance, and the bend of the lifted front paw, are shared with the winged lion in the Book of Armagh: they are reminiscent of Eastern compositions of lions/griffins flanking a tree of life.[139] The tail remains leonine, and recalls the oriental-looking frieze of pacing lions with leafy tails at Breedon-on-the-Hill (Fig. 4.28*a*).

Not all the animals of Series Y are static: some have one hind leg extended as if leaping, turning into fantastic winged and spread-eagle animals, in the distinctive fashion of contemporary art (Fig. 4.29).[140] Such changes testify to the die-cutters' ability to incorporate innovations, and also to the non-sacrosanct nature of the model.

East Anglian Lions

As Metcalf noted, there appear to be iconographic links between the 'heraldic' lions with long paws, elongated open jaws, and triple-tufted tail first used by Aldfrith on his coinage and coins of East Anglian origin (Fig. 4.30).[141] The link,

---

[135] Henderson 1999: 50. The lion of Series Y could be anachronistically described as 'lion passant'.
[136] Booth 1984.
[137] *T&S* iii. 576.
[138] The Book of Kells depicts several examples of lions with upright manes: see for instance fos. 114ʳ and 183ʳ (Meehan 1994: 83, fig. 54 and p. 83, fig. 113).
[139] Cf. Pugliese Carratelli 1982: figs. 149–52. These representations are common on textiles, probably common sources of inspiration.
[140] See the parallels cited in *MoE* 227.
[141] *T&S* i. 118.

Fig. 4.28. *a.* detail from the frieze from Breedon-on-the-Hill, Leicestershire, late 8th century (© The Conway Library, Courtauld Institute of Art); *b.* the lion, symbol of St Mark, fo. 32ᵛ, Book of Armagh, MS 52, 807, Trinity College Library, Dublin (The Board of Trinity College Dublin); *c.* tile from Brescia, 8th/9th century (per concessione dei Civici Musei d'Arte e Storia di Brescia, Italy).

illustrated here by a late Secondary Series coin, stretches back to animals featured on some coins with the reverse legend SAROALDO.[142] Sketchier renderings of the animal design were found in the Aston Rowant hoard of *c.*710, in two versions (Figs. 4.31*a–b*), linked by similar reverses combining crosses and pellets. On some coins the animal becomes just a series of strokes ending in pellets and topped by a cross (perhaps a misunderstanding of the tufted tail). A specimen from Coventry is hardly zoomorphic,[143] but the relation between the 'matchstick' animals seems evident.[144]

Metcalf classifies these coins with those of Series Z, Type 66,[145] labelling them 'Aston Rowant' type.[146] However, the iconography of the animals is quite distinct: the 'Aston Rowant' type have triple-tufted tails and other details close to the SAROALDO-related animals, including a pellet near the mouth, whilst those of Series Z hold their tails and muzzles low. On some specimens of Series Z, Type

[142] These SAROALDO-related coins are known to me from two fine specimens, one ex-Subjack, 72, and one in the de Wit collection, where there are also two coarser imitations. On the reverses: saltires without pellets in standard and legends degenerated, but clearly related to the SAROALDO type with portrait discussed in *T&S* i. 147–51. Some specimens share a further element with some of the coins of Aldfrith: in the mouth of the animal there is a pellet, a detail that Salin calls 'magic ball' and believes to be ultimately derived from ancient Eastern sources. See Salin 1949–59: iv. 94–6 and Whitfield 1995: 92–5. For its Christian transformation into a host, see the lion on fo. 29ʳ of the Book of Kells (Meehan 1994: 44, fig. 46).

[143] *T&S* i. 139, now de Wit collection.

[144] Cf. however Blackburn and Bonser 1986: 77, Royston find no. 47. The 'crossed' tail also features on some of Series Q.

[145] *T&S* i. 133–9, esp. 137.   [146] Ibid. 138–9.

Fig. 4.29. *a.* penny of King Eadberht of Northumbria (738–57), Series Y, Class B iv (3818, de Wit Collection); *b.* the central disc of the Witham pin-set, from Fiskerton, Lincolnshire late 8th century (MME 1856, 11-11, 4. © The British Museum, London).

Fig. 4.30. Series Q, Type QIII, silver penny, late Secondary (*T&S* 386. The Ashmolean Museum, Oxford).

Fig. 4.31. *a* and *b.* 'Aston Rowant' types, silver pennies, Intermediate (CM 1971, 2-16-117. The British Museum, London; 3542, de Wit collection).

Fig. 4.32. *a* and *b.* Series Z, Type 66, silver pennies, early/mid-Secondary (CM 1990, 2-12-2. The British Museum, London; 3587, de Wit collection).

66, the animals appear dog-like, as Metcalf puts it, following a scent;[147] this, however, may be due to the constriction of the pseudo-legend above the animal, which might also explain the position of the tail. On other coins (Fig. 4.32*b*),[148] the animals are fiercer, the body compressed and heavier, pellets near the snout, and paws well marked with digits/claws which call to mind the sharp claws of lions in illuminated books—but also of the wolves of the Franks Casket.[149]

One might wonder whether the animals of Series Z, which are early Secondary coins with a production centred on northern East Anglia, might represent wolves, with a local relevance as punning emblems.[150] Norfolk Celtic staters, breaking away from traditional horse prototypes, had a uniquely British design featuring a wolf (Fig. 4.33): it is conceivable that the design of Series Z may have

[147] Ibid. 134.

[148] Fig. 4.32*b* is the King's Lynn find (*T&S* i. 138), de Wit collection.

[149] See for instance p. 221 of the Lichfield Gospels and fo. 102 of the Hereford Gospels (*MoE* 126–7, nos. 90–1), and the examples illustrated at Figs. 4.26 and 4.28. With regard to the Franks Casket, bearing in mind the relative scale, it is interesting to compare the lions depicted on the back panel (see *MoE* 102, no. 70), with paws reminiscent of those of coins of Series Y (Figs. 4.27 and 4.29), with the rendering of the wolves' claws on the left-hand end-panel (Fig. 4.55), where some of the digits are detailed.

[150] See Hicks 1993: 69 n. 11.

Fig. 4.33. Norfolk wolf stater (British J), 1st century BC (Institute of Archaeology, Oxford).

Fig. 4.34. *a.* Series Q, Type QIVA, silver penny, mid/late Secondary (*BMC* 183. The British Museum. London); Byzantine enamel-inlaid disc, from Risan, Montenegro, 6th century (1896–1908 M 190. The Ashmolean Museum, Oxford).

been partly inspired by finds of this type.[151] Certainly the scattered pellets in the field are characteristic of the coins of Secondary Series Q, similarly produced in the western half of Norfolk.[152]

Series Q is a coinage with a very varied iconography, and in two styles of execution, linear or modelled. The eclectic character of the Series makes sequences problematic.[153] The coins, dated to the mid-720s, are believed to have been minted in the Wash area of Norfolk. Finds of these coins in Northumbria testify to the economic links between the areas,[154] as do the iconographic similarities already noted. Pellets in the field also became a feature on some of Eadberht's coins.[155]

The modelled style of Series Q presents a lion very near to Oriental prototypes, not only in stance and body mass, but in the bearing of the tail and the protruding tongue.[156] A Byzantine enamel pendant (or ear-ring) gives an idea of the sort of Oriental prototype that we must postulate to be behind the Anglo-Saxon rendering (Fig. 4.34).[157]

The lolling tongue might have reminded audiences of *Physiologus* and its legend of the lion breathing life into his cubs,[158] a Christological theme, or of an apocalyptic trumpet-blowing evangelist symbol.[159] Besides these allegorical ref-

---

[151] Finds of these coins are plentiful in the Icenian territory, including hoards (Philip de Jersey, personal communication).

[152] *T&S* iii. 483. Coins of Series Q draw their motifs from a variety of sources, but whatever the iconography, pellets do remain a constant feature.

[153] *T&S* iii. 483–501.   [154] *T&S* iii. 486; Carver 1990: 122.

[155] See Fig. 4.29, Booth Class B.

[156] This is a feature also of the lions on the back-panel of the Franks Casket and some coins of Series Y (cf. *T&S* iii, pl. 27, no. 454).

[157] The Byzantine enamel-inlaid disc, from Risan, Montenegro, is now in the Ashmolean Museum, Oxford (MacGregor 1997: 227–8, no. 112.1, for bibliography, and discussion regarding its dating).

[158] See Curley 1979: 4.

[159] As in the Lindisfarne Gospels: lion of St Mark, fo. 93ᵛ and man of St Matthew, fo. 25ᵛ (Backhouse 1981: 40, no. 23 and p. 46, no. 27) and on the Hartlepool fragment (*MoE* 141, no. 106*b*). Cf. also Haseloff 1990: 84 and 133, no. 61).

Fig. 4.35. *a*. fragment of
gold-glass, 4th century (The
Ashmolean Museum,
Oxford, Loan 65); *b*. Series
K, Type 33, silver penny,
mid/late Secondary (*T&S*
306. The Ashmolean
Museum, Oxford).

erences, the elegant design might have been enjoyed just for its rich and exotic
connotations: indeed some coins uniquely repeat the same lions on both sides.[160]
The impression given by Series Q is of a coinage that delighted in interaction and
experiment.

The Tale of Two Panthers

In their comparative study of coins of Series K, Metcalf and Walker labelled
Types 32a, 33, and 42 as 'The "Wolf" Sceattas'.[161] The animal of Type 32a may
be more aptly described as a long-jawed 'snake/lion', as is discussed below,
together with its ancient pedigree. The 'Wolf' label should again be questioned
for the animals of Types 33 and 42, as prototypes of both designs can be found
in the classical world as representations of panthers.

Type 33 shows the head of a fierce animal;[162] a fragment of gold-glass,[163] presumably from a bowl,[164] with the head of a panther, displays striking similarities
with certain details on our coins (Fig. 4.35).[165] The animal on our coin, though
translated into Anglo-Saxon idiom, with more pointed ears, angular eye, and
extended and curved lolling tongue,[166] has spots on the muzzle and triangles on
the body, presumably derived from the serration border of an original gold-glass
piece. This serration, which characterizes the so-called *Dignitas Amicorum* gold-
glass group,[167] also reappears on the outside of the pelleted frame of this and

[160] QIVe: *T&S* iii. 499 ff.   [161] Metcalf and Walker 1967.

[162] Ahead of the Series, with the lion facing right, is probably *BMC* 157 (= Metcalf and Walker 1967:
pl. 7, no. 7), discussed in Baldwin Brown 1903 (see below, p. 132 and Fig. 4.36a).

[163] 'Gold-glass', the ancient technique of sandwiching images cut in gold-leaf between two layers of
glass, commonly denotes third/fourth-century decorated bases of presentation cups utilized as tomb-
markers in catacombs. Painter 1987: 276–86.

[164] This medallion may be compared to those of the Saint-Severin bowl, late fourth century, part of
which was found in a sarcophagus near Cologne, with 21 medallions in gold backed with emerald-green
and cobalt-blue glass (Harden et al. 1968: 67, no. 88; Painter 1987: 277–9, no. 154).

[165] This roundel is illustrated in Garrucci 1872–80: iii, pl. 203, no. 2; Vopel 1899: no. 150; Morey
1959: 63, no. 382. From the private collection of T. Capobianco, it passed to the Wilshere collection,
Pusey House, Oxford at the beginning of the twentieth century, now kept in the Ashmolean Museum. It
is not however mentioned in Webster 1929.

[166] Compare Fig. 4.48.

[167] Morey 1959: 34 *et passim*. The serration is usually enclosed in a two-band border, as on the Oxford
fragment (Fig. 4.35). *Dignitas Amicorum* translates as 'doing friends proud'.

Fig. 4.36. *a*. Series K, Type 33 (*BMC* 157; drawing courtesy of Prof. Metcalf, by permission of the RNS); *b*. detail of fo. 124ʳ, the Book of Kells, MS A.1.6 (58), mid-8th century, Trinity College Library, Dublin (The Board of Trinity College Dublin); *c*. detail from the lion symbol, the Book of Durrow, MS A.4.5 (57), fo. 191ᵛ, mid-7th century, Trinity College Library, Dublin (The Board of Trinity College Dublin); *d*. Series K/L, Type 33 var., silver penny, mid/late Secondary (*BMC* 160. The British Museum, London).

other coins, and similar zigzags link coins reading (MONITA)SCORVM and SEDE.[168] Marion Archibald has proposed that the legend (MONITA)SCORVM could be expanded to read *moneta sanctorum*.[169] SCORVM might also be an echo of the inscription *Dignitas Amicorum* derived from a similar gold-glass fragment. Although none survives, we can postulate the presence in England of such pieces as easily portable relics, retrieved from catacombs and connected with saints, and we can imagine that they would have been treasured and imitated, including the inscription, especially appreciated among the literate.

Baldwin Brown regarded the coin in the British Museum (Fig. 4.36*a*) as one of the masterpieces of Anglo-Saxon designers, 'masterly in composition' and having 'some of the qualities of a fine early Babylonian seal in its force and accent'.[170] The iconography is indeed ultimately indebted to Sassanian motifs, widely known and imitated on textiles,[171] but the great influence that such fierce heads had on Insular art is evident from manuscripts, where similar iconography used as evangelists' symbols allow us to identify the animal on the coins with lions (Fig. 4.36).[172]

[168] See for instance Series K, Type 33 (Keary 1887: 17, no. 157, pl. III.23), (MONITA)SCORVM (*T&S* iii. 435); SEDE (Fig. 5.28*c*). A zigzag is of course an easy pattern, and it is also possible that it may have been derived from a 'rationalization' of a garbled inscription (see the coin in *T&S* ii, pl. 15, no. 263).

[169] Lecture at the Royal Numismatic Society (see Metcalf 1984*a*: 39 n. 27).

[170] Baldwin Brown 1903–37: iii. 100.

[171] See for instance Rice 1973: 112, figs. 96–7, where the wall painting from Balayk Tepe shows Soghdian fabrics influenced by Sassanian motifs related to the Sassanian textile fragment from Astana. Similar ancient prototypes may have also inspired Celtic coins (*pace* Dhénin 1987: 312 and fig. 3). It must be noted that the pelleted frames on the coins, comparable to the 'pearls' bordering the motifs on the roundels on the material, are also found framing other coin series, and are devices extensively used in metalwork.

[172] See for instance the 'portrait' roundels of St Mark carried with the other Evangelists' symbols, representing the concordance of the Gospels, on the wings of the eagle of St John in the Book of Armagh (Meehan 1994: 42, no. 41) and lion symbol in the Book of Durrow, fo. 191ᵛ (Fig. 4.36*c*), where, it may be argued, the serrations of the original mane have been rendered as an overall body pattern.

Fig. 4.37. *a*. Series K, Type 42, silver penny, mid/late Secondary (*T&S* 311. The Ashmolean Museum, Oxford); *b*. Roman engraved gemstone from Ham Hill, Somerset, 1st century AD (TTNCM A.1776. © Somerset County Museums Service).

The lion, however, is also a symbol of Christ, as the Lion of Judah, and of his Resurrection,[173] and rather than singling out an Evangelist's symbol, it is more probable that the coins intend to symbolize Christ.[174] This iconography should be compared to that of the coins with 'Facing Lions'.[175]

Type 42 features a backwards-looking animal in front of a plant: the prototype for this iconography is derived from representations of Bacchus' panther leaping in front of the *thyrsus*, a motif found on many Roman artefacts in Britain (Fig. 4.37).[176] On the gemstone Bacchus' panther is shown wearing its traditional collar, a detail reproduced on Anglo-Saxon coins by more than one die.[177] Although the source of the image is clear, the significance attached to it is certainly not related to the ancient cult of Bacchus, but must be sought in the contemporary artistic context.[178]

The *thyrsus* would have been understood as the artistic device against which animals were conventionally represented,[179] and its transformation into a fruiting bush from which the animal feeds points to a Christian context and recalls eucharistic images of animals feeding in the vine-scroll, as on the screen at Jedburgh. On some specimens of Type 42 the animal is seen feeding on the berry

[173] Meehan 1994: 53.

[174] Similar lions to the one represented on the coin of Fig. 4.36*d* appear on a looted Anglo-Saxon eighth-century gilt-bronze book-mount, now in the Historisk Museum, Bergen, Norway (see Graham-Campbell and Kidd 1980: 33, fig. 10, and Campbell 1982: 147, fig. 139): notice particularly the bifurcated tongue. The iconography on this lozenge-shaped piece—four lion heads, with prominent tongues, in the arms of a cruciform design—suggests a representation of the Creator-Logos from whom derive the Gospels, and ideas of quadripartite harmony and the spreading of salvation to the four corners of the world (Esmeijer 1978: 47–53; McEntire 1986: 349; O'Reilly 1998: 77–80).

[175] See below.

[176] Hutchinson 1986: 145 and 142. See Baldwin Brown 1903–37: iii. 103, pl. 9, fig. 2, and Smith 1923: 67, for a 'leopard' on a bronze pail found in a cemetery at Chessel Down, and Johns 1983: 120, fig. 34, no. 66, for the animal on the fourth-century AD spoon from the Thetford treasure. See Fig. 2.64 for the obverse of this coin, which also has a 'Bacchic' theme.

[177] Henig 1978: 121 and 264. On this account Metcalf (1993–4: iii. 391) had believed the animal to be a dog.

[178] A comparable iconography to that of our coins can be found on the 'Rupertus Cross' (*MoE* 152, no. 114; 171, no. 133).

[179] Henderson 1998: 110 ff.

Fig. 4.38. *a.* Series Q, Type QIIIA, silver penny, late Secondary (3885, de Wit collection); *b.* detail from the screen fragment from Jedburgh, Borders, early 9th century (© Corpus of Anglo-Saxon Stone Sculpture).

of the fruiting bush,[180] while a coin of Series Q reproduces the same creature, this time turning to its interlaced tail (Fig. 4.38).[181]

This elegant animal, though originally also a panther, cannot be said to share the majestic strength and connotations of the Type 33: its role is that of a tame partaker of salvation. Bacchus's panther has had his spots changed.[182]

Facing Lions

Coins collected under the label 'Animal Mask'[183] combine the design of a facing, alert-looking feline with a variety of well-known motifs (bird-in-vine, bird and cross, standing figure with bird and cross, backward-turning animal) plus an innovative reverse.[184] The wide distribution of the coins, and the varied styles of the animal, suggest that this was a powerful design chosen and executed for several substantial series. The design replaces the bust traditional on an obverse, and clearly portrays a creature of noble symbolic connotations: a lion (Fig. 4.39).

Facing lions are comparatively rare in Insular art.[185] A naive early portrayal comes from the Book of Durrow; later frontal representations are influenced by exotic exemplars of fabulous beasts, as on the Gandersheim Casket, the Larling Plaque, the Ormside Bowl, and the 'Rupertus Cross' and, in manuscripts, the Barberini Gospels.[186] Their often lugubrious countenance can be contrasted with the round-faced lion at Breedon.[187] These examples testify both to an interest in experimentation, and to the models available. The facing lion on our coins,

---

[180] For instance, *T&S* iii, pl. 18, no. 313. For variations on the *thyrsus*/bush, see ibid. 393.

[181] On the specimen, ex-Subjack 63, now de Wit collection, the tail forms a triquetra. Triquetras are combined to form crosses, and with bunches of grapes, in a complex eucharistic image (see Fig. 5.7). The coin therefore may be allusive to salvation in an abbreviated form of great sophistication.

[182] Jeremiah 13: 23.

[183] *T&S* iii. 446–8.

[184] *T&S* iii. 448, pl. 21, no. 356.

[185] Unlike the calf, symbol of St Luke, also often shown facing (e.g. G. Henderson 1987: St Cuthbert's coffin lid, p. 116, no. 168; Lichfield Gospels, fos. 218–19, pp. 123 and 44, nos. 180 and 44; Soiscél Molaise book-shrine, p. 46, no. 49).

[186] St Mark's symbol, Book of Durrow, fo. 2, seventh century (G. Henderson 1987: 42, no. 42); other examples: *MoE* 177, 179, 172, 170, and 207, nos. 138, 139, 134, 133, and 160.

[187] Cramp 1977: 203, no. 53*b*.

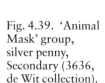

Fig. 4.39. 'Animal Mask' group, silver penny, Secondary (3636, de Wit collection).

Fig. 4.40. Detail from fo. 92ᵛ of the Sacramentarium Gellonense, MS lat.12048, end of the 8th century (Bibliothèque Nationale, Paris).

Fig. 4.41. Lion's muzzle from the Wolf Portal, Palatine Palace, Aachen (drawing courtesy of Prof. G. Henderson).

however, is more than a variation on the iconography of lions adopted by other Series, as in Series K, Type 33 with the animal shown in profile.[188] Not only does the image carry the symbolic and apotropaic value that the lion mask had in Antiquity,[189] but it must be understood in the context of the contemporary Christian symbolism,[190] as expressed in the *Physiologus*,[191] and portrayed in a miniature of the Sacramentarium Gellonense (Fig. 4.40).[192] The vigilant, wide-eyed,[193] prick-eared creature, having just breathed life into his cub,[194] is the spiritual lion of the tribe of Judah, and he is wreathed in glory, as on our coins.

This *imago clipeata* recalls the famous lion's muzzles on Charlemagne's portal (Fig. 4.41),[195] where to the religious symbolism of the lion as door-keeper is juxtaposed a political statement of *romanitas*.[196] We might equally perceive several levels of meaning in the iconography of our coins, as symbolic of Christ and his Redemption, and recalling Rome, the seat of his church.

[188] See Fig. 4.35.
[189] Mende 1981: 128–36.
[190] Ibid. 140–61.
[191] Curley 1979: pp. xiv ff. and 3 ff.
[192] MS lat. 12048, Bibliothèque Nationale, Paris, *c*.790–5, diocese of Meaux.
[193] Psalm 121: 4: 'Behold, he that keepeth Israel shall neither slumber nor sleep'.
[194] Curley 1979: 3 ff.
[195] Hubert, Porcher, and Volbach: 1970, figs. 1 and 205. Although these copies are generally considered as the 'icons' of the Carolingian Renaissance, our coins testify to the presence of this motif in Anglo-Saxon England in the first half of the eighth century, and allow us to speculate as to the possible existence of lion door-knockers in England before those of Charlemagne. The Donore 'handle assembly' (Youngs 1989: 69, no. 64) also testifies to its early use in Ireland (Gannon 2002).
[196] For lions as guardians of doors, see Mende 1981: 136–40.

SNAKES

Pattern-making snakes are ubiquitous in Anglo-Saxon art: sacred to the cult of Woden, and linked to chthonic evocations and ideas of fertility and healing, they appear simultaneously reviled and revered.[197] As decorations, they possibly served apotropaic functions, protecting the wearer against them, and the diseases they caused.[198] The Christian tradition is also ambivalent: snakes are portrayed as symbols of evil and wisdom, Fall and Resurrection.[199] *Physiologus*, however, reinforced the positive connotations,[200] as skin shedding and self-renovation were compared to rebirth at baptism and Christ's Resurrection.[201] On the coins, apart from the iconography of the Good-versus-Evil battle,[202] snakes appear benign. Following Germanic iconography traditions, snake-like bodies are often given large heads, with jaws and lolling tongues.

A passage in a letter of St Boniface has been interpreted by Speake as a condemnation of vestments bordered with worm-shaped decorations as heralding the Antichrist and leading to sin.[203] Higgitt, in spite of some reservations, has pointed out the importance of this contemporary comment by a Christian on the reception of zoomorphic ornament.[204] However, whether we can assume that Boniface was justified in fretting about the endurance of old pagan symbols amongst ordinary people (writing, as he was, from the experience of a Continental, rather than Anglo-Saxon perspective), or whether we witness another of his unfavourable outbursts, is debatable. In view of the uses and transformation of the motif in a Christian context, from Gospel illuminations to metalwork, including on the coinage, there is no doubt that 'snakes', well-established motifs from the traditional repertoire, were adopted as harbingers of Christian ideas. The complex paradoxes of the multifaceted 'snake' would no doubt have given much food for thought to those delighting in exegesis.

Motif-Encircling Snakes

Series B coins surround both obverses and reverses with an *uroborus*,[205] an apotropaic motif common as a border in English and Scandinavian metalwork (Fig. 4.42).[206]

---

[197] Speake 1980: 85–92.   [198] Cameron 1993. Snakes also appear on *caducei*.
[199] Schmidt and Schmidt 1982: 100–10.   [200] Curley 1979: 16–19.
[201] G. Henderson 1997: 6. For Speake 1980: 89, the continuity of snake ornamentation into Christian times was due to Woden, as god of the dead, being given Christ-like attributes.
[202] See 'Bird with Snakes'.
[203] Boniface's letters to Cuthbert, archbishop of Canterbury, 747 (Dümmler 1892: no. 78, pp. 349–56 at p. 355). It is interesting to compare Boniface's sentiments with those of St Nilus of Sinai, who rejects secular imagery in churches as distracting, whilst commending the didactical function of sacred art for the illiterate (Elsner 1995: 260), in words that will be echoed by Gregory the Great (see epistle 13 in *Patrologia Latina*, lxxvii, col. 1128).
[204] Higgitt 1982: 64.   [205] Speake 1980: 91.
[206] Further examples of snake borders are illustrated in Speake 1980: fig. 11.

Fig. 4.42. *a.* Series B, Type BIA, silver penny, Primary (*T&S* 103. The Ashmolean Museum, Oxford); *b.* animal motif from a C-bracteate, Lyngby, Jutland, Denmark (© Oxford University Press, 1980. Reprinted from George Speake, *Anglo-Saxon Animal Art and its Germanic Background* (1980) by permission of Oxford University Press, fig. 11*d*).

Bearing in mind this well-attested, traditional, iconography, the design of Series O, Type 38, commonly labelled 'bird in torque', needs reconsideration (Fig. 4.43).[207] Not only is the 'torque' asymmetrical, but it is clearly zoomorphic, with both the head and the tapering tail of a snake clearly differentiated in a double border of pellets, and the tame, forwards-facing crested bird happily nestling within it.[208] Unquestionably the role of the snake here is protective,[209] as is the interlace border on the obverse of the coins.[210]

Around the main motif on the reverse of certain coins of Series K, Type 32a, group E–F,[211] there is a thin snake with a body ending in a tiny head, this time viewed from above (Fig. 4.44), like the apotropaic zoomorphic finials on crests such as the Sutton Hoo and York helmets.[212] In front of the snout there is a pellet.[213] The prominent ears at the side of the head are a detail, albeit with variations, shared with animals seen from above in metalwork or manuscripts:[214] in a Christian context zoomorphic torques bearing sacred words work syncretically, unifying two worlds.

[207] The iconography of Anglo-Saxon Type 38 also found favour among Continental coinage (*MEC* 507 and pl. 29 no. 631). The popularity of the design on both sides of the Channel might perhaps be ascribed not just to commercial factors, but to the success of an iconography combining positive connotations both of Germanic and Christian imagery.

[208] For Metcalf (*T&S* iii. 470) the coin illustrated ibid. on pl. 22, no. 373, at the head of the series on account of its fineness, might show a bird in a vine-scroll with a garbled inscription around. On some specimens what was probably originally a *bulla* placed in front of the bird (ibid. i, pl. 22, no. 375) is transformed into a cross (pl. 22, no. 374).

[209] Unlike on Series J, Type 72 (see Fig. 4.11) where the iconography portrays a fight between a bird and a snake.

[210] The pelleted interlaced border which came to replace the original garbled legends on the obverses of Type 38 was interpreted as zoomorphic and apotropaic by analogy to the Bacton pendant border (see Fig. 2.17*a*). The snakes of the reverses could be seen to reinforce this interpretation.

[211] Metcalf and Walker 1967: 21. For the central motif, see below.

[212] Tweddle 1992: 1148 ff. and figs. 575–8. Representations of animals seen from above are rare until ninth-century strap-ends (ibid. 1148–9).

[213] For this important detail, which may be interpreted as a eucharistic symbol, see Whitfield 1995: 92–5, and Salin 1949–59: iv. 94–6, and above, n. 142.

[214] For instance, see the finials on the right limbs of the initial *Chi* on fo. 11 of the *Codex Aureus* (Stockholm, Royal Library, MS a.135), illustrated in *MoE* 199, no. 154. See Webster 2001*b*: 52–5.

Fig. 4.43. Series O, Type 38, silver penny, mid/late Secondary (*T&S* 374. The Ashmolean Museum, Oxford).

Fig. 4.44. Series K, Type 32a, silver penny, mid/late Secondary (*T&S*, 307. The Ashmolean Museum. Oxford).

The translation of the all-embracing, protective snake into Christian iconography reaches sophisticated exegetical heights as exemplified in many of the illuminations of the Book of Kells, where snakes, often surrounding text or motifs, are intended to signify Christ's Resurrection.[215] The underlying theological message becomes particularly apparent on some coins, where, surrounded by the protective snake, crosses replace the bird of Type 38,[216] or, as in a specimen from Hamwic, where the motif surrounds a figure standing between crosses.[217] The iconography here could be interpreted as a celebration of salvation, but we might perceive that the Germanic past also finds an echo in the Christian reading. By analogy to its role as keeper of treasures/protector of the hero in Germanic myths,[218] the snake could be read as Christ the protector of the bird/soul, for a Christian the treasure *par excellence*.

Rolled-Up 'Snakes'

Amongst the most ancient motifs on Anglo-Saxon coinage is one derived from an artistic heritage going back to Chinese and Scythian animal representation (Fig. 4.45*a*): the large-headed, rolled-up 'monster'.[219] According to Salin,[220] they were guardians of treasure, a role shared with the encircling snakes discussed above, whose apotropaic qualities were explored first in a pagan, then in a Christian context. The motif, ideal to fit on a roundel, had already been used on Celtic

---

[215] Meehan 1994: 53, with examples.

[216] On two specimens in the de Wit collection (one illustrated at Fig. 5.28*c*), the snake's head is clearly detailed and shown with jaws open around a disc, which may represent the Host (see n. 213 above). The snake has 'rays' around its body, which is curved over a cross, a design with strong Christological meaning.

[217] Series U, Hamwic 110 (Metcalf 1988*c*).   [218] Speake 1980: 85 ff.

[219] Brehm 1926: 46–51. The motif will here be referred to as 'snake', though the label of 'earth-lion', as used in Akkadian literature to refer to snakes (*Dictionary of Biblical Imagery*, 1998: 514, *Lion*) would be preferable when describing such composite mythical creatures.

[220] Salin 1949–59: iv. 241–4.

Fig. 4.45. *a.* Chinese decoration, Han Dynasty (206 BC–AD 220); *b.* Celtic stater from Austria (after Salin 1949–59: iv. 243, pl. K, 3–4); *c.* Celtic coin from Stradonitz, Bohemia (drawing courtesy of Prof. Metcalf, by permission of the RNS).

Fig. 4.46. *a.* bronze key-ring, Kingston Gr. 222, Kent (© Oxford University Press, 1980. Reprinted from George Speake, *Anglo-Saxon Animal Art and its Germanic Background* (1980) by permission of Oxford University Press, fig. 11*h*); *b.* Series K, Type 32, silver penny, mid/late Secondary (The Fitzwilliam Museum, Cambridge).

coinage (Fig. 4.45*b*) and also appears on Roman insignia.[221] Although Metcalf and Walker labelled as 'wolf-headed' the animals featured on reverses of coins of Series K,[222] Types 33 and 42 are derived from different prototypes,[223] whilst the creatures of Type 32, close to the motifs described here, are more aptly described as 'long-jawed', and considered in their Germanic artistic tradition (Fig. 4.46).[224]

Series K, Type 32 shows three variations on the rolled-up 'snake': with a body made up of pellets (Fig. 4.46*b*), a more substantial furry body and a body with limbs added (Fig. 4.47). Earlier numismatists believed in the theory of stylistic degeneration, so they envisaged the design to have devolved from a realistic animal (Fig. 4.47*c*), to one with only front paws (Fig. 4.47*b*), to simplified torques (Figs. 4.46 and 4.47*a*).[225] However, it can be argued that the sequence in Figure 4.47 shows traditional prototypes reinterpreted with new contents and

[221] See the insignia of the *Equites Taifali*, depicted in the *Notitia Dignitatum*, fo. 141ʳ, fifteenth-century copy, Oxford Bodleian MS Canon Misc. 378 (illustrated in Webster and Brown 1997: pl. 1: the insignia in question is on the second shield). The *Equites Taifali* (Salin 1939–43: i. 265) were stationed in Bohemia, an important cultural 'distributing centre' (Speake 1980: 13–14). See the same motif on the Celtic coin from Stradonitz, Bohemia (Fig. 4.45*c*) illustrated in *T&S* iii. 385. For the Celtic stater of Fig. 4.45*b*, see also Forrer 1908: fig. 485.

[222] Metcalf and Walker 1967.   [223] As discussed at 'Tale of Two Panthers'.

[224] See the examples discussed and illustrated in Speake 1980 and see Salin 1904: 214–90.

[225] Keary 1887: 75, thought that the wolf was derived from the 'She-wolf and Twins' of Series V, a point also made by Baldwin Brown 1903–37: iii. 99. Brooke 1950: 5–9, suggested that the animal head of Type 33 (see Fig. 4.35) was derived from an extreme simplification of Type 32a. See also Hill 1952: 4 and 17. Metcalf and Walker 1967 had found problems with this theory on account of numismatic evidence relating to the heavier weight of what they classify as the simpler design (fig. 1*a*, from Garton), but they too were prejudiced by the inclusion in the sequence of Types 33 and 42. See ibid. 21, for their interpretation of the relationship Type 32a/ 'She-Wolf' (see below).

Fig. 4.47. *a–c*. Series K, Type 32a, silver pennies, mid/late Secondary (*BMC* 154, 153, 151. The British Museum, London).

realism, so that the iconography of Figure 4.47*c* could be the point of arrival rather than departure. The elongated limbs compare well with representations on the Franks Casket and with those on some manuscripts' initials,[226] and whether the animals on the coins are meant to represent wolves or lions is of course debatable: they may be allusions to Rome and Divine Providence, or Christ as the Lion of Judah, or a synthesis of both.[227]

It will be noticed that tongues are a prominent feature on the Franks Casket both of the wolves, which use them to lick the twins, and of the lions on the back panel:[228] it is highly likely that a deep significance might be attached to such iconography. Curled tongues are prominently featured on the coins, and find good parallels in contemporary manuscripts and metalwork. On some coins the tongue is extremely long and knotted back on itself, suggesting the shape of a *Chi*-cross, whilst on others the tongue develops into a 'fruiting vine',[229] reinforcing the benign impression of these creatures, and possible salvific connotations implicit in the notion of 'tasting' (Fig. 4.48).[230]

As for the fur-like lines radiating from the backs of the creature of Figure 4.47*a*, this is a feature common to other 'snake' designs, as in the 'radiant' snakes surrounding crosses,[231] and which may have been conditioned by the 'porcupine' iconography.

[226] Compare, for instance, the long legs of the wolves on the left-hand panel of the Franks Casket (Fig. 4.55) and the limbs added to the animal-headed initial on fo. 102 of the Hereford Gospels, late eighth century (*MoE* 127, no. 91), also a feature on initials of the Book of Kells, fo. 188 and the Lichfield Gospels, 221 (G. Henderson 1987: 167, fig. 240, and p. 127, fig. 186).

[227] See the comments at 'Wolves' and 'Lions'.

[228] Webster 1999: figs. 19.4 and 19.5.

[229] See also *T&S* iii. 401.

[230] On a coin from north-east Lincolnshire, discussed and illustrated in Blackburn and Bonser 1984*b*: 235 and pl. 14, no. 8, the tongue finishes in a miniature snake-head, which perhaps also serves the function of the tiny creature noticed in the motif-encircling snakes, discussed above. It is possible that this coin might be an imitation of northern manufacture, as probably is the coin from Grimsby discussed in Metcalf and Walker 1967: no. 35, where the tongue creates a *Chi*-cross comparable to the iconography on the fragment of a looted mount found in Bjørke, Norway (Webster 2001*b*: 59, fig. 8*c*), and on a disc-head pin from Nevenby, Lincolnshire (Webster 2000: 68, fig. 11*a*).

[231] See for instance the coins in the CARIP group: *T&S* iii, pl. 20, nos. 337 and 340 and Hunterian 46 (Type 61) Fig. 5.28*c*.

Fig. 4.48. *a.* Detail of fragment of a fitting found in the River Thames, late 8th century (MME 1869, 6-10, 1. The British Museum, London); *b.* CARIP eclectic group, silver penny, Secondary (*BMC* 152. The British Museum, London).

Fig. 4.49. *a–b.* Type 23e and Series S, silver pennies, Secondary (*T&S* 360 and 438. The Ashmolean Museum, Oxford).

Whorls of Snakes

Coins classified as Series H, Type 48, Series S (the Female Centaur), Type 47, and Series U, Type 23e all show on their reverse a whorl of either three or four creatures, resembling the long-tongued snakes discussed above, with long tongues converging on a central pellet (Fig. 4.49).[232] The motif differs from the main body of Germanic metalwork,[233] and of Pictish snake bosses,[234] because the snakes' movement is centripetal rather than centrifugal. Celtic-inspired decorations, however, such as zoomorphic peltas and trumpets in the Lindisfarne Gospels and other manuscripts, tend to converge to the centre.[235] The closest comparisons to our coins are found on the reverse side to the *Chi* motif on the sword pommel from Fetter Lane,[236] and in several illuminations in the Book of Kells, which either form, or are framed by, a cross shape, stressing the sacred connotations of the motif.[237]

[232] For the symbolism of the pellet, see discussion above.
[233] See Speake 1980: fig. 13, and Klein-Pfeuffer 1993: 92 ff. Compare also Renner 1970: pl. 25, no. 526.
[234] For examples, see Henderson 1987.
[235] For instance, see the whorls in the Lindisfarne Gospels, fo. 29, *c.*698 (Backhouse 1981: 68, fig. 43) and the Barberini Gospels, fo. 125, eighth century (*MoE* 207, no. 160), and also the back of the Hunterston brooch (Spearman and Higgitt 1993: back cover).
[236] See *MoE* 221, no. 173, and Webster 2001*b*: 54, fig. 5*q–t*.
[237] See for instance fo. 291ᵛ, and fo. 114ʳ (Meehan 1994: figs. 37 and 54).

Fig. 4.50. *a*. Series J, Type 60, silver penny, early Secondary (CM 1935, 11-17-259. The British Museum, London); *b*. pin-head from Brandon (BRD018 2161, photograph by R. D. Carr, ©Suffolk County Council Archaeological Service).

The iconography of the coins suggest a religious equivalence for these too, especially through details such as the central pellet, or the rosette—probably representing a bunch of grapes of eucharistic significance[238]—and the shape of the cross formed by the tongues of the creatures. The symbolism might allude to death and Resurrection,[239] but the tongues could also literally express Psalm 34: 8 'taste and see that the Lord is good' and a message of salvation with eucharistic overtones.[240]

A related image is the whorl of two long-jawed snakes found on the reverse of Series J, Type 60. This version is known only from two unprovenanced coins.[241] Parallels are rare,[242] but the motif, which is reminiscent of spirals in the Book of Durrow, finds a good match on a pin found at Brandon (Fig. 4.50).[243]

Offa's Snakes

With the possible exception of the debased coin with backward-looking birds,[244] the only animals represented on coins struck for King Offa are snakes: as finials on the double-headed torques of the moneyer Alhmund, and the coins of the moneyers Ciolheard and Pendred (as main motif, and in a panel above the king's head) (Fig. 4.51).

Keary stressed the close relationship between Offa's coinage and native art,[245] but there are also important innovations. Just as portraiture received a fresh impulse from the conscious imitation of a variety of classical

---

[238] For rosette-shapes: see Figs. 5.7 and 5.8. The creatures on the coin in *T&S* iii, pl. 26, no. 441, and on coin no. 40A in Blackburn and Bonser 1986, appear to be bird-like and beaked, and although a firm identification with birds is difficult, they perhaps attempt a different iconography related to birds-in-vine motifs.

[239] MacLean 1993: 251–2.

[240] Casartelli Novelli 1992: 552–3, fig. 50, specifically on the iconography of lions with tongues out, feeding on grapes. The 'Female Centaur' (which appears on the obverse of Series S) could represent *caritas* or *Ecclesia* (see relevant section below).

[241] *T&S* iii. 354.

[242] Comparisons with common Romano-British 'dragonesque' brooches (Johns 1996: 151–3) or the rarer Anglo-Saxon S-brooches (MacGregor and Bolick 1993: 153, no. 21.2) are tenuous. On S-shaped, double-headed snakes: Klein-Pfeuffer 1993: 90 ff., and see the brooch from Crailsheim, Baden-Württemberg, ibid., pl. 9, no. 41.

[243] For instance, see fo. 3ᵛ of the Book of Durrow (G. Henderson 1987: 20, fig. 3).

[244] See Fig. 4.3*b*.   [245] Keary 1875.

Fig. 4.51. Pennies of Offa of Mercia (757–96). *a*. moneyer Alhmund (*MEC* 1123. The Fitzwilliam Museum, Cambridge); *b*. moneyer Ciolheard; *c*: moneyer Pendred (*BMC* 11 and 27. The British Museum, London).

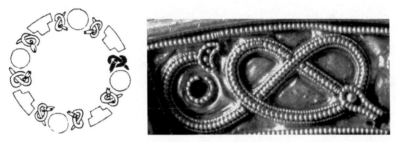

Fig. 4.52. *a*. disc-brooch from Faversham, Kent 6th century (© Oxford University Press, 1980. Reprinted from George Speake, *Anglo-Saxon Animal Art and its Germanic Background* (1980) by permission of Oxford University Press, fig. 9*f*); *b*. detail from the Hunterston brooch, late 7th century (photograph: Dr N. Whitfield, reproduced by courtesy of the Trustees of the National Museums of Scotland).

models,[246] not surprisingly even coiled snakes, at first glance traditional Anglo-Saxon motifs,[247] are innovative.

Ciolheard's designs (Fig. 4.51*b*) show a realistic animal (lacking the jaws and ears of earlier iconography), in a realistic position, without any interlacing. Traditionally, single snakes in metalwork, even in their simplest form, are knotted (Fig. 4.52), and in manuscripts they are even more convoluted and calligraphic.[248] When we also take into account the painstaking care Ciolheard took in the rendering of the texture of the scales, we might assume this is an experiment with natural forms rather than with patterns, parallel to other animal representations at the time,[249] but unlike the more playful creatures found on contemporary Mercian metalwork.[250]

---

[246] See Offa's sections in 'The Bust'.

[247] Keary (1875: 214 and pl. 5) suggested that the zoomorphic interlace was closely comparable to patterns in illuminated manuscripts.

[248] For example, see the initial S on fo. 179ʳ in the Book of Kells (Meehan 1994: 53, fig. 58). Whilst the general figure-of-eight shape is comparable to the design on the coin, the snake forming the letter is actually knotted on itself.

[249] See the comments on the interest in textured reptiles in late eighth-century art in *MoE* 178, especially when seen from above, and the comparisons drawn between the animals on the Gandersheim Casket, the Edda Stone, the St Petersburg Gospel, and the Rothbury Cross. A Carolingian equivalent study in natural forms can be seen in the representation of a salamander, fo. 17ᵛ, *Physiologus Latinus*, *c*.830 (Hubert, Porcher, and Volbach 1970: 113, fig. 99).

[250] For an extensive discussion, with examples, see Webster 2000, 2001*a*, and 2001*b*.

The same comment is also valid for the coins of Pendred, where two snakes are shown interlaced, a design at first sight traditional, and contrived to fill in a given space (Fig. 4.51c–d). Here too, however, although traditionally and formally confronted, the bodies of the snakes differ from comparable examples by being much more credible and naturalistic.[251] They also seem removed from the busy interlace of contemporary metalwork.[252]

For the double-headed and scaly torques on the reverses of some of Offa's coins by Alhmund, the moneyer might have wanted to transform the numismatic precedent of a laurel wreath around an inscription, a common reverse on Roman coins,[253] into something wittily Germanic. On the other hand, it is also feasible that Alhmund may have based his design on precious artefacts known and admired at Offa's court, perhaps newly discovered or acquired.[254]

As for the significance of the snake iconography on Offa's coinage, Pendred's coin with a miniature motif above the king's head on the obverse (Fig. 4.51d) seems to allude to the apotropaic role of snakes as traditional protectors of the warrior-hero,[255] not a resurgence of paganism, but a living ornamental tradition, as testified by the recurrence of snake iconography on weapons.[256]

WOLVES

Wolves are rare on Anglo-Saxon coinage. Earlier scholars had postulated that the she-wolf of Series V had 'through extraordinary morphological changes'[257] turned into other wolf types,[258] such as the animals featured on Series K,[259] but these can now be seen to derive from discrete prototypes.[260] Theories matching Series V and K 'wolves' to the East Anglian Wuffingas dynasty are untenable,[261]

---

[251] The gold bracteate from Kingston (Speake 1980: fig. 13o) offers a good traditional example of con-fronted interlaced snakes, which can be compared to those in the letter M on fo. 3 of the Lindisfarne Gospels (Backhouse 1981: 35, fig. 20).

[252] Compare the material in Webster 2001a and 2001b.

[253] See for instance the *siliqua* illustrated in Bland and Johns 1993: 16, no. 4.

[254] Metcalf 1963: 41 had suggested that the double-headed torque on Alhmund's coins represented eels, wealth of the Fens, and a pun on the moneyer's name. Eels, however, are smooth-skinned and have long dorsal fins. The motif between the snakes, rather than the fish-hooks he suggested, might reproduce the raised bezel of a Roman snake ring or bracelet of Type Biii (Johns 1996: 45, fig. 3.3, and p. 109). It is also possible to postulate exotic gifts as sources of inspiration. The spectacular gold bracelet from Hadra, Egypt, c.625 (Kent and Painter 1977: 101, no. 173) might serve as an example of the sort of elaborate arte-fact that may have served as prototype.

[255] Speake 1980: 86.

[256] See for instance *MoE* 60, 221, and 226, nos. 47, 173, and 181, and Webster 2001a: 272–3, fig. 18.6 on the sword pommel from the Beckley area.

[257] Baldwin Brown 1903–37: iii. 99.

[258] Keary 1887: 75; Baldwin Brown 1903–37: iii. 99–100; Hill 1952: 4–5 and 17–18, but see doubts in Metcalf and Walker 1967: 21.

[259] See Fig. 4.47.

[260] See discussion above.

[261] *T&S* iii. 385: distribution-patterns for Series V and K belong south of the Thames.

Fig. 4.53. Series V, silver penny, Secondary (*T&S* 453. The Ashmolean Museum, Oxford).

Fig. 4.54. The Undley bracteate, Lakenheath, Suffolk, 5th/6th century (MME 1984, 11-1, 1. The British Museum, London).

though an iconographical connection between the region and wolves could exist, as suggested above, through Celtic prototypes.[262]

The She-Wolf

Series V, *BMC* Type 7, a rare and distinctive coinage, although eschewing the classical bust, uses on its obverse an image strongly connected to Rome (Fig. 4.53). Its distribution pattern, mainly in East Kent,[263] makes it untenable to see in the choice of the motif an East Anglian badge derived from a punning allusion to Rædwald's great-grandfather's name, Wuffa, 'from whom the kings of the East Angles are called Wuffingas'[264]—and later dynastic claims to Roman descent.[265]

The iconography relates to the mythical foundation of Rome and the legend of Romulus and Remus fed by the she-wolf. First used on Roman coins on the reverse of silver didrachma of the mid-third century BC, it was subsequently employed on the Constantinian coinage of the *Urbs Roma* type, which, as finds testify, circulated widely in England.[266] Their obverse and reverse were combined and copied closely, including stars and wreath,[267] on the late fifth/early

[262] See Fig. 4.33.

[263] *T&S* iii, map p. 574.

[264] *HE* II, 15; Sisam 1953: 306–7.

[265] *T&S* iii. 385 and 570–1; *pace* Campbell 1982: 67, and Hicks 1993: 69, n. 11.

[266] See for example the South Italian *didrachma* (269–242 BC) in Sydenham 1952: pl. 13, no. 6, and the coin of Constantine I, struck at Trier (*c.*330) in *MoE* 105–6, no. 74*a*. Metcalf and Walker 1967: 21, suggest that the curved spine of the wolf is copied from earlier coins (Series K, Type 32a), rather than directly from a Roman prototype. However, this may be simply to do with the space available.

[267] One of the eight-pointed stars, with pellets as terminals, is clearly visible; the other and the wreath have been covered by the double-spiral below the loop.

Fig. 4.55. Details of the wolves   Fig. 4.56. Penny of Æthelberht of East Anglia (*BMC* 2.
from the left-hand panel of the   The British Museum, London).
Franks Casket, 8th century (MME
1867, 1-20, 1. © The British
Museum, London).

sixth-century bracteate from Undley (Fig. 4.54).[268] It may be argued that, having transformed Roma into a bearded male, the Undley bracteate represents the contemporary Germanic heroic ethos by compressing the double role of 'fighter' and 'provider' in an apotropaic context of prestigious resonance.

To a later Anglo-Saxon audience, Christian, and familiar with the exegetical works of Gregory, Augustine, Cassiodorus, and Bede,[269] the she-wolf would have been a powerful image, suggesting a sophisticated hologram of Rome and its might, Rome as the source of Christianity in Britain and Rome as *ecclesia*. All these different strands, synthesized in the transformation of the meaning of the visual idiom,[270] would have converged in a meditation on history as the unfolding of God's plan, and in a complex statement of awareness and belonging.[271] The ultimate meaning on our coins could be eucharistic, especially in view of the reverse, which presents the theme of the True Vine.[272] The iconography may represent the theme of Providence granting not only material sustenance, as with the she-wolf's milk and the berries, but spiritual growth and salvation through the Church of Rome. The scene on the left side of the Franks Casket (Fig. 4.55), although derived from a different iconographic tradition to our coins,[273] also presents the she-wolf as food-provider for the twins, and could equally be interpreted eucharistically.[274] The image of the saving milk is juxtaposed to the cup labelled 'biter' on the right-hand panel, contrasting a nourish-

---

[268] Webster and Brown 1997: 237 and p. 116, fig. 48.
[269] Lang 1999: 247.
[270] Barasch 1997: 38–9.
[271] The conscious reuse of Roman *spolia*, especially the use of ivory (see below), suggests emulation of Christian Rome.
[272] See Fig. 4.18*a*.
[273] Neuman de Vegvar 1999: 259–62.
[274] See Webster 1999: 239–41, for further connotations.

ing drink on which the twins thrive, to one presumably poisonous, bringing grief and death.

A Roman Constantinian coin,[275] probably newly found, and not any previous Anglo-Saxon rendering, must have served as model for the penny struck by the moneyer Lul for Æthelberht of East Anglia (Fig. 4.56). Æthelberht was executed at Offa's command in 794. The fact that he had started minting independently from Offa, and the particular iconography of this coin was the word REX, a provocative gesture of political independence from Mercia and a pun on the name of the Wuffingas dynasty, which claimed descent from Caesar,[276] have been interpreted as contributing to his fate.[277] Æthelberht was venerated as a saint in Herefordshire, where he had been murdered, and in East Anglia.[278] The fragment of an ivory plaque found at Larling, Norfolk, where a church was dedicated to him, also shows the she-wolf and twins motif nestling in a panel at the base of a cross:[279] its iconography has been related to that of Æthelberht's coinage, as a political statement of East Anglian *romanitas*.[280] However, in view of the context in which it was found, the likely function of the plaque and the associations of the motif with the vine-scroll, a religious interpretation is tenable, parallel to that discussed above.[281] Rather than a charged political gesture, Æthelberht's iconographical choice may simply have been a pious and enthusiastic response to the fortuitous find of a Roman coin and intended to display providential salvation through the mother Church of Rome.

Æthelberht's penny is known from three specimens,[282] one found in Rome, below the walls in Tivoli.[283] The large number of coins of this period that found their way to Italy invites caution;[284] however, it is tempting to speculate that the coin might have been deliberately taken there by an Anglo-Saxon pilgrim aware of the multi-layered she-wolf/Rome connection and deposited, in a sacred context,[285] in remembrance of Æthelberht.

---

[275] Specifically, provincial coins from Trier can be seen as very near prototypes: the coin of Constantine I (mentioned above, and illustrated in *MoE* 105–6, no. 74a) seems more convincing than those proposed by Kent 1961: pl. 2, no. 6, or Brooke 1950: pl. 1c. The distinctive treatment of pelt and pelleted border below the wolf's belly and hind leg is reminiscent of the conventional Germanic metalwork rendering of animals outlined by a double contour-line (see Whitfield 1995: 96); also, the tilt of the head turned to look at the twins is such that the wolf appears to be biting its legs.

[276] See Hicks 1993: 69 n. 11.

[277] Stenton 1971: 210; Blunt 1961: 49; Archibald 1985: 34.

[278] Thacker 1985: 5–7; Neuman de Vegvar 1999.

[279] *MoE* 179, no. 139; Green 1971; Neuman de Vegvar 1999: 257–8, fig. 21.2.

[280] Campbell 1982: 67; *T&S* iii. 571.

[281] *MoE* 179. We see a similar use of the iconography on a panel from the diptych of Rambona now in the Vatican Museum, of *c.*900, where the she-wolf figures prominently as the base of the Cross (Menz-Vonder Mühll 1981: pl. 27, no. 39a). See also Gannon forthcoming.

[282] *BMC* 2 (acquired 1803, not found at Tivoli, *pace MoE* 251); ex-Norweb collection (no. 105, reputedly found at Tivoli in 1908; same obverse as *BMC* 2); Hunterian 413a. According to a note in an old inventory, the Hunterian specimen is a cast of that in the British Museum. The editor of the Hunterian collection was unsure about it, so the specimen was labelled as 413a instead of 414.

[283] Blunt 1986: 164.

[284] Blunt 1986.

[285] Travaini, forthcoming.

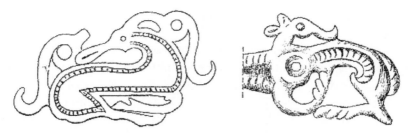

Fig. 4.57. Scythian and Sarmatian examples of backward-looking animals: 5th/6th and 3rd century BC (after Salin 1949–59: iv, pl. F, nos. 3–5).

BACKWARD-LOOKING ANIMALS

The crouched animals featured on Continental Series X and on the Secondary Series N, O, Q, and Type 40 turn their heads backwards, a traditional position of ancient animal representations in the art of the nomads of the Steppes (Fig. 4.57), and from them ultimately transmitted, via several mediators, to the Germanic repertoire.[286] Apart from any possible religious/magical connotation,[287] from the practical point of view of the die-cutter, the arrangement makes it easier for the animal to fit in a roundel.

The Early Secondary Series X (*c*.710–15), Danish in origin,[288] was a very substantial coinage, as the 173 specimens from the Hallum hoard (*c*.715–20), representing all its common varieties, testify.[289] These coins, widely used and copied in North Sea trade, and imitated wholly or partially in England,[290] carry animals comparable to those of Fig. 4.57. Noteworthy are the fronded feet, tucked under the beast in the manner of a horse or a deer, the lappet (elongated ear), the looped head and jaws, the tufted tail and the prominent sexual member (Fig. 4.58*a*). Anglo-Saxon Series N, an early Secondary (*c*.720) substantive issue also widely imitated,[291] presents in Varieties 41a and 41b a comparable animal, sometimes reversed. The body is outlined by dots, and head and jaws are more naturalistic; only 41a details genitals.[292] Some of the animals also show a prominent tongue (Fig. 4.58*b–c*).[293]

---

[286] Dalton 1924; Belaiew 1935: 177 ff.; Salin 1949–59: i. 315, and iv. 209–22; Whitfield 1995: 90–2 and fig. 3.

[287] Salin 1949–59: iv. 220–2.

[288] Bendixen 1981*b*; Metcalf 1984*c*: 161.

[289] *T&S* ii. 275–93.

[290] Royston 42 and 43 (*T&S* ii. 292). For the Insular copies varieties C–F, whose English attribution is debatable, see *T&S* ii. 286–9.

[291] *T&S* iii. 459–67. For the corpus, Metcalf 1974.

[292] See also the unique coin from Barking Abbey (*T&S* iii. 395; *MoE* 93, no. 67*w*). The animal on this coin seems to have more in common with Series N than Type 42 (*pace T&S*, ibid.).

[293] The animals with prominent tongue (among which a very fine one in the de Wit collection, and see *T&S* iii, pl. 22, no. 368) might be compared to a yet unpublished copper bracteate from Brixton Deverill. See also discussion in 'Rolled-up Snakes'.

Fig. 4.58. *a.* Series X, Type 31, Danish silver penny, Intermediate/Secondary(*BMC* 148. The British Museum, London); *b–c.* Series N, variety 41a, silver pennies, mid-Secondary (*BMC* 173. The British Museum, London and *MEC*, 704. The Fitzwilliam Museum, Cambridge).

Fig. 4.59. *a.* detail of the Pictish cross-slab at Aberlemno, Forfar, 8th century (photograph courtesy of Dr I. and Prof. G. Henderson); *b.* detail of fo. 129ᵛ, the Book of Kells, MS A.1.6 (58), mid-8th century, Trinity College Library, Dublin (The Board of Trinity College Dublin); *c.* Type 15/41, silver penny, mid-Secondary (*T&S* 352. The Ashmolean Museum, Oxford).

Crouching animals are comparatively rare in Insular art, and whilst the Pictish example from Aberlemno beautifully fits the available space under the 'eaves' of the slab, the forward-facing calf of St Luke on fo. 129ᵛ of the Book of Kells kneels uncomfortably.[294] However, other prototypes besides the Danish coins must have circulated, as the mannered beast with short curly tails of Type 15/41, framed by a triple border, testifies (Fig. 4.59).[295]

A very different backward-looking animal appears with early Type 40 and is then taken up by Series O and Q:[296] the creature balances on fronded back feet whilst sharply raising the front limb to the head, the short tail is curled, and from the pellets surrounding the animal depart rays—or a mane (Fig. 4.60*a*). The

[294] See Meehan 1994: 40, fig. 38.

[295] The silver brooch of the later ninth century illustrated in *MoE* 232, no. 190 may have been inspired by a similar prototype.

[296] Type 40 is unrelated to Series O but concurrent with Series N in distribution and silver content (*T&S* iii. 477–81). Series Q (first block) features the animal on Types QIʙ, QIᴅ, QIᴇ, and QIx (ibid. 488–91); see also *BMC* Type 43 (ibid. 482) and the similar creature of Series O, Type 57 (ibid. 474–5). QIᴀ copies Series N.

Fig. 4.60. *a.* Series O, Type 40, silver penny, mid/late Secondary (*BMC* 171. The British Museum, London); *b.* harness mount, unknown find place, Denmark (© Oxford University Press, 1980. Reprinted from George Speake, *Anglo-Saxon Animal Art and its Germanic Background* (1980) by permission of Oxford University Press, fig. 3*k*).

sinuous profile recalls late Roman metalwork,[297] and also occurs, with raised, interlacing forelimbs, in illuminated manuscripts,[298] and Scandinavian art. The animals on the Danish harness shown here (Fig. 4.60*b*) seem particularly close to those on the coins, and match stylistic elements on the Sutton Hoo metalwork:[299] the motif therefore belongs to an artistic repertoire already familiar in seventh-century England. For its iconography and interaction with Series N, then, Type 40 chose a discrete but related model, also of ultimate Scandinavian derivation. One may wonder if a particular significance is to be read in these peculiarly Germanic motifs in an iconography that is mainly derived from the Christian Mediterranean. If the traditional role of these backward-looking animals was that of 'custodians of treasure',[300] perhaps, in a metaphysical sense, they may have been regarded as guardians of the 'souls' on the obverse.

In another group of coins, bracketed under the general label of Series Q,[301] backward-looking animals with similarly long snouts stand on four slim legs, playfully interlacing either tails or lappets between their limbs. The design encapsulates several allusions: with muzzles, to the animals of Series X, N, and Type 40, and then to other standing quadrupeds of Series Q, and images of inhabited vine-scrolls found in other Series.[302] The animals' tails and lappets actually create the enmeshing vine-scroll, as in much art of the time.[303] Far from 'presumably deriving from the plant-scroll but now out of context',[304] this shows

[297] See for instance the S-shaped animals on the border of the Howletts quoit-brooch, fifth century (Smith 1923: 54, no. 58).

[298] See the detail of fo. 2 of the Durham Cathedral MS A.11.17 illustrated in Webster 1982: 23, fig. 2*c*.

[299] See the Sutton Hoo shield detail Fig. 2.3, and drinking cup mount (Speake 1980: fig. 3*j*; see also figs. 1*l* and 1*o*).

[300] Speake 1980: 90.

[301] Series Q (second block): see *T&S* iii. 492–5.

[302] See Fig. 4.38*a*.

[303] Webster 2001*b*: 44–5 and 47–50, with many examples specifically Southumbrian.

[304] Wilson 1984: 64–5.

Fig. 4.61. *a*. Q-related silver penny, Secondary (4314, de Wit Collection); *b*. detail from the nasal of the York helmet, second half of the 8th century (YORCM CA 665. © The Castle Museum, York).

a sophisticated visualization of John 15: 5: 'I am the vine, you are the branches'. On other coins in the Series, as we saw, the interlacing tail forms a triquetra or makes the sign of the cross,[305] and seems to respond to triquetras or Latin crosses on the obverse, thus confirming the religious allusion.[306] On another backward-looking animal seen on some Q-related, as yet unpublished coins we see a variation on the tucked-in legs, emphatically making up a *Chi*-cross, recalling the 'crossed paws' of the York helmet (Fig. 4.61).[307] The Christianization of the motif of the backward-looking animal seems now to be complete.

FANTASTIC HYBRIDS

The Female Centaur

The iconography of the obverse of Secondary Series coins of *BMC* Type 47 in Fig. 4.62 caused a lively debate among numismatists and art historians. Rigold had chosen S as a mnemonic label to the Series because he interpreted the design as that of a sphinx.[308] Metcalf originally supported this interpretation. As finds suggested an East-Saxon origin, he postulated a local political interest in the image: the classical sphinx—associated with heroic memories of an independent past, when Cunobelin, founder of Colchester, was king—'crossed' with a silver coin of Cunobelin himself, showing a male centaur carrying a branch, had

---

[305] See *T&S* iii. 492–6. However, the 'strange animal' of QIIIA discussed and illustrated ibid. at p. 496, is *not* scratching the back of his diminutive head, but is to be related to the leaping animals with raised forepaws at Fig. 4.37. See also ex-Subjack 63, 67, and 68, now in the de Wit collection, and Webster 2001*b*: 46, figs. 2*e*, *g*, and *n*.

[306] Lewis 1980 on sacred calligraphy and Stiegemann and Wemhof 1999: ii. 458 ff. on *Chi*-crosses made by interlace.

[307] There are two such coins in the de Wit collection, and one in the Abramson collection in Leeds. For 'crossed paws' and other *Chi*-crosses, see discussion at 'Birds in Vine-Scrolls'.

[308] Rigold 1977.

Fig. 4.62. Series S, silver penny, late
Secondary (*T&S* 441. The Ashmolean
Museum, Oxford).

Fig. 4.63. Detail of broad frieze at Breedon-on-
the-Hill, Leicestershire, late 8th century (© The
Conway Library, Courtauld Institute of Art).

furnished the East Saxons with an appropriate propaganda icon against
Æthelbald's Mercian drive for hegemony.[309]

From an art-historical stance, Morehart argued that the figure was not a
sphinx but a female centaur, and cited a number of artistic parallels.[310] She
rejected the possibility of any link to Celtic coinage, preferring other points of
entry for the image and, like Metcalf, interpreted the centaurs on the coins as
winged. She also suggested that the iconography would not have been understood as classical mythology but accepted within Germanic parameters.[311] The
link to Æthelbald having been demolished by Blackburn's revised coinage
chronology, her argument contributed to the acceptance of the figure as a female
centaur in its own right.[312] Some points however need addressing.

Celtic coinage, which, then as now, would have been commonly found, does
in fact play a part in the iconography of Anglo-Saxon coins.[313] The coin of
Cunobelin that Metcalf suggested could have served partly as a model for Series
S might in fact be a not-too-distant prototype: its classical flavour would have
made it particularly endearing to Anglo-Saxon patrons. Centaurs are commonly
portrayed with branches, their usual attributes,[314] as testified on Roman coins
and gems.[315]

---

[309] Metcalf 1976*a*: 8–13. For Cunobelin's coin, see ibid., pl. 1, no. 10.

[310] Morehart 1985: 3 ff. See also Baldwin Brown 1903–37: iii. 86 ff.

[311] Morehart 1985: 5–6 quotes the centaur on the lost horns from Gallehus and the horse-headed,
winged figure on the right-hand end of the Franks Casket as examples of how centaurs could have been
adopted within a mythology that already possessed hybrids.

[312] *T&S* iii. 538.

[313] See Figs. 2.20 and 4.33.

[314] For centaurs armed with pine-branches: March 1998: 100.

[315] See for instance the Cunobelin Centaur type (AD 10–20) in Metcalf 1976*a*: pl. 1, no. 10, compared
to the reverse of the Roman Republican coin (155–120 BC) of Hercules in a *biga* of centaurs (Sydenham
1952: pl. 18, no. 429), and the Etruscan scarab (third century BC) illustrated in Henig 1994: no. 111.

The carvings of Breedon-on-the-Hill testify to the interest in exotic creatures, and among these, one female centaur in a scroll of the broad frieze can be closely compared to those on our coins (Fig. 4.63). First, on the coins the centaurs seem to be 'stepping over', in a stance similar to that adopted straddling the carved vine-scroll. On the coins there is nothing to impede progress, but the long tail entwining with the hind legs recalls a vine-scroll. Secondly, both in the carving and on the coins the centaur's torso is turned frontally. Attached at the shoulders are arms, and behind the scroll, vegetation, analogous to the palm-branches brandished on the coins. I believe this is the only true centaur at Breedon, having four legs and two arms;[316] its slender waist and arms also suggest a female. Finally, the rolled haunches, which Steven Plunkett considers typically derived from quasi-Syrian exemplars,[317] are also characteristic of the coins cut in what Metcalf describes as 'best style'.[318]

We might therefore postulate similar models, whether derived from textiles or 'portable, durable, precious' artefacts both for the coins and the carving, testifying to the patrons' cultural tastes and to the display of patronage through the arts.[319] The mini-renaissance of classical scholarship and the interest in mythology must have been fuelled not only by literature,[320] but also by the desire to understand the exotic figures gracing prestigious imports.

We witness a switch in the perception of centaurs: from symbols of untamed barbarism,[321] said by *Physiologus* to 'represent the figures of devils',[322] they become worthy creatures, possibly through descriptions such as those of the good centaurs hoping in Christ's salvation encountered by Antony journeying in the desert.[323] Moreover, their iconography, with their traditional attributes reinterpreted as triumphal palm-branches brandished with arms raised in the *orans* position,[324] seamlessly transports them to a Christian context. The good, caring nature of centaurs organized in family groups or singly, with the female of the species attending to her young, is a common theme in Pictish sculpture, often associated with images of salvation.[325] A couple of centaurs are also to be found in the Earthly Paradise represented on an ivory leaf of the Carolingian Areobindus diptych, closely copied from antique prototypes.[326]

---

[316] Wings would be springing at shoulder level, as they do on the other creatures next to the centaur at Breedon-on-the-Hill (see Fig. 4.64c). See also the Celtic silver tetradrachm illustrated as no. 3 in Morehart 1985.

[317] Plunkett 1998: 217.

[318] Series S 'best style', as distinguished from that with thin haunches, is discussed and illustrated in *T&S* iii. 542.

[319] Cramp 1977: 207 sees the derivation from textiles: Morehart 1985: 6, and Jewell 1986: 108–9 favour objects as prototypes.

[320] Herren 1998.

[321] Pholus and Cheiron, both connected to Heracles, were civilized exceptions: March 1998: 100.

[322] Curley 1979: 24.

[323] Account from the *Life of St Paul* by Jerome; see Henderson 1996: 21 ff.

[324] Cabrol and Leclercq 1907–53: *Palm*; Milburn 1988: 3.

[325] Henderson 1996.

[326] See Hubert, Porcher, and Volbach 1970: 237, fig. 218; p. 355.

Fig. 4.64. *a.* Silver penny of King Eadberht of Northumbria (738–57), Series Y (3818, de Wit collection); *b.* Series Q, Type QIIA, silver penny, mid/late Secondary (Abramson collection); *c.* detail of broad frieze at Breedon-on-the-Hill, Leicestershire, late 8th century (© The Conway Library, Courtauld Institute of Art).

Iustus ut palma florebit:[327] the hopeful image of the centaur rejoicing in the promise of salvation, having come from barbarity to Christ, may have struck a sympathetic chord with the Anglo-Saxons. Besides the general connotations of virtue and salvation, we might see in the prominent breasts on the centaur an allusion to *caritas* or *Ecclesia*, caring and nourishing the faithful.[328] The image on our coins, to be appreciated for its prestige connections but also understood at deeper religious levels,[329] seems to be in keeping with other similarly complex iconographical choices.

Winged Quadrupeds and Other Hybrids

We have already encountered a Northumbrian winged, back-kicking variation on the formally posed lions in the coinage of Eadberht (738–57), and commented on the iconographic links between Northumbrian and East Anglian coinage,[330] reflecting close contacts of maritime neighbours.[331] Series Q presents us with a winged animal prancing among pellets, an answer perhaps to the surprisingly frivolous change to Series Y (Fig. 4.64).[332] Breedon-on-the-Hill has in its vine-scroll a winged quadruped (Fig. 4.64*c*), different from its centaur neighbour discussed above, and its suggested derivation from oriental textiles would also explain the 'heraldic' animals on our coins.[333] Comparisons with contemporary Anglo-Saxon art testify to a taste for exotic fauna, often winged and in

---

[327] Psalm 92: 12.
[328] See discussion at 'The She-Wolf'.
[329] Stevenson 1993: 24.
[330] See 'East Anglian Lions' and Fig. 4.29*a* and Newman 1999: 44.
[331] Carver 1990: 122.
[332] Abramson collection. Cf. also Hunterian 130, mentioned in *T&S* iii. 494, where the wing is interpreted as an incomplete cross.
[333] Plunkett 1998: 218, and Jewell 2001: 249–50, who sees stylistic analogies with Byzantine sculptures, as well as ivories and textiles from the Christian East.

Fig. 4.65. Series M, silver penny, mid-Secondary (obv: *BMC* 187. The British Museum, London; rev.: *T&S* 365. The Ashmolean Museum, Oxford).

Fig. 4.66. Series K-related silver penny (Abramson collection).

stylized positions,[334] and the plurality of models available,[335] to which must be added those derived from the Romano-Celtic tradition.[336]

As suggested above, Series Q, interlacing the animal in a demi-volute made of its own tail, alludes to the vine-scroll, a suitable haven for creatures of any kind, including hybrids. The prevalence of exotic hybrids in eighth-century Anglo-Saxon art, all enmeshed in their own trailing arranged so as to make a multitude of crosses,[337] indicates not only a fascination with the material wealth arriving in England, but a preoccupation with the exploration of the universality of the symbolism of salvation. Another winged animal, this time leaping forward, appears on the obverse of Series M coupled with a coiled fruiting branch, although in some variations the wings disappear (Fig. 4.65).[338] The spiralling branch and the pronouncedly arched body, curled tongue and tail of the animal seem to underline a correlation between the obverse and the reverse of the coin,[339] that is to say, the vine and the animal, inviting us to 'fit' the creature in the vine. Mental comparisons with animals interlaced in manuscripts, metal-work, sculpture, etc. would have suggested such a connection.

A fantastic creature, unique among Anglo-Saxon coinage, but which finds general counterparts in contemporary art,[340] belongs to the family that Leslie

---

[334] Webster 2001*a* for an analysis of the style, which is often labelled Anglian or Mercian.

[335] See the winged animals on the Gandersheim Casket, the Ormside Bowl (*MoE* 177, no. 138; p. 173, no. 134), the St Petersburg Gospel (Alexander 1978: no. 39), and also the creature in the top left scroll of cross-shaft from Croft on Tees (*MoE* 153, no. 115), where it is erroneously described as a bird.

[336] See for instance the bronze disc from Santon (Toynbee 1964: pl. 1*c* and p. 23). Roman engraved gems with Pegasus (e.g. Henig 1978: pl. 21, no. 662), possibly influential on the iconography of Celtic coinage (Dubnovellanus and Cunobelin: cf. Van Arsdell 1989: nos. 165-1 and 2053-1, and discussion at p. 101) would have presented prestigious prototypes, furthermore valued for their amuletic qualities (Henig 1978: 161).

[337] Stevenson 1981–2, Stiegemann and Wemhoff 1999: ii. 460, Webster 2000, and see above, Fig. 4.29*b*.

[338] *T&S* iii. 454–5.   [339] Gannon, forthcoming

[340] See for instance the detail from fo. 11ᵛ of the Barberini Gospel (Budney and Graham-Campbell 1981: 12, fig. 2*g*) for the long tripartite tails and the position of the forelimbs with differentiated digits, and the fragment in Tassilo Chalice style from Lippstadt illustrated in Stiegemann and Wemhoff 1999: ii. 464, no. VII, 24*b*.

Webster aptly describes as 'sportive beasts with streamlined bodies' (Fig. 4.66).[341] On account of the prominent triquetra and lively style, it recalls Series Q; however, it has a reverse modelled on a Series K, Type 33 lion, yet another example of the great variety and experiments pursued by die-cutters.

[341] Webster 2001*b*: 50–1, and fig. 4.

5

Reverses with Crosses, Standards/Saltires, and Porcupines

CROSSES

Originally from Constantinople, 'cross' type reverses began to be used on the reverses of the Merovingian 'National' gold coinage (*c*.570/80–670),[1] and the selection found in the Sutton Hoo hoard gives a good impression of their variety.[2] The majority of Anglo-Saxon gold coins (*c*.580–675) also have crosses on their reverses, but the treatment is often quite original. Apart from the practicality of conforming to a recognized iconography in the commercial sphere, crosses served as signifiers of adherence to Christianity and also as political statements. In the Secondary silver coinage crosses as reverses are fewer, the religious message being conveyed by an ambitious figural iconography of complex meaning.

Latin Crosses

The role of Bishop Liudhard, Queen Bertha's chaplain, in persuading King Æthelberht of Kent to accept St Augustine's mission and Christianity is not discussed by Bede,[3] but a find from the churchyard of St Martin's at Canterbury,[4] now firmly associated with him,[5] gives an insight into his position as a 'broker' for Christianity, *romanitas*, coinage, and literacy (Fig. 5.1). Liudhard's 'medalet', a looped pendant, was intended for presentation, yet it is coin-like, the first such object manufactured in England at a time when there was no independent currency. On the obverse it conforms to the norm of classical coinage, but, by adopting a patriarchal cross on the reverse, it breaks with the

[1] *MEC* 117 ff., especially p. 119 on 'cross' types.
[2] Kent 1975. See also Cabrol and Leclercq 1907–53: *Croix et Crucifix*, on coinage iconography.
[3] *HE* I, 25.
[4] St Martin's hoard: Grierson 1952; *MoE* 23, nos. 5a–h.
[5] The medalet is dated *c*.580 (Grierson 1979). The inscription was originally problematic to early scholars, who interpreted the initial character (now read as L) as 'X', a cross often preceding proper names on coins. On the refining of the reading for Liudhard, Sutherland 1948: 31 n. 3, and on the evolution of the character L and other examples of its occurrence, Evans 1942: 25–6.

Fig. 5.1. The Liudhard's 'medalet',
c.600 (M 7018, permission granted by
the Board of Trustees National
Museums and Galleries of Merseyside,
Liverpool Museum).

Fig. 5.2. *a*. 'Portrait-and-Cross'
type, gold shilling, *c*.640 (*T&S* 68
= Crondall 34. The Ashmolean
Museum, Oxford); *b*. Anglo-
Saxon gold solidus, mid-7th
century (*MEC* 665. The
Fitzwilliam Museum,
Cambridge).

contemporary numismatic tradition of portraying a 'Victory'.[6] The importance of this cross, its association with the True Cross and its relics sent to Poitiers in 569, and its allusions, have been persuasively argued by Werner,[7] who also postulates the existence of such an altar-cross at Canterbury.[8]

However, in spite of the rich symbolism and elegance, neither Liudhard's cross, nor the Merovingian-inspired 'Cross-on-Steps',[9] decorated with tau-shaped *pendilia* and topped by a star (Fig. 5.2*a*), were imitated among the immediately subsequent coinage.[10] It is simpler crosses-on steps that feature on the reverses of 'benutigo' coins, and Type BX.[11] Only Anglo-Saxon gold solidi of the seventh and the eighth centuries,[12] perhaps prestige medallic gifts, rather than

---

[6] Grierson 1952: 42.

[7] Werner 1991. See also Werner 1990, for the patriarchal cross as a carpet page design in the Book of Durrow and its symbolism.

[8] Werner 1991: 39.

[9] This is the 'Portrait-and-Cross' type from the Crondall hoard (34). Its 'rare delicacy and quality in style' suggests English workmanship to Sutherland 1948: 34.

[10] Arguably Liudhard's type of cross might be represented on the 'LEMC' coins (Crondall 27, 28, obverse and reverse, and obverses of 29 and 30, and possibly 31–3; Sutherland 1948: pl. 1, nos. 6–10) and among the 'Two Emperors' type, if we interpret the marks on the obverse on Sutherland 43 as crosses and not degenerated legends (ibid., pl. 2, no. 29). Crondall 35 has an *orbis cruciger* on steps.

[11] Sutherland 1948: pl. 1, nos. 23–6. For Type BX, see Fig. 4.1*a*.

[12] Stewart 1978. Apart from the 'skanomodu', the Valentinian and the Helena solidi (Sutherland 1948: nos. 20–2), which do not have crosses, there are three described by Grierson 1953, based on seventh-century Byzantine cross-potent-on-steps reverses (the Fitzwilliam specimen is illustrated here). The reverse of the CIOLH solidus, which Sutherland (1948: 94–5, pl. 4, no. 21) anachronistically believed to be of Ceol of Wessex (591–7), is also based on a Byzantine type of Heraclius (610–41), as Pagan 1965: 8, pointed out. Pagan reattributed it to Ciolheard, moneyer to Offa and Coenwulf, and drew attention to the two pellets featured at the top of the steps. For its obverse, see Fig. 2.24.

Fig. 5.3. *a.* WITMEN MONITA, gold shilling, *c.*640 (*T&S* 1 = Crondall 69. The Ashmolean Museum); *b.* AVDVARLÐ, gold shilling, by 640 (Tangmere find. The Fitzwilliam Museum, Cambridge); *c.* LVNDINIV, gold shilling, *c.*640 (*T&S* 52 = Crondall 54. The Ashmolean Museum, Oxford).

currency 'coins',[13] are modelled on seventh-century Byzantine 'Cross potent-on-Steps' (Fig. 5.2*b*).

On the reverse of the earliest identifiable English coin, the EVSEBII MONITA, struck at Canterbury (DOROVERNIS CIVITAS) in the early seventh century, now in Paris, there is a simple Latin cross *fourchée* on a step.[14] Similar terminals, but with the cross becoming equal-armed, perhaps because easier to fit in a circle, feature on the reverses of the WITMEN MONITA coins, also Kentish.[15] As on many Merovingian gold issues,[16] inscriptions, though often garbled, perhaps intended as Victory wreaths,[17] surround the composition of cross and circle (Fig. 5.3*a*). Presumably consciously different from Kentish reverses, issues struck at London, AVDVARLÐ REGES and LVNDINIV types, opted for a plain Latin cross on a globe and enclosed in a circle/wreath surrounded by hatching and lettering (Fig. 5.3*b*–*c*).[18]

Another coinage presumed to stem from London,[19] the CRISPVS/'delaiona' pale gold type of the second half of the seventh century, elaborates the Latin cross with ring-in-pellet ornaments as finials to the arms and top, and two small crosses set diagonally in the lower quarters,[20] inscribed in a triple dotted wreath with stylized knotted ties. The obverse is a fine imitation, albeit with the rich Anglo-Saxon texture of pellets and annulets, of a Roman coin of Crispus, and

[13] Sutherland 1948: 38; Stewart 1978: 154 n. 69.
[14] Paris, Bibliothèque Nationale (Sutherland 1948: pl. 1, no. 2). In *MEC* 160, Frankish workmanship is proposed for it.
[15] The coin illustrated here (Crondall 69), ahead of the series, clearly differentiates the base of the cross, but other specimens turn it into a forked terminal.
[16] Cf. *MEC* pls. 20–5.
[17] Stevenson 1981–2: 5.
[18] For the AVDVARLÐ obverse, see p. 46, Fig. 2.32, and for the legends, see Blackburn 1998*b*: 3, and Williams 1998: 139–40. One LVNDINIV variety in the de Wit collection (ex-Subjack 1) has an annulet and a mark below the cross's arms representing alpha and omega, but omits the globe.
[19] *T&S* i. 44. Four coins are known: one from St Albans (*BM*), two from Coddenham, and one from Eyke.
[20] On a specimen from Eyke, Suffolk (*Coin Register* 1993: no. 65) there are two annulets on top of the cross, which is in a double pelleted circle.

Fig. 5.4. CRISPVS/'delaiona', gold shilling (CM 1934, 10-13-1. The British Museum, London).

has a Latin inscription, while the reverse carries one in runic: a successful synthesis of coinage, Christianity, *romanitas*, and literacy (Fig. 5.4).[21]

Among the transitional series, some reverses of the VANIMUNDUS type have Merovingian-inspired crosses on a globe, with the letters C and A appended.[22] Later, in the silver coinage, we encounter Latin crosses, always associated with birds, on the reverses of Series BZ, Types 29a/b,[23] BIIIc and Series J, Type 85 and the obverses of Series J, Types 37 and 72.[24] They also often feature as attributes on obverses,[25] and as tall processional crosses/apotropaic symbols on the reverses of numerous Secondary Series.[26]

Greek Crosses

As WITMEN MONITA types evolved, the tendency was for the Latin cross to turn into a Greek one, forked on all limbs. This trend is common among Anglo-Saxon issues, gold and later: in contrast with the directionality of Merovingian designs, Anglo-Saxon crosses become patterns,[27] akin to those discernible on jewels, brooches, and pendants, though not all of the latter, of course, carry Christian connotations.[28] Sutherland had already identified similarities between jewelled disc brooches and coins;[29] parallels are indeed ubiquitous (Fig. 5.5).[30]

---

[21] See ex-Subjack 93 (Series W) for two similar crosses with prominent annulet terminals as hand-held attributes.

[22] These are believed to be derived from coins of Chalon-sur-Saône (*T&S* i. 81–2).

[23] Some specimens of Series BZ, Types 29a and 29b (*BMC* 143–4; Mack 320 and one in the de Wit collection) have Latin crosses *fourchées* and annulets, unlike those in *T&S* i, pl. 7, nos. 138–9 with plain Greek crosses.

[24] The obverses of Series J, Types 37 and 72 have tall crosses between confronting heads (Fig. 2.19), but the reverses have birds (see Figs. 4.3*a* and *b*, 4.11*a*).

[25] See e.g. Fig. 2.60.

[26] See Chapter 3 for relevant examples.

[27] For instance, the 'cross' types inspired by Merovingian *tremisses* (Crondall 39–53, Sutherland 1948: 77 and pl. 1, nos. 18–22) with on one side a simplified cross *ancrée* (a cross topped by a curved segment) on a linear base: on the other face this becomes a unidirectional cross moline, i.e. a Greek cross topped by four curved segments.

[28] MacGregor and Bolick 1993: 79.

[29] Sutherland 1937: fig. 1. His coin-evolution theories, however, are now superseded.

[30] The design of the coin Series R, Type R2z (Fig. 5.5*e*) might be a 'Greek cross version' of the 'delaiona' reverse, also in a triple border (above, Fig. 5.4). On the obverse it has a laterally reversed bust (see Fig. 2.30*b*), a variant of a find from Garton-on-the-Wolds and of one in Glasgow (Hunterian 15). Triple

Fig. 5.5. *a–c.* pendants from Compton Verney, Warwickshire; Ducklington, Oxfordshire; and Faversham, Kent, late 6th/early 7th century (1948.134, 1971.472, and 1942.223. The Ashmolean Museum, Oxford); *d.* jewelled disc brooch from Milton, Abingdon, Oxfordshire, mid-7th century (1836.123.59. The Ashmolean Museum, Oxford); *e.* Series R, Type R2z, silver penny, Secondary (3031, de Wit Collection); *f.* WITMEN MONITA, gold shilling, *c.*640; *g.* 'London-Derived', gold shilling, *c.*640; *h.* Series H, Type 48, silver penny, mid/late Secondary (*f, g,* and *h. T&S* 1 = Crondall 69; *T&S* 22 = Crondall 60; *T&S* 291. The Ashmolean Museum, Oxford).

The more elaborate patterns comprise more than one cross, and demand visual alertness. The stepped-cross pattern of Series E, Type 53[31] calls to mind, besides garnet jewellery,[32] multiple crosses on manuscripts' carpet pages.[33] The double cross with crosslets of Intermediate Series Z ('Aston Rowant' type) and Series W (with a *Chi*-cross) also recalls such geometry (Fig. 5.6). It is likely that this proliferation of crosses mirrors a form of devotion with a long history in Christian art.[34]

pelleted borders, on coins of Series R, Type R3, also feature on the LICINVS, WUNEETON, and 'æðiliræd' issues. The design is also found on Type 81 (Hamwic 124, *T&S* ii. 292). Cf. *T&S* iii. 510. The parallel with the seventh-century pendant from Compton Verney (and many others can be found) may be hoped to answer Prof. Metcalf's doubts concerning the cross design on the Garton find (*T&S* iii. 450).

[31] The English/Continental origin of the Type is debated (*T&S* ii. 243–5).

[32] Baldwin Brown 1903–37: iii. 89.

[33] Examples abound, but in particular see fo. 85[v] of the Book of Durrow (Meehan 1996: 47); fos. 94[v] and 210[v] in the Lindisfarne Gospels (Backhouse 1981: 48, fig. 28, and p. 56, fig. 34); the Nestorian manuscript in Stevenson 1981–2: 3, fig. 2; and also the crosses framing the eagle symbol of St John: Cambridge, Corpus Christi College, MS 197B, fo. 1 (G. Henderson 1987: 77, fig. 109).

[34] Stevenson, 1981–2: 15.

Fig. 5.6. *a.* Series E, Type 53, silver penny, Intermediate; *b.* Series W, silver penny, Intermediate (*T&S* 258 and 155. The Ashmolean Museum, Oxford).

Fig. 5.7. *a–b.* 'Triquetras' group, Type 52, silver pennies, Secondary (*BMC* 198. The British Museum, London; *T&S* 341. The Ashmolean Museum, Oxford); *c.* 'Celtic Cross with rosettes', Type 34b, silver penny, Secondary (*T&S* 346. The Ashmolean Museum, Oxford).

Comparisons have been drawn between Merovingian plaster-of-Paris sarcophagi of the Paris region and jewellery, especially pewter brooches, with crosses and rosettes inscribed in circles,[35] patterns that also relate to our coins. Although Patrick Périn, who replicated the technology, stresses the utilitarian simplicity of the shapes,[36] which in any case derive from shared Mediterranean designs, it is the enduring apotropaic appeal of the symbols and their application that are of interest.[37] However, if some designs only require the use of elementary tools and limited technical expertise,[38] the construction of the Celtic and Triquetras crosses of the Secondary Series is of great sophistication (Fig. 5.7), and it relates to manuscript illumination and stone carving,[39] which utilized complex patterns and templates.[40] When one considers that these designs, as with the

[35] Fossard 1963. Compare the reverse of the coins reading EAN (Crondall 94, Sutherland 1948: pl. 4, no. 27; however, it should be noted that the cross is mounted on a staff that breaks the circle) with the Merovingian sarcophagus panel and the Anglo-Saxon pewter brooch illustrated in Peroni 1967: figs. 4 and 7. See ibid. 21.

[36] Périn 1980: 36–42, especially p. 39. Crosses with pellets are used extensively for the Continental Series D (*T&S* ii. 184–95).

[37] See also Fossard 1963: 37, figs. 26–7, and Casartelli Novelli 1992: 544.

[38] Périn 1980: 39; *MEC* 119.

[39] The central motif on the cross at Northallerton (J. Lang 2001: figs 672–3) is germane to the iconography of the coins discussed here. I am grateful to Mr D. Craig, for having brought it to my attention.

[40] Wilson 1984: 38, figs. 28–9; Stevick 1994.

Celtic Cross and the bird-in-vine types, were produced concurrently at several mints, one cannot postulate a progressive simplification/rationalization among these designs.[41] Rather, it is a question of experimenting with different models and ideas. The combination of crosses, rosettes and triquetras, voids and solids, positive and negative,[42] crosses made up of simple lines or groupings of pellets, could be read as crosses or *Chi*-crosses, and the prominent five bosses or pellets as allusions to the wounds of Christ. These multi-directional crosses, as discussed for the motif of four birds-on-cross,[43] might also allude to the cosmological Cross, and the universality of redemption.[44] The complex geometry, like the comparable interlocking crosses on religious objects,[45] engages the attention and would have suggested meditations ('visual incantations', as Pirotte puts it)[46] on the centrality of the Cross. Its apotropaic value may have been paramount to personal devotion and in the continuation of the iconography on secular artefacts.[47]

By analogy with the eucharistic bunches of grapes in the Book of Kells, the pelleted rosettes that appear between the arms of the crosses on our coins can be interpreted as clusters of berries.[48] Similar bunches appear among the curling vine-scrolls decorating the Lowther Cross,[49] and the plant-scroll at Breedon: both compare to those in the coils of Series M, and point to a eucharistic reading for this design (Fig. 5.8).[50]

Variations are ever possible: some coins combine various Greek crosses inscribed in circles with elements such as trefoils, which may be interpreted as simplified triquetras,[51] or groups of three pellets.[52] Although arguably traditional decorative space fillers,[53] the four triads might have become significant.[54]

[41] *T&S* iii. 424–5, 430, 432, and 553.

[42] Visually one can focus on the designs under the arms of the crosses dividing the field. Figure-ground illusion (Bradley and Dumais 1975) is characteristic of carpet page layouts and of other compositions, as on discs and brooches (e.g. *MoE* nos. 66c, 170–1, 184–7, 189, 194, 198, etc., dating eighth/ninth century). See also Pirotte 2001: 204–5 on Gestalt Theory.

[43] See Fig. 4.3.

[44] Esmeijer 1978: 47–53, esp. 50; McEntire 1986: 349; O'Reilly 1998: 77–94.

[45] See the Ormside Bowl and the copper-alloy mount, Whitby (*MoE* 173, no. 134, and p. 142, no. 107a).

[46] Pirotte 2001: 204.

[47] As on the ninth-century silver openwork disc-brooch from Beeston Tor, Staffs. (*MoE* 270, no. 245a). Nestled between the arms of the cross there are four trefoils, a motif perhaps related to the *crux foliata*. A similar trefoil appears on a copper-alloy stud from Appleby, Lincs., comparable to a Carolingian enamelled plaque from Borken (Stiegemann and Wemhof 1999: i. 343, no. VI.24, where the motif is described as a lilyform cross).

[48] Rosettes of pellets also feature on some obverses: see Fig. 2.69.

[49] For similar renderings of grape bunches at Hexham: Bailey and Cramp 1988: pl. 175, figs. 926–7, and pl. 176, figs. 929–30. Wilson 1984: 75, suggests the Lowther Cross represents 'both the Cross and Christ in almost iconoclastic vein on one monument'.

[50] See also *T&S*, iii, pl. 26, no. 441 for creatures pecking at a rosette-shaped bunch.

[51] See the coin from Barking Abbey (*MoE* 93, no. 67w), and that from near St Neots (*T&S* iii. 448), which Metcalf, however, interprets as 'four letters T in the segments of a circle'.

[52] *T&S* iii, pl. 22, no. 378, and pp. 478–80.

[53] Compare the trefoil motif on the Manton Common escutcheon (Brenan 1991: 247, no. 41).

[54] Klein-Pfeuffer 1993: 131–2, on triquetras under the arms of crosses paralleled on German brooches (e.g. Pfalheim, ibid., pl. 56, no. 260), and as symbols of the Trinity on many artefacts. The eighth-century Sacramentarium Gellonense, fo. 37ᵛ (Dumas 1981: fig. 35) has a comparable roundel with a cross and triquetras. Hopper 1969: 70–4 and 83–4, discusses the symbolism of the numbers three and four in early medieval Christian thought.

Fig. 5.8. *a*. detail of the Lowther Cross, Lowther, Westmorland, 8th century (© The British Museum, London); *b*. Series M, silver penny, Secondary (*T&S* 366. The Ashmolean Museum, Oxford); *c*. detail of *fo*. 32ᵛ, the Book of Kells, MS A.1.6 (58), mid-8th century, Trinity College Library, Dublin (The Board of Trinity College Dublin); *d*. detail from the plant-scroll at Breedon-on-the-Hill, Leicestershire, late 8th century (© The Conway Library, Courtauld Institute of Art).

Fig. 5.9. *a*. 'Saltire-standard', Type 51, silver penny, Secondary (4458, de Wit collection); *b*. detail from the pendant from Faversham, Kent (MME 11-45, 70. The British Museum. Photograph: Dr N. Whitfield, reproduced by courtesy of the Trustees of the National Museums of Scotland).

On some coins the pattern of the cross is made up of four V-shaped scrolls (Fig. 5.9),[55] often found in seventh-century filigree jewellery and combined in a cross shape on early brooches, but with no Christian connotations.[56] This composition, of late Roman provincial origin, and pleasing pattern for a round shape, is sometimes described as a floriate cross or *Ankerkreutz*.[57]

Another form of Greek cross is the simple quatrefoil 'Solomon's knot'[58] of Type 43 (Fig. 5.10*a*), used on Anglo-Saxon and Frisian coins.[59] Compared to the angular designs of Continental coins, the Anglo-Saxon pattern is rounded and regular, with five pellets placed within the design and with additional segments

---

[55] These coins are mentioned in *T&S* iii. 531, where the specimen from Tilbury, with a saltire on its reverse, is illustrated. On the reverse of the coin illustrated here, in the de Wit collection, there are groups of three pellets under the arms of a Greek cross inscribed in a circle.

[56] See for instance the applied saucer-brooch pair from Highdown, Sussex, mid-fifth century (Welch 1983: no. 3403–4, p. 626, fig. 110*c*), and the gold brooch from Dürrmenz (Klein-Pfeuffer 1993: pl. 87, no. 53). See also *MoE* 275, no. 249*a*.

[57] Welch 1983: 39–41. Klein-Pfeuffer 1993: 141 interprets the pattern as heart-shaped.

[58] Stevenson 1981–2: 24 n. 52. The motif is ancient and widely used: Holmqvist 1939: 61; Salin 1949–59: iv. 129–30, and could have been familiar to the Anglo-Saxons from Roman mosaics.

[59] The Continental issues are sometimes labelled as 'Maastricht' types (*MEC* 151–2, pl. 30, no. 634; *T&S* ii. 258–62; Zedelius 1980: 145; Op den Velde, De Boone, and Pol 1984: 138).

Fig. 5.10. *a*. Type 43, 'Monster/Interlace' silver penny, Secondary; *b*. penny of King Beonna of East Anglia, Interlace type, *c*.760? (Royston 45 and *MEC* 1121*a*. The Fitzwilliam Museum, Cambridge).

Fig. 5.11. 'Constantine' type from Caistor, very debased gold shilling or silver penny (3414, de Wit collection).

between the arms. The pattern, which already on the seventh-century pendant from Ash may be taken to signify Christian belief,[60] can be perceived as the dominant shape formed by the zoomorphic interlace in the filigree vine-scroll on the Windsor pommel.[61] Another type of cross, based on a more elaborate interlaced pattern, is featured on some of Beonna's coins (Fig. 5.10*b*). The pattern, sometimes further entwined in a circle, forms continuous positive crosses by its own interlace; in Germanic Western Europe it is traditionally zoomorphic,[62] but, as its use on Christian artefacts testifies, no doubt invested with Christian significance. [63]

Already experimented with as a traditional jewellery pattern, easy to execute and ideal to fit on a flan, the Greek cross is, with the bust, the most long-lived of designs. The Anglo-Saxons would have enjoyed the endless possibility for visual play and for sophisticated renderings of the Christian message.

Marigolds

A very debased *tremissis* of the 'Constantine' type from Caistor-by-Norwich has on its reverse an eight-rayed motif (Fig. 5.11).[64] It recalls Merovingian coins with a Christogram in a wreath,[65] but differs both in the number of arms and in their terminals. The symbol might be related to those found on the obverses of two 'Constantines' (Billockby and Coddenham 285), and suggests an eight-pointed

[60]   This is also argued for Continental metalwork such as the Bartenbach pendant (Klein-Pfeuffer 1993: 121–3 and p. 474, no. 348), though for earlier pieces (like inlaid sixth-century buckles) the intention would have been generically decorative/apotropaic. For the Ash pendant, see *MoE* 25, no. 8.

[61]   The Windsor sword-pommel, second half of the eighth century (*MoE* 226, no. 180). See also the interlace on the Gandersheim Casket and one of the Witham pins (Fig. 4.29*b*) and its interpretation.

[62]   Stevenson 1981–2: 9; Smith 1923: pl. 3, no. 2.

[63]   The motif appears on a panel of the Chur reliquary (Poeschel 1948: 149, fig. 151), and also on an unparalleled Lombard bracteate cross from Zanica (Bergamo), sixth/seventh century (Menis 1990: 228, V13).

[64]   *T&S* i. 47–8. For 'Constantines', see Figs. 2.59 and 2.72.

[65]   For example, the coin from the Rheims region (*MEC* pl. 28, no. 607). These designs are echoed on Merovingian plaster sarcophagi (Périn 1980: 39, fig. 29).

Fig. 5.12. *a*. detail from the
front panel of the Franks
Casket, Northumbrian, 8th
century (MME 1867, 1-20, 1.
© The British Museum,
London); *b*. lead ampulla
from Palestine, 6th century
(no. 1, Museo del Duomo,
Monza, Italy).

star,[66] but its symmetry and use of pellets aligns it with the geometrical crosses found on other *tremisses*,[67] so that it reads as a complex cross, perhaps a marigold.[68] Marigolds were classical ornamental motifs, known from imported goods and imitated on brooches,[69] but are also often met in Anglo-Saxon illuminated Gospel books and sculpture.[70]

Another marigold appears on the Franks Casket to represent the star guiding the Magi, traditionally used to accompany representations of the Epiphany in the Palestinian tradition (Fig. 5.12).[71] This enriches the reading of the other marigolds noted in Gospel books: far from being just decorative, they allude to the Incarnation of Christ, so the cross of St Luke in the Lichfield Gospels unites both ideas of Christ, his birth and his death.

The juxtaposition of a marigold on the reverse and cross on the obverse of the coin may have been intentional, and such rich allusions might have occurred to the more sophisticated. To the majority the symbol was more probably read simply as a variation on a cross, with no further exegetical thought. The marigold-motif is not used in the Secondary Series, and is not encountered again until Offa's time, when it features on some coins of Archbishop Iænberht.[72]

---

[66] Discussed at "Bust and Star".   [67] Cf. *MEC* pl. 28, no. 607.

[68] For marigold crosses: Stevenson 1981–2: 2 ff.

[69] A marigold forms the central motif on one of the silver bowls from Sutton Hoo (Carver 1998: 133, fig. 83). Many saucer-brooches in Anglo-Saxon England have classically derived decorations, such as spirals, stars, rosettes, etc., as on the fifth-/sixth-century Anglo-Saxon saucer-brooches from Kempston, Bedfordshire (MacGregor and Bollick 1993: 47, no. 2.27, and see ibid. 42 ff.). The motif is also found on the Continent: Klein-Pfeuffer 1993: 142–5.

[70] Among the manuscripts, the marigold features at the centre of the Cross of St Luke, p. 218 of the Lichfield Gospels (G. Henderson 1987: 122, fig. 180); other instances include the Lindisfarne Gospels, fo. 26ᵛ, the Book of Kells, fo. 8, the Echternach Gospels, fo. 18ᵛ (G. Henderson 1987: 103, 143, and 74, nos. 145, 208, and 102), the Codex Aureus, fo. 8ᵛ (Wilson 1984: 92, fig. 101) and in the eighth-century Sacramentarium Gellonense, at fos. 38ᵛ, 54ᵛ, 90, 91, and 164ᵛ (Dumas 1981: figs. 37, 43, 75, 77, and 104). Among the sculpture, see the examples at Lastingham and Middleton (Lang 1991: pls. 582 and 694).

[71] See also the fragment of a bronze cross, Palestinian, sixth century (Ross 1962–5: i. 56, pl. 40, no. 65).

[72] For Archbishop Iænberht's coins see Blunt 1961: pl. 7, nos. 130–1.

Fig. 5.13. *a–b*. 'Abbo' and 'Bust/LOND',
gold shillings, *c*.640 (*T&S* 72 = Crondall
25 and 71 = Crondall 36. The Ashmolean
Museum, Oxford).

Crossed Instruments

The reverses of the Gold phase, as we have seen, tend to experiment with the design of crosses. Two coins in the Crondall hoard (*c*.640), one with the legend ABBONI MANET, probably a direct copy from a Merovingian coin of Abbo of Chalon,[73] and one among the 'Bust/LOND' issues, also close to Merovingian prototypes, arrange disparate objects in cross-like compositions (Fig. 5.13).

Sutherland interpreted the ABBONI MANET reverse as a superimposition of three discrete objects: a processional cross, a crozier, and a 'trident'.[74] Because of its association with other religious objects, he tentatively suggested the 'trident' might be a *candelabrum*.[75] Indeed, on some Merovingian reverses, crosses are dressed with candles balanced at the extremities of their arms, resembling a trident, and bifurcate bases are also known;[76] Bailey has also argued for the possibility that the series of holes on the fragment of the cross-head from Rothbury may have held candles.[77] Sutherland also relates it to the 'trident' shown on the obverse of the WITMEN group,[78] though the WITMEN 'trident', with a further bifurcation on the central prong, may well be an unrelated object.[79]

In a Christian context tridents are rare;[80] however, they would have been known from Roman coinage, as attributes of Neptune normally accompanied by dolphins, and also from Celtic coins, either in a plain field or hand held,[81] and familiar also from mosaic floors or tombstones.[82] A fine Romano-British bronze

[73] The English origin is debated: *MEC* 162. On Abbo, presumed master of Eligius, see Sutherland 1948: 33, and *MEC* 98–9.

[74] Sutherland 1948: 33, rejected the previous interpretation of the design as a six-armed cross with degenerate alpha and omega *pendilia* (a common Merovingian detail). His new reading bears 'no relationship with anything devised in Gaul at any time', hence the Anglo-Saxon attribution.

[75] Sutherland, ibid., n. 5.

[76] For instance see the Merovingian reverse (Cabrol and Leclercq 1907–53: *Croix et Crucifix*, fig. 3391, no. 14 and col. 3097) which shows a cross on a globe, with candles on top of the arms and symmetrical letters below; and the Merovingian coin obverse (?Tours area) from the Sutton Hoo purse (Kent 1975: pl. 27, no. 34) with a cross on a splayed bifurcate base with *pendilia* below the arms.

[77] Bailey 1996: 9.   [78] Sutherland 1948: 33.

[79] See discussion at 'Bust and "Tridents"'.   [80] Cabrol and Leclercq 1907–53: *Trident*.

[81] See for instance the Roman *denarius* of Pompey, *c*.38 BC (Reece 1983: 169, no. 139*a*) and the Celtic coins of Verica, first century AD (Van Arsdell 1989: 161, no. 486-1, and p. 462, no. 487-1). Also the Celtic trident on the Farley Heath sceptre binding (Goodchild 1947: 83–5; Green 1976: 219).

[82] See the tombstone of Titus Valerius Pudens, 2nd Legion 'Adiutrix', from Lincoln, with a trident and mattock (Brailsford 1951: 60, fig. 28, VI*b*), and the representation on the third-century mosaic from Withington, Glos. (ibid. 58, pl. 23.4). Tridents are also shown on *terra sigillata* ware as weapons of gladiators (Oswald 1964: 51).

Fig. 5.14. Romano-British bronze bowl, Nun's Bridge, Hinchinbrooke, Huntingdon (D.1967 4. Museum of Archaeology and Anthropology, University of Cambridge).

bowl, with smith's and other tools between bearded heads,[83] makes an interesting comparison with the motifs on our coins (Fig. 5.14).

A crossed hammer and arrow (punch?) forming the reverse of the 'Bust/LOND' coin—similar to the combination on the bowl of a decussate hook and trident, plus a hammer, the trade tools, or perhaps the 'badge' of a moneyer or die-cutter, may have been the prototype for the arrangement on the reverse of the ABBONI MANET. Perhaps the idea of transforming the original arrangement of die-cutter's tools sealed by a cross into a Christian composition may have been suggested by the similarity between these 'tools' and those of a bishop: the hook would easily turn into a crozier, and the 'trident' into a *candelabrum*. Whatever the origin of the composition, 'Abbo's coin' is certainly a most elegant and effective exercise in cross-shaped designs, which furthermore echoes the sacred monogram.

Offa's Crosses

The introduction of an epigraphic coinage is one of Offa's innovations conforming to current Anglo-Saxon and Continental practice,[84] but the integration of the lettering into the overall pattern of the reverses is distinctive,[85] and the variations on the design extraordinary. As Blunt pointed out, such vitality is in marked con-

---

[83] For the bronze bowl see discussion in Green 1976: 25 and 209 on possible interpretations in a Romano-Celtic iconographical context, and p. 110 on smiths' tools as pottery decoration.

[84] I shall here concentrate simply on the iconography of the coins, with no distinction between light coinage (*c.*765–92) and heavy coinage (*c.*792–6). See discussion on Offa's coinage in Williams 2001*a*: 212–19.

[85] Whereas it was usual in Northumbria (from the time of Aldfrith: 685–704: see Fig. 4.25) for the royal name to be arranged around a central feature on reverses (Northumbrian Series Y and the 'Moneyer's-Name Series': *T&S* iii. 576–600), in the south the complex iconography of the coins of the Secondary Series left little space for lettering, the main exceptions being the London inscribed Series and runes representing moneyers' names on the obverses of Series R (*T&S* iii. 502–23). Towards the end of Series R, characteristic of the work of the moneyers Wigræd and Tilbeorht (ibid. 520) is the integration of runes and design. In Wigræd's case the drapery incorporates the shape X (see Fig. 2.31*a*) whereas the final runes of Tilbeorht's name are arranged as to suggest a chin beard (Fig. 2.31*b*). The coins of King Beonna

trast with the uniformity of contemporary Continental coinage,[86] especially considering how closely Offa's coinage shadowed economic changes in fabric and weight across the Channel,[87] and all the more remarkable in its permutations when considering that Offa's issues were striving towards standardization.[88] That Offa's coinage mirrors the richness of Anglo-Saxon art has been recognized many times,[89] and the present study stresses the experimental, even the exotic, besides the traditional in some designs: thus one can postulate the wealth of models available, and the taste and curiosity of the king.[90]

Few of Offa's coins conform to Continental contemporary reverses, where inscriptions form a continuous border around the central motif:[91] the majority are based on variations on a cross quartering the legend, which may be seen as traditionally organizing motifs into panels.[92] Among these is a cross with annulets struck for Offa by the moneyer Eoba, a design also used for the coins Eoba struck in the name of two Kentish kings, Headberht and Ecgberht.[93] The cross with annulets as terminals is a traditional pattern,[94] but the addition of a central boss, and the emphasis placed on its subsequent expanded version, will be influential in anchoring the focus of the composition to the centre of the coin. It is from this centre that the additional elements making up the arms of the cross and the letters forming the inscription depart, playing visually on the positive/negative possibilities of the composition, so that one can concentrate either on the cross or on the lettering.[95] Having established the basic model, whilst still retaining a distinctive look, all manner of inventive variations are possible, either by changing the terminals of the crosses,[96] or by turning the centre into a lozenge. On some coins the expanded cross is reminiscent of the 'Celtic Cross and Rosettes' type of the Secondary Series (Fig. 5.15).[97]

(Archibald 1985), which replaced the debased East Anglian issues of Series R in the mid-eighth century, although not directly associated, show certain affinities in type and detail to the Northumbrian issues (ibid. 31 on questions of fineness and dating): the king's name and title, sometimes mixing runic and Roman characters, are arranged around a central feature. Characteristic of these compositions is the geometrical subdividing of the lettering in sectors. Legends and monograms were used on Carolingian, Lombard, and papal coinages.

[86] Blunt 1961: 42–3, stresses the utilitarian nature of the Continental coinage.

[87] *MEC* 277 ff. Offa's coins, however, were always lighter than the contemporary Carolingian issues.

[88] Stewart 1986: 28.

[89] Beginning with Keary 1875, stating that the art on Offa's coins was entirely native (p. 214) and showing points of contact with the style of illuminated manuscripts, all the major studies stress the artistic qualities of the coinage (Lockett 1920, Blunt 1961, Stewart 1986, Chick 1997).

[90] As discussed above, for the iconography of his coinage.

[91] See for instance Blunt 1961: pl. 7, nos. 110–23.

[92] As discussed above under 'Encircled Heads'.

[93] Blunt 1961: 40–1 (the Kentish coins are illustrated ibid., pl. 1, nos. 1 and 3); Chick 1997: 49–50. Chick 1997: 60 n. 14 considers the coin of Offa (Blunt 1961: pl. 1, no. 10) as later than the specimen he illustrates on pl.1, no. 6, which he believes also to predate Ecgberht's.

[94] See Fig. 5.5*e* and n. 30 above.

[95] A traditionally complex way of seeing (see p. 163).

[96] See the coins of Eoba, Ealred, and Alhmund (Blunt 1961: nos. 13, 15, 9, and 43).

[97] For the 'Celtic Cross' as prototype: Blunt 1961: 13, and see the coins in the name of Pehtwald and of Tirwald (ibid., nos. 73–5 and 79–80).

Fig. 5.15. Pennies of Offa of Mercia (757–96). *a–b.* moneyers Eadhun and Eoba (*MEC* 1126, 1127 The Fitzwilliam Museum, Cambridge); *c.* moneyer Wihtred (*BMC* 55. The British Museum. London).

Fig. 5.16. Pennies of Offa of Mercia (757–96). *a–b.* moneyers Dud and Alhmund (*BMC* 13 and 8. The British Museum, London); *c.* moneyer Ethilvald (*MEC* 1128. The Fitzwilliam Museum, Cambridge).

Amongst the most interesting designs on coins of Offa are four-lobed crosses, a classical pattern of segments of arches touching at one point and forming linked chains, often found on mosaics and other artefacts.[98] Four-lobed crosses are sometimes combined with delicate trefoils,[99] and vegetation motifs are also used as terminals in their own right, and on some coins of Dud and Ethilvald a triple-branched sprig is placed in front of Offa's bust on the obverse, which Lockett interprets as a palm, a sign of victory and peace (Fig. 5.16).[100]

Whilst one could look to traditional jewellery for precedents for the Greek crosses of the Secondary Series, the subdivision of the field by means of lobes and lozenges on Offa's coins looks forward to early ninth-century metalwork, anticipating the lentoid and subtriangular fields preferred by the Trewhiddle style,

[98] For instance, see the running decoration on the arms of the crosses on the silver bowls from Sutton Hoo (Care Evans 1994: 60–1, figs. 44–5). See also the fragment reputedly from the Cross of Eligius, now in the Bibliothèque National in Paris (*Les Francs* 1997: 32, fig. 32).

[99] Compare the coin from Barking Abbey (*MoE* 93, no. 67*w*).

[100] Lockett 1920: 78. The coins of Dud and Ethilvald (ex-Lockett 350 and 2643) are illustrated as nos. 31 and 58 in Blunt 1961. Four-lobed crosses appear on a new variety of Archbishop Iænberht and Offa: (*EMC* number: 2000.0049).

Fig 5.17. The right-hand disc of the Witham pin-set, from Fiskerton, Lincolnshire late 8th century (MME 1856, 11-11, 4. © The British Museum, London).

Fig. 5.18. Series Pa, transitional pale gold shillings of Pada, *c*.670–80 (*a*. PaIB, 4307, de Wit collection; *b*. PaIIA, *MEC* 668. The Fitzwilliam Museum, Cambridge).

testifying to the innovative work of the ateliers. The Pentney hoard of brooches offers many points of comparison,[101] as does the right-hand disc, believed to be a replacement, in the set of the Witham Pins, where a lobed-cross emerges in the negative, behind one with expanded terminals (Fig. 5.17).[102] Details in manuscript illumination also testify to the legacy of a much richer corpus of art from Offa's time,[103] of which little besides the coins remains as testimony to an innovative vigour too often ascribed *tout court* only to the Carolingian school.

STANDARDS AND SALTIRES

We saw how, when copying the 'Two Emperors' type, the Anglo-Saxon die-cutters, limited by the size of the flans, chose to select just part of the Roman prototype.[104] It is again a detail from Roman coinage that furnished material for a reverse used both in the pale gold and the silver coinage: the lettering TOT XX in a square,[105] normally referred to as a 'standard'. Whilst it is certain that the origin is Roman, it is debatable from which amongst the many possible

---

[101] *MoE* 229–30, nos. 187*a–f*. See also the division of the field on the Strickland brooch (*MoE* 232–3, no. 189).

[102] The lobed-shaped 'arm-pit' is innovative compared to the more usual round ones deployed on the other two.

[103] See the detail on the right-hand side roundel on the canon table of the Canterbury Bible (London, British Library, Royal I.E.VI) illustrated in Wilson 1984: 95, fig. 103.

[104] See Fig. 3.8.

[105] It is usually believed that the substitution TOT for VOT is due to assimilation, maybe for symmetry; however, the inscription TOT appears on the bezel of Roman rings found in Britain, and it is thought to stand for Toutatis, the principal Celtic deity in Gaul and Britain (Johns 1996: 59 and fig. 3.19; Marshall 1911: 185, ring, no. 1169; Walters 1921: plaque, no. 230). The Ts may also have been considered Tau crosses.

prototypes bearing the inscription VOT XX it was derived.[106] It is first adopted as a reverse on the transitional coinage of Pada, and the design is commonly referred to as a 'standard' (Fig. 5.18a). If, however, we consider chronologically the juxtaposing of types with inscriptions contained either in a square 'standard' or in a circular wreath, it appears that it is TOT XX, not the 'standard', that is the innovative borrowing, and that Pada's coinage was experimenting with organizing lettering in shapes. On the earliest type from Finglesham, Pada's name (in runes) is in a square;[107] it is then presented in a circular wreath (Fig. 5.18b), and other types shows it outside a circle—or on the side of the 'standard'.[108] The triangular appendages (perhaps stylized wreath-ties, by analogy with the earlier 'Constantine' type, though usually interpreted and described as a *tufa*)[109] are framed between symmetrical letters.[110] It is also worth noticing how the contours of both square and circle are rendered with pellets, unlike the solid Roman contours, but very much in the Anglo-Saxon tradition.[111]

The TOT inscribed 'standard', a successful and respected design with strong Roman echoes, became a very influential reverse in Anglo-Saxon coinage and its imitations. It continued in the coinage succeeding Pada's in Kent, that of Series A,[112] whose importance in the iconography of Series C and R (Fig. 5.19),[113] and related later Series,[114] has rightly been stressed.[115]

Endless permutations of the basic design are employed for the reverses of the plentiful, though artistically indifferent, Continental Series E and D, Type 8. Whether these reverses are derived from Series A or Series C is unsure.[116] The relief, both on coins of Series E and D, is characteristically very deep. In Series E (porcupines, Fig. 5.20a), there is usually a geometrical arrangement of marks

---

[106] One could quote: FELICITAS ROMANORVM (shield: Kent and Painter 1977: 185, no. 822), BEATA TRANQUILLITAS (inscribed altar), CONSTANTINI MAX AVG (inscription in wreath), VICTORIAE LAETAE (standard between two standing figures), and VIRTVS EXERCIT (standard between two prisoners: these four types are illustrated in Casey 1994: pl. 19, nos. 4, 6, 2, and 3). VIRTVS EXERCIT is the prototype suggested by Hill 1951: 251, and Kent 1961: 11. The coin bears on the obverse a helmeted Crispus, on which the Anglo-Saxon obverse was modelled (see Fig. 2.42a). However, as Kent himself notes (ibid. 10), mixed copying from several prototypes was the norm, so this argument is not conclusive.

[107] Rigold 1960: pl. 2: —, 2 Finglesham.

[108] *T&S* i, 4, nos. 82–3, and for the 'standard', pl. 4, no. 81.

[109] For the 'Constantine' type coin, see Fig. 2.71, and its discussion.

[110] An unconventional orientation of Pada's coin Pa III (*T&S* i, pl. 4, no. 82 and *MEC* pl. 31, no. 669), will show Pada's name inscribed in a wide triangular field. Also, on Rigold 1960: PIA, 1 Pada's name is inscribed in an oblong but it appears upside-down to the pelleted cross outside the oblong. This again testifies to the experimental character of the coinage.

[111] It is intriguing to find the only other 'square' on a reverse of a pale gold issue from York, now in the British Museum (Fig. 2.4b). The four faces and arms around the square bear comparison with those elements of Pada's and later standards usually described as *tufa* and horns, and particularly with the imitation of Series R, ex-Subjack, 74.

[112] See Rigold's scheme (Rigold 1960: p. 10, fig. 1, and above, Fig. 2.28).

[113] The division between Series C and R is disputed (see Ch. 2 n. 144).

[114] Other early Anglo-Saxon series that adopt the motifs are the VERNUS and SAROALDO types (*T&S* i. 140–6 (but see Blackburn and Bonser 1984a) and *T&S* i. 147–51.

[115] *T&S* i. 86.

[116] *T&S* ii. 197 and 211. As they do not reproduce the triangular element (ribbon/*tufa*), they seem closer to Series C; however, some specimens of the Kloster Barthe hoard do (*T&S* ii. 235, fig. die A).

Fig. 5.19. *a*. Series A, Type 2a, silver penny, Primary; *b*. Series C, silver penny, late Primary; *c*. Series R, silver penny, Secondary (*BMC* 22; CM 1935, 11-17-290; *BMC* 43. The British Museum, London).

Fig. 5.20. Series E, silver penny, Intermediate. *a*. 'Aston Rowant' variety; *b*. VICO type (CM 1971, 12-16-41 and 1935, 11-17-238. The British Museum, London); Series D, 'Continental Runic' type, late Primary/Intermediate; *c*. Type 2c; *d*–*e*: Type D8, obverse and reverse (*BMC* 4 and CM 1971, 12-16-68. The British Museum, London).

within a square, but some early reverses have lettering, interpreted as VICO (Fig. 5.20*b*),[117] an appropriate legend for the coinage of a *wic*.[118] Among the later varieties, those from the later phase (represented in the Kloster Barthe hoard)[119] present the most symmetrical designs. The other very prolific Continental coinage, that of Series D, Type 2c, copies the crowned bust of Series C in a degenerate style, but replaces the standard with a Continental cross-and-pellet reverse

---

[117] Perhaps more properly VIC, however, as what is generally read as O is actually the central annulet of the design.

[118] *T&S* ii. 211. The first to suggest this was John Kent. On *wics*: Lebecq 1997*a*: 73–5. See also the discussion on porcupines (obverses) below.

[119] *MEC* 151 and 153–4; *T&S* ii. 227–37.

Fig. 5.21. *a.* Series G, Type 3a, silver penny, early Secondary; *b.* Series E 'plumed bird' variety, Intermediate (CM 1922, 11-5-45 and *BMC 75.* The British Museum, London).

(Fig. 5.20*c*). Series D, Type 8, however, combines that cross-and-pellet design with a standard derived from Series E (Fig. 5.20*d–e*). Hence, it could be said to bring together two commercially prestigious reverses.

Metcalf attributes Series G to Quentovic,[120] although the distribution of finds is widespread throughout England, and points perhaps to an origin in the north Midlands. The coins, combining often sensitive portraits on the obverses with careful geometric reverses,[121] have affinities with English issues. The arrangement on the 'standard' of Series G, Type 3a (Fig. 5.21*a*), may be compared to that of Series E, 'plumed bird variety' (Fig. 5.21*b*),[122] but also to the arrangement on Secondary Series H, with cross and rosettes.

In the Anglo-Saxon silver coinage, 'standards' are used perhaps with an eye to international commercial types, but they are usually of finer workmanship than the Continental equivalent, as in the VERNVS group, and for Type 30, an Anglo-Saxon response to Series X,[123] with standards as an alternative reverse to its backward-looking animals.[124] In addition to the square with symbols described as a standard, we should consider the 'saltire-standard' label given to another arrangement within a square: an X, with groups of three pellets between the arms. The design can be read as a Greek cross or *Chi*-cross, and is met first surrounded by a SAROALDO inscription.[125] Type 51 features essentially the same saltire as the SAROALDO type, but within a double contour (Fig. 5.22). This reverse also combines with well-known types, such as 'Two Standing Figures' , backward-looking animals, or a Series R bust. On the obverse of the latter the crosses by the bust also have pellets, recalling the design on the reverse, and

---

[120] *T&S* ii. 266–74. For Quentovic: Leman 1990; Weiller 1999: 222–3.

[121] For a sensitive portrait, see Fig. 2.36, and ex-Subjack 36.

[122] Arguably, an English Series: see *T&S* ii., 209 and discussion at 'Porcupines'.

[123] *T&S* i. 140–51 for the VERNVS type; ii. 275–93 for the Danish Series X, and iii. 527–31 for Type 30.

[124] Other Insular derivations of Series X use backward-looking animals or the 'Two Standing Figures' reverses (*T&S* ii. 292–3 and iii. 528–31).

[125] See *T&S* i, pl.8, nos. 151–3. The same obverse design is also teamed with a bust from Series O (cf. *T&S* iii. 475 and pl. 8, no. 151) and lion obverse (de Wit collection, unpublished, and see ex-Subjack collection, no. 72), in the latter case with a legible SAROALDO inscription, but omitting the pellets in the square.

Fig. 5.22. *a* and *b*. Type 51 (*BMC* 197. The British Museum, London; 4458, de Wit collection).

justifying our religious reading.[126] Geometrical designs are also combined with the saltires of Type 51, juxtaposing ornate crosses with scrolls or annulets within double square or double circle contours and groups of pellets between the arms (Fig. 5.22*b*): the impression is of a carefully organized design, far from the utilitarian Continental types. Type 70 combines a saltire—although smaller and with single contour and additional ribbon/*tufa*—with geometrical obverses.[127] Some of these are 'standards', with additional zigzags on one side, reminiscent of the crowns of Series D or R.[128]

The simple but effective design of a cross with annulets as terminals is a design found on several coin types.[129] A version inscribed within a small standard is combined with rolled snakes of Series K, Type 32a,[130] a geometrical design,[131] a bird related to Series O with a MONITA SCORVM inscription (Type 46),[132] and a MONITA SCORVM inscription around a square-and-pellet motif (Fig. 5.23).[133] Connections between these variations clearly extend widely.

Some rare coins combine a backward-looking animal with an elaborate reverse; Metcalf classifies the Type as QIx, but notes its affinity to Type 70.[134] The specimen illustrated here is very ornate, indeed jewel-like, recalling fine garnet-inlaid brooches, and incorporates a zigzag as border (Fig. 5.24*a*). The small square with radiating arms in Figure 5.24 can be compared with the geometrical reverses, albeit with different central motifs, of the coins of King Beonna, which,

[126] These types, which Metcalf terms an eclectic group (*T&S* iii. 524), are the product of a small mint probably in the East Midlands (Mark Blackburn, personal communication).

[127] *T&S*, iii, pl. 26, no. 437, is classified by Metcalf as Type 70, as it only has one pellet within the arms of the cross. However, the saltire is large and double-contoured; perhaps it ought to be regarded as a mule 70/51.

[128] Ibid. no. 436.

[129] See Fig. 5.5*e*.

[130] Metcalf labels these K/R 'mules' (Rigold and Metcalf 1977: pl. 2, no. 26; *T&S*, iii, pl. 21, no. 358, and pp. 449–50);

[131] On this coin, a find from St Albans (*Coin Register* 1987: no. 91), the standard is probably die-identical to that of Type 46 (*T&S* iii. 53–5), whilst on the other side five annulets and pellets disposed as a cross are contained in a double border with four annulets, similar to that of Fig. 5.24*a*.

[132] *T&S* iii. 436 and 534–5.

[133] Prof. de Wit collection, and Woodham Walter hoard, both unpublished. Conceptually, and via the MONITA SCORVM inscription, these and the other coins mentioned above can be related to the SEDE coins teamed with a radiant snake surrounding a cross (see Fig. 5.28*c*).

[134] *T&S* iii. 490. The coins are probably East Anglian.

Fig. 5.23. MONITA SCORUM type, silver penny, obverse and reverse, Secondary (3801, de Wit collection).

Fig. 5.24. *a*. Series Q, type QIx, silver penny, mid-Secondary (3870, de Wit collection); *b*. jewelled disc brooch from Sarre, Kent, early 7th century (1934.202. The Ashmolean Museum, Oxford); *c*. penny of King Beonna of East Anglia, *c*.760? moneyer Efe (CM 1982, 4-9-4. The British Museum, London).

about the middle of the eighth century, replaced the debased East Anglian issues of Series R with finer issues on a broader flan (Fig. 5.24*c*).[135] The design seems to have found favour in East Anglia.

As far as Anglo-Saxon England is concerned, it seems clear that even relatively simple designs were executed with care and probably invested with a significance above the practical needs of a mint. This seems to suggest that the Anglo-Saxon issues had to meet greater expectations of patrons and public.

PORCUPINES

The coins discussed so far display a rich iconography which comparisons with other artefacts and literary evidence show was highly sophisticated. The care lavished on their designs, and the variations on the themes, as we have noticed, suggest expectations beyond the purely practical, yet, the coins were undoubtedly used for financial transactions, not only internally,[136] but across the North Sea and beyond.

---

[135] Archibald 1985 and 1995.   [136] Lebecq 1999: 55.

From around AD 600 sea-routes across the North Sea began to be systematically exploited,[137] and new trading ports, *wics*, proliferated.[138] Anglo-Saxon coins are found in the Low Countries and beyond, whilst the presence of Frisian merchants is well attested in France and England, coin finds suggesting not only routes, but that they moved with money.[139] This is also the case for Scandinavian traders:[140] the Ribe excavations have yielded coins of exactly the same types as other West European hoards and stray finds from important trading places.[141] The attribution of certain coin types, found on both sides of the sea and often imitative, is problematic,[142] but it indicates that by the late seventh century one can refer to a 'common market' around the North Sea.[143]

The dramatic increase in minting in Frisia at the end of the eighth century may have called for distinctive, easily executed types. Utilitarian reasons could perhaps have favoured types with little artistic pretence, such as Series D and E, which, as we saw, contrast noticeably with the fine coins produced in England and Denmark.

Coins of Series E are known from several thousand specimens struck over a considerable span of time in numerous varieties found in England, Frisia, Francia, Germany, and Scandinavia, and they are gathered under the collective label of 'porcupines',[144] a name referring to the characteristic design of quills on the obverse (Fig. 5.25a). Its place of origin has long been debated:[145] it is now attributed to Frisia, particularly the lower Rhine—Dorestad being a possible mint—but the obverse design was also copied on certain independent English types.[146] The iconography has also proved controversial. Some scholars, beginning with Dirks,[147] believed the porcupines were derived from the degeneration of a 'she-wolf and twins' Roman prototype,[148] the lines below the curved, shaggy back of the wolf being the twins. Baldwin Brown proposed a coin from the Museum of Middelburg as intermediary, a still legible stage before the design turns into a typical 'porcupine'.[149] This design is now classified as variety G4

---

[137] Carver 1990; Lebecq 1999: 54. This is also due to developments such as the shift from rowing to rigging and different building techniques for boats suitable for 'blue sea sailing' or 'coastal crawling', which makes it necessary to rethink geographical distances, 'near-neighbours' and cultural influences, with the sea as a means of easier contacts rather than a hindrance.

[138] Initially on a modest scale. Lebecq 1997a: 73–5; Lebecq 1999: 54–5, and see the thought-provoking collection of essays in Anderton 1999.

[139] Lebecq 1983: 49. Lebecq 1997b and 1999 are updating. For surveys of finds from the Low Countries, see Op den Velde, de Boone, and Pol 1984, and for finds along the Rhine, Zedelius 1980.

[140] Hines 1984: 280 and 294; Callmer 1984: 44–56.

[141] Bencard 1981; Bendixen 1984: 152.

[142] See for instance the debated English origin of Series F or the SAROALDO type (*T&S* i. 125 and 147) and the attribution of Series D, E, and X (Metcalf 1966b: 179–205 and *T&S* ii. 182; Lebecq 1997b: 998–9).

[143] *T&S* ii. 170. The choice of established and respected designs (such as standards on the reverses of Series E, ultimately derived from Series A, see above), or the use of names of well-known moneyers (as probably the SAROALDO type, *T&S* i. 147) is part of the trend of assimilation.

[144] This term was coined by Sutherland 1942: 64, 'in order to avoid controversial alternatives'.

[145] Metcalf 1966b and 1984a: p. 32; see now *T&S* ii. 174–83.

[146] *T&S* ii. 182. See below for the English types.   [147] Dirks 1870: 87.

[148] See *MoE* 105–6, no. 74a.   [149] Baldwin Brown 1903–37: iii, pl. 7, and pp. 96–7.

Fig. 5.25. *a–c.* Series E 'porcupines', silver pennies, Intermediate (CM 1935, 4-9-6; CM 1986, 8-46-15; CM 1935 11-17-240. The British Museum, London).

(Fig. 5.25*b*), a late development of the earlier 'porcupines' variety G, where the 'limbs of the twins' are derived from a pseudo-runic inscription.[150] Dirks, however, was bemused by the fact that whilst some specimens have two lines below the 'she-wolf', representing the twins, others have three or four.[151] He therefore postulated that such inflation might have originated from another fairly common Roman coin type, showing a galley (the hair being the oars, and the twins, increased to four, the oarsmen):[152] this time the coin needs to be viewed from a different perspective (Fig. 5.25*c*). Although a boat would make an excellent badge for sea-faring merchants, similarities are tenuous.

The 'general English theory', as Baldwin Brown put it, saw the design as a degeneration of a profile head with a spiky hairstyle.[153] Recently Michel Dhénin has suggested a derivation from a bronze coin of the Carnutes, itself a degenerated bust, adducing other examples of what he names 'homotypies anachroniques', borrowings of typology from the past.[154] The comparisons he makes are interesting, but debatable: as with the other examples Dhénin quotes, in order to span the geographical/chronological chasm, one can postulate common but discrete prototypes.[155] If one accepts the derivation of porcupines from degenerated busts, the shared fascination with certain details of the image, such as the hair, may explain why other Anglo-Saxon issues imitated Celtic coinage.[156]

[150] Variety G has been subdivided into four subclasses (G1, G2, G3, and G4) by Blackburn and Bonser 1987. See also Op den Velde, De Boone, and Pol 1984: 136 and fig. 2 on coin types that might have influenced the development of Series E, variety G.

[151] Dirks 1870: 87, comparing Hallum and Franeker finds.

[152] A beautiful *sestertius* of Hadrian (AD 132–4) was found in the river Tyne, and is now in the Museum of Antiquities in Newcastle upon Tyne. Another possible prototype may have been found amongst gemstones: see the first century BC Roman ringstone with a comparable boat motif in Henig 1994: no. 164.

[153] Baldwin Brown 1903–37: iii. 95, on Evans, and Keary (1887: i. 7). See also Hill 1952: 13. For Sutherland 1942: 64, there is an 'infusion of influence from the "wolf and twins" '.

[154] Dhénin 1987. His theory is applauded by Metcalf (*T&S* ii. 206).

[155] Or indeed find them, as in the case of Series K, Type 33, and the coin of the Bituriges Cubi (*T&S* iii. 314, fig. 3), which, are we saw, are related to ancient Eastern prototypes (see Fig. 4.35).

[156] See Ch. 4 n. 313.

Fig. 5.26. Series E 'porcupines', silver pennies, Intermediate. *a*. 'plumed bird'; *b*. VICO type; *c–d*. varieties D and G (*BMC* 75; CM 1935, 11-17-238; *BMC* 54; CM 1986, 8-46-15. The British Museum, London).

Many theories proposed for the design ignored the chronological sequence of types; moreover, postulating degeneration from images to patterns has proved to be erroneous.[157] Metcalf states 'the wide currency and acceptability of the "porcupines" no doubt made it advisable for the later copyists to keep fairly closely to their model'.[158] However, the opposite flow also seems to have been true: several busts turn into porcupines by adopting a characteristically spiky hairstyle, presumably for credibility reasons.[159] The 'porcupine' design is still as inexplicable as it must have been for the die-cutters themselves from an early stage: the permutations into insects, birds, worms, or heads were probably intended to make sense of the baffling pattern.

In 1966, and before the discovery of at least 324 coins of the Aston Rowant hoard (*c*.710),[160] which showed the range of Intermediate phase coinage in southern England, and included about seventy early 'porcupines' in four varieties ('plumed bird', VICO,[161] and classes D and G), Metcalf attempted a classification of 'porcupines' into classes.[162] This proved unsatisfactory, as the classes only accommodate half of the known types, whilst many coins straddle two, or do not fit any. Whereas the four earlier types are distinctive and consistent (Fig. 5.26), later varieties used many hundreds of dies, and it is difficult to find a pattern among the design variations.[163]

The four early varieties of Series E are commonly found in England, and Metcalf originally postulated that these were Anglo-Saxon in origin,[164] but evidence now seems to indicate Frisia and its booming trade early in the eighth century.[165] The attribution of the 'plumed bird' variety, with 25 specimens from

---

[157] See for instance the 'man in the moon' (*BMC* Type 10) in *T&S* ii. 249, and also the interesting comments in Davis 1989: 186.

[158] Metcalf 1966*b*: 197.   [159] See Figs. 2.34–2.37*a*.

[160] The precise number is uncertain, as some of the coins were dispersed.

[161] Originally interpreted as VOIC, now VICO, however VIC (= *wic*) may be preferable, as the O seems to be part of the design, not a letter (see Fig. 5.20*b*).

[162] Metcalf 1966*b* and *T&S* ii. 181–3, on earlier attempts at classification.

[163] *T&S* ii. 222–3. Hoards' evidence confirms the distinct chronological phases (ibid. 181).

[164] Metcalf 1966*b*: 192–7.

[165] Metcalf 1984*a*: 32; *MEC* 167; *T&S* ii. 196–206.

Fig. 5.27. 'æðilræd', runic silver
penny, early Secondary, obverse
and reverse (*BMC* 4. The British
Museum, London).

England (including four from Hamwic) versus nine from Domburg,[166] still seems
open to question, not only because of similarities with the iconography of
Secondary Series H (*c*.720),[167] which may be explained as 'paying homage' to a
successful international type, but because the naturalistic rendering fits in well
with representational Anglo-Saxon motifs in coinage and metalwork. The
brooch found at Southampton makes an interesting comparison: the 'hatched
lines within a segmental field above the bird' might deliberately recall the
'plumed bird' of the coins.[168]

   Some 'porcupines' are securely attributed to England: among these, the Intermediate VER group, whose internal sequence is debated among scholars,[169] with
several specimens found in the Aston Rowant hoard.[170] The 'æðilræd' runic porcupines (Type 105; Fig. 5.27), assigned to Kent or the Thames Valley, carry not
the name of a king, but, following Kentish practice, that of a moneyer.[171] As for
the dating, their silver content, and their absence from the Aston Rowant hoard,
point to *c*.715. The triple dotted border on the reverse finds parallels not so much
in the later Series J, Type 37,[172] as Metcalf suggested, but rather in the earlier
LICINIVS, VANIMVNDVS, and CRISPVS 'delaiona' coinages.[173]

   The 'porcupine' is continued in the Secondary Series of Anglo-Saxon coinage,
but changes character. Series T (coins with the legend LEL or TANUM), has a distinctive 'knob', probably a head, at one end and pellets below the curve: the
impression is zoomorphic, sometimes with four 'beaked' strokes below, suggesting young feeding (Fig. 5.28*a*). Coins with the legend MONITA SCORVM (Fig.
5.28*b*) have a finer version usually with the addition of a zigzag border. Certain

---

[166] *T&S* ii. 205.
[167] Birds of Series H are teamed with annulets or crosses. The Celtic Cross design of the reverses of
Series H, Type 39, compares with variety L reverses (5 annulets with central pellets in square), and the
'tubular style' bird as obverse (cf. *T&S* ii. 202 and 208).
[168] See Ch. 4 n. 45. In view of the correspondences found between artefacts and coins, the sceptical
comment in Hinton 1996: 103, seems unjustified.
[169] See Fig. 2.37*a*, and its discussion.
[170] *T&S* i. 140.
[171] Blackburn 1991: 157–8. Originally ascribed to King Æthelræd of Mercia (674–704), but now
believed more likely to name the moneyer.
[172] *T&S* i. 121.
[173] See *T&S* i, pl. 2, nos. 36–41; pl. 4, nos. 84–6 and see Fig. 5.4.

Fig. 5.28. *a.* Series T, silver penny, early/mid-Secondary (*BMC* 85. The British Museum, London); *b.* MONITA SCORUM type, silver penny, Secondary (3808, de Wit collection); *c.* SEDE type, silver penny, early Secondary, obverse and reverse (4303, de Wit collection).

coins reading CARIP transform the 'porcupine' into a snake-like creature, which we also find on some 'London related imitations',[174] and, teamed with Celtic Cross reverses, surrounding a cross.[175] Coins inscribed ELVNDONIA and SEDE have both 'porcupine' and snake versions.[176] Series O has a bird surrounded by what can be interpreted by analogy as a related motif.[177] The connections are again complex, but all these coins have in common inscriptions, outstanding workmanship, and zigzag borders,[178] and seem to have transformed the 'porcupine' into a *radiant* snake.[179]

Whatever its real original meaning, the numerous variations suggest that the 'porcupine' design was understood to have a significance, though interpreted in various ways. On account of the literacy displayed by the coinage and the combination with religious motifs we might speculate that the sense of the image among the derivatives should be sought in exegetical interpretations. It is possible that the rich symbolism of snakes, invested with Christian overtones, gave the key to a peculiar understanding and reinterpretation of the motif, perhaps with a Christological meaning, or as *Ecclesia/Caritas*, in line with the iconography of other coins.[180]

[174] CARIP and imitation: *T&S* iii, pl. 20, nos. 337 and 340.

[175] Prof. de Wit collection.

[176] Two coins with the legends ELVNDONIA on the obverse and SCORVM on the reverse below a 'porcupine' are known to me: one in Prof. de Wit's collection, the other illustrated in *T&S* iii. 435, with additional zigzag border and pellet for eye. In the de Wit collection there is also a SEDE coin teamed with a 'porcupine', albeit of inferior workmanship.

[177] *T&S* iii, pl. 22, nos. 373–5. See also ex-Subjack 54 with 'beaked' snake.

[178] On the SEDE coin at the Ashmolean Museum (*T&S* ii, pl. 15, no. 263) there is a garbled legend instead of the zigzag.

[179] The transformation of the quills into 'rays' may have been derived from solar symbols (Salin 1949–59: iv. 124–5, fig. 27*d*).

[180] See 'She-Wolf' and 'The Female Centaur'.

6

Conclusion

The 'third way' we have been following in this study of the coins has of necessity been a collection of 'cameos', often diachronic. Whilst this approach has allowed imagery and themes to be examined, understood, and placed firmly within the visual culture of the time, it has also provided firm foundations for addressing a number of issues posed at the beginning of the work, concerning sources, context, and meaning. We can now proceed to draw some conclusions, which will broadly cover artistic, numismatic, and historical questions.

The study of the iconography of the early coinage has highlighted the eclectic use of a great variety of sources beyond those of purely numismatic derivation, and indicated that the particular choice of idiom was symptomatic of the change in the perceived function of the coins. Within the period, distinctions can be made between the earlier and later coinages. Although a desire to conform to monetary types respected on the Continent, including Visigothic and Byzantine issues,[1] suggests that commercial credibility was important at the inception of Anglo-Saxon coinage, an analysis of the iconography expands this picture.

Early independent Anglo-Saxon coinage (c.630–700) appears to be relatively conservative, modelled on Roman prototypes via Merovingian issues showing busts on the obverse, and reverses with crosses.[2] The classical bust, on account of its charisma and tradition, was clearly felt to be an important part of the iconography, and was reproduced on the majority of issues. Unlike classical prototypes, however, it was rarely accompanied by identifying legends. When these occur, they are reproduced in an increasingly degenerated manner, until they turn into patterns, perhaps pseudo-magical.[3] Inscriptions may have been superfluous in an illiterate society, or perhaps it might have been considered more beneficial for all concerned for the bust to represent 'authority' in general, rather than a particular person.[4] It is interesting to notice runic and Latin characters coexisting, and perhaps even challenging each other.

---

[1] See Figs. 2.35*b* and 2.49.
[2] The reader is referred to the relevant chapters and subchapters in the work.
[3] See for instance Fig. 2.2.
[4] While traders stood to benefit from the goodwill and protection of the authorities, the latter also flourished through the commercial activities of the merchants. Sawyer 1977: 158; Woolf 1999: 67.

Rigold's scheme of the various elements derived from the gold coinage which eventually conflated in Series A shows the creative use of disparate elements, *insignia*, attributes, and details which, as with other 'barbarian' coinages, were selectively copied,[5] and sometimes replaced with native equivalents. Although we can only speculate about how these were understood, we can challenge the often-repeated *horror vacui* explanation for the saturated surfaces of Anglo-Saxon and Germanic artefacts, by considering the simultaneous rendering of both obverse and reverse of the *Urbs Roma* type on the Undley bracteate.[6] This synthesis suggests that the coin prototype was read as a three-dimensional object and translated onto a single surface dense with meaning.

The Crondall hoard (*c.*640)[7] testifies to the artistic vitality of the first experimental gold coins by the presence of three different portrait renderings. The LICINIVS types are deep-relief imitation with sensitive modelling of the Roman prototype with a bust in profile;[8] 'Portrait-and-Cross' types show a Merovingian-inspired rendering of a face broken into its salient traits, with little modelling;[9] whilst LVNDINIV coins have frontal, linear portraits, sober and classicizing, independent of numismatic precedents.[10] The same versatility in the reproduction of portraits is apparent in Anglo-Saxon illuminated books, which, rather like the coinage, can be considered as innovations responding to prototypes from overseas. Both coins and manuscripts involved a creative exploration and blending of many available traditions, Germanic, Celtic, and Roman. These were derived from different media, and translated in a variety of idioms, including the making of facsimiles. We can see how the iconography of the early coinage mirrors Anglo-Saxon England at the crossroads, the dialectic tension between the old and new order, and the formidable changes occurring at the time of the Conversion.

It is no surprise that drapery and hair on the early coins essentially reproduce the texture of much metalwork,[11] as the two productions were cognate.[12] Traditional metalwork had provided an endless supply of motifs and even 'techniques' for the new art forms of manuscripts and stone carvings,[13] and itself proved to be equally dynamic.[14] Whilst it could readily produce suitably Christian versions of secular-style jewels,[15] it was equally capable of absorbing

[5] Arslan 1992: 796–7. For Rigold's scheme see Fig. 2.28.

[6] See Fig. 4.54.

[7] Sutherland 1948.

[8] See Fig. 2.26*b*.

[9] Compare the 'Portrait-and-Cross' (Crondall 36, *T&S* i, pl. 3, no. 71) with the Merovingian coin from Saint-Bertrand-de-Comminges, by the moneyer Nonnitus, illustrated in *MEC* pl. 31, no. 1816-1.

[10] See Fig. 2.1.

[11] See for instance, Figs. 2.4 and 2.42.

[12] See 'Die-Cutters and Moneyers'.

[13] G. Henderson 1987: 105–9; Hawkes 2001: 236.

[14] G. Henderson 1987: 32; Peroni 1967: 21; Casartelli Novelli 1992: 541–5.

[15] See the Ixworth and Wilton Crosses and that of St Cuthbert (*MoE* 26–7, nos. 11–12; p. 133, no. 98, second quarter to second half of the seventh century).

and mastering new styles, as evident in the linearity of the plaque from Hexham.[16] The common denominator connecting all the arts of time, from manuscript illumination to metalwork, from sculpture to architecture, and of course the making of coins, was a cultural drive towards all things *iuxta morem Romanorum*. The response was richly original.

From the very beginning, through to the debased gold issues of the mid-seventh century,[17] and in the Primary and Intermediate phases of the silver coinage (*c*.675–710),[18] Roman influence was strong. This was due not only to the political appeal of *Romanitas*, or the idea that real coins should look like Roman ones,[19] but particularly because of the Christian significance of Rome. Innovative designs, such as the bird-on-cross of Series B, herald an iconography that, whilst oscillating between traditional classical images or novel and exotic motifs, was deeply religious, and both aesthetically and intellectually pleasing. One of the possible sources of this motif could have been derived from what was possibly amongst the earliest necessary imports for a new church: lamps, such as the richly symbolic Coptic examples mentioned earlier.[20] This was the time when travellers of 'impressionable and acquisitive minds'[21] brought back so much from the Continent to furnish the early churches.

Next to such attractive and allusive designs, the 'porcupines' from Frisia (whatever the design meant) appear aniconic, and baffle us as they must have baffled the Anglo-Saxon die-cutters that imitated them. The copying of 'porcupines' and the modelling of many issues in the Intermediate phase on Merovingian types show the need for monetary conformity in overseas trade, which was at this stage dominated by Francia and Frisia.[22] The trend was also paralleled early in the next phase of the coinage, with the Scandinavian early Secondary Series X, Type 31 (*c*.710–15) and its Anglo-Saxon counterpart, Type 30.[23] In both cases, a delicacy of execution is apparent for the Anglo-Saxon versions, which seem to have been expected to live up to certain standards of craftsmanship.

As for the Secondary phase of the coinage (*c*.710–50), the pinnacle of the artistic production, the systematic study of the sources of the motifs has served to bring some order to the vast array of designs that characterize it, particularly among the animals. This allows us to perceive greater unity in the iconography of the Secondary Series, with birds, snakes, and other creatures being represented, albeit expressed through different designs, across the whole of the

---

[16] *MoE* 138, no. 104 (seventh-eighth century).

[17] e.g. CRISPVS 'delaiona', 'Clasped Hands', the 'Two Emperors', and 'Constantine' issues.

[18] See the VANIMVNDVS issues, the 'Standards', the modelled heads with crowns or diadems of Series A and C and Pada and B, and also some of the very beautiful portraits of Series G.

[19] *MoE* 105.

[20] See Fig. 4.1*c*.

[21] G. Henderson 1999: 74.

[22] Cf. the VER and SAROALDO types and Series F.

[23] *T&S* ii. 275–93.

coinage and political borders. Within substantive coinages, e.g. Series U, V, and H, Type 39, all with bird-in-vine motifs, the concept is subordinate to the at-a-glance recognition of the Series, so that even though they respond to each other, they proclaim themselves discrete. They find close counterparts in other media, and regional trends are discernible.[24]

Conceptually, we could reorder the coinage according to the one common message that is apparent throughout—the promise of salvation—and how this was visualized, through crosses, vine-scrolls, symbolic animals, etc. This may well have been how the Anglo-Saxons themselves would have perceived their coinage, and it has the advantage of rendering the coinage more approachable and attractive to scholars in general. The current, painstaking classification of the coins in Series, types, and subtypes is desirable from a numismatic point of view, in order to map and research mint-attributions, monetary affairs, and political questions:[25] however, whilst it is intriguing to pursue such matters, we should not miss the wood for the trees.

Iconographically, lions emerge as a particularly strong group, represented widely among many Series, with a pedigree stretching back to Aldfrith's and the SAROALDO-related coins,[26] and with many interesting variations. The similarity between the lions featured on the Northumbrian coinage and those on Northumbrian manuscripts allow us to postulate an identity also between the lions featured on East Anglian coins (Series Q) that survive, and those on manuscripts from the region that do not.[27] Equally, the striking image of the full-face lion featured by several Series,[28] which is an adaptation of the classical iconography of the lion as a doorkeeper, well ahead of those of Charlemagne at Aachen, lets us postulate the existence of now lost Anglo-Saxon door knockers.[29] Other motifs that appear quite commonly across the Series, such as crosses, birds in the vine, snakes, figures holding crosses, etc. are equally fascinating in their variations and allusions. They all find counterpart in the arts of the time.

The wide-ranging nature of the sources and the quality of execution presuppose a highly sophisticated patronage,[30] enjoying access to materials such as Roman gems and jewellery, gold-glass, Oriental textiles and artefacts,[31] and,

---

[24] Webster 2001*b*.

[25] Metcalf 2000.

[26] See Figs. 4.25 and 4.31.

[27] Gannon 2002.

[28] *T&S* iii. 446–8.

[29] Gannon 2002.

[30] There seems to be an evolution in taste and expectations between the 'translation' of motifs, e.g. the York group, which transforms Byzantine coin prototypes into the tradition of fine metalwork (p. 28), and the adoption of foreign models, as for instance the exotic lion of Series Q (p. 130) or the 'Female Centaur' and other fantastic animal.

[31] For instance, two Roman gems connected with the cult of Bacchus were the source for obverse and reverse of Series K, Type 42 (see Figs. 2.64 and 4.37*b*), and one with Heracles for a coin of Series L (see Fig. 3.18*b*). The influence of valuable imported textiles, which by their fragile nature do not survive, is more difficult to demonstrate; however, it is possible it may have influenced a few designs, as has been suggested for other artefacts (Plunkett 1998: 218 n. 22).

indeed, imported illuminated manuscripts.[32] As in other media, exotic new influences were eagerly adopted, as is testified by comparing for instance the playful fauna on the Ormside Bowl, or at Breedon-on-the-Hill,[33] to the animals on the coins. The visual connections apparent with other prestigious Anglo-Saxon art forms, such as sculpture, carvings, metalwork, and manuscripts suggests a repository shared amongst craftsmen presumably working for the same patron.[34] The coins take their place among all these 'related sets of objects within a single standard and context of patronage',[35] which suggests an exalted position for the coinage, on a par with major arts of the period, and hence perceived not merely as functional,[36] but testifying to prestige and refinement.

The coins, as argued above, often testify to the currency of certain iconography lost in other media,[37] and this is important, as it contributes to the refining of our knowledge of the period, and of the stature of the culture. Hawkes's arguments in redating the Rothbury Cross,[38] and Jewell's definition of Southumbrian classicism,[39] can be further buttressed in claiming independence from, and, indeed, primacy over the Carolingian Renaissance for Insular classical culture by the legacy of the coins. This is the proud background to the confident coinage of Offa, closely modelled on Roman imperial precedents, and showing him as an ambitious player on the European scene.[40]

Having established the origin and 'etymology' of the motifs, one may wonder whether the purpose for such variety and richness was visual gratification and display, or whether the coinage was meant to convey some special meaning. If the religious significance of the bird-in-vine motif, or of crosses, is transparent, whilst other iconographies are fully apparent only to the 'initiated eye',[41] it is clear that theological themes can be identified behind most of the coinage of the Secondary Series and that it works at more than one level of reading. 'Symbols in art are notoriously easy to identify and very difficult to interpret correctly',[42] hence the need for a methodological justification for the bases for interpretations.[43]

---

[32] Not all necessarily religious: Aldfrith's lion (Fig. 4.25) may be drawn from an illumination of the 'Cosmographers' (Henderson 1999: 94–5). It is difficult for us to appreciate the full impact of such cultural 'novelties' at the time.

[33] *MoE* 173, no. 134 (second half of the eighth century); Jewell 1986; Plunkett 1998: 215–20; Jewell 2001: *passim*; Webster 2001*b*: 43–5.

[34] It is interesting to note that coins do not seem to take native brooches as models (*pace* Smedley and Owles 1965: 167, fig. 22, and Hills 1983: 105, both specifically on East Anglian 'animal' brooches, which seem totally unrelated to the sources of our coins). The reason must be a difference in patronage.

[35] Plunkett 1998: 210. Besides metalwork, sculpture, carving and manuscripts, we should also include textiles amongst the related objects testifying to the visual culture of the time. The embroidery from the Convent of SS Harlindis and Relindis (*MoE* 184, no. 143, *c*.800) is one of the few survivals. See Dodwell 1982: 129–34.

[36] There is no doubt that the use of coins was widespread, and economy monetized in the eighth century (Metcalf 2000: 1).

[37] Gannon, forthcoming.   [38] Hawkes 1996: 91.   [39] Jewell 2001: 262.

[40] Williams 2001*a*: 216–19; Nelson 2001.

[41] Lewis 1980: 141. See 'Birds with Cross and Fledgling', and the reference to Deut. 32: 11.

[42] Janes 1998: 116.   [43] Niles 1998: 181–5.

The iconography of the coins has been approached as another manifestation of a culture that delighted in paradox and metaphor. This statement can be readily justified in literature, and particularly in poetry, where texts such as *The Dream of the Rood* actively play on juxtapositions of potent images to elicit deeper responses, presenting readers with hermeneutical challenges.[44] This use of layers of meaning in imagery can be compared to the way riddles present ordinary objects in an extraordinary way.[45] In the visual arts, scholarly opinion is divided over the interpretation of the maze of allusions in the iconography of the Ruthwell Cross, even though a runic version of the *Dream of the Rood* accompanies the carved images. The Franks Casket, by bringing together disparate themes and legends from the classical, Christian, and Germanic worlds, invites similar leaps in understanding, working as a three-dimensional riddle guided by the inscriptions and the arrangements of the panels.[46] Illuminations in manuscripts, such as the Passion image in the Book of Kells (fo 114[r]), evoke the several layers of meaning suggested by exegetical readings 'unifying and harmonising the visual and verbal in expression of complex thought'.[47] It does therefore seem appropriate to test the iconography of the coinage within the parameters suggested by other contemporary sources, and to propose a range of possible allusions that would have been apparent to the beholder. We can be sure that people handling the coins would have been familiar with complex exegesis as displayed and made available already in a variety of matching media.[48]

The obverses of Series K, with their attributes prominently displayed, have yielded particularly interesting comparative material, which has been discussed under the relevant sections.[49] A related type with a facing bust and two knotted wreath-ties,[50] classified in the 'Triquetras' eclectic group on account of its reverse,[51] might belong with the others. When one considers them together (Fig. 6.1), the coins appear to represent the Five Senses:[52] Touch (the cross), Taste (the cup), Smell (the sprig), Hearing (the bird), and Sight (frontal gaze). If this is the case—and the fact that they are all associated by interlaced wreath-ties and comparable drapery seems to bracket them as a group—the coins would be a remark-

---

[44] It is interesting to compare this to the genesis of Christian viewing and exegesis as explored by Elsner 1995: 249–87.

[45] Niles 1998: 200–1; Whitehurst Williams 1992: 25–30.

[46] Webster 1999: 246 and 230–5.

[47] Farr 1997*b*: 157.

[48] Elsner 1995: 251.

[49] See Ch. 2, 'Attributes': 'Hands Holding Crosses', 'Hands Holding Cups', 'Hands Holding Sprigs', 'Bust and Bird'.

[50] Fig. 2.39.

[51] *T&S* iii. 422–5.

[52] Described in Isidore of Seville (*Etymologiarum, Lib.XI.i*, Lindsay 1911: l. 18): 'sensus corporis quinque sunt: visus, auditus, ododratus, gustus et tactus', the Five Senses were the subject of many Patristic commentaries well known in Anglo-Saxon England (Thorpe 1844) and of a riddle by Tatwine, monk at Breedon-on-the-Hill and archbishop of Canterbury 731–4 (Glorie 1968: 193, no. 26). For comparative accounts of the iconography of the Five Senses in Antiquity, Nordenfalk 1976 and 1985.

Fig. 6.1. The Five Senses: Series K, silver pennies, Secondary: Type 32a (*BMC* 151. The British Museum, London); Type 20/18, Type 42, Type 42, and 'Triquetras' type (*T&S* 317, 311, 313, and 344. The Ashmolean Museum, Oxford).

able precursor of the iconography of the Fuller Brooch (Fig. 6.2).[53] In a homily Ælfric interpreted the parable of the Five Talents as signifying the five bodily senses,[54] so a sophisticated allegorical programme might lie behind the set of the five coins/talents. In the same Series,[55] the remarkable coin with the raised hand and cross in front of the bust in a rhetorical gesture may indicate Speech guided by Wisdom,[56] and perhaps be connected with the set. The reverse of this coin bears a fierce lion's head, whose long tongue connects it to other reverses of Series K with emphasis on tongues and tasting, literally *Sapientia*.[57]

Who commissioned the coinage? Metcalf has argued in favour of royal

---

[53] For its interpretation as a representation of the Five Senses: Bruce-Mitford 1956: 173–90. Pratt (forthcoming) interprets the figure of Sight on the Fuller Brooch as depicting the 'mind's eyes', Reason, with the ability to perceive wisdom. As on the Fuller Brooch and in Tatwine's riddle, the Senses on our coins are personified by men, and the symbolism is explicitly expressed by the hands, or in the frontal position in the case of Sight. The two triskeles at the side of Sight on the brooch might be compared to the duplicated wreath-ties on the coins with frontal busts and considered to have the same apotropaic value. It is possible that the iconography might have been derived from an illustrated medical or philosophical treatise (Nordenfalk 1976: 21), or it may even have been an Anglo-Saxon innovation.

[54] Thorpe 1844: ii. 551.

[55] Fig. 2.58.

[56] Nordenfalk 1976: 28 n. 23, on a Carolingian poem where the Five Senses are guided by Reason. On Gregory the Great's attitude to the Five Senses, that if unbridled may lead to sin, which was followed by Bede, see Nordenfalk 1976: 19, and Pratt (forthcoming).

[57] See 'Whorls of Snakes' and 'Rolled-Up Snakes'.

Fig. 6.2. The Fuller Brooch, end of 9th
century (MME 1952, 4-4, 1. © The British
Museum, London).

control.[58] Indeed, the right to coin was a recognized royal prerogative throughout the Middle Ages and, as the tenth-century Grateley decrees testify, it was the
king who granted it to others, such as bishops and abbots.[59] However, Grierson
and Blackburn have argued that the situation in Anglo-Saxon England during
the seventh and eighth centuries may have mirrored that of Merovingian France,
where the organization of minting was initially in the hands of moneyers and
only slowly came under royal control.[60] Although one should beware of putting
excessive weight on a single aspect of the question, as very few of our coins
explicitly carry names of kings or moneyers, it is the iconography that in an age
of limited literacy should be seen as the bearer of meaning.[61] The iconography of
the Secondary Series suggests a patronage, to some extent literate,[62] with access
to rich artefacts and good craftsmen, enjoying a sophisticated, religious, and
over-regional iconography, able to organize wealth into coinage and manage the
necessary bureaucracy. Although kings or merchants might fulfil some of these
requirements, and it could be argued, as indeed I have, that religion was the preoccupation of the age, the designs of the Secondary Series point to a third con-
testant: the Church.

The economic role of minsters (*monasteria*), ecclesiastical complexes housing
religious communities endowed with lands and commanding a well-organized

[58] *T&S* i. 10–25.
[59] Decrees of Athelstan (925–39), Attenborough 1922: 115. Blunt 1960: p. ii, on the origins of ecclesiastical coinage.
[60] A situation due to the weakness of the monarchy. *MEC* 139; *T&S* i. 11.
[61] *T&S* i. 24, invites caution, as 'an understanding derived only from the design of the coins may turn
out to be superficial'.
[62] Literacy links the issues with the legend SEDE (interpreted as 'seat' or 'see', arguably stemming from
Canterbury) and MONITA SCORUM; shared reverses and details such as the serration borders provide
further connections with Series K, Type 33, 'Celtic Cross', CARIP, and Series L and O (see discussion in
'Porcupines' and Figs. 5.28 and 2.66).

workforce, needs careful consideration. The concept of the minster as *civitas sancta* is based on theological writing:[63] it has been argued that in terms of size, population, buildings, economic importance, and wealth, minsters were the closest thing to towns eighth-century Anglo-Saxons would have known,[64] much more impressive than the utilitarian *wics*. The late seventh century saw minsters lavishly endowed by kings, indeed headed by royal ladies, with many eventually developing into 'alternative courts',[65] as ways for aristocratic groups to gain privileges and exemptions from the king and enjoy a civilized lifestyle of culture, prestige, and increasing wealth.[66] Their wealth was augmented by taxes,[67] and their position near road crossings and waterfronts, nodal points in the communication system, not only allowed the acquisition of prestige goods, but the marketing of the surplus produced.[68]

Many Secondary Series coin finds are from minster sites,[69] and also from the course of the middle and upper Thames, where thirty-three important minsters existed:[70] it seems probable that at least some of the coinage served and was produced at minsters, even as a special royal concession, as they would have commanded the economic power, craftsmanship, and artistic/intellectual flair for such a distinguished production.[71] One might wonder if the function of the religiously charged designs on the coins was a way of preaching the gospel,[72] part of pastoral commitment, as sermons in miniature for edifying meditations. Coins, like the didactic high crosses,[73] were public, and ideal for teaching the illiterate,[74] as Gregory the Great had recommended.[75] The use of religious iconography may also have been a way of justifying the possession of a wealth that was becoming embarrassing.[76]

The worldly sophistication of these establishments, apart from the vibrant art they produced, is testified to by numerous archaeological finds,[77] and also

---

[63] Gem 1996: 1.   [64] Blair 1996a: 9.

[65] See Parsons 2001: 62–3, on 'lax' monasteries and aristocratic family homes.

[66] Blair 1996b: 6.

[67] Bede's letter to Ecgberht testifies to this (McClure and Collins 1994: 347).

[68] *MoE* 133; Blair 1996b: 8 and 17.   [69] Newman 1999: 44–5.

[70] Metcalf 1984a: 40; Blair 1996b: 5.

[71] Marion Archibald's reading of the legend MONITA SCORVM as *moneta sanctorum* (lecture at the Royal Numismatic Society; see Metcalf 1984a: 39 n. 27) would support the claim that these coins and the related issues stem from Canterbury.

[72] Minsters are here discussed as economic centres, supporting a genuinely religious community whose achievements in the pastoral and intellectual spheres are immense.

[73] Mitchell 2001: 95–109. Gannon, forthcoming.

[74] As for their reception, it is interesting that the three coins found in Italy, two coins of the scarce Type 48, and one of Eadberht, Series Y, 'presumably losses by English pilgrims or travellers to Italy' (*T&S* iii. 334; Orlandoni 1988), all had crosses, and that Rome was the find-spot of the coin of Æthelberht, with the she-wolf motif (Fig. 4.56). Beside apotropaic functions, for the people using them, memory and meaning were attached to the coins and their iconography (Travaini, forthcoming).

[75] See Gregory's epistle 13 in *Patrologia Latina*, lxxvii, col. 1128: 'pro lectione pictura est'.

[76] Bede, *Letter to Ecgbert* (McClure and Collins 1994: 355).

[77] For instance the quality of finds from Hartlepool (Daniels 1988); Brandon, Barking Abbey, Whitby, and York (*MoE* 81–94, nos. 66a–y and 67a–w; pp. 141–7, nos. 107a–q and 108a–e).

by criticism in contemporary sources.[78] The letters of Bede to Ecgberht, and Boniface to Æthelbald,[79] as well as the provisions of the Council of Clovesho (746/7),[80] and Æthelbald's concessions at the synod of Gumley in 749,[81] alert us to the fact that the second quarter of the eighth century was a time of self-questioning and trouble. As Bede saw it, the problem was twofold: the church was in need of internal reform, with so many spurious monasteries occupying land, and lay society lacked the means to support itself.[82] For Boniface and other religious leaders, kings and nobles, having been protectors and givers to the church, had become envious of its wealth and organization, and had begun to covet the resources of minsters, reducing their privileges and conscripting their manpower.[83]

As far as the coins can testify, we witness a great economic upheaval in the middle of the eighth century, with crisis and debasement in south-eastern England already evident from the second quarter of the century, and a much reduced volume of the coinage.[84] The crisis might be linked to the problems outlined above, if we assume that the monasteries had been behind part of the coinage but then lost minting-rights. Judging from the lack of coins, output must have ceased at many mints.[85] One may wonder if Æthelbald's concessions at the synod of Gumley in 749[86] were not only in answer to Boniface's accusations,[87] but a belated attempt at restarting the economy by removing some of the burdens that had impoverished monasteries—and Mercia generally.

Do we witness a dramatic unfolding of the crisis in East Anglia, where two very different types of coins circulated, and apparently were freely exchanged?[88] There exists a great contrast between the rich and very varied iconography of Series Q, and the geometric designs of Series R, obstinately non-classical and runic:[89] it is likely that Series Q was monastic, and Series R civil.[90] The rather

---

[78] See Bede's letter to Ecgberht (McClure and Collins 1994: 350), Aldhelm's *De Virginitate*, dedicated to Barking's abbess, condemns 'dressed-up impudence'; Boniface's letter to Cuthberht of Canterbury (Talbot 1954: 133, no. 35) and later Alcuin's letters on the fashion and literature enjoyed by Lindisfarne monks (Whitelock 1968: 776, no. 193; Dümmler 1895: 183, no. 124). See also Wormald 1978: 42–5 and 50–4.

[79] McClure and Collins 1994: 343–57; Talbot 1954: 120–6, no. 32.

[80] Keynes 1994: 4–6; Cubitt 1995: 99–124.

[81] Cubitt 1995: 112–13.

[82] Bede to Ecgberht (McClure and Collins 1994: 350–1); Wormald 1982: 100; Williams 2001*b*: 301.

[83] See the letters of Abbess Eangyth and her daughter Heaburg to Boniface (Emerton 1940: 36–40, no. 6). One of the accusations of Boniface to Æthelbald regards the forced employment of the monasteries' manpower on royal building projects. On the problems associated with bookland, see Brooks 1971: 76–7; John 1996: 51–2 and Williams 2001*b*: 295–301.

[84] *MEC* 187–9; Metcalf 1988*a*: 236–9.

[85] *MEC* 187–9.

[86] These declare publicly that monasteries are free from taxes and other onuses, apart from the common burdens (see Brooks 1971: 71, and Williams 2001*b*: 297).

[87] Cubitt 1995: 112; John 1996: 52; Williams 2001*b*: 301.

[88] Metcalf 2000: 4–5.

[89] Both coinages are very complex, and are subdivided in many types, with discrete distribution patterns (Metcalf 2000).

[90] Newman 1999: 41–4 supports the idea of the monastic site at Ely as a likely mint place for Series Q (p. 43); see, however, Metcalf 2000: 5, where distribution patterns are taken to indicate a more northerly site for the mint. Series R is probably mainly from Ipswich (*T&S* iii. 523)

Fig. 6.3. Series Q/R mule, silver penny, late
Secondary (ex-Subjack collection, 69).

debased mules Q/R (one of which is from Brandon, a high-status site, most probably monastic)[91] had Metcalf wondering if they might 'signal an extension of
East Anglian political control over the mint-place of Series Q' (Fig. 6.3).[92]

North of the Humber, Eadberht (738–58) revived the royal coinage of Series
Y to better standards and weight than in the south,[93] after a gap of about thirty-
five years. Some of the coins were struck with his brother Ecgberht, archbishop
of York, the recipient of Bede's letter mentioned above: the restoration of a
regular royal and archiepsicopal coinage may be seen as one of the measures
taken to counteract the problems referred to by Bede.[94] Eadberht's coins carry his
name and a lion, like those of King Aldfrith before him, and set a pattern that will
be followed by his successors for about fifty years.[95]

In East Anglia, the reformed royal coinage of King Beonna (750s–60s),[96] on
improved standards and on broader flans, a coinage that replaced the debased
Series R,[97] is epigraphic, and displays the names of the king and his moneyers,
but, with one exception,[98] no pictorial images.

By the time Offa became king in 757, therefore, the coinage of Anglo-Saxon
England declared itself clearly royal, and is mainly epigraphic.[99] Offa's coinage,
too, made a decisive break with the past, as he took full control of the coinage,
not only in Mercia, but in Kent and East Anglia. His reformed coins carried his
name and title, and here also, whilst maintaining the high standards of craftsmanship, the iconography became standardized, with a strong preference for
geometric designs. Compared to Carolingian coinage, and indeed to that of
other Anglo-Saxon rulers, his production is most inventive and attractive, not
only for his busts, but for the innumerable variations that his die-cutters

[91] *MoE* 81–8, no. 66 (*a–y*).
[92] *T&S* iii. 498.
[93] *MEC* 173, Booth 1984: 72.
[94] Booth 1984: 72–4. Pepin's reform of the coinage of 754–5 clearly post-dates Eadberht's. Whether it
was influential on Beonna's, given the strong links between the coinages of Northumbria and East Anglia,
is debatable.
[95] With the subsequent royal coinage of Northumbria, from Ælfwald (779–88) onwards, the pictorial
reverse will give way to an epigraphic one, carrying the moneyers' names.
[96] Archibald 1985; *T&S*, iii. 601–7.
[97] The Middle Harling hoard shows coins of Series R and of Beonna together (*MEC* 173 and 189).
[98] The interlace type, see Fig. 5.10*b*.
[99] See the chronology scheme in *MEC* 188. The situation in Kent and whether the reformed coinage on
a broad penny was produced first by Heahberht *c.*765 (as argued persuasively in Chick 1997), or under
Offa's control in the 770s (Blunt 1961), is still unclear. See comments in Williams 2001*a*: 213–16.

managed to achieve on the geometric reverses. There is no doubt that his designs were the richly endowed legacy of a visually alert society, but now with different priorities. Although the need to impress, as testified by his image-making portraiture, was a foremost concern for Offa,[100] in the changing conception of kingship the duty to preach the Good News was certainly not.

The coinage we have examined was the product of a complex age, which relied on the visual to convey messages: the dramatic change in the iconography of the second half of the eighth century seems to stress that coinage had reverted to being a totally royal prerogative.

[100] Nelson 2001. In the elegance of his coinage and richness of classical allusions, Offa undoubtedly shows himself superior to Charlemagne.

Bibliography

ÅBERG, N. (1943–7), *The Orient and the Occident in the Art of the Seventh Century* (3 vols.), Stockholm.

ADELSON, H. (1957), *Light Weight Solidi and Byzantine Trade during the Sixth and Seventh Centuries*, Numismatic Notes and Monographs 138, New York.

ALCOCK, L. (1993), 'Image and Icon in Pictish Sculpture', in Spearman and Higgitt 1993: 230–6.

ALCOCK, S. E. (ed.) (1997), *The Early Roman Empire in the East*, Oxford.

ALEXANDER, J. J. G. (1976), 'The Illustrated Manuscript of the *Notitia Dignitatum*', in Goodburn and Bartholomew 1976: 11–25.

——(1978), *Insular Manuscripts 6th to 9th Century* (A Survey of Manuscripts illustrated in the British Isles, vol. 1), London.

——and PULLINGER, J. (eds.) (2000), 'Roman Cambridge: Excavations on Castle Hill 1956–1988', *Proceedings of the Cambridge Antiquarian Society*, 48 (for 1999), ed. Alison Taylor.

ALEXANDER, M. (ed.) (1995), *Beowulf*, London.

ALEXANDER, S. (1997), 'Daniel Themes on the Irish High Crosses', in Karkov, Ryan, and Farrell 1997: 99–114.

ALFÖLDI, A. (1934), 'Eine spätromische Helmform und ihre Schicksale im Germanisch-Romanischen Mittelalter', *Acta Archaeologica*, 5: 99–144.

ALKEMADE, M. (1997), 'Elite Lifestyle and the Transformation of the Roman World in Northern Gaul', in Webster and Brown 1997: 180–93.

ALLASON-JONES, L. (1996), *Roman Jet in the Yorkshire Museum*, York.

ALMGREN, B. (1983), 'Helmets, Crowns and Warrior's Dress: From the Roman Emperors to the Chieftains of Uppland', in Lamm and Nordström 1983: 11–16.

AMÉCOURT, G. (de Ponton d'Amécourt) (1872), 'Farther Notes on the Gold Coins Discovered in 1828 at Crondall, Hants', *Numismatic Chronicle*[2] 12: 72–82.

——(1877), 'Type de l'orant sur les monnaies mérovingiennes', *Annuaire de la Sociéte Française de Numismatique*, 5: 175–7.

ANDERSON, A. O., and ANDERSON, M. O. (1991), *Adomnán's life of Columba*, Oxford.

ANDERTON, M. (ed.) (1999), *Anglo-Saxon Trading Centres: Beyond the Emporia*, Glasgow.

ANDRÉN, A. (1991), 'Guld och makt—en tolkning av de skandinaviska guldbrakteaternas funktion', in Fabech and Ringtved 1991: 245–56.

ANDREWS, P. (ed.) (1988), *Southampton Finds: The Coins and Pottery from Hamwic* (vol. i), Southampton.

ANGENENDT, A. (1986), 'The Conversion of the Anglo-Saxons Considered against the Background of the Early Medieval Mission', *Angli e Sassoni al di qua e al di là del mare: Settimane di Studio del Centro Italiano di Studi sull'Alto Medioevo (1984)*, Spoleto, 747–81.

ARCAMONE, M. G. (1980), 'Antroponimia altomedievale nelle iscrizioni murali', in Carletti and Otranto 1980: 257–317.

ARCHIBALD, M. M. (1985), 'The Coinage of Beonna in the Light of the Middle Harling Hoard', *British Numismatic Journal*, 55: 10–54.

——(1991), *Coinage and Currency*, in Webster and Backhouse 1991: 35–7, 62–7, 155–6, 189–92, 247–53, 284–9.

——(1997), Review of D. M. Metcalf, *Thrymsas and Sceattas in the Ashmolean Museum, Oxford*, *British Numismatic Journal*, 67: 150–3.

——BROWN, M., and WEBSTER, L. (1997), 'Heirs of Rome: The Shaping of Britain, AD 400–900', in Webster and Brown 1997: 208–48.

——and FENWICK, V. with COWELL, M. R. (1995), 'A Sceat of Ethelberht I of East Anglia and Recent Finds of Coins of Beonna', *British Numismatic Journal*, 65: 1–19.

——LANG, J., and MILNE, G. (1995), 'Four Early Medieval Coin Dies from the London Waterfront', *Numismatic Chronicle*, 155: 163–200.

ARNOLD, C. J. (1997), *An Archaeology of the Early Anglo-Saxon Kingdoms*, London.

ARNOLD, T. (ed.) (1882–5), *Simeonis Monachi Opera Omnia* (2 vols.), Rolls Series, London.

ARSLAN, E. (1984), 'La monetazione', in Pugliese Carratelli 1984: 413–44.

——(1992), 'Emissioni monetarie e segni del potere', *Committenti e produzione artistico-letteraria nell' alto medioevo occidentale: Settimane di Studio del Centro Italiano di Studi sull' Alto Medioevo (1991)*, Spoleto, 791–854.

ATCHLEY, E. G. (1909), *A History of the Use of Incense in Divine Worship*, London.

ATHERTON, M. (1993), 'The Figure of the Archer in *Beowulf* and the Anglo-Saxon Psalter', *Neophilologus*, 77: 653–7.

ATTENBOROUGH, F. L. (1922), *The Laws of the Earliest English Kings*, Cambridge.

ATSMA, H. (ed.) (1989), *La Neustrie: Les pays au Nord de la Loire de 650 à 850. Colloque historique international*. Francia Beihefte 16/1 and 16/2, Sigmaringen.

AXBOE, M. (1991), 'Guld og guder i folkevandringstiden', in Fabech and Ringtved 1991: 187–202.

BACKHOUSE, J. (1981), *The Lindisfarne Gospels*, London.

——(1989), 'Birds, Beasts and Initials in Lindisfarne Gospel Books', in Bonner, Rollason, and Stancliffe 1989: 165–74.

——TURNER, D. H., and WEBSTER, L. (eds.) (1984), *The Golden Age of Anglo-Saxon Art 966–1066*, London.

BADAWY, A. (1978), *Coptic Art and Archaeology*, Boston, Mass.

BAILEY, R. N. (1996), *England's Earliest Sculptors*, Toronto.

——and CRAMP, R. (1988), *British Academy Corpus of Anglo-Saxon Stone Sculpture in England*, vol. ii: *Cumberland and Westmorland*, Oxford.

BAKER, E. P. (1949), 'St Oswald and his Church at Zug', *Archaeologia*, 93: 103–23.

——(1951), 'The Cult of St Oswald in Northern Italy', *Archaeologia*, 94: 167–94.

BALDWIN BROWN, G. (1903–37), *The Arts in Early England* (6 vols.), London.

BAMMESBERGER, A. (ed.) (1991), *Old English Runes and their Continental Background*, Heidelberg.

BARASCH, M. (1997), *The Language of Art: Studies in Interpretation*, New York.

BASTIEN, P. (1992), *Le Buste monétaire des empereurs romains* (3 vols.), Wetteren.

BATTISCOMBE, C. F. (ed.) (1956), *The Relics of St Cuthbert*, Oxford.

BECKWITH, J. (1963), *Coptic Sculpture*, London.

BECKWITH, J. (1966), 'A Rediscovered English Reliquary Cross', *Victoria & Albert Museum Bulletin*, 11: 117–23.
——(1989), *Studies in Byzantine and Medieval Western Art*, London.
BELAIEW, N. T. (1932), 'Frisia and its Relations with England and the Baltic Littoral in the Dark Ages', *British Archaeological Association*, 37: 190–215.
——(1935), 'On the "Wodan Monster" or the "Dragon" series of the Anglo-Saxon sceattas', *Seminarium Kondakovianum, Recueil d'Études Archaeologie, Histoire de l'Art, Études Byzantines, Institut Kondakov*, vol. vii (Prague), 169–84.
BELFORT, A. (1892–95), *Description générale des monnaies mérovingiennes* (5 vols.), Paris.
BÉMONT, C. (ed.) (1987), *Mélanges offerts au Docteur J.-B. Colbert de Beaulieu*, Paris.
BÉNAZETH, D. (1992), *L'Art du métal au début de l'ère chrétienne*, Catalogue du département des antiquités égyptiennes, Musée du Louvre, Paris.
BENCARD, M. (ed.) (1981), *Ribe Excavations 1970–76*, vol. i, Esbjerg.
BENDIXEN, K. (1974), 'The First Merovingian Coin-Treasure from Denmark' *Medieval Scandinavia*, 7: 85–101.
——(1981a), 'The Currency in Denmark from the Beginning of the Viking Age until *c.*1100', in Blackburn and Metcalf 1981: 405–14.
——(1981b), 'Sceattas and Other Coin Finds', in Bencard 1981: 63–101.
——(1984), 'Finds of Sceattas from Scandinavia', in Hill and Metcalf 1984: 151–7.
BIDDLE, B., and KJØLBYE-BIDDLE, B. (1985), 'The Repton Stone', *Anglo-Saxon England*, 14: 233–92.
BIEDERMANN, H. (1992), *Dictionary of Symbolism*, New York.
BINSKI, P., and NOEL, W. (2001), *New Offerings, Ancient Treasures: Studies in Medieval Art for George Henderson*, Stroud.
BLACKBURN, M. (1984), 'A Chronology for the Sceattas', in Hill and Metcalf 1984: 165–74.
——(ed.) (1986), *Anglo-Saxon Monetary History (Essays in Memory of Michael Dolley)*, Leicester.
——(1991), 'A Survey of Anglo-Saxon and Frisian Coins with Runic Inscriptions', in Bammesberger 1991: 137–89.
——(1994), 'A Variant of the Seventh-Century "York" Group of Shillings Found in Lincolnshire', *Numismatic Chronicle*, 154: 204–8.
——(1995), 'Money and Coinage', in McKitterick 1995: 538–59.
——(1998a), 'The London Mint in the Reign of Alfred', in Blackburn and Dumville 1998: 105–23.
——(1998b), 'A New Coin of King Eadbald of Kent (616–40)', *Chris Rudd List*, no. 34: 2–4.
——and BONSER, M. (1984a), 'A Derivative of the *VER* Group of Intermediate Sceattas Found at Springfield, Essex', in Hill and Metcalf 1984: 229–31.
————(1984b), 'Sceattas, a Styca, and Other Coin Finds from a Site in North-East Lincolnshire', in Hill and Metcalf 1984: 233–7.
————(1985), 'Single Finds of Anglo-Saxon and Norman Coins—2', *British Numismatic Journal*, 55: 55–78.
————(1986), 'Single Finds of Anglo-Saxon and Norman Coins—3', *British Numismatic Journal*, 56: 64–96.

——— (1987), 'The "Porcupine" Sceattas of Metcalf's Variety G', *British Numismatic Journal*, 57: 99–103.

——and DUMVILLE, D. N. (eds.) (1998), *Kings, Currency and Alliances*, Woodbridge.

——and LYON, S. (1986), 'Regional Die-Production in Cnut's *Quatrefoil* Issue', in Blackburn 1986: 223–72.

——and METCALF, D. M. (eds.) (1981), *Viking Age Coinage in the Northern Lands*, 6th Oxford Symposium on Coinage and Monetary History (2 vols.), BAR International Series 122, Oxford.

BLAIR, J. (1994), *Anglo-Saxon Oxfordshire*, Stroud.

—— (1996*a*), 'Churches in the Early English Landscape: Social and Cultural Contexts', in Blair and Pyrah 1996: 6–18.

—— (1996*b*), 'The Minsters on the Thames', in Blair and Golding 1996: 5–28.

——and GOLDING, B. (eds.) (1996), *The Cloister and the World: Essays in Medieval History in Honour of Barbara Harvey*, Oxford.

——and PYRAH, C. (eds.) (1996), *Church Archaeology: Research Directions for the Future*, CBA Research Report 104, York.

BLAND, R., and JOHNS, C. (1993), *The Hoxne Treasure: An Illustrated Introduction*, London.

——and ORNA-ORNSTEIN, J. (eds.) (1997), *Coin Hoards from Roman Britain*, vol. x, London.

BLUNT, C. E. (1960), 'Ecclesiastical Coinage in England—Part One: To the Norman Conquest' (The President's Address to the Royal Numismatic Society, Session 1959–60, delivered 15 June 1960), *Numismatic Chronicle*[6] 20: pp. i–xviii.

—— (1961), 'The Coinage of Offa', in Dolley 1961: 39–62.

—— (1986), 'Anglo-Saxon Coins Found in Italy', in Blackburn 1986: 159–69.

——and DOLLEY, M. (1968), 'A Gold Coin of the Time of Offa', *Numismatic Chronicle*[7] 8: 151–60.

BONNER, C. (1950), *Studies in Magical Amulets*, Ann Arbor.

BONNER, G., ROLLASON, D., and STANCLIFFE, C. (eds.) (1989), *St Cuthbert, his Cult and his Community to AD 1200*, Woodbridge.

BONSER, W. (1935), 'The Magic of St Oswald', *Antiquity*, 9: 418–23.

BOON, G. C. (1992), 'Towards a Numismatic History of the Kingdom of Serendip, II', *Numismatic Circular*, Apr.: 82.

BOOTH, J. (1984), 'Sceattas in Northumbria', in Hill and Metcalf 1984: 71–111.

BOURKE, C. (1993), 'The Chronology of Irish Crucifixion Plaques', in Spearman and Higgitt 1993: 175–81.

—— (ed.) (1995), *From the Isles of the North: Early Medieval Art in Ireland and Britain*, Belfast.

BRADLEY, D. R., and DUMAIS, S. R. (1975), 'Ambiguous Cognitive Contours', *Nature*, 257: 582–4.

BRAILSFORD, W. (1951), *Guide to the Antiquities of Roman Britain*, London.

BRAILSFORD, W. (ed.) (1968–76), *Lexicon der christlichen Ikonographie* (8 vols.), Freiburg i. B.

BRÉHIER, L. (1903), 'Les Colonies d'Orientaux en Occident au commencement du moyen-âge', *Byzantinische Zeitschrift*, 12: 1–39.

BREHM, B. (1926), 'Der Ursprung der germanischen Tierornamentik', in Strzygowski 1926: 37–95.

BRENAN, J. (1991), *Hanging Bowls and their Context*, BAR British Series 220, Oxford.

BRENK, B. (1977), *Spätantike und frühes Christentum*, Frankfurt.

BROOKE, G. C. (1950), *English Coins from the Seventh Century to the Present Day* (3rd edn.), London.

BROOKS, N. (1971), 'The development of military obligations in eighth- and ninth-century England', in Clemoes and Hughes 1971: 69–84.

——(1984), *The Early History of the Church of Canterbury*, Leicester.

BROWN, D., CAMPBELL, J., and CHADWICK-HAWKES, S. (eds.) (1981), *Anglo-Saxon Studies in Archaeology and History* 2, BAR British Series 72, Oxford.

BROWN, M. P., and FARR, C. A. (eds.) (2001), *Mercia, an Anglo-Saxon Kingdom in Europe*, Leicester.

BRUCE-MITFORD, R. L. S. (1956), 'Late Saxon Disc-Brooches', in Harden 1956: 171–201.

——(1964), 'A Hiberno-Saxon Bronze Mounting from Markyate, Hertfordshire', *Antiquity*, 38: 219–20.

——(1974), *Aspects of Anglo-Saxon Archaeology*, London.

——(ed.) (1975), *The Sutton Hoo Ship-Burial*, vol. i: *Excavations, Background, the Ship, the Coins, Dating and Inventory*, London.

——(ed.) (1978), *The Sutton Hoo Ship-Burial*, vol. ii: *Arms, Armour and Regalia*, London.

——(ed.) (1983), *The Sutton Hoo Ship-Burial*, vol. iii: *Silver, Hanging-Bowls, Drinking Vessels, Containers, Musical Instruments, Textiles, Minor Objects*, London.

BUCKTON, D. (ed.) (1994), *Byzantium: Treasures of Byzantine Art and Culture*, London.

BUDNEY, M., and GRAHAM-CAMPBELL, J. (1981), 'An Eighth-Century Bronze Ornament from Canterbury and Related Works', *Archaeologia Cantiana*, 97: 7–25.

BULLOUGH, D. (1975), '"*Imagines Regum*" and their Significance in the Earliest Medieval West', in Robertson and Henderson 1975: 223–76.

——(1993), 'What has Ingeld to do with Lindisfarne?', *Anglo-Saxon England*, 22: 93–125.

BUSCHHAUSEN, H. (1995), *Der Lebenskreis der Kopten*, Vienna.

CABROL, F., and LECLERCQ, H. (eds.) (1907–53), *Dictionnaire de archéologie chrétienne et de liturgie* (15 vols.), Paris.

CAGNAT, R., and CHAPOT, V. (1916–20), *Manuel d' archeologie romaine*, Paris.

CALLMER, J. (1984), *Sceatta Problems in the Light of the Finds from Åhus*, Scripta Minora Regiae Societatis Humaniorum Litterarum Ludensis, Lund.

CAMERON, M. L. (1993), *Anglo-Saxon Medicine*, Cambridge Studies in Anglo-Saxon England, Cambridge.

CAMPBELL, J. (ed.) (1982), *The Anglo-Saxons*, Oxford.

CARE EVANS, A. (1994), *The Sutton Hoo Ship Burial*, London.

CARLETTI, C., and OTRANTO, G. (eds.) (1980), *Il Santuario di S. Michele sul Gargano dal VI al IX secolo*, Bari.

CARLYON-BRITTON, P. W. P. (1908), 'The Gold Mancus of Offa, King of Mercia', *British Numismatic Journal*, 5: 55–72.

CARRADICE, J. (1995), *Greek Coins*, London.

CARSON, R. A. G., and KRAAY, C. M. (eds.) (1978), *Scripta Nummaria Romana: Essays Presented to Humphrey Sutherland*, London.

CARVER, M. O. H. (1990), 'Pre-Viking Traffic in the North Sea', in McGrail 1990: 117–25.

——(ed.) (1992), *The Age of Sutton Hoo*, Woodbridge.

——(1998), *Sutton Hoo: Burial Ground of Kings?*, London.

CASARTELLI NOVELLI, S. (1992), 'Committenza e produzione scultorea "bassa"', *Committenti e produzione artistico-letteraria nell' alto medioevo occidentale, Settimane di Studio del Centro Italiano di Studi sull' Alto Medioevo (1991)*, Spoleto, 532–67.

CASEY, J. (1994), *Roman Coinage in Britain*, Princes Risborough.

——and REECE, R. (eds.) (1988), *Coins and the Archaeologist* (2nd edn.), London.

CHADWICK-HAWKES, S. (1981), 'Recent Finds of Inlaid Iron Buckles and Belt Plates from Eighth-Century Kent', in Brown, Campbell, and Chadwick-Hawkes 1981: 49–70.

——ELLIS DAVIDSON, H. R., and HAWKES, C. (1965), 'The Finglesham Man', *Antiquity*, 39: 17–32.

——MERRICK, J. M., and METCALF, D. M. (1966), 'X-Ray Fluorescent Analysis of some Dark Ages Coins and Jewellery', *Archaeometry*, 9: 98–138.

CHALLIS, C. E. (ed.) (1992), *A New History of the Royal Mint*, Cambridge.

CHANEY, W. A. (1962), 'Grendel and the Giftstol: A Legal View of the Monster', *Publications of the Modern Language Association of America*, 77: 513–20.

——(1970), *The Cult of Kingship in Anglo-Saxon England*, Manchester.

CHARLES-EDWARDS, T. (1998), 'Alliances, Godfathers, Treaties and Boundaries', in Blackburn and Dumville 1998: 47–62.

CHERRY, J. (1999), 'Antiquity Misunderstood', in Henig and Plantzos 1999: 143–7.

CHICK, D. (1989), 'A Portrait Coinage for Offa in East Anglia', *Numismatic Circular*, 97, July/Aug.: 191–2.

——(1997), 'Towards a Chronology for Offa's Coinage: An Interim Study', *Yorkshire Numismatist*, 3: 47–64.

CLEMOES, P. (1983), *The Cult of St Oswald on the Continent*, Jarrow Lecture.

——(1995), *Interactions of Thought and Language in Old English Poetry*, Cambridge.

——and HUGHES, K. (eds.) (1971), *England before the Conquest: Studies in Primary Sources Presented to Dorothy Whitelock*, Cambridge.

COCKAYNE, T. O. (1864–6), *Leechdoms, Wortcunning and Starcraft of Early England*, London.

COLGRAVE, B., and MYNORS, R. A. B. (eds.) (1969), *Bede's Ecclesiastical History of the English People*, Oxford.

COLGRAVE, B. (ed. and trans) (1956), *Felix's Life of Saint Guthlac*, Cambridge.

CONTI, R. (1983), *Il Tesoro: Guida alla conoscenza del Tesoro del Duomo di Monza*, Monza.

CONTICELLO DE'SPAGNOLI, M., and DE CAROLIS, E. (1986), *Le Lucerne di Bronzo: Musei della Biblioteca Apostolica Vaticana, Inventari e Studi I*, Città del Vaticano.

COWIE, R. (2001), 'Mercian London', in Brown and Farr 2001: 194–209.

CRAMP, R. J. (1977), 'Schools of Mercian Sculpture', in Dornier 1977: 191–233.

——(1984), *British Academy Corpus of Anglo-Saxon Stone Sculpture* (vol. 1.i–1.ii): *County Durham and Northumberland*, Oxford.

CRAWFORD, B. (ed.) (1994), *Scotland in Dark Age Europe*, St Andrews.

CRUIKSHANK DODD, E. (1961), *Byzantine Silver Stamps*, Washington, DC.

CUBITT, C. R. E. (1995), *Anglo-Saxon Church Councils c.650–c.850*, London.

CURLEY, M. J. (trans.) (1979), *Physiologus*, Austin, Tex.

DALTON, O. M. (1901), *Catalogue of Early Christian Antiquities and Objects from the Christian East* (British Museum), London.

——(1924), 'Sarmantian Ornaments from Kerch in the British Museum Compared with the Anglo-Saxon and the Merovingian Ornaments in the same Collection', *Antiquarian Journal*, 4: 259–62.

DANIELS, R. (1988), 'The Anglo-Saxon Monastery at Church Close, Hartlepool, Cleveland', *Archaeological Journal*, 114: 158–210.

DAVIS, W. (1989), 'Finding Symbols in History', in Morphy 1989: 179–89.

DEANESLY, M. (1943), 'Traditionalist Influence among the Anglo-Saxons', *English Historical Review*, 58: 129–46.

DE JERSEY, P. (1996), *Celtic Coinage in Britain*, Princes Risborough.

DE LASTEYRIE (1855), 'Notice sur une lampe chrétienne en forme de bélier', *Mémoires de la Société Imperiale des Antiquaires de France*, 3rd Series, 22: 224–39.

DEONNA, W. (1949), 'Daniel, le "maitre des fauves" ', *Artibus Asiae*, 12: 119–374.

DE WIT, G. W. (1984), 'Some Questions about the Primary Series (a Contribution to the Discussion)', in Hill and Metcalf 1984: 147–8.

DHÉNIN, M. (1987), 'Homotypies anachroniques', in Bémont 1987: 311–13.

Dictionary of Biblical Imagery (1998), ed. Ryken, Wilhoit, and Longman III, Downers Grove, Ill.

Die Alamannen (1997), (Catalogue of the exhibition 'Die Alamannen' 1997–8), Stuttgart.

Die Franken (1996), (2 vols. Catalogue of the exhibition 'Die Franken, Wegbereiter Europas. 5. bis 8. Jahrhundert n.Chr.—Les Francs, Précurseurs de L'Europe.Ve–VIIIe s.'), Mainz.

DIRKS, J. (1870), *Les Anglo-Saxons et leur petits deniers, dits sceattas: Essai historique et numismatique*, Brussels.

DIXON, P. (1991), 'Secular Architecture', in Webster and Backhouse 1991: 67–70.

DODWELL, C. R. (1982), *Anglo-Saxon Art: A New Perspective*, Manchester.

DOLLEY, M. (1988), 'Some Thoughts on the Manner of Publication of Coins Found in the Course of Archaeological Excavations', in Casey and Reece 1988: 254–63.

DOLLEY, R. H. M. (ed.) (1961), *Anglo-Saxon Coins*, London.

DORNIER, A. (ed.) (1977), *Mercian Studies*, Leicester.

DRANSART, P. (2001), 'Two Shrines Fragments from Kinneddar, Moray', in Redknap et al. 2001: 233–40.

DUBOIS, A. E. (1954), 'Giftstool', *Modern Language Notes*, 69: 546–9.

DU BOURGUET, P. (1964), *Catalogue des étoffes coptes: Musée National du Louvre*, Paris.

DUMAS, A. (ed.) (1981), *Liber Sacramentorum Gellonensis (alias Sacramentarium Gellonense)*, Corpus Christianorum, Series Latina, vol. 159 A, Turnhout.

DÜMMLER, E. (ed.) (1892), *Epistolae Merowingici et Karolini Aevi* I, Monumenta Germaniae Historica, *Epistolae III*, Berlin.

——(ed.) (1895), *Alcuini Epistolae; Epistolae Karolini Aevi* II, Monumenta Germaniae Historica *Epistolae IV*, Berlin.

DYNES, W. (1981), 'Imago Leonis', *Gesta*, 20/1: 35–41.

ELLIS DAVIDSON, H. R. (1967), *Pagan Scandinavia*, London.

ELLMERS, D. (1986), 'Schiffsdarstellungen auf skandinavischen Grabsteinen', in Roth 1986: 342–62.

ELSNER, J. (1995), *Art and the Roman Viewer: The Transformation of Art from the Pagan World to Christianity*, Cambridge.

——(1997), 'The Origins of the Icon: Pilgrimage, Religion and Visual Culture in the Roman East as "Resistance" to the Centre', in Alcock 1997: 178–99.

——(1998), *Imperial Rome and Christian Triumph*, Cambridge.

EMERTON, E. (trans. with introd.) (1940), *Boniface: Letters*, New York.

ENGEMANN, J. (1968–9), 'Bemerkungen zu Spätromischen Gläsern mit Goldfoliendekor', *Jahrbuch für antike und Christentum*, 11–12: 7–25.

——and RÜGER, C. B. (eds.) (1991), *Spätantike und frühes Mittelalter: Ausgewälte Denkmäler im Rheinischen Landesmuseum Bonn*, Bonn.

ESMEIJER, A. C. (1978), *Divina Quaternas: A Preliminary Study in the Method and Application of Visual Exegesis*, Assen.

ESTRICH, R. M. (1944), 'The Throne of Hrothgar—Beowulf, LL. 168–169', *Journal of English and German Philology*, 384–9.

EVANS, A. (1942), 'Notes on Early Anglo-Saxon Gold Coins', *Numismatic Chronicle*[6] 2: 19–41.

EVERSON, P., and STOCKER, D. (1999), *British Academy Corpus of Anglo-Saxon Stone Sculpture in England*, v: *Lincolnshire*, Oxford.

EVISON, V. (1979), *Wheel-Thrown Pottery in Anglo-Saxon Graves*, Royal Archaeological Institute Monograph, London.

FABECH, C., and RINGTVED, J. (eds.) (1991), *Samfundsorganisation og regionalvariation*, Jysk Archeologisk Selskab 27, Copenhagen.

FAEDO, L. (1978), 'Per una classificazione preliminare dei vetri dorati tardo-romani', *Annali della Scuola Normale di Pisa*, Series 3, vol. 3.3: 1025–70.

FARMER, D. H. (1978), *The Oxford Dictionary of Saints*, Oxford.

——(ed.) (1988), *The Age of Bede*, London.

FARR, C. A. (1997a), 'Worthy Women on the Ruthwell Cross: Woman as Sign in Early Anglo-Saxon Monasticism', in Karkov, Ryan, and Farrell 1997: 45–61.

——(1997b), *The Book of Kells: Its Function and Audience*, London.

FARRELL, R. T. (ed.) (1978), *Bede and Anglo-Saxon England* (Papers in honour of the 1300th anniversary of the birth of Bede, given at Cornell University in 1973–4), BAR British Series 46, Oxford.

——(ed.) (1982), *The Vikings*, London.

——(1986), 'Reflections on the Iconography of the Ruthwell and Bewcastle Crosses', in Szarmach and Oggins 1986: 357–76.

FAULL, M. L. (1977), 'British Survival in Anglo-Saxon Northumbria', in Laing 1977: 1–57.

FELL, C. (1984), *Women in Anglo-Saxon England*, London.

FENNELL, K. R. (1969), 'The Loveden Man', *Frümittelalterliche Studien*, 3: 211–15.

FENSKE, L., ROSENER, W., and ZOTZ, T. (eds.) (1984), *Institutionen, Kultur und Gesellschaft im Mittelalter: Festschrift J. Fleckenstein*, Sigmaringen.

FLETCHER, E. (1980), 'The Influence of Merovingian Gaul on Northumbria in the VII Century', *Medieval Archaeology*, 24: 69–86.

FLINT, V. (1991), *The Rise of Magic in Early Medieval Europe*, Oxford.

FORRER, R. (1908), *Keltische Numismatik der Rhein- und Donauland*, Straßburg.

FOSSARD, D. (1963), 'Décor mérovingiens des bijoux et des sarcophages de plâtre', *Art de France*, 30–9.

FOSTER, S. M. (ed.) (1998), *The St Andrews Sarcophagus*, Dublin.

GABORIT-CHOPIN, D. (1989), 'Les Trésors de Neustrie du VIIe au VIIIe siècle d' apres les sourses écrites: orfèvrerie et sculpture sur l' ivoire', in Atsma 1989: 259–94.

GAIMSTER, M. (1992), 'Scandinavian Gold Bracteates in Britain: Money and Media in the Dark Ages', *Medieval Archaeology*, 36: 1–28.

GAMESON, R. (1997), *Saint Augustine of Canterbury* (Photographic exhibition catalogue), Canterbury.

——(1999*a*), 'The Earliest Books of Christian Kent', in Gameson 1999*b*: 313–73.

——(ed.) (1999*b*), *St Augustine and the Conversion of England*, Stroud.

——and LEYSER, H. (eds.) (2001), *Belief and Culture in the Middle Ages. Studies Presented to Henry Mayr-Harting*, Oxford.

GANNON, A. (2002), 'King of all Beasts—Beast of all Kings: Lions in Anglo-Saxon Coinage and Art', in *Archaeological Review from Cambridge*, 18: 22–36.

——(forthcoming), 'A Chip off the Rood: The Cross in the Early Anglo-Saxon Coinage' (Kalamazoo 2002 paper, publication pending).

GARIPZANOV, I. H. (1999), 'The Image of Authority in Carolingian Coinage: The *Image of a Ruler and Roman Imperial Tradition*', *Early Medieval Europe*, 8 (2): 197–218.

GARRUCCI, R. (1858), *Vetri ornati di figure in oro trovati nei cimiteri cristiani primitivi di Roma*, Rome.

——(1872–80), *Storia dell' arte cristiana nei primi otto secoli della Chiesa* (6 vols.), Prato.

GEAKE, H. (1997), *The Use of Grave-Goods in Conversion-Period England, c.600–c.850*, BAR British Series 261, Oxford.

GELLING, M. (1978), *Signposts to the Past*, London.

GEM, R. (1996), 'Church Buildings: Cultural Location and Meaning', in Blair and Pyrah 1996: 1–6.

GLORIE, F. (ed.) (1968), *Tatwine Aenigmata*, C.C.S.L. 133, Turnhout.

GODEL, W. (1963), 'Irishes Beten im frühen Mittelalter', *Zeitschrift für Katholische Theologie*, 83: 261–321.

GOODBURN, R., and BARTHOLOMEW, P. (eds.) (1976), *Aspects of the Notitia Dignitatum*, BAR Supplementary Series 15, Oxford.

GOODCHILD, R. G. G. (1947), 'Farley Heath Sceptre', *Antiquaries Journal*, 27: 83–5.

GRABAR, A. (1971), *L'Empereur dans l' art byzantin*, London; first pub. 1936.

——(1966), *Byzantium: From the Death of Theodosius to the Rise of Islam*, London.

GRAHAM-CAMPBELL, J. (2001), 'National and Regional Identities: The "Glittering Prizes"', in Redknap et al. 2001: 27–38.

——and KIDD, D. (1980), *The Vikings*, London.

GREEN, B. (1971), 'An Anglo-Saxon Bone Plaque from Larling, Norfolk', *Antiquaries Journal*, 51: 321–3.

GREEN, M. (1976), *A Corpus of Religious Material from the Civilian Areas of Roman Britain (The Religion of Civilian Roman Britain)*, BAR 24, Oxford.

——(1992), 'The Iconography of Celtic Coins', in Mays 1992: 151–63.

GRIERSON, P. (1952), 'The Canterbury (St. Martin's) Hoard of Frankish and Anglo-Saxon Coin-Ornaments', *British Numismatic Journal*, 27: 39–51.

—— (1961), 'La Fonction sociale de la monnaie en Angleterre aux VIIe–VIIIe siècles', *Moneta e scambi nell'Alto medioevo, Settimane di Studio del Centro Italiano di Studi sull' Alto Medioevo*, Spoleto, 341–85.

—— (1953), 'A New Anglo-Saxon Solidus', *Numismatic Chronicle*[6] 13: 88–91.

—— (1967), 'The Volume of Anglo-Saxon Coinage', *Economic History Review*, 20: 153–60.

—— (1970), 'The Purpose of the Sutton Hoo Coins', *Antiquity*, 44: 14–18.

—— (1974), 'The Sutton Hoo Coins again', *Antiquity*, 48: 139–40.

—— (1975), *Numismatics*, London.

—— (1979), *Dark Age Numismatics*, London.

—— (1982), *Byzantine Coins*, London.

—— and BLACKBURN, M. (1986), *Medieval European Coinage 1: The Early Middle Ages (5th–10th Centuries)*, Cambridge.

GUNN, V. A. (1993), 'Bede and the Martyrdom of St Oswald', in Wood 1993: 57–66.

HARBISON, P. (1986), 'A Group of Early Christian Carved Stone Monuments in County Donegal', in Higgitt 1986: 49–85.

HARDEN, D. B. (ed.) (1956a), *Dark Age Britain (Studies presented to E. T. Leeds)*, London.

—— (1956b), 'Glass Vessels in Britain and Ireland AD 400–1000', in Harden 1956a: 132–67.

—— (ed.) (1987), *Glass of the Cæsars* (catalogue of the exhibition at the Corning Museum of Glass, Corning, NY), Milan.

HARDEN, D. B., PAINTER, K. S., PINDER-WILSON, R. H., and TAIT, H. (1968), *Masterpieces of Glass* (British Museum), London 1968.

HARMAN, M. MOLLESON, T. I., and PRICE, J. L. (1981), 'Burials, Bodies and Beheadings in Romano-British and Anglo-Saxon Cemeteries', *Bulletin British Museum Natural Hisory* (Geol.) 35, 3: 45–88.

HASELOFF, G. (1990), *Email im frühen Mittelalter: Frühchristliche Kunst von der Spätantike bis zu den Karolingern*, Marburg.

HAUCK, K. (1976), 'Bilddenkmäler zur Religion', *Reallexikon der Germanischen Altertumskunde, begr. von Johannes Hoops, Band 2, Lieferung 4/5*, pp. 577–98, New York.

—— (1984), 'Missiongeschichte in veränderter Sicht', in Fenske, Rosener, and Zotz 1984: 1–34.

—— and AXBOE, M. (1985), *Die Goldbrakteaten der Völkerwanderungzeit*, Munich.

HAWKES, J. (1993), 'Mary and the Cycle of Resurrection: The Iconography of the Hovingham Panel', in Spearman and Higgitt 1993: 254–60.

—— (1995), 'The Wirksworth Slab: An Iconography of Humilitas', *Peritia*, 8: 1–32.

—— (1996), 'The Rothbury Cross: An Iconographic Bricolage', *Gesta*, 35: 77–94.

—— (1999), 'Anglo-Saxon Sculpture: Questions of Context', in Hawkes and Mills 1999: 204–15.

—— (2001), 'Constructing Iconographies: Questions of Identity in Mercian Sculpture', in Brown and Farr 2001: 231–45.

—— and MILLS, S. (eds.) (1999), *Northumbria's Golden Age*, Stroud.

—— and Ó CARRAGÁIN, É., with TRENCH-JELLICOE, R. (2001), 'John the Baptist and the *Agnus Dei*: Ruthwell (and Bewcastle) Revisited', *The Antiquaries Journal*, 81: 131–53.

HENDERSON, G. (1972), *Early Medieval*, Harmondsworth.

HENDERSON, G. (1980), *Bede and the Visual Arts*, Jarrow Lecture.

——(1987), *From Durrow to Kells*, London.

——(1993), 'Cassiodorus and Eadfrith once again', in Spearman and Higgitt 1993: 82–91.

——(1999), *Vision and Image in Early Christian England*, Cambridge.

HENDERSON, I. (1983), 'Pictish Vine Ornament', in O'Connor and Clarke 1983: 243–68.

——(1986), 'The "David Cycle" in Pictish Art', in Higgitt 1986: 87–123.

——(1987), 'The Book of Kells and the Snake-Boss Motif on Pictish Cross Slabs and the Iona Crosses', in Ryan 1987: 56–65.

——(1994), 'The Insular and Continental Context of the St Andrews Sarcophagus', in Crawford 1994: 71–102.

——(1996), *Pictish Monsters: Symbol, Text and Image*, H. M. Chadwick Memorial Lectures 7, Cambridge.

——(1998), '*Primus inter pares*: The St Andrews Sarcophagus and Pictish Sculpture', in Foster 1998: 97–167.

HENDY, M. F. (1988), 'From Public to Private: The Western Barbarian Coinages as a Mirror of the Disintegration of Late Roman State Structures', *Viator*, 19: 29–78.

HENIG, M. (1975), *The Lewis Collection of Gemstones*, BAR Supplementary Series 1, Oxford.

——(1978), *A Corpus of Roman Engraved Gemstones from British Sites*, BAR British Series 8, Oxford.

——(ed.) (1983), *A Handbook of Roman Art*, London.

——(1994), *Classical Gems*, Fitzwilliam Museum, Cambridge.

——and PLANTZOS, D. (eds.) (1999), *Classicism to Neo-classicism: Essays Dedicated to Gertrud Seidmann*, BAR International Series 793, Oxford.

HERREN, M. W. (1998), 'The Transmission and Reception of Graeco-Roman Mythology in Anglo-Saxon England, 670–800', *Anglo-Saxon England*, 27: 87–103.

HICKS, C. (1986), 'The Birds on the Sutton Hoo Purse', *Anglo-Saxon England*, 15: 153–65.

——(1993), *Animals in Early Medieval Art*, Edinburgh.

HIGGITT, J. (1982), Review of G. Speake, *Anglo-Saxon Animal Art and its Germanic Background*, *Journal of the British Archaeological Association*, 135: 62–4.

——(ed.) (1986), *Early Medieval Sculpture in Britain and Ireland*, BAR British Series 152, Oxford.

HIGHAM, N. (1992), *Rome, Britain and the Anglo-Saxons*, London.

——(1993), *The Kingdom of Northumbria AD 350–1100*, Stroud.

——(1997), *The Convert Kings*, Manchester.

HILL, D. H., and METCALF, D. M. (eds.) (1984), *Sceattas in England and on the Continent*, BAR British Series 128, Oxford.

HILL, P. V. (1950), 'Saxon Sceattas and their Problems', *British Numismatic Journal*, 26 (1949–51), 129–55.

——(1951), 'The "Standard" and "London" Series of Anglo-Saxon Sceattas', *British Numismatic Journal*, 26: 1949–51, pp. 251–79.

——(1952), 'The Animal, "Anglo-Merovingian", and Miscellaneous Series of Anglo-Saxon Sceattas', *British Numismatic Journal*, 27, 1952–54, pp. 1–38.

——(1953), 'Uncatalogued Sceattas in the National and Other Collections', *Numismatic Chronicle*[6] 13: 92–114.

HILLS, C. (1979), 'The Archaeology of England in the Pagan Period: A Review', *Anglo-Saxon England*, 8: 297–329.

——(1983), 'Animal Stamps on Anglo-Saxon Pottery in East Anglia', *Studien zur Sachsenforschung*, 4: 93–110.

——(1990), 'Anglo-Saxon Chairperson', *Antiquity*, 54: 52–4.

HINES, J. (1984), *The Scandinavian Character of Anglian England in the Pre-Viking Period*, BAR British Series 124, Oxford.

——(1993), 'A Gold Bracteate from Kingston Bagpuize, Oxfordshire', *Medieval Archaeology*, 37: 219–22.

——(1997), *A New Corpus of Anglo-Saxon Great Square-Headed Brooches*, Woodbridge.

HINTON, D. A. (1974), *A Catalogue of the Anglo-Saxon Ornamental Metalwork in the Department of Antiquities, Ashmolean Museum, Oxford*, Oxford.

——(1982), 'Hamwic', in Campbell 1982: 102–3.

——(1986), 'Coins and Commercial Centres in Anglo-Saxon England', in Blackburn 1986: 11–26.

——(1996), *The Gold, Silver and other Non-ferrous Alloy Objects from Hamwic*, Southampton Archaeological Monographs 6, Southampton.

HODGES, R. (1982), *Dark Age Economics: The Origins of Towns and Trade* AD *600–1000*, London.

——(1989), *The Anglo-Saxon Achievement: Archaeology and the Beginnings of English Society*, London.

HOLMQVIST, W. (1939), *Kunstprobleme der Merowingerzeit*, Stockholm.

HOPE-TAYLOR, B. (1977), *Yeavering: An Anglo-British Centre of Early Northumbria*, London.

HOPPER, V. F. (1969), *Medieval Number Symbolism*, Oxford.

HOWLETT, D. R. (1974), 'The Iconography of the Alfred Jewel', *Oxoniensia*, 39: 44–52.

HÜBENER, W. (ed.) (1975), *Die Goldblattkreuze des frühen Mittelalters*, Veröffentlichung des Alemannischen Instituts Freiburg i. Br. 37, Bühl/Baden.

HUBERT, J. (1977), 'Les Routes du Moyen Age', *Arts et vie sociale de la fin du monde antique au Moyen Âge*, Geneva.

——PORCHER, J., and VOLBACH, W. F. (1969), *Europe in the Dark Ages*, London.

————(1970), *Carolingian Art*, London.

HUNTER, M. (1974), 'Germanic and Roman Antiquity and the Sense of the Past in Anglo-Saxon England', *Anglo-Saxon England*, 3: 29–50.

HUNTER BLAIR, P. (1971), 'The Letters of Pope Boniface V and the Mission of Paulinus to Northumbria', in Clemoes and Hughes 1971: 5–13.

HUTCHINSON, V. J. (1986), *Bacchus in Britain: The Evidence for his Cult*, BAR British Series 151, Oxford.

JAMES, E. (1988), *The Franks*, Oxford.

JANES, D. (1998), *God and Gold in Late Antiquity*, Cambridge.

JANSEN, A. (1995), 'The Development of the St Oswald Legends on the Continent', in Stancliffe and Cambridge 1995: 230–40.

JELLEMA, D. (1955), 'Frisian Trade in the Dark Ages', *Speculum*, 30: 15–36.

JENNBERT, K., ANDRÉN, A., and RAUDVERE, C. (eds.) (2002), *Plats och praxis: Studier av nordisk förkristen ritual*. Vägar till Middgård 2, Lund.

JESSOP PRICE, M. (1991), *The Coinage in the Name of Alexander the Great and Philip Arrhidaeus* (2 vols.), Zurich/London.

JESSUP, R. (1950), *Anglo-Saxon Jewellery*, London.

JEWELL, R. H. I. (1986), 'The Anglo-Saxon Friezes at Breedon-on-the-Hill, Leicestershire', *Archaeologia*, 108: 95–115.

——(2001), 'Classicism in Southumbrian Sculpture', in Brown and Farr 2001: 247–62.

JOHN, E. (1996), *Reassessing Anglo-Saxon England*, Manchester.

JOHNS, C. (1983), *The Thetford Treasure*, London.

——(1996), *The Jewellery of Roman Britian*, London.

JØRGENSEN, L. (2002), 'Kongsgård—kultsted—marked: Overvejelser omkring Tissøkompleksets struktur og funktion', in Jennbert, Andrén, and Raudvere 2002: 215–47.

KANTOROWICZ, E. H. (1960), 'The Archer in the Ruthwell Cross', *Art Bulletin*, 42: 57–9.

——(1965), 'Gods in Uniform', *Selected Studies*, New York: 7–24.

KARKOV, C. E. (1997), 'The Bewcastle Cross: Some Iconographical Problems', in Karkov, Ryan, and Farrell 1997: 9–26.

——and FARRELL, R. (eds.) (1991), *Studies in Insular Art and Archaeology*, American Early Medieval Studies 1, Oxford, Oh.

——RYAN, M., and FARRELL, R. T. (eds.) (1997), *The Insular Tradition*, New York.

KEARY, C. F. (1875), 'Art on the Coins of Offa', *Numismatic Chronicle*[2] 206–15.

——(1887), *A Catalogue of English Coins in the British Museum, Anglo-Saxon Series*, vol. i, London.

KEMPSHALL, M. (2001), 'No Bishop, No King: The Ministerial Ideology of Kingship and Asser's *Res Gestae Ælfredi*', in Gameson and Leyser 2001: 106–27.

KENT, J. P. C. (1961), 'From Roman Britain to Anglo-Saxon England', in Dolley 1961: 1–22.

——(1972), 'The Aston Rowant Treasure Trove', *Oxoniensia*, 37: 243–4.

——(1975), 'The Date of the Sutton Hoo Hoard' and 'Catalogue of the Sutton Hoo Coins, Blanks and Billets', in Bruce-Mitford 1975: 588–647.

——and PAINTER, K. S. (eds.) (1977), *Wealth of the Roman World AD 300–700*, London.

KER, N. R. (1957), *Catalogue of Manuscripts Containing Anglo-Saxon*, Oxford.

KEYNES, S. D. (1994), *The Councils of Clofesho*, Eleventh Brixworth Lecture, Brixworth.

KING, M. D. (1988), 'Roman Coins from Early Anglo-Saxon Contexts', in Casey and Reece 1988: 224–9.

KIRBY, D. P. (1991), *The Earliest English Kings*, London.

KITZINGER, E. (1936), 'Anglo-Saxon Scroll Ornament', *Antiquity*, 10: 61–71.

——(1940), *Early Medieval Art at the British Museum*, London.

——(1980), 'Christian Imagery: Growth and Impact', in Weitzmann 1980: 141–63.

——(1993), 'Interlace and Icons: Form and Function in Early Insular Art', in Spearman and Higgitt 1993: 3–15.

KLEIN-PFEUFFER, M. (1993), *Merowingerzeitliche Fibeln und Anhänger aus Preßblech*, Marburg.

KOCH, U. (1976), 'Frümittelalterliche Brakteatenfibeln—christliche oder heidnische Amulette?', *Jahrbuch für Historischen Verein*, Heilbronn 28: 19–28.

——(1982), *Die Fränkischen Gräberfelder von Bargen und Berghausen in Nordbaden*, Forschungen und Berichte zur Vor- und Frügeschichte in Baden-Würtenberg, Stuttgart.

KRAUSE, O. (ed.) (2001), *Tiere, Menschen, Götter: Wikingerzeitliche kunstile und ihre neuzeitliche Rezeption*, Hamburg.

KÜHN, H. (1941–2), 'Die Danielschnallen der Völkerwanderungszeit', *Jahrbuch für Historische und Ethnographische Kunst (IPEK)*, 140–69.

——(1974), *Die Germanischen Bügelfibeln der Völkerwanderungzeit in Süddeutschland* (2 vols.), Graz.

KYBALOVÁ, L. (1967), *Coptic Textiles*, London.

LAFAURIE, J. (1961), 'Les Routes commerciales indiquées par les trésors et trouvailles monétaires mérovingiennes', *Monete e scambi nell' Alto medioevo, Settimane di Studio del Centro Italiano di Studi sull' Alto Medioevo*, Spoleto, 231–78.

——(1963), 'Trésor de deniers mérovingiens trouvé à Savonières (Indre-et Loire)', *Revue Numismatique*[6] 5: 65–81.

——(1974), 'Les Animaux dans la numismatique mérovingienne', *Le Bestiaire des monnaies, des sceaux et des médailles*, Hôtel de la Monnaie exhibition, Paris, 137–50.

——JANSEN, B., and ZADOKS-JOSEPHUS JITTA, A. N. (1961), 'Le Trésor de Wieuwerd', *Oudheidkundige Mededelingen*, 42: 78–107.

LAING, L. (1977), *Studies in Celtic Survival*, BAR 37, Oxford.

——LAING, J. (1996), *Early English Art and Architecture*, Stroud.

LAMM, J. P., and NORDSTRÖM, H. Å. (eds.) (1983), *Vendel Period Studies: Transactions of the Boat-Grave Symposium in Stockholm, February 2–3 1981*, Stockholm.

LANG, J. (1988), *Anglo-Saxon Sculpture*, Aylesbury.

——(1991), *British Academy Corpus of Anglo-Saxon Stone Sculpture*, iii: *York and Eastern Yorkshire*, Oxford.

——(1999), 'The Imagery of the Franks Casket: Another Approach', in Hawkes and Mills 1999: 247–55.

——(2001) *British Academy Corpus of Anglo-Saxon Stone Sculpture in England* (vi): *Northern Yorkshire*, Oxford.

LAPIDGE, M., and HERREN, M. (1979), *Aldhelm: The Prose Works*, Ipswich.

——and ROSIER, J. L. (1985), *Aldhelm: The Poetic Works*, Cambridge.

LEBECQ, S. (1983), *Marchands et navigateurs frisons du haut moyen âge* (2 vols.), Lille.

——(1990), 'On the Use of the Word "Frisian" in the 6th–10th Centuries Written Sources: Some Interpretations', in McGrail 1990: 85–90.

——(1997*a*), 'Routes of Change: Production and Distribution in the West (5th–8th Century)', in Webster and Brown 1997: 67–78.

——(1997*b*), 'Le Grand Commerce frison au début du Moyen Age: Une mise à jour', *Revue du Nord*, 89, no. 322: 995–1005.

——(1999), 'England and the Continent in the Sixth and Seventh Centuries: The Question of Logistics', in Gameson 1999*b*: 50–67.

LECLERCQ, J. (1957), *L'Amour des lettres et le désir de Dieu: Initiation aux auteurs monastiques du Moyen Age*, Paris.

LEEDS, E. T. (1949), *A Corpus of Early Anglo-Saxon Great Square-Headed Brooches*, Oxford.

LEIGH, D. (1980), 'Ambiguity in Anglo-Saxon Style I Art', *Antiquaries Journal*, 64: 34–42.

LEMAN, P. (1990), 'Quentovic: État des recherches', *Revue du Nord*, 72, no. 286: 175–8.

Les Francs (1997), special edition of *Connaissance des Arts* for the exhibition 'Les Francs, Précurseurs de l'Europe', Paris.

LEVISON, W. (1946), *England and the Continent in the VIII Century*, Oxford.

LEWIS, A. R. (1958), *The Northern Seas: Shipping and Commerce in Northern Europe AD 300–1100*, Princeton.

LEWIS, S. (1980), 'Sacred Calligraphy: The Chi-Rho Page in the *Book of Kells*', *Traditio*, 36: 139–59.

LEYERLE, J. (1967), 'The Interlace Structure of Beowulf', *University of Toronto Quarterly*, 37: 1–17.

LINDSAY, W. M. (ed.) (1911), *Isidori Hispalensis Episcopi Etymologiarum sive Originum* (2 vols.), Oxford.

LOCKETT, R. C. (1920), 'The Coinage of Offa', *Numismatic Chronicle*⁴ 20: 57–89.

LONGWORTH, I., and CHERRY, J. (eds.) (1986), *Archaeology in Britain since 1945*, London.

LOTHER, H. (1929), *Der Pfau in der Altkristichen Kunst*, Leipzig.

LOWE, E. A. (1934–72), *Codices Latini Antiquiores: A Paleographical Guide to Latin Manuscripts Prior to the Ninth Century* (11 vols. and supplement), Oxford.

LOWRIE, W. (1947), *Art in the Early Church*, New York.

LUISELLI FADDA, A. M., and Ó CARRAGÁIN, É. (eds.) (1998), *Le isole britanniche e Roma in età romanobarbarica*, Rome.

LUKMAN, N. (1958), 'The Raven Banner and the Changing Ravens', *Classica et Mediaevalia*, 19: 133–51.

MCCLURE, J., and COLLINS, R. (trans.) (1994), *Bede: The Ecclesiastical History of the English People*, Oxford.

MCENTIRE, S. (1986), 'The Devotional Context of the Cross before AD 1000', in Szarmach and Oggins 1986: 345–56.

MCGRAIL, S. (ed.) (1990), *Maritime Celts, Frisians and Saxons*, CBA Research Report 71, London.

MACGREGOR, A. (1997), *A Summary Catalogue of the Continental Archaeological Collections (Roman Iron Age, Migration Period, Early Medieval)*, British Archaeological Reports, International Series 674, Oxford.

——(1998), 'A Viking Age Brooch from Berinsfield', *The Ashmolean*, 35: 9.

——(1999), 'The Afterlife of Childeric's Ring', in Henig and Plantzos 1999: 149–62.

——and BOLICK, E. (1993), *A Summary Catalogue of the Anglo-Saxon Collections (Non-ferrous Metals), Ashmolean Museum Oxford*, Oxford.

MACKEPRANG, M. B. (1952), *De Nordiske Guldbrakteater*, Århus.

MCKITTERICK, R. (1989), 'The Diffusion of Insular Culture in Neustria between 650 and 850: The Implications of the Manuscript Evidence', in Atsma 1989: 395–432.

——(1989), 'Anglo-Saxon Missionaries in Germany: Reflections on the Manuscript Evidence', *Transactions of the Cambridge Bibliographical Society*, 9: 291–329.

——(1991), *Anglo-Saxon Missionaries in Germany: Personal Connections and Local Influences*, 8th Brixworth Lecture 1990, University of Leicester Vaughan Paper 36, Leicester.

——(1994), *Books, Scribes and Learning in the Frankish Kingdoms, 6th–9th Centuries*, Aldershot.

——(ed.) (1995), *The New Cambridge Medieval History II: c.700–c.900*, Cambridge.

MACLEAN, D. (1993), 'Snake-Bosses and Redemption at Iona and in Pictland', in Spearman and Higgitt 1993: 245–53.

MAGNUS, B. (1997), 'The Firebed of the Serpent: Myth and Religion in the Migration Period Mirrored through some Gold Objects', in Webster and Brown 1997: 194–207.

MAGNUSSON, M., and FORMAN, W. (1976), *Viking Hammer of the North*, London.

MARCH, J. (1998), *Dictionary of Classical Mythology*, London.

MARSDEN, R. (1999), 'The Gospels of St Augustine', in Gameson 1999*b*: 285–312.

MARSHALL, F. H. (1911), *Catalogue of the Jewellery (Greek, Etruscan and Roman) in the Department of Antiquities, British Museum*, London.

MARTH, R. (ed.) (2000), *Das Gandersheimer Runenkästchen, Internationales Kolloquium Braunschweig, 24.–26. März 1999*, Braunschweig.

MASTRELLI, C. A. (1980), 'Le iscrizioni runiche', in Carletti and Otranto 1980: 321–32.

MATHEWS, T. F. (1993), *The Clash of Gods: A Reinterpretation of Early Christian Art*, Princeton.

MATTINGLY, H. (1937), 'The Roman "Virtues"', *Harvard Theological Review*, 30: 103–17.

MAY, J. (1977), 'Romano-British and Saxon Sites near Dorchester on Thames, Oxfordshire', *Oxoniensia*, 42: 42–79.

MAYR-HARTING, H. (1972), *The Coming of Christianity to Anglo-Saxon England*, London.

MAYS, M. (ed.) (1992), *Celtic Coinage: Britain and Beyond*, BAR British Series 222, Oxford.

MAZO KARRAS, M. (1985), 'Seventh-Century Jewellery from Frisia: A Re-examination', *Anglo-Saxon Studies in Archaeology and History*, 4: 159–77.

MEANEY, A. (1964), *A Gazetteer of Early Anglo-Saxon Burial Sites*, London.

——(1981), *Anglo-Saxon Amulets and Curing Stones* BAR British Series 96, Oxford.

MEEHAN, B. (1994), *The Book of Kells*, London.

——(1996), *The Book of Durrow*, Dublin.

MEGAW, R., and MEGAW, V. (1989), *Celtic Art*, London.

MENDE, U. (1981), *Die Türzieher des Mittelalters* (Denkmäler deutscher Kunst) (Bronzegeräte des Mittelalters, 2), Berlin.

MENENDEZ PIDAL, R. (ed.) (1980), *Historia de España*, iii: *España Visigoda*, Madrid.

MENIS, G. C. (1990), *I Longobardi*, Milan.

MENZ-VONDER MÜHLL, M. (1981), 'Die St. Gallen Elfenbeine um 900', *Frühmittelalterlichen Studien*, 15: 387–434.

METCALF, D. M. (1963), 'Offa's Pence Reconsidered', *Cunobelin*, 9: 37–52.

——(1965), 'How Large was the Anglo-Saxon Currency?', *Economic History Review*, 18: 475–82.

——(1966*a*), 'A Coinage for Mercia under Æthelbald', *Cunobelin*, 12: 26–39.

——(1966*b*), 'A Stylistic Analysis of "Porcupine" Sceattas', *Numismatic Chronicle*[7] 6: 179–205.

——(1972), 'The "Bird and Branch" Sceattas in the Light of a Find from Abingdon', *Oxoniensia*, 37: 51–65.

——(1974), 'Sceattas Found at the Iron-Age Hill Fort of Walbury Camp, Berkshire', *British Numismatic Journal*, 44: 1–12.

——(1976*a*), 'Twelve Notes on Sceattas Finds', *British Numismatic Journal*, 46: 1–18.

——(1976*b*), 'Sceattas from the Territory of the Hwicce', *Numismatic Chronicle*[7] 16: 64–74.

METCALF, D. M. (1982), 'Anglo-Saxon Coins I: Seventh to Ninth Centuries', in Campbell 1982: 62–3.

——(1984a), 'Monetary Circulation in Southern England in the First Half of the Eighth Century', in Hill and Metcalf 1984: 27–69.

——(1984b), 'Twenty-five Notes on Sceattas Finds', in Hill and Metcalf 1984: 193–205.

——(1984c), 'A Note on Sceattas as a Measure of International Trade, and on the Earliest Danish Coinage', in Hill and Metcalf 1984: 159–64.

——(1988a), 'Monetary Expansion and Recession: Interpreting the Distribution Patterns of Seventh and Eighth-Century Coins', in Casey and Reece 1988: 230–53.

——(1988b), 'A Sceat of Series K Minted by Archbishop Berhtwald of Canterbury (693–731)', *British Numismatic Journal*, 58: 124–6.

——(1988c), 'The Coins', in Andrews 1988: 17–59.

——(1993–4), *Thrymsas and Sceattas in the Ashmolean Museum Oxford* (3 vols.), London.

——(2000), 'Determining the Mint-Attribution of East-Anglian Sceattas through Regression Analysis', *British Numismatic Journal*, 70: 1–11.

——and WALKER, D. R. (1967), 'The "Wolf" Sceattas', *British Numismatic Journal*, 36: 11–28.

MICHELLI, P. (1999), 'What's in the Cupboard? Ezra and Matthew Reconsidered', in Hawkes and Mills 1999: 345–64.

MILBURN, R. (1988), *Early Christian Art and Architecture*, Aldershot.

MILES, G. C. (1952), *The Coinage of the Visigoths of Spain: Leovigild to Achila II*, New York.

MILNE, G. (1990), 'Maritime Traffic between the Rhine and Roman Britain', in McGrail 1990: 82–4.

MITCHELL, J. (2001), 'The High Cross and Monastic Strategies in Eighth-Century Northumbria', in Binski and Noel 2001: 88–114.

MOREHART, M. J. (1970), 'Some Dangers of Dating Sceattas by Typological Sequences', *British Numismatic Journal*, 39: 1–5.

——(1984), 'Anglo-Saxon Art and the "Archer" Sceat', in Hill and Metcalf 1984: 181–92.

——(1985), 'Female Centaur or Sphinx? On Naming Sceat Types: The Case of *BMC* Type 471', *British Numismatic Journal*, 55: 1–9.

MOREY, C. F. (1959), *The Gold-Glass Collection of the Vatican Library*, Vatican City.

MORPHY, H. (ed.) (1989), *Animals into Art*, London.

MORTON, A. (1999), 'Hamwic in its Context', in Anderton 1999: 48–62.

MUNDELL MANGO, M. (1986), *Silver from Early Byzantium*, Baltimore.

MURAWSKI, P. (2000), *Benet's [sic]. Artefacts of England & the United Kingdom, Current Values*, Cambridge.

MUTHESIUS, A. (1997), *Byzantine Silk Weaving AD 400 to AD 1200*, Vienna.

NAU, E. (1982), 'Ein angelsächsischer Sceatta und das Goldblattkreutz von Ulm-Ermingen', *Fundberichte aus Baden-Württenberg*, 7: 475–9.

NELSON, J. L. (1995), 'Kingship and Royal Government', in McKitterick 1995: 383–430.

——(2001), 'Carolingian Contacts', in Brown and Farr 2001: 126–43.

NEUMAN DE VEGVAR, C. (1986), 'The Iconography of Kingship in Anglo-Saxon Archaeological Finds', in Rosenthal 1986: 1–15.

——(1997), 'The Echternach Lion: A Leap of Faith', in Karkov, Ryan, and Farrell 1997: 167–88.

——(1999), 'The Travelling Twins: Romulus and Remus in Anglo-Saxon England', in Hawkes and Mills 1999: 256–67.

NEWMAN, J. (1999), 'Wics, Trade, and the Hinterlands: The Ipswich Region', in Anderton 1999: 32–47.

NILES, J. D. (1977), *Beowulf: The Poem and its Tradition*, Cambridge, Mass.

——(1998), 'Exeter Book Riddle 74 and the Play of the Text', *Anglo-Saxon England*, 27: 169–207.

NORDENFALK, C. (1976), 'Les cinq sens dans l'art du Moyen Age', *Revue de l'Art*, 34: 17–28.

——(1985), 'The Five Senses in Late Medieval and Renaissance Art', *Journal of the Warburg and Courtauld Institutes*, 48: 1–22.

NORTH, J. J. (1980), *English Hammered Coinage*, vol. i, London.

Ó CARRAGÁIN, É. (1986), 'Christ over the Beasts and the Agnus Dei: Two Multivalent Panels on the Ruthwell and Bewcastle Crosses', in Szarmach and Oggins 1986: 377–403.

——(1987), 'A Liturgical Interpretation of the Bewcastle Cross', in Stokes and Burton 1987: 15–42.

——(1987–8), 'The Ruthwell Crucifixion Poem in its Iconographic and Liturgical Contexts', *Peritia* 6–7: 1–71.

——(1988), 'The Meeting of St Paul and St Anthony: Visual and Literary Uses of a Eucharistic Motif', in Wallace and MacNiocaill 1988: 1–58.

——(1999), 'The Necessary Distance', in Hawkes and Mills 1999: 191–203.

O'CONNOR, A., and CLARKE, D. V. (eds.) (1983), *From the Stone Age to the 'Forty Five': Studies Presented to R. B. K. Stevenson*, Edinburgh.

ODDY, A. (1991), 'Arab Imagery on Early Umayyad Coins in Syria and Palestine: Evidence for Falconry', *Numismatic Chronicle*, 151: 59–66.

OGGINS, R. S. (1984), 'Falconry in Anglo-Saxon England', *Mediaevalia*, 7: 173–208.

O'MAHONY, F. (ed.) (1994), *The Book of Kells*, Proceedings of a Conference at Trinity College Dublin, 6–9 Sept. 1992, Dublin.

OP DEN VELDE, W., DE BOONE, W. J., and POL, A. (1984), 'A Survey of Sceatta Finds from the Low Countries', in Hill and Metcalf 1984: 117–45.

O'REILLY, J. (1998), 'Patristic and Insular Traditions of the Evangelists: Exegesis and Iconography', Luiselli Fadda and Ó Carragáin 1998: 49–94.

ORLANDONI, M. (1988), 'La via commerciale della Valle d'Aosta nella documentazione numismatica', *Rivista Italiana di Numismatica*, 90: 433–48.

ORTON, F. (1999), 'Northumbrian Sculpture (the Ruthwell and Bewcastle Monuments): Questions of Difference', in Hawkes and Mills 1999: 216–26.

OSBORN, M. (1991), 'The Lid as Conclusion of the Syncretic Theme of the Franks Casket', in Bammesberger 1991: 249–68.

OSWALD, F. (1964), *Index of Figure Types on Terra Sigillata*, London.

OWEN-CROCKER, G. R. (1986), *Dress in Anglo-Saxon England*, Manchester.

——(1991), 'Hawks and Horse Trappings; The Insigna of Rank', in Scragg 1991: 220–37.

PAGAN, H. E. (1965), 'A Third Gold Coin of Mercia', *British Numismatic Journal*, 34: 8–10.

PAGAN, H. E. (1986), 'Coinage in Southern England, 796–874', in Blackburn 1986: 45–65.

PAGE, R. I. (1990), *Matthew Parker and his Books*, Sanards Lectures in Bibliography, Cambridge.

PAINTER, K. (1987), 'Gold-Glass', in Harden 1987: 276–86.

PANAZZA, G., and TAGLIAFERRI, A. (1996), *Corpus della scultura altomedievale Italiana*, iii: *La diocesi di Brescia*, Spoleto.

PARKER PEARSON, M., VAN DER NOORT, R., and WOOLF, A. (1993), 'Three men and a Boat: Sutton Hoo and the East Saxon Kingdom', *Anglo-Saxon England*, 22: 27–50.

PARSONS, D. (1976), 'A Note on the Breedon Angel', *Transactions of the Leicestershire Archaeological and Historical Society*, 51: 40–3.

——(2001), 'The Mercian Church: Archaeology and Topography', in Brown and Farr 2001: 50–68.

PEDERSEN, A. (1994–6), 'A Striding Man from Tissø: A Rare Imitation of Charlemagne's Dorestad-Coinage', *Nordisk Numismatisk Årsskrift*, 22–40.

——(2001), 'Rovfugle eller Duer. Fugleformede Fibler fra den Tidlige Middelalder', *Aarbøger for Nordisk Oldkyndigheid og Historie 1999*, Copenhagen: 19–66.

PEERS, C., and RADFORD, C. A. R. (1943), 'The Saxon Monastery at Whitby', *Archaeologia*, 89: 27–88.

PÉRIN, P. (1980), *Paris Mérovingien*, Bulletin du Musée Carnavalet, 33e Année, 1980, Nos. 1 et 2, Paris, 7–52.

——(1996), *L'Art mérovingien: Permanences et innovations*, Liege.

PERONI, A. (1967), *Oreficerie e metalli lavorati tardoantichi e altomedievali del territorio di Pavia*, Spoleto.

PESCHECK, C. (1975), 'Germanische Gräberfelder in Kleinlangenheim, Lk. Kitzingen', Kat. RGZM 1975 *Ausgrabungen in Deutschland*, ii. 211–23.

PIRIE, E. J. E. (1992), 'The Seventh-Century Gold Coinage of Northumbria', *Yorkshire Numismatist*, 2: 11–15.

PIROTTE, E. (2001), 'Hidden Order, Order Revealed: New Light on Carpet Pages', in Redknap et al. 2001: 203–7.

PLUNKETT, S. J. (1998), 'The Mercian Perspective', in Foster 1998: 202–26.

——(2001), 'Some Recent Metalwork Discoveries from the Area of the Gipping Valley, and their Local Context', in Binski and Noel 2001: 61–87.

POESCHEL, E. (1948), *Die Kunstdenkmäler des Kantons Graubünden*, vii: *Chur und der Kreis fünf Dörfer*, Basel.

PORSIA, F. (1976), *Liber Monstrorum: introduzione, versione e commento*, Bari.

POTTER, T. W. (1997), *Roman Britain*, London.

PRATT, D. R. (forthcoming), 'Persuasion and Invention at the Court of King Alfred the Great', in C. Cubitt (ed.), *Court Culture in the Early Middle Ages*, Turnhout.

PROU, M. (1892), *Les Monnaies mérovingiennes (Catalogue des monnaies françaises de la Biblithèque Nationale)*, Paris.

PUGLIESE CARRATELLI, G. (ed.) (1982), *I Bizantini in Italia*, Milan.

——(ed.) (1984), *Magistra Barbaritas: I Barbari in Italia*, Milan.

RASPI-SERRA, J. (1974), *Corpus della scultura altomedievale Italiana*, viii: *Alto Lazio*, Spoleto.

RAW, B. C. (1967), 'The Archer, the Eagle and the Lamb', *Journal of the Warburg and Courtauld Institutes*, 30: 391–4.

——(1970), 'The *Dream of the Rood* and its Connections with Early Christian Art', *Medium Ævum*, 30, no. 3: 239–56.

——(1992), 'Royal Power and Royal Symbols in Beowulf', in Carver 1992: 167–74.

REDKNAP, M., EDWARDS, N., YOUNGS, S., LANE, A. and KNIGHT, J. (eds.) (2001), *Pattern and Purpose in Insular Art*, Oxford.

REECE, R. (1983), 'Coins and Medals', in Henig 1983: 166–78.

RENNER, D. (1970), *Die Durchbrochenen Zierscheiben der Merowingerzeit*, Mainz.

REUTER T. (ed.) (1980), *The Greatest Englishman: Essays on St Boniface and the Church at Crediton*, Leicester.

RICE, D. T. (1956), 'New Light on the Alfred Jewel', *Antiquaries Journal*, 36: 214–17.

RICE, T. T. (1973), *Ancient Arts of Central Asia*, London.

RICHARDS, P. (1980), 'Byzantine Bronze Vessels in England and Europe', University of Cambridge unpublished Ph.D. dissertation.

RICHARDSON, H. (1984), 'Number and Symbol in Early Christian Irish Art', *Journal of the Royal Society of Antiquaries of Ireland*, 114: 28–47.

RIDDLE J. M. (1965), 'The Introduction and Use of Eastern Drugs in the Early Middle Ages', *Sudhoffs Archiv für Geschichte der Medizin und der Naturwissenschaften*, 49: 185–98.

RIEMER, E. (1997), 'Im Zeichen des Kreuzes', *Die Alamannen*, Stuttgart.

RIGOLD, S. E. (1960), 'The Two Primary Series of English Sceattas', *British Numismatic Journal*, 30: 6–53.

——(1975), 'The Sutton Hoo Coins in the Light of the Contemporary Background of Coinage in England', in Bruce-Mitford 1975: 653–77.

——(1977), 'The Principal Series of English Sceattas', *British Numismatic Journal*, 47: 21–30.

——and METCALF, D. M. (1977), 'A Check-List of English Finds of Sceattas', *British Numismatic Journal*, 47: 31–52.

RITCHIE, A. (1989), *The Picts*, Edinburgh.

RIVES, J. B. (trans.) (1999), *Tacitus 'Germania'*, Oxford.

ROBERTSON, A. S. (1961), *Hunterian and Coats Collection, University of Glasgow. Sylloge of Coins of the British Isles*, 2, London.

ROBERTSON, G., and HENDERSON, G. (eds.) (1975), *Studies in Memory of D. T. Rice*, Edinburgh.

ROGERSON, A., and DALLAS, C. (eds.) (1984), *Excavations in Thetford 1948–59 and 1973–80*, East Anglian Archaeological Report 22, Dereham.

ROLLASON, D. (1989), *Saints and Relics in Anglo-Saxon England*, Cambridge, Mass.

——with GORE D., and FELLOWS-JENSEN, G. (1998), *Sources for York History to AD 1100*, York.

ROSENBAUM, E. (1955), 'The Vine Columns of Old St. Peter's in Carolingian Canon Tables', *Journal of the Warburg and Courtauld Institutes*, 18: 1–15.

ROSENTHAL, J. (ed.) (1986), *Kings and Kingship*, Acta for 1984, Center for Medieval and Early Renaissance Studies, vol. 11, Binghampton.

ROSS, M. C. (1962–5), *Catalogue of the Byzantine and Early Medieval Antiquities in the Dumbarton Oaks Collection* (2 vols.), Washington, DC.

ROTH, H. (ed.) (1986), *Zum Problem der Deutung frümittelalterlicher Bildinhalte*, Sigmarigen.

ROTILI, M. (1966), *Corpus della scultura altomedievale*, v: *Diocesi di Benevento*, Rome.

RYAN, M. (ed.) (1987), *Ireland and Insular Art AD 500–1200*, Dublin.

——(1990), 'The Formal Relationships of Insular Early Medieval Eucharistic Chalices', *Proceedings of the Royal Irish Academy*, vol. 90, Series C, no. 10: 281–356.

RYAN, M. (1991), 'Links between Anglo-Saxon and Irish Early Medieval Art: Some Evidence of Metalwork', in Karkov and Farrell 1991: 117–26.

RYNNE, E. (1994), 'Drolleries in the Book of Kells', in O'Mahony 1994: 311–21.

SALIN, B. (1904), *Die altgermanische Thierornamentik*, Stockholm.

SALIN, E. (1939–43), *Rhin et l' Orient* (2 vols.), Paris.

——(1942–3), 'Sur quelques images tételaires de la Gaule Mérovingienne. Apports orientaux et survivances sumeriennes', *Syria*, 23: 201–43.

——(1949–59), *La Civilisation mérovingienne* (4 vols.), Paris.

SALZMAN, M. R. (1990), *On Roman Time: The Codex-Calendar of 354 and the Rhythms of Urban Life in Late Antiquity*, Berkeley, Calif.

SAWYER, P. H. (1977), 'Kings and Merchants', in Sawyer and Wood 1977: 139–58.

——and WOOD, I. N. (eds.) (1977), *Early Medieval Kingship*, Leeds.

SAXL, F. (1943), 'The Ruthwell Cross', *Journal of the Warburg and Courtauld Institutes*, 6: 1–19.

SCHARER, A. (1999), 'The Gregorian Tradition in Early England', in Gameson 1999*b*: 187–201.

SCHEERS, S. (1992), 'Celtic Coin Types in Britain and their Mediterranean Origins', in Mays 1992: 33–46.

SCHILLER, G. (1971), *Ikonographie der Christlichen Kunst*, iii: *Die Auferstehung und Erhöhung Christi*, Gütersloh.

SCHMIDT, H., and SCHMIDT, M. (1982), *Die vergessene Bildsprache Christlicher Kunst*, Munich.

SCHMIDT, V. M. (1995), *A Legend and its Image*, Groningen.

SCHRAMM, P. E. (1954), *Herrschaftszeichen und Staatssymbolik*, Schriften der Monumenta Germaniae Historica, 13: 1, Stuttgart.

——and MÜTHERICH, F. (1962), *Denkmale der deutschen Könige und Kaiser*, Munich.

SCRAGG, D. (ed.) (1991), *The Battle of Maldon AD 991*, Manchester.

SEEWALD, C. (1981), 'Ein alamannisches Kriegergrab mit Goldblattkreutz von Ulm-Ermingen', *Fundberichte aus Baden-Würtenberg*, 6: 667–715.

SELLWOOD, L., and METCALF, D. M. (1986), 'A Celtic Silver Coin of Previously Unpublished Type from St. Nicholas at Wade, Thanet: The Prototype for Anglo-Saxon Sceattas of *BMC* Type 37?', *British Numismatic Journal*, 56: 181–2.

SENA CHIESA, G. (1978), *Gemme di Luni*, Archaeologica 4, Rome.

SETTIS-FRUGONI, C. (1973), *Historia Alexandri elevati per griphos ad aerem*, Rome.

SHAPIRO, M. (1963), 'The Bowman and the Bird on the Ruthwell Cross and Other Works', *Art Bulletin*, 45: 351–5.

SIMS-WILLIAMS, P. (1990), *Religion and Literature in Western England 600–800*, Cambridge.

SISAM, K. (1953), 'Anglo-Saxon Royal Genealogies', *Proceedings of the British Academy*, 39: 287–346.

SMEDLEY, N., and OWLES, E. (1965), 'Some Anglo-Saxon "Animal"-Brooches', *Proceedings of the Suffolk Institute of Archaeology and Natural History*, 30: 166–74.

SMITH, R. A. (1923), *British Museum Guide to Anglo-Saxon Antiquities 1923*, London.

SMITH, W., and CHEETHAM, S. (1875–80), *A Dictionary of Christian Antiquities* (2 vols.), London.

SPEAKE, G. (1970), 'A Seventh-Century Coin-Pendant from Bacton, Norfolk, and its Ornament', *Medieval Archaeology*, 14: 1–16.

——(1980), *Anglo-Saxon Animal Art and its Germanic Background*, Oxford.

SPEARMAN, R. M., and HIGGITT, J. (eds.) (1993), *The Age of Migrating Ideas*, Edinburgh.

STAFFORD, P. (2001), 'Political Women in Mercia, Eighth to Early Tenth Centuries', in Brown and Farr 2001: 34–49.

STANCLIFFE, C., and CAMBRIDGE, E. (eds.) (1995), *Oswald, Northumbrian King to European Saint*, Stamford.

STENTON, F. (1971), *Anglo-Saxon England* (3rd edn.), Oxford.

STEUER, H. (1987), 'Helm und Ringschwert: Prunkbewaffung und Rangbezeichen germanischer Krieger. Eine Übersicht', *Studien zur Sachsenforschung*, 6: 189–236.

STEVENSON, R. B. K. (1981–2), 'Aspects of Ambiguity in Crosses and Interlace' (the Oliver Davies Lecture for 1981), *Ulster Journal of Archaeology*, 44–5: 1–27.

——(1993), 'Further Thoughts on some Well-Known Problems', in Spearman and Higgitt 1993: 16–26.

STEVICK, R. D. (1994), *The Earliest Irish and English Bookarts: Visual and Poetic Forms before AD 1000*, Philadelphia.

STEWART, B. H. I. H. (1978), 'Anglo-Saxon Gold Coins', in Carson and Kraay 1978: 143–72 (with appendix by W. A. Oddy).

——(1984), 'The Early English Denarial Coinage, *c*.680–750', in Hill and Metcalf 1984: 5–25.

——(1986), 'The London Mint and the Coinage of Offa', in Blackburn 1986: 27–43.

——(1992), 'The English and Norman Mints', in Challis 1992: 1–82.

STEWARTBY, LORD (1998), 'Moneyers in the Written Records', in Blackburn and Dumville 1998: 151–3.

STIEGEMANN, C., and WEMHOFF M. (eds.) (1999), *799 Kunst und Kultur der Karolingerzeit (Karl der Große und Papst Leo III. in Paderborn)* (2 vols.), catalogue of the 1999 Paderborn exhibition, Mainz.

STOKES, M., and BURTON, T. L. (eds.) (1987), *Medieval Literature and Antiquities, Studies in Honour of Basil Cottle*, Woodbridge.

STRZYGOWSKI, J. (1926), *Der norden in der Bildenden Kunst Westeuropas: Heidnisches und Christliches um das Jahr 1000*, Vienna.

SUTHERLAND, C. H. V. (1937), 'Numismatic Parallels to Kentish Polychrome Brooches', *Archaeological Journal*, 94: 116–27.

——(1942), 'Anglo-Saxon Sceattas in England: Their Origin, Chronology and Distribution', *Numismatic Chronicle*[6] 2: 42–70.

——(1948), *Anglo-Saxon Gold Coinage in the Light of the Crondall Hoard*, Oxford.

——(1973), *English Coinage 600–1900*, London.

SWAN, L. (1995), 'Fine Metalwork from the Early Christian Site at Kilpatrick, Co Westmeath', in Bourke 1995: 75–80.

SWANTON, M. (ed.) (1996), *The Dream of the Rood*, Exeter.

SYDENHAM, E. A. (1952), *The Coinage of the Roman Republic*, Oxford.

SZARMACH, P. E., and OGGINS, V. D. (eds.) (1986), *Sources of Anglo-Saxon Culture*, Kalamazoo.

TALBOT, C. H. (ed.) (1954), *The Anglo-Saxon Missionaries in Germany*, London.

THACKER, A. (1985), 'Kings, Saints and Monasteries in Pre-Viking Mercia', *Midland History*, 10: 1–25.

——(1995), '*Membra disjecta*: The Division of the Body and the Diffusion of the Cult', in Stancliffe and Cambridge 1995: 97–127.

THOMAS, C. (1998), *The Christian Celts: Messages and Images*, London.

THOMPSON, D. (1971), *Coptic Textiles in the Brooklyn Museum*, New York.

THORPE, B. (ed.) (1844), *The Homilies of the Anglo-Saxon Church* (2 vols.), London.

TOMASINI, W. H. (1964), *The Barbaric Tremissis in Spain and Southern France, Anastasius to Leovigild*, American Numismatic Society 152, New York.

TOYNBEE, J. M. C. (1964), *Art in Britain under the Romans*, Oxford.

——(1973), *Animals in Roman Life and Art*, London.

TRAVAINI, L. (forthcoming) 'Saints and Sinners: Coins in Medieval Italian Graves', in M. A. S. Blackburn and K. Bornholdt (eds.), *Gods, Graves and Numismatics: Interpreting Early Medieval Coins Finds in Sacred Contexts*, Leiden.

TUDOR, V. (1995), 'Reginald's *Life of St Oswald*', in Stancliffe and Cambridge 1995: 178–94.

TWEDDLE, D. (1992), *The Anglian Helmet from 16–22 Coppergate*, York Archaeological Trust, The Archaeology of York (general ed. P. V. Addyman), vol. 17, fasc. 8: *The Small Finds*, York.

——BIDDLE, M., and KJØLBYE-BIDDLE, B., (1995), *British Academy Corpus of Anglo-Saxon Stone Sculpture*, iv: *South-East England*, Oxford.

VAN ARSDELL, R. D. (1989), *Celtic Coinage of Britain*, London.

VECCHI, I. (1998), *Nvmmorvm Avctiones 11: The William L. Subjack Collection of Thrymsas and Sceattas*, London, 5 June 1998 (catalogue of the Sale), London.

VERHULST, A. (1970), 'Der Handel in Merovingerreich: Gesamtdarstellung nach scriftlichen Quellen', *Early Medieval Studies*, 2: 2–54.

VERMEULE, C. C. (1957), 'Aspects of Victoria on Roman Coins, Gems, and in Monumental Art', *Numismatic Circular* Sept.: 357–62.

VERZONE, P. (1967), *From Theodoric to Charlemagne*, London.

VIERCK, H. E. F. (1975), 'Folienkreuze als Votivgaben', in Hübener 1975: 125–43.

——(1978), 'La Chemise de Sainte Bathilde à Chelles et l'influence byzantine sur l'art de court mérovingienne au VIIè siecle', *Centenaire de l'Abbé Cochet, Actes du Colloque International d'Archéologie 1975: La période mérovingienne*, vol. iii, Rouen, 521–64.

VINCE, A. (1990), *Saxon London: An Archaeological Investigation*, London.

——(2001), 'The Growth of Market Centres and Towns in the Area of the Mercian Hegemony', in Brown and Farr 2001: 183–93.

VOLBACH, W. F. (1961), *Early Christian Art*, London.

VÖLKL, L. (1963), 'Zusammenhängen zwischen der antiken und der früchristlichen Symbolwelt', *Das Münster*, 7/8: 233–82.

VON FREEDEN, U., KOCH, U., and WIECZOREK, A. (eds.) (1999), *Völker an Nord- und Ostsee und die Franken*, Bonn.

VOPEL, H. (1899), *Die Altchristlichen Goldgläser: Ein Beitrag zur altchristlichen Kunst- und Kulturgeschichte, Archäologische Studien zum christlischen Altertum und Mittelalter*, Freiburg.

WALLACE, P., and MacNIOCAILL G. (eds.) (1988), *Keimelia: Studies in Medieval Archaeology in Memory of Tom Delany*, Galway.

WALLACE-HADRILL, J. M. (1971), *Early Germanic Kingship in England and on the Continent*, Oxford.

——(1975), *Early Medieval History*, Oxford.

WALTERS, H. B. (1921), *Catalogue of the Silver Plate (Greek, Etruscan and Roman) in the British Museum*, London.

WAMERS, E. (1993), 'Insular Art in Carolingian Europe: The Reception of Old Ideas in a New Empire', in Spearman and Higgitt 1993: 35–44.

WARD-PERKINS, B. (2000), 'Why did the Anglo-Saxons not become more British?', *English Historical Review*, 115: 513–33.

WEBSTER, L. (1982), 'Stylistic Aspects of the Franks Casket', in Farrell 1982: 20–31.

——(1986), 'Anglo-Saxon England AD 400–1100', in Longworth and Cherry 1986: 119–59.

——(1999), 'The Iconographic Programme of the Franks Casket', in Hawkes and Mills 1999: 227–46.

——(2000), 'Style and Function of the Gandersheim Casket', in Marth 2000: 63–72.

——(2001*a*), 'Metalwork of the Mercian Supremacy', in Brown and Farr 2001: 263–77.

——(2001*b*), 'The Anglo-Saxon *Hinterland*: Animal Style in Southumbrian Eighth-Century England, with Particular Reference to Metalwork', in Krause 2001: 39–62.

——and BACKHOUSE, J. (eds.) (1991), *The Making of England: Anglo-Saxon Art and Culture AD 600–900*, London.

——and BROWN, M. (eds.) (1997), *The Transformation of the Roman World AD 400–900*, London.

WEBSTER, T. B. L. (1929), 'The Wilshere Collection at Pusey House in Oxford', *Journal of Roman Studies*, 19: 150–4.

WEILLER, R. (1999), 'Un sceat trouvé au Grand-Duché de Luxembourg', *Revue Belge de Numismatique*, 145: 219–30.

WEITZMANN, K. (ed.) (1980), *Age of Spirituality: A Symposium*, New York.

WELCH, M. G. (1983), *Early Anglo-Saxon Sussex*, BAR British Series 112, Oxford.

——(2001), 'The Archaeology of Mercia', in Brown and Farr 2001: 147–59.

WERNER, J. (1961), 'Fernhandel und Naturwirtschaft im oestlisch Merovingerreich nach archaeologischen und numismatischen Zeugnissen', *Bericht der romischgermanischen Kommission*, 42: 307–46.

WERNER, M. (1990), 'The Cross-Carpet Page in the Book of Durrow: The Cult of the True Cross, Adomnan and Iona', *Art Bulletin*, 72: 174–223.

——(1991), 'The Liudhard Medalet', *Anglo-Saxon England*, 20: 27–41.

WHITE, R. H. (1988), *Roman and Celtic Objects from Anglo-Saxon Graves. A Catalogue and Interpretation of their Use*, BAR British Series 191, Oxford.

WHITEHURST WILLIAMS, E. (1992), 'Sacred and Profane: A Metaphysical Conceit upon a Cup', *In Geardagum*, 13: 19–30.

WHITFIELD, N. (1993), 'The Filigree of the Hunterston and Tara Brooches', in Spearman and Higgitt 1993: 118–27.

——(1995), 'Formal Convention in the Depiction of Animals on Celtic Metalwork', in Bourke 1995: 89–104.

WHITELOCK, D. (ed.) (1955), *English Historical Documents*, i: *c.500–1042*, London.

WHITTING, P. D. (1961), 'The Byzantine Empire and the Coinage of the Anglo-Saxons', in Dolley 1961: 23–38.

WICKER, N. L. (1999), 'Archaeology and Art History: Common Ground for the New Millennium', *Medieval Archaeology*, 43: 161–71.

WILLIAMS, G. (1998), 'The Gold Coinage of Eadbald, King of Kent (AD 616–40)', *British Numismatic Journal*, 68: 137–40.

——(2001*a*), 'Mercian Coinage and Authority', in Brown and Farr 2001: 210–28.

——(2001*b*), 'Military Institutions and Royal Power', in Brown and Farr 2001: 295–309.

WILLIAMSON, C. (ed.) (1977), *The Old English Riddles of the Exeter Book*, Chapel Hill.

WILSON, D. (1992), *Anglo-Saxon Paganism*, London.

WILSON, D. M. (1980), *The Vikings and their Origins*, London.

——(1984), *Anglo-Saxon Art: From the Seventh Century to the Norman Conquest*, London.

——and KLINDT-JENSEN, O. (1966), *Viking Art*, London.

WITTKOWER, R. (1977), *Allegory and the Migration of Symbols*, London.

WOOD, D. (ed.) (1993), *Martyrs and Martyrologies*, Studies in Church History 30, Oxford.

WOOD, I. (1983), *The Merovingian North Sea*, Alingsaas.

——(1990), 'Ripon, Francia and the Franks Casket in the Early Middle Ages', *Northern History*, 26: 1–20.

——(1997), 'The Transmission of Ideas', in Webster and Brown 1997: 111–27.

WOOD, M. (1981), *In Search of the Dark Ages*, London.

WOOLF, A. (1999), 'The Russes, the Byzantines, and Middle-Saxon Emporia', in Anderton 1999: 63–75.

WORMALD, P. (1978), 'Bede, Beowulf and the Conversion of the Anglo-Saxon Aristocracy', in Farrell 1978: 32–95.

——(1982), 'The Age of Bede and Æthelbald' and 'The Age of Offa and Alcuin', in Campbell 1982: 70–128.

WULFF, O. K., and VOLBACH, W. F. (1926), *Spätantike und koptische Stoffe aus Ägyptischen Grabfunden* (Kaiser-Friedrich Museum), Berlin.

YORKE, B. (1990), *Kings and Kingdoms of Early Anglo-Saxon England*, London.

YOUNGS, S. (ed.) (1989), *'The Work of Angels': Masterpieces of Celtic Metalwork, 6th–9th centuries AD*, London.

——(1999), 'A Northumbrian Plaque from Asby Winderwath', in Hawkes and Mills 1999: 281–95.

——(2001), 'Insular Metalwork from Flixborough, Lincolnshire', *Medieval Archaeology*, 45: 210–20.

ZEDELIUS, V. (1980), 'Neue Sceattas aus dem Rheinland—Bonn und Xanten', *Zeitschrift für Archäologie des Mittelalters*, 8: 139–52.

ZIPPERER, S. (1999), 'Coins and Currency: Offa of Mercia and his Frankish Neighbours', in Von Freeden, Koch, and Wieczorek 1999: 121–7.

Index of Anglo-Saxon Coins

Solidi 158–9, Fig. 5.2b
  Helena 40, 54 n. 212, 55 n. 214, 158 n. 12, Fig. 2.22
  'skanomodu' 80 n. 8, 158 n. 12
  Valentinian 158 n. 12
Gold Coinage (Shillings *Thrymsas*) 10–12, 182–4
  AVDVARLÐ 46, 159, Fig. 2.32, Fig. 5.3b
  'benutigo' 34, 158
  Bust/LOND 167, Fig. 5.13b
  EAN 51, 162 n. 35, Fig. 2.41
  EVSEBII MONITA/DOROVERNIS CIVITAS 159
  London derived 30, Fig. 2.9a and c, Fig. 5.5g
  LEMC 42, 158, n. 10, Fig. 2.26a
  LVNDINIV 31, 42, 44, 54 n. 212, 55 n. 220, 180, 183,
    Fig. 2.26b
  LVNDINIV 25, 30, 159, 183, Fig. 2.1a, Fig. 5.3c
  Portrait-and-Cross 24 n. 15; 158, 183, Fig. 5.2a
  'Victory' 80, 80 n. 9, Fig. 3.2
  WITMEN MONITA 47, 55 n. 213 and 214, 72–3, 159,
    167, Fig. 2.33, Fig. 2.70, Fig. 5.3a, Fig. 5.5f
  WUNEETTON 47, 73, Fig. 2.34
  York Type 27–8, 62, 88, 172 n. 111, 185 n. 30,
    Fig. 2.4
Pale Gold 12, 184
  Concordia Militum/Clasped hands 43, 54 n. 212,
    55, 63, 184 n. 17, Fig. 2.27, Fig. 2.57
  'Constantine' 62, 65, 73, 74, 165, 184 n. 17 Fig. 2.59,
    Fig. 2.71, Fig. 2.72
  CRISPVS/'delaiona' 52–3, 54 n. 212, 58, 159, 172,
    180, 184 n. 17, Fig. 2.42a, Fig. 5.4
  'Two Emperors' 17 n. 86, 44 n. 146, 49, 52, 62, 81 n.
    13, 82, 84–7, 171, 184 n. 17, Fig. 2.37c, Fig. 3.8
Transitional 12
  debased 'Constantine' 165, Fig. 5.11
  'pada' 44, 47, 52–3, 57, 172, 184 n. 18, Fig. 2.35,
    Fig. 2.42b, Fig. 5.18
  VANIMVNDVS MONE 53, 58–9, 75–6, 160, 180,
    184 n. 18, Fig. 2.43, Fig. 2.51a, Fig. 2.73
Silver pennies (*sceattas*):
Primary 12–3, 184
  Series A 43–4, 43 n. 144, 47, 48 n. 173, 55, 172, 177
    n. 143, 183, 184 n. 18, Fig. 2.29a, Fig. 5.19a
  Series B 36, 47, 48 n. 173, 107–10, 112, 136, 184,
    184 n. 18, Fig. 2.18a, Fig. 4.1b, Fig. 4.5
  Series B, Type BX 35, 158, Fig. 2.13a
  Series C 43–4, 43 n. 144, 48 n. 173, 55, 172–3,
    184 n. 18, Fig. 2.29b, Fig. 5.19b
  Series D 162 n. 36, 172–4, 175,177, 177 n. 142,
    Fig. 5.20c and d–e
Intermediate 12–3, 184
  Aldfrith's of Northumbria 12, 125–6, 185, 186 n. 32,
    Fig. 4.25
  SAROALDO and related 49, 128, 172 n. 114, 174, 177
    n. 142 and 143, 184 n. 22, 185, Fig. 4.31

Series BZ (Types 29 a/b) 26, 28 n. 38, 29, 39,
  107 n. 5, 160, Fig. 2.2
Series E (Porcupines) 176–81, 177 n. 144, 184,
  189 n. 6, Fig. 5.20, a–b, Fig. 5.25, Fig. 5.26
Type 53 161, Fig. 5.6a
'Plumed Bird' 48 n. 173, 113, 172–4, Fig. 4.7a,
  Fig. 5.21b, Fig. 5.26a
VICO Variety 173, 179, Fig. 5.20b, Fig. 5.26b
Series F (Type 24) 49, 177 n. 142, 184 n. 22,
  Fig. 2.37b
Series W 62, 65, 87, 160 n. 21, 161, Fig. 2.56,
  Fig. 5.6b
Series X—Woden Type (Danish Type 31) 29,
  148–50, 177 n. 142; 184, Fig. 4.58a,
Series Z (Type 66) 28, 29, 128–9, 161, Fig. 2.7a,
  Fig. 4.32
VER 48, 48 n. 173, 172 n. 114, 174, 180, 184 n. 22,
  Fig. 2.37a
Secondary 13, 184–6
  'ædilræd' 180, Fig. 5.27
  'Animal Mask' (Facing lion) 133, 134–5, 185,
    Fig. 4.39
  'Archer' Type 105–6, Fig. 3.29, Fig. 3.31
  CARIP 76, 87, 95, 98, 140 n. 231, 181, 189 n. 62,
    Fig. 3.19c, Fig. 3.22a, Fig. 4.48b
  'Celtic Cross and Rosettes' Types 53 n. 206,
    57 n. 227, 87, 101 n. 159, 162–3, 169, 189 n. 62,
    Fig. 5.7c
  DELVNDONIA/ELVNDONIA 53 n. 206, 168 n. 85,
    181
  MONITA SCORVM 17 n. 84, 132, 175, 180–1,
    189 n. 62, 190 n. 71, Fig. 5.23, Fig. 5.28b
  SEDE 132, 138, 175 n. 133, 181, Fig. 5.28c
  Series G 48, 48 n. 170, 65, 174, 184 n. 18, Fig. 2.36,
    Fig. 5.21a
  Series H (Type 39) 113, 119, 120, 123, 180, 185,
    Fig. 4.16
  Series H (Type 48) 174, 180, Fig. 5.5
  Series H (Type 49) 28, 36, 113, 120, 123, 180,
    190 n. 74, Fig. 2.6, Fig. 4.19
  Series J 47
  Series J (Type 36) 48 n. 170; 55 n. 215, 114–5,
    Fig. 4.8
  Series J (Type 37) 37–9, 73, 86 n. 51, 107 n. 5,
    110–11, 160, Fig. 2.19, Fig. 4.3a
  Series J (Type 60) 142, Fig. 4.50a
  Series J (Type 72) 116, 137 n. 209, 160, 180,
    Fig. 4.11a
  Series J (Type 85) 36, 48 n. 170, 107 n. 5, 109–12,
    Fig. 2.18b; Fig. 4.2a
  Series K 49, 55 n. 218, 56, 65, 87, 94, 97,
    97 n. 131, 131–4, 144, 187–8, Fig. 4.66 (K-
    related)

Secondary (*cont.*):
  Series K (Type 20 and 20/18) 66, 97 n. 131, 187–8,
    Fig. 2.61, Fig. 3.20b, Fig. 6.1
  Series K (Type 32a) 35, 71, 72, 131, 137, 139–40,
    175, 187–8, Fig. 2.15, Fig. 2.48a, Fig. 4.44,
    Fig. 4.46b, Fig. 4.47, Fig. 6.1
  Series K (Type 33) 59 n. 237, 64–5, 131–2, 134, 135,
    139, 156, 178 n. 155, 189 n. 62, Fig. 2.48b,
    Fig. 2.49a, Fig. 2.58, Fig. 4.35b, Fig. 4.36a,
    Fig. 4.36d (Series K/L)
  Series K (Type 42) 58–9, 67, 71, 72, 77, 131, 132–4,
    139, 185 n. 31, Fig. 2.38, Fig. 2.51b, Fig. 2.63,
    Fig. 2.74, Fig. 4.37a
  Series K/N related 87, Fig. 3.10b
  Series L 51, 87, 189 n. 62
  Series L (Type 13) 51, Fig. 2.40, Fig. 3.22b
  Series L (Type 18) 56 n. 222,
  Series L (Type 15) 59, 60, 70–2, Fig. 2.67, Fig. 268a
  Series L (Type 16) 59, 60, 70–2, 97 n. 131, Fig. 2.68b;
    Fig. 2.69; Fig. 3.19a–b
  Series L (Type 18) 95–7, 97 n. 131, Fig. 3.20a
  Series L (Type 19) 95–7, Fig. 3.20c
  Series L (Type 20/18) 95–7, Fig. 3.20b
  Series M 155, 164, Fig. 4.65, Fig. 5.8
  Series N 101, 103, 104 n. 177 and 179, 148–50,
    Fig. 3.24, Fig. 3.26, Fig. 4.58 b–c
  Series O (Type 20) 89 n. 74
  Series O (Type 38) 35–6, 61, 174 n. 125, 175, 181,
    189 n. 62, Fig. 2.16
  Series O (Type 40) 137, 148–50, Fig. 3.17, Fig. 4.43,
    Fig. 4.60
  Series Q 28–9, 39, 53, 65, 87, 101 n. 159, 113, 116–7,
    128, 130–1, 134, 148–50, 151 n. 305, 154–6, 175,
    185, 185 n. 30, 191–2, Fig. 2.7b, Fig. 2.44,
    Fig. 4.7b and c, Fig. 4.30, Fig. 4.34a, Fig. 4.30,
    Fig. 4.34a, Fig. 4.38a, Fig. 4.64b,
  Q-related Fig. 4.6, Fig. 4.17a, Fig. 4.22a, Fig. 4.61a
  Series R 24, 43–5, 43 n. 144, 45 n. 151, 55, 56, 60,
    160 n. 30, 168 n. 85, 172, 174, 175–6, 191,
    Fig. 2.30, Fig. 2.31, Fig. 2.46, Fig. 2.47, Fig. 5.5e,
    Fig. 5.19c

  Mule Q/R 191–2, Fig. 6.3
  Series S (Female Centaur) 141, 142 n. 240, 151–4,
    185 n. 30, Fig. 4.49b. Fig. 4.62
  Series T (LEL and TANUM) 48 n. 173, 53, 53 n. 206,
    180, Fig. 5.28a
  Series U 66, 87, 89, 91 n. 86 and 88, 93, 117–19, 138
    n. 217, 141, 185, Fig. 3.10a; Fig. 3.14, Fig. 3.18a,
    Fig. 4.13, Fig. 4.49a
  Series V (She-Wolf and Twins) 119, 139 n. 225,
    144–5, 185, Fig. 4.18a, Fig. 4.53
  Series Y 87, 91 n.83, 92, 127, 129 n. 149, 154, 167 n.
    85, 190 n. 74, 192, Fig. 3.16, Fig. 4.27, Fig. 4.29a,
    Fig. 4.64a
  Victory Type (Type 22) 70; 81–2; 87, Fig. 3.3a,
    Fig. 3.5
  'Triquetras' 27, 49, 83, 162, 187, Fig. 2.39, Fig. 3.6,
    Fig. 5.7a–b; Fig. 6.1
  Type 15/41 149, Fig. 4.59
  Type 23e 93, 185 n. 31, Fig. 3.18a
  Type 30a and b 29, 101 n. 159, 103–4, 104 n. 179,
    174, Fig. 2.8, Fig. 3.27, Fig. 3.28
  Type 43 164, Fig. 5.10a
  Type 51 (saltire standard) 101 n. 159, 104 n. 177,
    164, 174, Fig. 5.9a, Fig. 5.22
  Type 70 175, Fig. 5.22
Offa's Coinage 13–14; 16, 18 n. 92, 51, 59–62, 111,
    142–4, 168–71, 192
  Penny (pre-reform) of Offa of Mercia 111, 142,
    Fig. 4.3b
  Penny of Offa and Archbishop Iænberht 170 n.
    100
  Pennies of Cynethryth 40–1
  Penny of Æthelberht of East Anglia 147, 190 n. 74,
    Fig. 4.56
  Pennies of Beonna of East Anglia 165, 168 n. 85,
    175–6, Fig. 5.10b, Fig. 5.24c (reform of coinage)
    13, 192
  Penny of Alfred of Wessex 'Two Emperors Type' 85–6,
    Fig. 3.9

General Index

Aachen, *see* Charlamagne
Aaron's rod 69 n. 301, 71
    see also Flowering Rods
Abbo, *see* Moneyers
Adam 104
    Adam and Eve 104
Adlocutio 63
'Aduluald' 12 n. 51, 46 n. 157
Adventus 63
    see also Eadbald
Ælfric 188
Ælfwald, King of Northumbria 192 n. 95
Æthelbald, King of Mercia 54, 91 n. 86, 96, 152, 191
    see also Sculpture at Repton
Æthelberht, King of East Anglia 13, 147, 190 n. 74,
    Fig. 4.56
Æthelberht, King of Kent 10, 15, 46, 86 n. 53, 96
Æthelred, King of Northumbria 50 n. 185
Agilulf, King of the Lombards, *see* Helmets
Alcuin 32, 40 n. 124, 50 n. 185
    see also Letters
Aldfrith, king of Lindsay 12
Aldfrith, king of Northumbria 12, 19, 125–7,
    168 n. 85, 185, 186 n. 32, 192, Fig. 4.25
Aldhelm 94 n. 108, 89 n. 70, 122 n. 98, 191 n. 78
Alexander the Great 23 n. 1, 89, 92 n. 95
Alfred, King of Wessex 55 n. 216, 61 n. 247, 85
    (Fig. 3.9)
    Alfred's Jewel 89 n. 71
    see also Fuller Brooch
Allegory 67, 69, 72
Alloy 11, 12, 14
    as help to chronology 11, n. 46
    see also Fineness
Al Mansur, Calif 33
Alpha and *Omega* 87, 112, 159
    see also Crosses
Alrachsheim Plaque 63, 88
Altar 70, 81 n. 13, 82, 99
    Altar of Ratchis 84 n. 34
Ampullæ, pilgrims' flasks 70, 75 n. 343, 83, 88–90,
    Fig. 267b, Fig. 3.12, Fig. 5.12b
Amulet 9, 29, 75
    see also Apotropaic
Angels, Archangels and Seraphim 68 n. 296, 70, 79–84,
    86 n. 51, 87, 101
    see also St Michael
Animal Iconography 107–56
Animals 88 n. 61, 89, 90, 107
    backward-looking 104 n. 179, 148–51
    crouching 149
    masks 134–5
    see also Animal Iconography

Annunciation 82
Antiquity, *see* Classical influences
Antoninus Pius 31 n. 66
Apostles, *see* Sts Peter and Paul
Apotheosis 89
Apotropaic 8, 9, 27, 34–5, 36, 50, 52 n. 194, 57 n. 229,
    63, 87–8, 104, 107, 112, 113, 120, 135, 136, 137–8,
    144, 160, 162, 163, 182, 188 n. 53
    see also Amulet; Magic
Appendice perlée 53, 91
Arcades 35, 35 n. 90, 59
Archer 105–6, 119
Arculf 95 n. 116
Armour 62–3
Arrows 106
Artemis, temple of 14 n. 69
Ascension 115
Ash Tree 95 n. 111, 97
Asia Minor 14 n. 69
Athelstan, King, Grateley decrees 17 n. 82, 189
Attributes 63–78
Audience 94, 97, 105, 126, 132, 166, 186
Augustine (mission) 2, 25 n. 24
    Gospel-book, *see* Manuscripts: Cambridge, Corpus
    Christi College, MS 286
Aylesford Bucket 24 n. 17

Babylonian seals 132
Bacchus (gem) 59 n. 236, 68, 133, 185 n. 31, Fig. 2.64
Bacchus' panther (gem) 133–4, 185 n. 31, Fig. 4.37b
Balance 91
Baptism 86
Bases 70, 70 nn. 305 and 307, 72, 73, 82, 167
Bathilda/Baldehildis Ring bezel (Postwick Matrix)
    29–30, 29 n. 51, 30 n. 52
    see also *Chemise*
Battle of Good and Evil 116
Beadohild 66 n. 286
Beagifa 10, 99 n. 144
Beaks 112, 113, 114, 118 n. 76, 142 n. 238, 180
Beards 24, 29–30, 31 n. 66, 39, 62, 146, 168 n. 85
Bede, the Venerable 32, 46 n. 157, 73, 97, 106, 125, 146,
    157, 188 n. 56, 191, 192
Bells 92
Belt-chape (Northumbria) Fig. 4.2c
Belts 56 n. 222, 64 n. 267
Benedict Biscop 3, 27 n. 35
Benevento, Duchy of 84
Beonna, king of East Anglia 12 n. 51, 13, 41 n. 135,
    168 n. 85, 175–6, Fig. 5.10b, Fig. 5.24c
    reform of coinage 13, 192
Beowulf 10, 62 n. 287, 89 n. 70, 94, 96, 99
Berhtwald, Archbishop of Canterbury 64

Bertha 10, 157
Berries 68, 117 n. 69, 133, 163
Biblical quotations:
  Gen 49: 9 125 n. 120
  Deut 32:11 114 n. 53
  Ps 34: 8 142
  Ps 90 104 n. 178
  Ps 91 106 n. 188
  Ps 92; 12 154
  Ps 121 4:135 n. 193
  Prov 16:2 91 n. 85
  Is 11:1 72 n. 318
  Jer 13 23 134 n. 182
  Hab (3rd Canticle) 90, 106
  Rev 22:2 68 n. 296
  Mt 23 37 124
  Lk 12 24 123
  Lk 13; 34 124
  Jn 15 95 n. 112, 117, 157
  'Parable of the Sower' 125 n. 118
  'Parable of the Five Talents' 188
Billockby, coins from 74–5
Birds 76 n. 355, 70 n. 310, 77–8, 95–7, 98, 100–1,
    105–6, 107–25, 175, 184, 187
  Backward-looking birds 113, 116, 119, 134, 148–51,
    174, 179, Fig. 4.11, Fig. 4.17
  Birds in torque 136–8, Fig. 4.42a, Fig. 4.43
  Birds in vine-scroll 117–20, 134, 137 n. 208, 185, 186
  see also Brooches; Doves; Eagles; Falcons; Hawks;
    Hens; Peacocks; Ravens; Swans
Bishop seats 99, 99 n. 148
Blessing (gesture) 63, 64–5
  Trinitarian Blessing 64
Boat symbolizing the Church 90 n. 77
  Nordic mythology 90
  as origin of 'porcupine' 178
Boniface, Bishop and Saint 96, 112, 136, 191
  see also Letters
Books 25, 71–2, 125
  see also Manuscripts
Bracteates 9–10, 24, 30 n. 57, 35 n. 94, 39, 39 n. 116, 50,
    50 n. 182, 56 nn. 222 and 223, 58, 64, 64 n. 268,
    67 n. 287, 77, 77 n. 363, 88 n. 65, 98, 102, 111,
    124 n. 52, 144 n. 251, 165 n. 63, 182
  Lyngby Fig. 4.42b
  Undley 24, 74, 145–6, 187, Fig. 4.54
  see also Pendants and Gold-leaf Crosses
Braids 60
Branches 151–2
  see also Vegetation Motifs
Brandon site 192
  pin 142, Fig. 4.50b
Breasts 89 n. 74, 104, 154
Breedon-on-the-Hill 187 n. 52
  see also Sculpture
Brescia, tile, Fig. 4.28c
Bronze Age 90
Brooches 26 n. 32, 29 n. 45, 38, 55–6, 56 n. 223, 57, 61,
    61 n. 247, 162, 164, 166, 166 n. 69, 171
  Bird brooches 115, 115 nn. 57–8; Berinsfield 115,
    123 n. 108, Fig. 4.10; Darmsheim and
    Deidesheim 114, Fig. 4.9a–b; Hamwic 113, 123,
    180; Obrigheim 116, Fig. 4.11b; Fig. 4.12a

Button brooches 26 n. 32
  East Anglian 'animal' brooches 186 n. 34
  Fuller Brooch 60, 188, Fig. 6.2
  Great square-headed brooches 26 n. 32,
    30 nn. 56–7, 64, 64 n. 267
  Hunterston Brooch 141 n. 235, Fig. 4.52
  Jewelled disc brooches 160, 163 n. 42; Milton
    brooches Fig. 5.5d; Sarre brooches Fig. 5.24b
  Penanular 39
  Quoit brooches 30 n. 56; 150 n. 297
Buckles 30 nn. 56 and 57, 88 nn. 61 and 65;
    Finglesham 52, 76 n. 354, 88, 90 n. 75, 104
Bullæ 137 n. 208
Burials, see Graves
Busts 23–78, 182
Byzantine (influences) 45, 54, 55–6, 58, 65, 65 n. 280,
    74–5

Cæsar 74
Calligraphy 118, 120, 168–9
Cambridge, see gems and Manuscripts
Camels 90
Cameos 30
Candelabra 167–8
Canon Tables 35 n. 90
Canopy, see arcade
Canterbury 10, 13, 17 n. 82, 77, 86, 86 n. 51, 157–
    8
  see also Mints
Caps 51–2, 53 n. 206
  Frigian 103
Caritas 142 n. 240, 154, 181
Carlisle, coin from 29
Carolingian period 41, 120 n. 88, 135 n. 195, 153,
    188 n. 56
Carpet pages 161, 163 n. 42
Cassiodorus 141
Catacombs 83, 132
Celtic influences 24, 28 n. 42, 30, 31, 76, 183
Centaurs, see Female Centaur
Chalices 66–7, 87, 122
  Hexham 66 n. 285
  Tassilo Chalice 65, 66 n. 285
Charlemagne 13 n. 63, 32, 32 n. 72, 135, 190 n. 100
  palace at Aachen 135 185, Fig. 4.41
Charon's Obol 9
Charters 10 n. 35, 16 n. 78
Chasuble Sts Harlindis and Relindis 35 n. 90,
    65 n. 273, 100, 186 n. 35
Chemise of St Bathilda 111 n. 36, 121 n. 94
Chiffelet 17 n. 86
Childeric 75–6
Chi-Rho initial, Christogram 118, 137 n. 214, 165,
    168
Christ, Christological 30 nn. 53 and 55, 34 n. 86, 50,
    66, 75, 86, 86 n. 51, 87 n. 60, 90, 93, 104, 114, 115,
    116, 117, 120, 123–4, 125, 130, 133, 136, 138, 14 0,
    153–4, 166
  'Lion of Judah' 133, 135, 140
Christianity (advent, influences, etc.) 9, 10, 17, 23, 28,
    30 nn. 53 and 55, 46, 66–7, 68 n. 296, 72, 75–6,
    79, 83, 87–8, 99, 105, 107, 120, 121, 135, 136, 146,
    153, 157, 160, 165, 183

Chronology 18
    see also Alloy and Fineness
Church 46, 73, 90, 124, 189–90
    see also *Ecclesia*
Church apparel 25, 70, 70 n. 304, 87, 184
Classical influences 2, 9, 25, 33, 34, 37, 42, 51, 55, 56,
    58, 60, 63, 65, 67–8, 74, 93, 95, 105, 115, 122, 125,
    135, 142, 152, 166, 170, 184, 185, 193 n. 100
Claws 129
Cloisonné 28, 36, 62, 161, 175
Clothing 51, 68 n. 292, 91–3, 95; 101 n. 163, 103, 122,
    136
Clovis II, King of the Merovingians 29 n. 51
Coddenham, coins from 73, 74
Coelwulf, King of Mercia 85
Coenwulf, King of Mercia 158 n. 12
Coinage and Coins as brooches 57 n. 229; as pendants 8,
    9; pierced 8; reforms: 13–14, 16, 111 n. 28; 169; 192
    Abbasid, dinar 33, 33 n. 82
    Alemannic 80
    Barbarian 23, 77, 80, 183
    Burgundian 80
    Byzantine 8; Heraclius 24 n. 10; 27, 28, 30 n. 53,
        34 n. 85; 37; Heraclius 37 n. 100; Justinian II 58,
        n. 231; Heraclius 65 n. 278; 80; Constans II 87;
        157, 158 n. 12; Heraclius 158 n. 12; 159, 182, 185
        n. 30
    Carolingian 13, 23 n. 6, 158, 168 n. 85, 192
    Celtic 17 n. 86, 24; Commius and Tasciovanus
        24 n. 16; Taurisci and Cunobelin 30 n. 57; Iceni
        31; 37, 98; Norfolk wolf staters 129–30; 132 n.
        171; Austrian and Bohemian 138–9; 145;
        Cunobelin 151–3, Dubnovellanus and
        Cunobelin 155 n. 336; 167; Verica 167 n. 81;
        Carnutes 178; 183, Fig. 2.20, Fig. 4.33,
        Fig. 4.45b–c
    Danish 29–30, 148–9, 177, Fig. 4.58; *see also* Series X
    Frisian 12, 164, 184; Maasticht type 164 n. 59
    Greek 98
    Lombard 79–80; Cunincpert 79, 79 n. 6, 168 n. 85;
        Liutprand Fig. 3.1
    Lydian 14 n. 69
    Merovingian 8–13, 15 n. 74, 30, 34; *Vellevorum
        civitas* and Savonnière 37–8; 49 n. 175; Bertulfus
        at Orlèans 53 n. 207; 54, Moutiers-en-
        Tarenntaise 57 n. 227; 63 n. 261, 70 n. 305;
        Rodez, Saint-Bernard-de-Comminges 70 n. 311;
        80, 83, 87, 101, 107–8; Laon 108 n. 7; Bordeaux
        113; 157–9; Abbo 167, 183–4, 189, 192 n. 99,
        Fig. 3.11; *see also* Sutton Hoo
    Papal 168 n. 85
    Roman 7–10, 23; *Vrbs Roma* 24 n. 11; Hadrian 31;
        Hadrian, Antoninus Pius, Marcus Aurelius 31 n.
        66; Justinian 24; Constantine and Licinius 37 n.
        101; Helena 40; *Concordia Militum* 43; 46; 49;
        Eudoxia 50 n. 181; 55; 53, 54 n. 212, 56; Eudoxia
        57 n. 224; Majoran 58, n. 231; 59; Majorian and
        Honorius 60 n. 245; *Concordia Militum* 63;
        Marius 63 n. 264; *Vrbs Roma* 74; Trajan 74 n. 338;
        75–6, 79; Licinius 80; 'Two Emperors' 80,
        80 n. 39, Valentinian I and Theodosius 84 n. 39;
        87, 89, Hadrian 98 n. 136; *Gloria Exercitus* 101;
        119, *Vrbs Roma* 145–7; 152; Crispus 159; 167;

'Two Emperors' 171; Hadrian 178 n. 152; 184;
    Constantine the Great 7 n. 5, 27, 33 n.79,
    37 n. 101, 48, 51, 64, 65, 75, 87 n. 58; Constantius
    II 34 n. 85, 49 n. 177, 60 n. 245, 89 n. 73
    Umayyad 95–6
    Visigothic 8; Egica and Wittiza 37–8, 37 n. 103;
        47 n. 165, 57, 80; 182
Colchester 151
Collar 133
Commerce 114
'Common burden' 191 n. 86
Constantine the Great, *see coins*
Constantinople 70
    treasure 74
    see also Byzantine Coins and Byzantine Influences
Constantius II *Calendar of 354* 58 n. 231
    see also Byzantine Coins
Continental influences 2, 7, 8, 10–11, 12, 19, 28, 48, 63,
    73, 111
Control stamps 75
Council of Clovesho 191
Covenant 72
Cowls 28, 34
Crondall Hoard, *see* Hoards
Crosses 46, 48, 64–5, 71, 75, 76 n. 355, 77, 87, 95, 97,
    100, 122–3, 157–71, 182
    Adoration of Crosses 104
    Altar Cross 158; Eligius Cross 70 n. 306
    Apotropaic 27, 35, 82, 101
    As Tree of Jesse 72 n. 318
    Benediction cross 65
    Bird on Crosses 26 n. 30, 70 n. 310, 107–12, 163
    Cross on birds 123 n. 108, 127, 128 (as tail),
        154 n. 332 (as wing), 155 (trailings), 173–5, 185,
        186, 187
    Chi-Cross 51, 72, 74, 86 n. 51, 118, 140, 140 n. 230,
        141, 151, 161, 174
    Cross anchrée/Ankerkreutz (floriate crosses)
        160 n. 27, 164
    Cross *fourchée* 159, 160, Fig. 5.3a
    Cross-on-globe 65 n. 281, 158 n. 10, 159, Fig. 5.3b
    Cross-on-steps 9 n. 20, 158–9, 158 n. 10, Fig. 5.2
    Cross sceptre 69, 76
    Cross *candelabrum*, with *pendilia/alpha* and *omega*
        73, 87, 88 n. 61, 158, 159 n. 18, 160, 167, 167 n. 74
    Crux Foliata 68, 70–1, 70 n. 310, 163 n. 47
    Crux Gemmata 73
    Decussate Crosses 72, 118 n. 74
    Figure between Crosses 27, 28 n. 38, 37, 37 n. 101,
        57 n. 229, 62–3, 82, 87–94, 101–5, 138, 185
    Four-lobed Crosses 170–1, Fig. 5.16, fig. 5.17
    Gold-leaf, *see* Gold-leaf Crosses
    Multiple Crosses 161
    On heads 30 n. 52
    On helmets 52 n. 195, 151 163, Fig. 4.61b
    On Merovingian coins 34, 107, 157–9, 160
    Oswald's Cross 71 n. 313, 97
    Patriarchal Crosses 157, 158 n. 7 and 10, Fig. 5.1
    Pectoral Crosses: Cuthbert's Cross, Ixworth Cross,
        and Wilton Cross 9, 183 n. 15; Pope Vitalian's
        Cross 38; Processional Crosses 70, 79, 160, 167;
        Rupertus Cross 70 n. 304, 133 n. 178, 134;
        She-Wolf and Cross (Rambona Diptych) 147,

Pectoral Crosses (*cont.*)
    147 n. 281; Solomon Knot 164; Tau cross
    96 n. 120, 171 n. 105; True Cross 40, 158;
    Triquetras 49, 134 n. 181; With annulets 159,
    160 n. 30, 169, 175, Fig. 5.4, Fig. 5.5e, Fig. 5.23;
    With Evangelists' Symbols 111 n. 27
Crozier 72, 91 n. 83, 167–8
Cunobelin 151–2
Cups, *see* Palm cups
Cuthbert, Archbishop of Kent 136 n. 203
Cynehelm 91
Cynethryth, wife of Offa of Mercia 13, 40–1, 61
Cyprus, Second Treasure 32 n. 70

Daniel (in the lion's den) 89 n. 69, 90
Dankirke 29 n. 48, 39 n. 116
David, King 31–3, 65, 82, 100, 103
    on St Andrews Sarcophagus Fig. 2.11
    Plates (Second Cyprus Treasure) 32 n. 70
Debasement 11, 13, 47, 191
    see also Fineness
Decrees, *see* Grateley
Dedications to St Michael 84, 84 n. 36
Devil 106
Dextrarum iunctio 63 n. 264
Diadems 45–51
Dies 10, 14, 16, 40, 47, 51
    die-chains, die-links 11, 12, 15, 17
    die-cutters 12, 15, 24, 53, 114, 115, 127, 148, 171, 192
Display of wealth 8–10
Domburg 180
Door-knockers 135, 135 n. 195, 185
Dorchester barrel-lock 30, Fig. 2.9b
Dorestad 177
Dover 10, 10 n. 35
Doves 77–8, 107–9, 112, 112 nn. 40 and 41
Drapery 54–61, 80–1, 85, 85 n. 47
    saddle-back drapery 57
Dream of the Rood 71, 94, 187
Drinking 66–7
    see also Nourishment

E-shapes 88
Eadbald, King of Kent 12 n. 51, 46, 46 n. 157, 159
Eadberht, King of Northumbria 12 n. 51, 91 n. 83, 127,
    130, 154, 190 n. 74, 192, Fig. 4.27, Fig. 4.29,
    Fig. 4.64a
Eadriht 84 n. 35
Eagles 77 n. 367, 96, 107 n. 4, 112, 112 nn. 40–1,
    114–15, 116, 119–20
East Anglia 11, 11 n. 44, 12, 13, 14, 18, 24, 27, 29 n. 48,
    43 n. 144, 45, 47, 59, 60 nn. 239–40, 127–31,
    144–7, 154, 175–6, 185, 191–2
East coast 11
East Kent 78 n. 369, 145
East Mediterranean influences 41
East Midlands 12, 47
East Saxons 25, 151–2
Ecclesia 88 n. 61, 142 n. 240, 146, 154, 181
Ecgberht, Archbishop of York 91 n. 83, 92–3,
    190 nn. 67 and 76, 191, 192, Fig. 3.16
Ecgberht, King of Kent 169

Edwin. King of Northumbria 17, 73, 73 n. 333, 86 n. 53
Eels 144 n. 254
Egil 106
Elizabeth 86
Embroidery 40, 107
    see also *Chasuble; Chemise*
Encircled heads 34–6, 116 n. 65
Ephesus 14 n. 69
Epiphany 166
Essex 11, 12, 18
Eucharist 67, 72, 120, 133, 134 n. 181, 137 n. 213, 142,
    146, 163
Eusebius, *see* Moneyers
Evangelists and their symbols 107, 130, 132–3
    Luke 25, 32 n. 69, 71, 100, 134 n. 185, 166
    Matthew 32 n. 69, 71, 100, 130 n. 159
    Mark 32 n. 69, 100, 119, 130 n. 159, 132 n. 172,
        134 n. 186
    John 77, 77 n. 367, 96, 97, 101, 116 n. 62,
        132 n. 172
Evil eye 9
Exegesis 72, 110, 187, 187 n. 44

Falconry 96, 100
Falcons 77, 96
Faversham, Kent 8, 10 n. 35
    see also Pendants
Feeding, *see* Nourishment
Female Centaur 141, 142 n. 240, 151–4
Fertility 104, 136
Fetters 38
Filigree 52, 111, 164, Fig. 4.4, Fig. 4.52b, Fig. 5.5a–d,
    Fig. 5.9b
Fineness 11, 13, 16, 25, 27 n. 33, 28 n. 43, 35 n. 89,
    46 n. 153, 47, 47n. 165, 51 n. 193, 53, 82, 84, 109,
    137 n. 208, 149 n. 296, 168 n. 85, 180
    see also Alloy and Debasement
Fitting, River Thames, London Fig. 4.48a
Five Senses 187–8, Fig. 6.1
Flans 14, 121
Flasks, see *Ampullæ*
Fledglings 114–15
Fleury, Abbey, Saint-Benoît-Sur Loire 26 n. 29
Flowering Rods 71, 89 n. 71
    see also Vegetation Motifs
Frames 116, 131, 136
    apotropaic, *see* Arcades
Francia 9, 10, 14, 83, 177, 184
    see also Merovingian and Carolingian coinage
Frankincense 69
Franks Casket 39, 53, 61 n. 247, 62, 66, 69, 87, 91–2,
    93 n. 103, 99, 103, 105–6, 109, 129, 140, 146–7,
    152 n. 311, 166, 187, Fig. 2.45, Fig. 2.55, Fig. 2.62,
    Fig. 2.65, Fig. 3.15, Fig. 3.23, Fig. 3.31, Fig. 4.2b,
    Fig. 4.55, Fig. 5.12
Friðstol 99 n. 148
Frisia 12 n. 53, 29 n. 48, 177, 179
    see also Coins

Gallehus Horn   152 n 311
Gandersheim Casket 118, 134, 143 n. 249, 155 n. 335,
    165 n. 61

Garnets 27
  see also Cloisonné
Gems Bacchus 68
  Jupiter Serapis 68 n. 294
  Heracles 93; 119, 125 n. 122
  Bacchus's panther 133; 152, 155 n. 336, 178 n. 152,
    185, Fig. 2.64, Fig. 3.18b, Fig. 4.37b
Genoels-Elderen bookcover 39 n. 117, 75 n. 349, 82
Germanic influences 29–30, 66, 67, 77, 110, 114, 146,
    148
  metalwork techniques 147 n. 275, 165, 183
Gesture of Speech 65, 82, 188
Gifts 10, 17, 95, 99, 144 n. 254, 158
Giftstol 99
Gifu 99
Gilgamesh 89 n. 69
God 69, 79, 86, 100, 106, 146
  as Creator-Logos 133 n. 174
Gold foil 38–9, 49, 50, 64 n. 267, 111
Gold-glass 38, 81, 83, 86, 131–2, 131 n. 163, 185,
    Fig. 3.12, Fig. 4.35
Gold-leaf Crosses Spötting 50
  Ulm-Ermingen 38–9, 111, Fig. 2.21
Goldsmiths 8, 15, 16 n. 78
Gospel-books, *see* Manuscripts
Gotland 90 n. 78
Grapes, bunches and harvest 103, 112, 134 n. 181, 142,
    163, 163 nn 49–50
Grateley decrees 17 n. 82, 189
Graves, burials 8, 9, 76 n. 354, 88 n. 68, 101, 124
Graving tools 14, 168
Grézin plaque 104
Griffins 89, 89 n. 73, 122 n. 101, 127
Grips 87
  see also Hands
Guilloche-hatching 25, 30, 34
Guldgubbar 49

Hadrian 31
Hair and hairstyles 24, 28, 29–30, 31, 31 n. 66, 33, 39,
    42 n. 140, 45, 45 n. 151, 47, 48, 49–51
  knotted hair 50 n. 185; 51 n. 193, 85, 87, 91, 178–9,
    183
Halo 31, 34, 47, 53 n. 206, 85, 91 n. 89, 103
Hammer 14, 167–8
Hammered coinage 14
Hamwic (Southampton) 28 n. 41, 29 n. 48, 113, 138,
    180
  see also Bird Brooches, *Hamwic*, Mints)
Hands 63–9, 87
  see also Grips
Hatching 117, 159, 180
  see also Guilloche-hatching
Hawks 77
Headberht, King of Kent 169, 192 n. 99
Heads 25–54
Heads between beaks 104–5
  Bird-like heads 104
Healing 136
Helena, Empress 40
Helios 42
Hellenistic, *see* Oriental

Helmets 51–3; crest 53; see also *Cynehelm*; *Kammhelme*
  Agilulf, Val di Nievole 63, 76 n. 354, 99
  Benty Grange 52 n. 194, 53
  Sutton Hoo see Sutton Hoo
  Vendel 30 n. 57
  Woolastone 53, 54 n. 210
  York, Coppergate 35, 52 n. 194, 53, 54 n. 120,
    118 n. 76, 137, 151, Fig. 4.61b
Hens 123–5; Theodolind's Hen (Monza) Fig. 4.23b
Heracles and Hydra (gem) 93, 185 n. 31, Fig. 3.18b
Herodotus, 14 n. 69
Hessen 112
Hexham oratory 84; silver plaque 26, 93, 184
  see also Sculpture and Chalices
Hoards:
  Aston Rowant 19, 49 n. 175, 128, 161, 179, 180, 177,
    Fig. 4.31, Fig. 5.20a
  Canterbury, St Martin's 8, 101, 157; Liudhard's
    'medalet' Fig. 5.1
  Crondall 11, 11 nn. 40 and 43, 19, 24 n. 15, 25, 25 n.
    25, 27, 30, 42, 46–7, 47 nn. 159 and 160, 48 n. 171,
    51, 72, 73 n. 324, 84, 158 n. 9, 159, 167, 183
  Finglesham 9
  Garton-on-the-Wolds 9, 45 n. 149, 73 n. 327
  Hallum 29 n. 48, 148
  Hoxne 7 n. 7, 76
  Kloster Barthe 172 n. 116, 173
  Middle Harling 192 n. 97
  Pentney (brooches) 171
  Terwispel 29 n. 48
  Thames 53 n. 206
  Wieuwerd 36, 58, Fig. 2.17b, Fig. 2.49b–c
  Woodham Walter 57 n. 228, 83 n. 29, 175 n. 133
Holy Land, *see* Palestine
Holy Spirit, as dove 77, 108
Homotypies anachroniques 178
Horror Vacui 44, 69, 116, 183
Host (represented by 'pellet') 126 n. 130, 128,
    128 n. 142, 137, 138 n. 216, 141–2
Hrabanus 106
Human Figures 79–106
Hunt 77
Hybrids 151–6

Iænberht, Archbishop of Canterbury 166
Imperial iconography 75 n. 349, 89
Ingeld 90
Inscriptions 2, 10, 12, 13
  MONITA SCORUM 17 n. 84; 26 n. 30, 28 n. 38, 30 n. 53
  Kufic 33 n. 82; 34, 35; 40–1, 43
  AVÐVARLÐ 46, 46 n. 155, 48, 48 n. 173, 52 n. 195, 53,
    53 n. 206, 56, 57 n. 299, 68
  VANIMVNDVS 75 N. 345; 82, 84, 98, 107, 126, 127,
    128
  Dignitas amicorum 131–2; 132, 137, 138, 157 n. 5,
    159–60, 168 n. 85, 169, 171–2
  TOT/VOT 171–2
  VIC(O) 173, 173 n. 117; 174, 175, 180, 181, 182
  SEDE: 189 n. 62; 192
  see also Runic inscription
Interlace 49, 25 n. 85, 50 n. 185, 94, 116, 119 n. 80, 144,
    150, 165

Ireland 135 n. 195
Irene, Byzantine Empress 40
Ishmael 106
Isidore of Seville 121 n. 96, 187 n. 52
Islamic influences 33, 95–6
Ivory carvings '?Ariadne' Diptych 50 n. 181, 57 n. 224;
    98–9; 146 n. 271
    Rambona Diptych 147 n. 281
    Aerobindus Diptych:153
    see also Franks Casket; Genoels-Elderen bookcover;
    Gandersheim Casket; Larling Plaque

Jaws 126 n. 132, 127, 131, 136, 138 n. 216, 140, 142,
    143, 148
Jesus, *see* Christ
Jet 30
Jewellers 15
    see also Moneyers Abbo of Chalon and Eligius
Jewellery, influences and techniques 8, 8 n. 16, 10, 11
    n. 46, 15, 27, 33, 34, 43, 45, 48 n. 173, 63, 74, 92,
    102, 125, 144 n. 254; 183, 185
    see also Cloisonné; Garnets; Guilloche-hatching;
    Hatching and Metal)
Justus 46 n. 157

Kammhelme 52
Kent 8, 10, 11, 43 n. 144, 46, 46 n. 157, 47, 169, 180, 192
    see also Canterbury; Dover; Faversham;
    Lullingstone; Rochester; Sarre; Wantsum
    Channel
'Keyhole effect' 59
Kilts, *see* Clothing
Kings and coinage 16–17, 189
    see also under individual names
Kingship 32 n. 72, 32–3, 38, 41, 54, 62, 70, 76, 86–7, 97,
    99, 104, 189–90
Knotted hair see Hair and Hairstyles
Knots 27, 49–50, 50 n. 185

Lamps 108, 184, Fig. 4.1c
Lance 76
Lappet 148, 150
Larling Plaque 134, 147
Laurentius, Archbishop of Canterbury 46 n. 157
Laws of Æthelberht of Kent 15, 16
Legends Saints and birds 97
    St Oswald's Legends 97
Letters:
    Alcuin to Æthelred of Lindisfarne 50 n. 185,
    191 n. 78
    Alcuin to Bishop Speratus 90 n. 76
    Alcuin to Charlemagne 32 n. 72
    Aldhelm to Abbess of Barking 191 n. 78
    Archbishop Boniface 111 n. 30
    Archbishop Boniface to king Æthelbald of Mercia
    96, 191
    Archbishop Boniface to king Æthelberht of Kent 96
    Archbishop Boniface to Cuthbert, Archbishop of
    Kent 136 n. 203, 191 n. 78
    Bede to Ecgberht, Archbishop of York 190 n. 76, 191
    Charlemagne to Offa 13 n. 65
    Eangyth and Heaburg to Archbishop Boniface
    191 n. 83

Letter of Pope Gregory the Great 190 n. 75
    Letters to Charlemagne 32 n. 75
    Pope Boniface to Justus 46 n. 157
Libertas 102
Linear style 26, 103, 109, 130, 183
Lions 89 n. 69; 90, 125–35, 140, 156, 174 n. 125, 185,
    188
    Facing lions 134–5
    Lion's cub 130–5
    Lion's mane 125, 127
    Lion's triple tail 126
Literacy 157, 160, 181, 189
Liudhard Bishop and Liudhard's 'medalet' 157–8,
    Fig. 5.1
London, *see* Mints
'Long arms' 101
Loops 8, 9, 11 n. 46, 111, 145 n. 267
Lorica, *see* St Patrick
Lorica Hamata/squamata 62, 62 n. 253
Loros 58
Loveden man 90 n. 75
Lullingstone, Kent 83 n. 33
Lunette 90, 95, 101
Lysimachus of Thrace 23

Magi, see Wise Men
Magic 9, 35, 68 n. 296, 74, 110 n. 26, 148
    magic spell (Nine Herbs Charm) 117 n. 68
Mailcoat 62
Manerbio disk 28 n. 42
Manufacturing of coins 14–15
Manuscripts:
    Amiens, Bibliothèque Municipale, MS 18 (Corbie
    Psalter) 86
    Berne, Bürgerbibliothek, Cod. 318 143 n. 249
    Cambridge, Corpus Christi College, MS 197 B
    (Gospel-book) 161 n. 33
    Cambridge, Corpus Christi College, MS 286 (St
    Augustine's Gospel-book) 25, 68 n. 291, Fig. 2.1b
    Dublin, Trinity College, MS 52 (Book of Armagh)
    127, Fig. 4.28b
    Dublin, Trinity College, MS A.4.5 (57) (Book of
    Durrow) 27, 119, 125–6, 134, 142, 158 n. 7,
    161 n. 33, Fig. 2.5, Fig. 4.36c
    Dublin, Trinity College, MS A.1.6 (58) (Book of
    Kells) 39 n. 117, 68 n. 296, 82 n. 20, 89 n. 71,
    118 n. 76, 122, 125, 127, 127 n. 138, 128 n. 142,
    140 n. 226, 143 n. 248, 149, 163, 166 n. 70, 187,
    Fig. 4.20, Fig. 4.24, Fig. 4.36b, Fig. 4.59, Fig. 5.8c
    Durham, Cathedral Library, MS A.II.17 (Durham
    Gospels) 150 n. 298
    Durham, Cathedral Library, MS B.II.30
    (Cassiodorus, *Commentary on the Psalms*)
    31 n. 68, 82
    Hereford, Cathedral Library, MS P.I.2 129, n. 149
    Lichfield, Cathedral Library (Lichfield Gospels) 71,
    71 n. 316, 100, 129 n. 149, 134 n. 185, 140 n. 226,
    166
    London, British Library, Cotton MS Nero D.IV
    (Lindisfarne Gospels) 32, 55 n. 215, 113, 125,
    130 n. 159, 141, 144 n. 251, 161 n. 33, 166 n. 70
    London, British Library, Royal MS I.E.VI
    (Canterbury Bible) 171 n. 103

Manuscripts (*cont.*)
London, British Library, Stowe 944 70 n. 306
London, British Library, Cotton MS Vespasian A.I
 (Vespasian Psalter) 31 n. 68, 103
London, British Library, Cotton MS Vitellius A.XV
 (Nowell Codex) 89, n.70
Paris, Bibliothèque Nationale, MS lat. 9389
 (Echternach Gospels) 60, 60 n. 243, 92 n. 96, 100,
 138, 141, 166 n. 70, Fig. 4.26
Paris, Bibliothèque Nationale, MS lat.1141 (Metz
 Sacramentary) 77 n 368
Paris, Bibliothèque Nationale, MS lat. 12048
 (*Sacramentarium Gellonense*) 135, 166 n. 70,
 Fig. 4.40
Rome, Biblioteca Apostolica, Barberini MS Lat.
 570 (Barberini Gospels) 60 n. 243, 68 n. 291,
 95 n. 113, 134, 141 n. 235, 155 n. 340
St Gall, Monastery Library, Codex 567 (*Liber Beati
 Gregorii* 'Life' of Whitby) 77
St Petersburg, Lat. Q.v.I (Bede' *Historia
 Ecclesiastica*) 46 n. 157, 65 n. 280
St Petersburg, Cod.F.v.I.8 (St Petersburg Gospels)
 143 n. 249, 155 n. 335
Stockholm, Royal Library MS A.135 (*Codex Aureus*)
 65 n. 272, 68 n. 291, 71, 72 n. 317, 137 n. 214,
 166 n. 70
Trier, Stadtbibliothek 171/1626 (*Registrum
 Epistorarum*) 77 n. 368
Venice, Biblioteca Marciana, Cod. Gr. Z. 479
 (= 881) (*Cinetico*) Fig. 4.23a
Marigolds 166
Marriage 38, 63, 86, 102
Mary 86
Masks 105
Master of the Beasts 89 n. 69, 90
Medallions 9
Medeshamstede 65 n. 277
Medicine 68–9
 medicinal plants 68
Medusa 29–30
Mellitus, Archbishop of Canterbury 25
Menhir 101
Merchants 177, 178, 182 n. 4
Mercia 12, 18, 33, 35 n. 89, 60, 85, 97, 143, 147, 192
Metal, and metalwork techniques 7, 10, 14, 52, 55, 56,
 132 n. 171, 183–4
 see also Cloisonné; Garnets; Guilloche-hatching;
 Hatching; Jewellery
Metaphors 90, 107, 187
Mid Anglia 49 n. 175
Migration period 61 n. 247
Milk 146
Minting authorities 16–17, 188–9, 192
Mintmarks 43, 74, 123, 127
Mints 18
 Canterbury 10, 17 n. 82, 18, 60 n. 239, 78 n. 369,
 159, 190 n. 71
 Dorestad 177
 Ely 191 n. 90
 Hamwic (Southampton) 18, 28 n. 41, 113
 Ipswich 13, 191 n. 90
 London 13, 15 n. 77, 18, 33 n. 80, 60, 60 nn. 239 and
 241, 85 n. 47, 159

 Ribe 29 n. 48, 177
 Rochester 17 n. 82, 18
 Winchester 18
 York 18, 27, 38, 192
Missions: St Augustine's to the Anglo-Saxons 2
 Anglo-Saxon Missions to the Continent 97, 111,
 112
Modelled style 26, 28, 44, 130, 183
Monasteries, minsters 3, 17, 65 n. 277, 86, 103,
 103 n. 176, 104, 109 n. 14, 190 n. 77, 190–92,
 191 n. 90
Moneyers 10, 11, 13, 15; as witnesses 16; 47 n. 163, 60,
 75 n. 345, 168 n. 85, 180, 189
 Abbo (of Chalon, master of Eligius) 15 n. 74, 167,
 167 n. 73
 Abbo (ABBONI MANET) 72, 167–8, Fig. 5.13a
 Alhmund 31 n. 65, 33, 33 n. 78 and 80, 61, 142, 144,
 Fig. 2.13b, Fig. 4.51a, Fig. 5.16b
 Babba 61 n. 249 and 252
 Bertulfus 53 n. 207
 Cenred Fig. 3.9
 Ciolheard 41, 143, 158 n. 12, Fig. 2.24, Fig. 4.51b
 Dud 51 n. 189, 60, 60 n. 245, Fig. 2.12c, Fig. 2.53,
 2.54a, Fig. 5.16a
 Eadhun 31 n. 65, 33 n.80, 60, Fig. 2.10, Fig. 5.15a
 Efe Fig. 5.24c
 Eligius (Saint, bishop, jeweller and moneyer)
 15 n. 74, 167 n. 73, (cross) 170 n. 98
 Eoba 40, 51 n. 189, 169, Fig. 2.23, Fig. 5.15b
 Ethilvald 61 n. 249, 170, Fig. 2.54b, Fig. 5.16c
 Eusebius, 10, 159
 Ibba 60, Fig. 2.12b, Fig. 2.52b
 Nonnitus 24 n. 15
 Œthilred 60 n. 240
 Pada 44, 47, 52–3, 57, 172, 184 n. 18, Fig. 2.35,
 Fig. 2.42b, Fig. 5.18
 Pehtwald 31 n. 65, 33 n. 80, 60 n. 245
 Pendred 36, 40 n. 127, 142, 144, Fig. 4.51c
 Tilbeorht 24, 45, 168 n. 85, Fig. 2.31b
 Tirwald 60 n. 245
 Udd 59, Fig. 2.52a
 Vanimundus 11, 53, 58–9, 75–6, 160, 180, 184 n. 18,
 Fig. 2.43, Fig. 2.51a, Fig. 2.73
 Wigræd 45, 56, 168 n. 85, Fig. 2.31a, Fig. 2.47
 Wihtred Fig. 5.15c
 Wilred 13
 Witmen (WITMEN MONITA) 47, 55 n. 213 and 214,
 72–3, 159, 167, Fig. 2.33, Fig. 2.70, Fig. 5.3a,
 Fig. 5.5f
Monogram 13, 74–5, 87, 88, 113, 168 n. 85
 see also *Chi-Rho*
Monza 124
Mosaics 167, 170
 Beith Alpha 124 n. 133
Moustaches 24, 29–30, 30 n. 57, 39, 89, 89 n. 74, 104
'Mules' 41
Myrrh 69
Mystical gaze 33, 48
Mythology 9, 66, 90, 93, 95 n. 111, 102, 153

Neck 25, 40, 41, 44–5, 47, 55, 56, 57, 59
 triangular neck 44, 56, 59–60
Norfolk 28 n. 43, 29, 29 n. 51, 129–30

North Sea trade 148, 176–7
Northumbria 12, 12 n. 51, 13, 24 n. 18, 27, 29,
    47 n. 167, 50 n. 185, 72 n. 320, 97, 125–7, 130,
    154, 167 n. 85, 185, 192
Notitia Dignitatum 139 n. 221
Nourishment 119, 120, 133, 146–7, 154, 180
Nude 59, 61, 104
Numbers, sacred 99 n. 149

Offa, King of Mercia 12 n. 51, 13, 13 n. 65, 31–3, 35,
    40–1, 54, 55, 59–61, 111, 142–4, 147, 158 n. 12,
    166, 168–71, 186, 192
Orans 26 n. 30, 50, 83, 87, 88, 153
Orb 85, 87
    orb cruciger 95
Oriental influences 23, 33 n. 83, 51, 70, 89 n. 71, 130,
    132, 138, 153, 178 n. 155
Orientation:
    of coins 8
    of image 8 n. 17, 9 n. 20, 81–2, 112
Ormside Bowl 119 n. 83, 134, 155 n. 335, 163 n. 45
Oswald, King of Northumbria 67 n. 287, 68 n. 294,
    71 n. 313, 96–7, 86 n. 53
Oswiu, King of Northumbria 38, 97

Paganism and pagan customs 50 n. 185, 52 n. 195, 72,
    76, 79, 97, 99, 105, 107, 114, 124, 130
Palestine 70, 75, 95, 166
    see also *Ampullæ*
Pallium 25 n. 24
Palm branches 61 n. 249, 79–80, 81, 85 n. 47, 88,
    153–4, 170
Palm cups 66, 77, 97, 146, 187
Panther 68, 131–4
    Bacchus' panther 133–4, Fig. 4.37b
Paradise 88, 91, 93, 117, 153
Patronage 16–17, 97, 105, 114, 126, 152–3, 185–6, 189,
    190
Pavia 70, 122, 122 n. 105, Fig. 4.21
Peacocks 107, 113, 120–3
Peada, King of the Middle Angles and the Mercians
    47 n. 163, 86 n. 53
Pellets as contour 121
    on the field for Celtic coins, Series Q and
        Northumbrian coins 129–30, Fig. 4.29a,
        Fig. 4.30, Fig. 4.33
    see also Host
Peltas 141
Pendants 8, 26 n. 32, 49, 61, 101, 111, 165; coin 101,
    Fig. 5.25a; pseudo-coin, see also Liudhard
    'medalet' 84, 84 n. 42, Fig. 3.7, Fig. 3.25b; on
    crosses 87
    Bacton 36, 137 n. 210, Fig. 2.17a, Fig. 4.12c
    Compton Verney Fig. 5.5a
    Ducklington 5.5b
    Faversham Fig. 5.5c, Fig. 5.9b
    Risan 130, Fig. 4.34b
    Winkel 111, Fig. 4.4
Pendilia 45, 46, 50 n. 181, 158
Penes 104 n. 178, 148
Pepin the Short 13, 16, 192
Perches 95–6

Persian dress 58
Petra nigra 13 n. 65
Physiologus 108 n. 12, 130, 135, 136, 153
Pietas 83
Pile, see Tools
Pilgrim*s* 48 n. 171, 70
    badges:75
    flasks 83; 84, 95, 122 n. 105, 147, 190 n. 74
Plant scrolls, *see* Vine-scrolls
Pope Boniface 46 n. 157
Pope Gregory the Great 25, 65 n. 280, 77–8, 124,
    136 n.203, 146, 188 n. 56, 190
Pope Vitalian 38
Porcupines 48–9, 48 n. 173, 53 n. 206, 140, 172,
    176–81
Ports 48, 177
    see also Domburg; Ribe; Quentovic
Postwick Matrix, *see* Bathilda
Preacher 106
'Private viewing', *see* Orientation of image
Propaganda 2, 23, 79, 85
Psalters 32 n. 70
    see also Manuscripts

Quadripartite schemes 110–11, 133 n. 174, 162–3
Quentovic 48, 48 nn. 170 and 171, 174

Rædwald, King of East Anglia 11 n. 40, 86 n. 53, 145
Ravenna 50 n. 181, 57 n. 224, 70, 99 n. 150
Ravens 77–8, 96–7
Rays 149
Reginald of Durham 97
Resurrection 70, 115, 121, 133, 136, 138, 142
Rhine 111, 112, 177
Ribe 29 n. 48, 177
Riddles 94, 97 n. 134, 187, 188 n. 53
Rigold's Chart 43, 47, 183, Fig. 2.28
Rings 38, 63, 63 n. 246, 88 n. 61, 89 n. 73, 99
    Æthelwulf Rings 122 n. 101
    Childeric Rings 75–6
    see also *Beagifa*
Risley Man 90 n. 75
Rochester 46 n. 157
    see also Mints
Roman Britain 7, 30, 101, 117 n. 70, 121, 155, 167–8,
    Fig. 5.14
Romanitas 46, 76 n. 353, 80, 147, 157, 160, 184
Rome 7, 48 n. 171, 70, 120, 122 n. 105, 125, 135, 145–6,
    146 n. 271
    see also Celtic influences
Romulus and Remus 144
Rosettes 122–3, 123 n. 108, 142, 162–3, 174
Ruminatio 97 n. 134
Runic inscriptions 2, 9, 11, 11 n. 39, 13, 44; 45, 56,
    66 n. 286, 84 n. 35; 't' 88 n. 68; 146, 168 n. 85,
    172, 178, 180, 182–3, 191
    see also Anglo-Saxon Coins 'skanomodu';
    'benutigo'; 'pada'; CRISPUS/delaiona; 'æðilræd';
    Series C and Series R

Sæberht, King of the East Saxons 25 n. 21, 86 n. 53
Sailing 90

St Anthony of Egypt 77, 153
St Augustine of Hippo 121 n. 96, 146
St Cuthbert 77, 90 n. 80, 96 n. 122
  coffin 26 n. 32, 39 n. 117, 50, 55 n. 215, 89 n. 71, 103, 134 n. 185
  Gospel-book binding 68 n. 291, 95 n. 113
St Guthlac 9 n. 122
St Menas 88–90, 89 n. 53, Fig. 3.12
St Michael 79, 79 n. 6, 83–4
St Mumma Reliquary, 26
St Patrick's *lorica* 87 n. 60
St Paul the First Hermit 77
St Peter 90, n. 80
St Radegund reading desk 113
St Thecla 89 n. 69
Saints 17, 34 n. 86, 37–8, 40, 69 n. 299, 77, 86, 90, 96, 132
Sts Gervasius and Protasius 37, 37 n. 105
Sts Peter and Paul 38 n. 109, 81 n. 12, 86, 86 n. 51, 103
Saltire standard, Type 51 171–6
  see also Anglo-Saxon coins
Sarre 8, 10 n. 35; necklace 8, n. 16
Savonnière 37–8
Scandinavian influences, etc. 9, 29–30, 49, 50 n. 182, 52, 56 n. 223, 64, 90, 150, 177, 184
Sceattas 12, 12 n. 49
  see also Anglo-Saxon Coins, silver pennies
Sceptre 75–6, 89 n. 73
  see also Staff
Sculpture:
  Aberlemno, Forfar 149, Fig. 4.59a
  Bath, Temple of Sulis Minerva 30 n. 56
  Beverley, Humberside bishop's seat 99
  Bewcastle, Cumbria 96–7, 120 n. 88, Fig. 3.21
  Breedon-on-the-Hill, Leics. 31 n. 68, 33 n. 83, 35 n. 90, 39 n. 117, 41, 65, 103, 118, 119, 127, 134, 153, 154, 163, 186, Fig. 2.25, Fig. 3.26, Fig. 4.17c, Fig. 4.22b, Fig. 4.28a, Fig. 4.63, Fig. 4.64c, Fig. 5.8
  Brixworth, Northants 120
  Castor, Northants 35 n. 90
  Croft on Tees, North Yorks. 118, 155 n. 335, Fig. 4.15
  Easby, North Yorkshire 120, Fig. 4.18
  Fletton, Cambs 82, Fig. 3.4
  Gloucester, cross shaft 35 n. 90
  Hedda Stone, Peterborough, Northants. 35 n. 90, 103, 143 n. 249
  Hexham, Northumberland 66 n. 285, 97 n. 128; 163 n. 49; bishop's seat 99
  Hilton of Cadboll, Easter Ross 39 n. 118
  Hoddom 50
  Hornby, Lancashire 103
  Hovingham, North Yorks. 81–2, Fig. 3.3b
  Italian 70, 70 n. 310; *see also* Monte S. Michele, Pavia
  Jedburgh, Borders 120, 133, Fig. 4.18c, Fig. 4.38b
  Lastingham, North York. 100, 166 n. 70
  Lowther Cross, Cumbria 163, Fig. 5.8a
  Middleton, North Yorks. 166 n. 70
  Monkwearmouth, Tyne and Wear 100, 118 n. 76
  Monte S. Michele, Puglia 83–4
  Narbonne slab 65 n. 280

Niederdollendorf, stele 35 n. 91
Northallerton, North Yorkshire 162 n. 39
Otley, West Yorkshire Fig. 2.14
Papil slab 104
Pavia 83–4, 122; Theodata sarcophagus 122, Fig. 4.21
Pictish 153; snake bosses 141; *see also* Aberlemno, Hilton of Cadboll, St Andrews
Repton Cross, Derbyshire 54, 62, 96 n. 123
Rothbury Cross, Northumberland 50, 143 n. 249, 186
Ruthwell Cross, Dumfriesshire 39 n. 117, 101 n. 158, 106, 118 n. 76, 120 n. 88, 187, Fig. 3.30
St Andrews, Sarcophagus, Fife 32 n. 74, 126 n. 132, Fig. 2.11
Wirksworth slab, Derbyshire 103, Fig. 3.27
York 119, Fig. 4.17b
Sella curulis 98, 100
Sermons 91, 94, 190, 188
She-Wolf 119–20, 139 n. 225, 144–7, 177
Shield from Stabio 67 n. 290
Shillings, *see* Anglo-Saxon Coins, gold coinage
Sight 51 n. 187
Silks 38, 122 n. 105
Smiths 15, 168, Fig. 5.14
  see also Goldsmiths
Snake rings and bracelets 144 n. 245
Snakes 136–44
  Knotted 143
  Motif 136–38, 140 n. 230
  Radiant 140, 175 n. 133, 181
  see also Whorls
Sol Invictus 64
Solomon knot, *see* Cross
Soul 88, 91, 115, 117, 138, 150
Spears 75–6, 88 n. 68
Sphinx 151–2
Spolia 146 n. 271
Spong Hill, cremation urn—lid 99
Sponsorship (baptisimal) 86, 86 n. 53
Staffs 82, 104, 108
Standards on reverses 48 n. 170, 81 n. 13, 171–6, 184 n. 18
  as banners 73
Stars 74–5, 145, 158, 166
Steppes influences (Scythian and Sarmatian) 138, 148, Fig. 4.57
Style I 56
Sutton Hoo:
  Anastasius Dish 75
  Bird mount (shield) 26, 27, 150 n. 299, Fig. 2.3
  Bowls 166 n. 69, 170 n. 98
  Clasps 62 n. 257,
  Helmet 30 n. 57, 53, 137; helmet plaques 27, 58, 76 n. 354, Fig. 2.50
  Mail coat 62
  Merovingian coins 9, 11, 11 n. 40, 48 n. 171, 157, 167 n. 76
  Stand 73, 73 n. 333
  Wand 75
  Whetstone 24, 27, 28, 39 n. 118, 75, 76 nn. 353 and 358

Swans 108 n. 12
Sword pommels:
    Fetter Lane, London 141
    Windsor 165
Synod of Gumley 191
Syria 95

Tails 126, 148–9
Tangemere find Fig. 2.32
Tassilo Chalice 65, 66 n. 285
    style 155 n. 340
Tasting 140, 188
Tatwine, Archbishop of Canterbury 87 n. 52,
        187 n. 152, 188 n. 53
Textiles 51, 63, 73, 89, 89 n. 71, 92, 92 n. 95; 103, 112,
        115, 125–6, 126 n. 133, 132, 152 n. 171, 153, 154,
        185, 186 n. 35, Fig. 3.13
    see also *Chemise; Chasuble*
Thames 11, 12, 144 n. 261, 180, 190
    Fitting Fig. 4.48a
    see also Hoards
Theodolind 124
Theodora, Empress 50 n. 181, 57 n. 224
Theodore of Tarsus, Archbishop of Canterbury
        48 n. 171, 64
Thrones 82, 84, 98–101
    of Dagobert 100
Thrymsas, see Anglo-Saxon Coins, gold coinage
Thyrsus 68, 133
Tilbury 53, 56 n. 222
Tongues 130, 131, 133 n. 174, 136, 140, 141, 142, 148,
        155, 188
Tools 14, 167–8
    hammer 14, 167
    pile (anvil die) 14, 15
    punches 14
    trussel (upper die) 14, 15
Torques 35, 61, 82, 91, 107, 137, 139, 144
TOT, *see* Inscriptions
Trabea 58
Trade 10, 12, 48 n. 170, 54 n. 211, 58, 11, 177, 184
Treasure 7, 9, 91
    keeper of treasure 138, 150
    Constantinople 74
    Cyprus (Second Treasure) 32 n. 70
    Esquiline 26 n. 27, 98 n. 137
    Hoxne 126
    Thetford 126 n. 133, 133 n. 176
Tree of Life 38, 69 n. 301, 70, 73, 102, 117–8, 122 n. 99,
        127
Trees 71, 94–5, 97
Trefoils 163, 170
Tremissis 10
    see also Anglo-Saxon Coins, gold coinage;
        Merovingian Coins
Trewhiddle style 170–1
Tridents 72–3, 167–8
Trinity 17 n. 86, 163 n. 54
Triquetras 49, 113, 134 n. 181, 151, 163, 188 n. 53
    see also Anglo-Saxon Coinage and Crosses
Triumph 79, 82 n. 18
'True Vine' 117, 119, 146, 151

see also Biblical quotations, Jn.15
Tufa 73, 172, 175
Tunics, *see* Clothing

Undley Bracteate 24, 74, 145–6, 183, Fig. 4.54
Uroborus 36, 136

Valkyries 49
Vanimundus, *see* Moneyers
Vegetation Motifs 67, 70, 90, 93–5, 112, 133–4, 152–4,
        170, 187
    see also Branches; Flowering rods; Tree of Life;
        Trees; Vine-scrolls
Victory 70, 77, 79–82, 87, 98, 102, 158, 159
Vine-scrolls 68, 68 n. 296, 71, 90, 95, 105–6, 107,
        117–20, 117 n. 69, 120, 123, 133, 147, 150, 153,
        155, 163, 185
    fruiting vine 140, 155
Visual ambiguities 82–3, 119, 123 n. 106, 161, 163,
        165, 169, 171
Vivarium 82 n. 21

Wagons, Dejbjerg Mose, Oseberg 30 n. 57
Wall paintings 83
    Balayk Tepe 132 n. 71
Wantsum Chanel, Kent 10, 78 n. 369
Weland 66 n. 286
Wergild 11 n. 43, 15
Wessex 12, 35 n. 89, 89 n. 70
Whorls:
    of birds 110, Fig. 4.3
    of snakes 141–2, Fig. 4.49, Fig. 4.50
Wics 12, 19, 173, 177, 190
Wilbald 95 n. 116
Wilfrid 26, 27 n. 35, 48 n. 171, 90 n. 80, 97 n. 128
Wilred, *see* Moneyers
Wilton Cross, *see* pectoral Crosses
Winchester 16 n. 78
Wings 70, 77, 80–3, 85, 101 n. 165, 110, 113, 117,
        121–2, 152, 154–5
    wing scroll 110, 117 Fig. 4.2
Wisdom 69, 136, 188
Wise Men 66 n. 286, 69, 166
Witham Pins 165 n. 61, 171, Fig. 4.29b, Fig. 5.17
Woden 9, 76 n. 354, 77–8, 88 n. 68, 95 n. 111, 97, 99,
        136
    see also Anglo-Saxon Coins Series X
Wolves and She-Wolf 129, 131, 140, 144–47
    see also Anglo-Saxon Coins, Series V
Women 29, 39–41, 103
Wounds of Christ (five bosses on crosses) 163
Wreaths 34, 70, 79, 80–1, 120, 135, 144, 145 n. 267,
        159, 165, 172
Wreath-ties 27, 35, 43, 45–51, 52, 57 n. 229, 68 n. 292,
        75–6, 91, 159, 187188 n. 53
    see also Knots
Wuffa and Wuffingas 144–5, 147
Wulfhere, King of Mercia 65 n. 277

Yeavering 99
Yggdrasil 95 n. 111, 102 n. 166
York 17 n. 82, 18, 27, 38, 47 n. 168, 192
    see also Mints